THE FRENCH MONARCHICAL COMMONWEALTH, 1356–1560

How does authority become power? How does power justify itself to achieve its ends? For over two hundred years, the Valois kings relied on a complex mixture of ideologies, ruling a monarchical commonwealth with a coherent theory of shared governance. Forged in the Hundred Years War, this commonwealth built on the defense of the public good (*bien public*) came undone both practically and theoretically during the Wars of Religion. Just as certain kings sought to expand the royal prerogative, so, too, elites fought to preserve their control over local government. Using town archives from more than twenty cities to complement traditional sources of political theory, *The French Monarchical Commonwealth, 1356–1560* establishes the relationship between seemingly theoretical constructs, like the Salic Law, and the reality of everyday politics.

JAMES B. COLLINS is Professor of History at Georgetown University. His seven books include *The State in Early Modern France* (Cambridge University Press, 1995; 2nd ed. 2008) and *La monarchie républicaine* (2016), based on his lectures at the Collège de France. His work has been translated into French, Spanish, Polish, and Chinese.

T0384844

THE FRENCH MONARCHICAL COMMONWEALTH, 1356–1560

JAMES B. COLLINS

Georgetown University, Washington DC

CAMBRIDGE
UNIVERSITY PRESS

Shaftesbury Road, Cambridge CB2 8EA, United Kingdom

One Liberty Plaza, 20th Floor, New York, NY 10006, USA

477 Williamstown Road, Port Melbourne, VIC 3207, Australia

314–321, 3rd Floor, Plot 3, Splendor Forum, Jasola District Centre, New Delhi – 110025, India

103 Penang Road, #05–06/07, Visioncrest Commercial, Singapore 238467

Cambridge University Press is part of Cambridge University Press & Assessment,
a department of the University of Cambridge.

We share the University's mission to contribute to society through the pursuit of
education, learning and research at the highest international levels of excellence.

www.cambridge.org
Information on this title: www.cambridge.org/9781108461283

DOI: 10.1017/9781108593045

First published 2022
First paperback edition 2024

A catalogue record for this publication is available from the British Library

Library of Congress Cataloging-in-Publication data
Names: Collins, James B, author.
Title: The French monarchical commonwealth, 1356–1560 / James B Collins, Georgetown
University, Washington DC.
Description: Cambridge ; New York : Cambridge University Press, 2022. | Includes
bibliographical references and index.
Identifiers: LCCN 2021045504 (print) | LCCN 2021045505 (ebook) | ISBN 9781108473309
(hardback) | ISBN 9781108461283 (paperback) | ISBN 9781108593045 (ebook)
Subjects: LCSH: Monarchy – France – History. | Political science – France – History. | France –
History – House of Valois, 1328–1589. | France – Politics and government – History. | BISAC:
HISTORY / Europe / General
Classification: LCC JN2358 .C65 2022 (print) | LCC JN2358 (ebook) | LCC 320.444/0903–
dc23/eng/20211128
LC record available at https://lccn.loc.gov/2021045504
LC ebook record available at https://lccn.loc.gov/2021045505

ISBN   978-1-108-47330-9   Hardback
ISBN   978-1-108-46128-3   Paperback

CONTENTS

ILLUSTRATIONS

PREFACE

This project began innocently enough: colleagues in France invited me to a conference in Vervins, for the 400th anniversary of the peace signed there in 1598. I still have the warmest memories of the fabulous concert provided by Jordi Savall and Hesperion in the Église Notre-Dame, and of the poor mayor and good citizens of Vervins drenched in a downpour during the reenactment. My paper, on the "bien public" vocabulary of the 1590s, got me started on a project about political vocabulary in Henry IV's France. A few years later, at a conference on Philippe Duplessis Mornay organized by Hugues Daussy and Véronique Ferrer, I joined Mack Holt and Mark Greengrass for a sumptuous dinner at a restaurant in Saumur. They, too, were working on related subjects, which turned into prize-winning books: Mack's *The Politics of Wine* and Mark's *Governing Passions*. Sharing ideas with them, I was hooked.

What began as a book on political vocabulary and practical politics in late sixteenth- and early seventeenth-century France led in unexpected directions. I kept wondering whence came this vocabulary of the "bien public?" And I kept moving backwards, finally landing in the 1350s. French political society had long had various phrases for the interests of the community as a whole, of course, but I found that the phrase "bien de la chose publique" took over mainstream political discourse in lands controlled by the royal family, and in Brittany, in the 1350s and 1360s. I set out to trace the evolution of this vocabulary down to the period of my initial interest. This book follows the trail I found; a second book picks up the story in 1560–1561 and examines how the vocabulary of the "bien public" turned into a discourse of the "bien de l'Estat," with the word *Estat* now capitalized and with a specific new meaning.

My parents were professional politicians, so I learned to understand politics from the ground level. As friends and colleagues know, I learned a cold-blooded analysis of contemporary politics from my parents, and I have brought that characteristic to this consideration of late medieval and Renaissance France's political life. I urge readers to remember that I offer here a different perspective from the one developed by historians like Quentin Skinner or Jacques Krynen, one I view as complementary, not contradictory. Remember, too, that my examination of political practice has relied throughout on the scholarship of colleagues working in the history of political thought and of law: with respect to the French monarchy, the remarkable work of scholars like Krynen, Jean Barbey, Jean Bart, Michel Hébert, and Éliane Viannot quite literally made this book possible. A new generation of scholars have brought out in the last decade important works, both in French and English, covering so many aspects of this project, from royal entries to religious reform, to gender and politics, the latter made possible by outstanding scholarship recently produced on medieval Frenchwomen – Jeanne de Penthièvre, Isabeau of Bavaria, Yolande of Aragon, Anne of Brittany, et al. – involved in politics. Considerations of space made it impractical to follow up as deeply as I would have liked on women, gender, and French politics, but I hope to be able to do so in a book that is already in progress.

My previous work as a historian undergirds this book. Yes, I have read major (and minor) works of political philosophy, law, and history, and many Parisian records, but I have spent most of the last five decades in local archives, reading tax rolls, municipal deliberations, local court records, notarial archives, civil registers, and a host of other documents generated out in the field. My goal here is to relate the political vocabulary found in intellectual treatises and in royal actions to the vocabulary used in actual politics, from the local level up to the kingdom-wide stage. If I start by trying to understand why given political actors took given actions, I also want to understand why they justified those actions with the rhetoric they chose. Words matter; they have a life of their own and become political contexts in their own right. Moreover, the most contentious political words, like 'justice' or even the broader concept of the political community itself, defy easy definition.

The works of people from Nicole Oresme to Christine de Pizan to Jean Bodin play their part, but my primary focus lies with the use to which others put their terminology. This book – like the second one (1560–1651) – interacts with the historiography of political philosophy, but I seek here to get outside that field's boundaries, to show what the history of politics can teach us about political theory. The chosen vocabulary – what Pierre Bourdieu called the *langage*, or specialized vocabulary – often circumscribed later actions within the realm of politics. Political actors usually pursued specific practical ends, which fundamentally varied little, but their chosen method of justifying those actions evolved considerably and, in the end, helped change the nature of the polity.

A project that has gone on as long as this one builds up a list of obligations impossible to be given in detail, but I do want to offer some specific thanks. First of all, my thanks to Georgetown University for financial support of much of the research done for the book. The Leverhulme Trust enabled me to be a Research Professor in the UK for a semester; many colleagues in England and Scotland offered insights and, beginning with Peter Campbell, sponsored some of my talks there. Through the kindness of Élie Barnavi, Fanny Cosandey, and Robert Descimon, I was a *professeur invité* at their Friday morning seminar at the École des Hautes Études; I profited greatly from the feedback I received there, particularly in the post-seminar café. Thanks to the late Marc Fumaroli and Daniel Roche, the Collège de France gave me the great honor of presenting lectures as a *professeur invité*, truly one of the highlights of my academic life: those lectures, two of which sketch out the broad lines of this project c. 2013, were published as *La monarchie républicaine* by Odile Jacob.

Creating a final text involves many people, starting with those who offered criticisms and suggestions. My thanks to Jim Shedel, who organizes our departmental faculty seminars, and to the many colleagues who contributed to the discussion of part of the manuscript. As a long-time editor, I especially appreciate editorial work, in this case by Cambridge: many thanks to the wonderful team of Elizabeth Friend-Smith, Atifa Jiwa, Angela Roberts, Melissa Ward, and Michael Watson, and to the anonymous readers, whose comments led to important improvements. I remain solely responsible for what remains.

Historians rely on the professionalism and generosity of spirit of archivists to accomplish our research. I spent time in over twenty French archives doing this research, and I relied on research done in many other archives for previous projects. In Paris, may I single out the staffs of the Bibliothèque Nationale's branches at the Richelieu site and at the Arsenal, who have been unfailingly helpful. Out in the provinces, in recent years, I spent more time in Burgundy than any other region, so special thanks to the staffs of the departmental archives of Côte d'Or and Saône-et-Loire (the latter of whom generously allowed me to work through an elevator breakdown that meant fourteen storeys of documents were only available via the stairs!). I also spent many hours in the municipal archives in Dijon and some time in those of Macon and Chalon-sur-Saône. To the archival teams in cities like Lyon, Blois, Arles, Rennes (where I also spent many a day in years gone by), and Toulouse, who have digitalized the municipal deliberations: bravo!

The names of colleagues who have discussed this project with me runs into scores of people. Andrzej Kamiński, who has been my teacher, later colleague, and friend for nearly fifty years deserves special mention for all the times we have hashed out the contrast between the Polish and French monarchies. A fair number of those conversations have taken place over Lucullan feasts prepared by Maria Pryshlak, with whom I sat in Andrzej's classes at Columbia nearly fifty years ago. My History Department colleagues at Georgetown, and the Old Regime historians group of the DC Area have also been a fantastic help in honing my ideas on this project, and others. Because of our consonance of interests, Mack Holt has been especially helpful. French historians are blessed to be able to share ideas at two wonderful annual conferences in the US, and the UK's Society for the Study of French History has honored me with invitations to be one of their keynote speakers (in 2006 and 2016). I have also spoken on topics closely related to this project in many other venues; let

me make special mention of conferences in Amsterdam and Bergen, and of my
friend Robert von Friedeburg, who made my presence possible at each. Robert
and Peter Campbell have probably listened to more versions of this project
than anyone else. Thanks as well to Denis Crouzet for invitations to the
Sorbonne, and to Philippe Hamon for a talk at Rennes, which was one of the
highlights of my Collège de France visit, returning to the scene of my earliest
research in France. To walk the streets of Rennes was to remember the
neophyte graduate student who researched his dissertation there in 1975.

Talking with medievalists like Tracy Adams and John Watts at conferences
makes all the difference in developing a broader context for such a large topic.
Scholars working on other European polities, like my friends Wojciech
Falkowski in Warsaw, or John Morrill in Cambridge, have broadened my
horizons about developments in France, enabling me to have a better com-
parative framework. A special shout-out to all those with whom I have shared
the experience of the Recovering Forgotten Histories project in Poland, especially to John Merriman, whose company has brightened many a day, and to
my friends and colleagues Maurice Jackson, Marcus Rediker, and Bob Weiner
for so many conversations, both live and digital, that have revived my spirits in
some of America's darkest days.

Those of us getting on in years have both regrets and hopes related to any
long project. So many of those with whom I shared extensive conversations on
this topic are no longer with us: John Salmon and Marc Fumaroli come
immediately to mind. My dear friends Bill Beik and Al Hamscher have also
recently passed away. I'll have more to say about them when the second book
appears.

On the more hopeful side, I have learned much from the Ph.D. students it
has been my privilege to teach while working on this project. They include
medievalists like Guy Lurie, Darcy Kern, and Sylvia Mullins, the first two of
whom – entirely coincidentally – wrote dissertations closely related to this
book, as the notes make obvious. In several decades of training early modern-
ists, I have had three large clusters, the third of which are in the midst of
writing (or have just finished): Jakob Burnham, Ashleigh Corwin, Natalie
Donnell, Andrey Gornostaev, Sukhwan Kang, Leigh Stephens, and our
adopted colleague, Nathan Michalewicz, who just defended at George
Mason. Thanks to all of them for questions and insights that have made me re-
examine so many assumptions.

A family, too, has its regrets and hopes. My mother wanted to live long
enough to see this book: she did not quite make it, much to my regret. On the
hopeful side, two new granddaughters have appeared in 2019 and 2021. My
immediate circle – daughters, sisters, grandson, Jennifer – have given for many
years the support that makes any project of this magnitude possible. Thanks to
them all.

~

Introduction

For by Art is created that great Leviathan called a Common-wealth, or State, (in latine Civitas) which is but an Artificiall Man.

T. Hobbes, Leviathan (1651).

L'État est la chose de tous, la res publica, que l'on traduit parfois par "république" et plus souvent par la chose publique.

François Olivier-Martin, Histoire du droit français. (1948)

The centralizing monarchical discourse has long dominated our perception of the kingdom of France. Jacques Krynen, Jean Barbey, Arlette Jouanna, and many others have traced the evolution of this discourse between the fourteenth and seventeenth centuries, when, in their view, it led to a Bourbon "absolute monarchy," but one whose relationship to the concept "absolute" differed substantially in their presentations.[1] Jouanna has added important correctives to the earlier narrative, both in her insistence on the importance of a noble ideology of resistance and in her careful presentation of "puissance absolue" as an "extraordinary weapon" [arme extraordinaire] in the sixteenth century.[2] Kings did not issue legislation on the basis of "puissance absolue," but relied on their "certain science" and "pleine puissance," terms used by other rulers, such as the Pope. The king used his "puissance absolue" to force registration of acts to which sovereign courts had objected – above all tax edicts.

The jurists believed "puissance absolue" meant that the king was the ultimate source of law in his kingdom, but they objected strongly to its use to avoid the "forms of justice." As Jouanna rightly emphasizes, "absolu(e)" took on a new meaning in the seventeenth century, and we must avoid the temptation to view early sixteenth-century developments as the germ of what happened in

[1] J. Krynen, L'empire du roi: Idées et croyances politiques en France XIIIᵉ–XVᵉ siècle (Paris: Gallimard, 1993); J. Barbey, Être roi. Le roi et son gouvernement en France de Clovis à Louis XVI (Paris: Fayard, 1992).

[2] A. Jouanna, Le devoir de révolte (Paris: Fayard, 1989); Le pouvoir absolu (Paris: Gallimard, 2013), esp. ch. 2; and Le prince absolu: apogée de déclin de l'imaginaire monarchique (Paris: Gallimard, 2014).

the middle of the seventeenth century.[3] Barbey, in contrast, questions the utility of a distinction between the "absolutism" of Louis XIV and the theoretical powers of late medieval and Renaissance kings. Up through the late sixteenth century, "absolue" carried the sense of independent, and "puissance absolue" formed the logical extension of the doctrines that the king of France was "Emperor in his kingdom," had no earthly superior, and held his kingdom by virtue of his sword and of a direct anointing by God.[4]

Recent historiography has privileged a perspective on medieval France that seeks the origins of the "absolute monarchy" of the Bourbons. Nineteenth-century historians, like Leopold von Ranke, or Georges Picot, in his monumental five-volume study of the Estates General, or Augustin Thierry, in his vast *Histoire du Tiers État*, placed developments such as the 1356–1358 crisis, or the Estates Generals of 1560–1561, in the context of the bourgeoisie seeking, but failing to "share in the sovereignty" [Thierry]. The cahiers of 1484 and of 1560–1561 seemed to them precursors of the demands made in 1789.[5] Thierry, writing during the final days of the Second Republic (1852), with respect to the assembly at Pontoise (1561), spoke of "nobles and bourgeois presenting themselves imbued with the innovative spirit, and agreeing to try, not just for simple reforms, but the beginning of a revolution."[6] Jules Michelet, in the 1837 preface to volume four of his *Histoire de France*, began with the comment that "The national era of France is the 14th century. [...] The bourgeoisie appeared in the revolution of Marcel."[7]

In his preface to the second of his volumes on "the municipal history of l'ancienne France," Thierry argued that it had only recently (1852) got the great attention it deserved from public opinion, because of "modern revolutions, taking place before our eyes," which encouraged people to understand "medieval revolutions."[8] Picot completed his work in the 1860s, in response to a competition sponsored (1866) by the Académie des sciences morales et

[3] Jouanna, *Le pouvoir absolu*, 316.

[4] Rulers throughout Europe borrowed both words and images from each other. Phrasing from the presumed *ordo* of Louis the Stammerer (877, manuscript source from c. 1000), king of the Franks, popped up in England (twelfth century) and Sicily (1130, Roger II). At the Martorana in Palermo, a mosaic shows Roger II in Byzantine imperial robes, receiving his crown directly from Christ. [Clear image available in Wikipedia's entry on Roger II of Sicily.] French monarchs would later borrow from Frederick II of Sicily in their justifications of royal power vis-à-vis the Pope, and they would emphasize that the king of France, unlike the Emperor, was not crowned by the Pope. [Roger II, like the king of France, got his crown from a local archbishop.]

[5] L. von Ranke, *Civil Wars and Monarchy in France in the Sixteenth and Seventeenth centuries*, trans. M. Garvey (New York: Harper, 1853), 194–198, on the estates at Pontoise (August 1561).

[6] A. Thierry, *Recueil des monuments inédits de l'histoire du Tiers État* (Paris, 1850–1870) II, xcix.

[7] J. Michelet, *Histoire de France* (Paris, 1857), IV, 1.

[8] In his long introduction Thierry has a citation from an 1837 speech by Guizot, given "15 years ago." Louis Napoléon Bonaparte carried out his coup in December 1851, but the

politiques, and approved by them in February 1870.[9] The five volumes appeared in 1872 – he claims much changed from the text of 1869 – and he added the comment, in his preface, that "The importance of the subject offered by our study, far from diminishing in the midst of public agitations, took from these events an unanticipated interest and even a grandeur." [ii]

The Third Republic emphasized this tradition, not simply in the statue (1888) of Étienne Marcel outside Paris' Hôtel de Ville, but in the murals lining the walls of its salon Lobau, two of which depict Marcel – "saving the future Charles V from the mob" – and the execution of Jean Des Mares and the Maillotins (January 1383), who had rebelled against the imposition of permanent taxation. The two paintings formed part of a series on "the conquest and the defense of municipal liberties, the glorification of the people in its incessant and heroic fights against the despotism of royalty."[10] Marcel, in his statue – finished just in time for the centennial of the Revolution – bears a copy of the great ordinance of March 1357, issued in response to claims by the Estates General of Languedoïl to a share of governance.[11] Michelet claimed this ordinance "changed with a blow the government. It put the administration in the hands of the Estates, substituting the republic for the monarchy."[12] Even in the 1920s, Lucien Romier would cite the nobles' cahier at Pontoise as evidence of France seeking the "installation of a constitutional regime" a century before England did so.[13] (See Illustration 0.1.)

The connection between the events of 1356–1357 and those of 1560–1561 provides the chronology for this book. Rather than seeking to foreshadow the Revolution, and thus to establish historical roots for a republican regime that sorely needed legitimacy in 1852, or in 1872, I want to analyze these developments on their own terms, in their own historical context. I begin with the premise that a focus on the theoretical makes us too divorced from the

---

plebiscite creating the Second Empire did not take place until a year later, so France was technically a republic when Thierry was writing.

[9] He mentions the critiques from François Guizot, who had re-established the Academy in 1832 when a minister of Louis-Philippe, and François-Auguste Mignet, permanent secretary of the Academy in 1870, and says he made major revisions between 1870 and 1872. Guizot took a hard line against Étienne Marcel and suggested fourteenth-century France was not ready to govern itself; for him, "the government of the *pays* by the *pays* itself" had still not come about in the nineteenth century, "despite all the progress of the French nation." F. Guizot, *Histoire de France* (Paris, 1873), II, 155.

[10] Jean-Paul Laurens' murals, executed in the 1890s.

[11] King John then being a captive of the English, his son Charles, duke of Normandy, ruled in his name; the Estates established a commission of thirty-six men – twelve from each order – to supervise the government and the collection of taxes for a new army, and dismissed leading royal councilors. See Chapter 1 for details.

[12] Michelet, *Histoire de France*, IV, 273. Michelet then asks, "In reality, did France exist as a political person?" For him, in the absence of a common will [*volonté commune*], royalty provided the sole authority.

[13] L. Romier, *Catholiques et Huguenots à la cour de Charles IX* (Paris, 1924), 157ff. Romier here paraphrases Alphonse Ruble's book on Antoine de Bourbon and Jeanne d'Albret.

practical: the administrative apparatus of a Charles V (1364–1380) differed radically from that of Francis I (1515–1547), let alone Henry IV (1589–1610). Quite apart from the implementation differences, they lived in vastly different societies, whose political systems reflected changed socioeconomic, and cultural, realities. As Henri Pirenne put it, discussing the towns of the Low Countries, "in the High Middle Ages, as in our day, politics is not arbitrary, it must adapt everywhere to local circumstances."[14] The same word could, and often did, mean something different depending on context or audience, and the conceptual framework of political discussions evolved in parallel with the social changes of which it formed a part. Jouanna's *Pouvoir absolu* provides a detailed textual analysis of precisely such a change between the sixteenth and seventeenth centuries with respect to that important monarchical concept.

François Olivier-Martin, in his classic synthesis on the history of French law, recognized that the king did not "absorb" the State: "The king distinguished perfectly his interest and the interest of the chose publique." Robert Descimon and Fanny Cosandey have turned Olivier-Martin's formula on its head, suggesting that rather than the king absorbing the State, the State absorbed the king.[15] Barbey, following in the footsteps of Olivier-Martin, François Dumont, and many others, focused on the legal powers of the king, and has insisted that the nominal powers of the king of France scarcely varied from the time of Saint Louis (Louis IX, r. 1228–1270). In Anglophone scholarship, a parallel view received a classic statement in Joseph Strayer's remarkable *Medieval Origins of the Modern State* (1970), lectures given in the 1960s that reprised themes from his doctoral dissertation on the administration of Normandy under Saint Louis and emphasized the centralizing tendencies of the French monarchy.[16]

Olivier-Martin recognized that the monarchy emphasized different terminology in its references to the common interest: in medieval times the king typically referred to the "common utility." He claims the king emphasized the "interest of us and our kingdom" in the fifteenth and sixteenth centuries, shifting to an emphasis on "his service" or on "the good of his State" [*bien de son Estat*] in the seventeenth and eighteenth centuries.[17] The sources tell a different story. They show that the king often used that "common utility" phrase up through the early 1350s; he then shifted, in the late 1350s and early 1360s, to the "bien de la chose publique." This phrase remained normative

---

[14] H. Pirenne, *Les anciennes démocraties des Pays-Bas* (Paris: Flammarion, 1910), 86.

[15] R. Descimon and F. Cosandey, *L'absolutisme en France* (Paris: Seuil, 2002).

[16] J. Strayer, *The Administration of Normandy under Saint Louis* (Cambridge, MA: Mediaeval Academy of America, 1932). Strayer constantly stressed the "growing tendency to centralization" and went so far as to say that "the royal administration would control the towns in all important matters." [106] *On the Medieval Origins of the Modern State* (Princeton, NJ: PUP, 1970, reissued 2005).

[17] F. Olivier-Martin, *Histoire du droit français des origines à la Révolution* (Paris: Domat Monchrétien, 1948), both quotations on 307.

until the 1580s, although in the sixteenth century in particular the monarchy spoke often instead of the "bien public" and, in some cases, of the "respublique."

The greater use of the term "respublique," drawn from elite legal culture, in place of the simple vernacular "chose publique" began among those with a Latin education, especially the judicial elite, such as the Parlement of Paris, which prided itself on being the "Senate" of France. By the third quarter of the sixteenth century, "respublique" had become fairly common, although it had by no means completely displaced "chose publique." Here we need to keep in mind one important caveat: many of the key documents, such as renewal of municipal rights, liberties, and privileges, or of guild statutes, deliberately reprised the specific language of the initial or other earlier charters. Guild statutes, in particular, kept the usage of the "bien de la chose publique" or the "bien public" for a long time. The Catholic League of the late 1580s and 1590s made extensive rhetorical use of the "bien public," and Henry IV largely banished it from royal discourse. At the beginning of the seventeenth century, governments at all levels opted for a sly linguistic legerdemain: "bien public" (public good) became "bien du public" [good of the public].

After a brief period of "le bien du service du roi" [the good of the king's service] under the last Valois kings, the monarchy shifted to "le bien de mon Estat" and finally to "le bien de l'Estat," thus shifting from a meaning rooted into personal possession (mon = my) to one emphasized an abstract entity, **the** State. Royal documents standardized at this time [1580–1600] the spelling "Estat," with a capital letter, for this specific meaning of the older word "estat."[18] Other political actors shifted their vocabulary in the same chronology, in large measure because these general phrases most often came up in their negotiations and communications with the king.[19] Yet these actors had their own discursive needs, and to them the "chose publique" often carried an economic dimension. That the "chose publique" vocabulary emerged precisely at the intersection of

---

[18] Writers continued to use the spelling "estat" for these earlier meanings. **I refer here and elsewhere to the most common usage of each time; usages obviously overlapped,** but the ruptures of the 1350s and the 1590 were quite dramatic. Kings – Louis XIII in particular – often used "mon Estat" in their private letters, but public documents shifted from "son Estat" [his State] to "l'Estat" in the first decade of the seventeenth century, a process I will examine in a second volume, *From Monarchical Commonwealth to Royal State, 1561–1651* (Cambridge: CUP, forthcoming). "L'Estat" became the term of choice in the private letters of secretaries of state like Pomponne de Bellièvre and Nicolas de Neufville (Villeroy) from the late 1570s.

[19] Seventeenth-century municipal deliberations show urban governments using the "bien de l'Estat" when in dialogue with the royal government, but sometimes keeping to the "bien public" vocabulary when discussing local issues.

the political and the economic – in a discussion about coinage – reflected the dual purposes to which the various actors put this new vocabulary.[20]

The assumption that the State and the Republic are the same has long created a problem in our analysis of the French monarchy: they are not coterminous. Throughout the period covered here the central government used two political discourses: the monarchical one analyzed by scholars like Barbey, Krynen, and Tyler Lange, and a competing political discourse, built around the concept of a monarchical commonwealth.[21] Here Michelet's formula – of that 1357 ordinance substituting a republic for a monarchy – shows the anachronism of this contrast: political actors in sixteenth-century France believed they lived in a "respublique françoyse," whose form was a monarchy, to them one of the three legitimate forms of polity. I will argue that this commonwealth discourse was, in fact, France's primary *language of politics*, which exists at the intersection of actual, practical politics and the language of political justification. This discourse lasted between 1356 and the third quarter of the sixteenth century, when it gave way to a new paradigm, built around the State. Politicians negotiate in the language of politics, which has a symbiotic relationship to the language used in the discourse of political language, because politicians borrow and adapt language from theoretical sources, choosing the vocabulary and arguments that best suit the moment. Politics is about getting results; language provides one of the politician's most important tools. As Louis Le Roy told Henry III in the dedication to his 1576 translation of Aristotle's *Politics*: "Politics or the science of governing public states consists principally in practice [*usage*]."[22]

In the period covered here, 1356–1561, political language often combined with visual imagery, as in royal entry ceremonies or inaugurations of new municipal governments.[23] Virtually every major political writer of this period was also a politician, and I will argue their needs as politicians led them to seek justifications in a given corpus of writings drawn from Classical authors, from some religious sources, and from recent history. French people from outside this learned elite had their own ideas of self-governance – which the presence of members of the legal profession among them helped articulate in terminology – and visual images, often borrowed from royal discourse, especially when in dialogue with the royal government.

---

[20] *Res publica* had been around since Roman times, but the use of the term *chose publique* in this sense became normative only in the late 1350s.

[21] T. Lange, *The First French Reformation. Church Reform and the Origins of the Old Regime* (NY and Cambridge: CUP, 2014).

[22] Loys Le Roy (Regius), *Les Politiques d'Aristote* (Paris, 1576), "la Politique ou science de gouverner les estats publiques consiste principalement en l'usage". [on Gallica, image 11, not paginated]

[23] The municipal archives of Toulouse have a magnificent series of the illuminated portraits of the capitouls of Toulouse, going back to the group of 1352–1353, accessible online: www.archives.toulouse.fr

Specific people and writings defined the French monarchical common-wealth. Three key figures introduced this new discourse: Robert le Coq, bishop of Laon, in his speeches to the Estates General of Languedoïl in November 1356 and March 1357; Jean Buridan; and, most importantly, Nicole Oresme. Two writings of Oresme, *De moneta* (1355–1356), and his translations of Aristotle's *Ethics* and *Politics* (1370–1373), provided the essential vocabulary for commonwealth ideology. Oresme's glossary to *The Politics* defined key new words like aristocracy and oligarchy, and provided precise French definitions for old favorites like tyrant. In Oresme's *Politiques*, he made the radical statement that the kingdom itself was a vast "*cité*," composed of individual *cités*. He further distinguished between those who were political citizens of the kingdom-as-*cité* – the high clergy, the nobles, and the men of counsel – and those who were not – merchants, artisans, and peasants. This kingdom-level distinction made sense within the Aristotelian definition of citizen – those who rule and are ruled in turn.[24]

The post-1355 assemblies, however, revealed the conflict hidden by this formulation. Town governments included those – merchants, some artisans, even the odd *laboureur* – whom Oresme excluded from citizenship.[25] These men, especially the merchants and lawyers, demanded a share of political power, and the assemblies between 1356 and 1413 often witnessed a violent power struggle on their behalf. I would particularly emphasize the underappreciated events of 1380–1383, culminating in the executions ordered by Charles VI, which the Paris town government of the 1890s believed to be one of the defining moments of the city's history. Why? The taxes created for the ransom of King John II (1360) – the aides – had ceased their initial function by 1380, because John's ransom had been paid: according to the universally accepted principle of *cessante causa* (when the cause ceases, the effect ceases), they should have ended. Charles V, on his deathbed, abolished the hearth tax (*fouage*), which was borne mainly by the countryside and small towns; his urban subjects, however, believed he had abolished all "new" taxes, thus the aides as well. Riots broke out when the government tried to continue the collection; after a brief respite (and some violence at Rouen), the government tried, and failed, again. When Charles VI returned from his triumph at Roosebeke, in February 1383, he and his army entered Paris through a city gate that had been removed from its hinges, and now lay on the ground as if battered by a conqueror. The events of 1380–1383

---

[24] The *cité/civitas* was the political community of citizens. In Ambrogio Calepino's multilingual dictionary, he drew the parallel *polis-civitas-cité*.

[25] Municipal governance involved scores of people, not simply council members: guild inspectors and those responsible for upkeep of the streets, the lazar house, the bread supply, walls, paving stones, and the town militia. Thierry, *Recueil des monuments . . .*, IV, Abbeville, 187–190 has Abbeville's list from 1408. These men would have been local "citizens" in the Aristotelian sense.

Illustration 0.1a–b Citizens (*Gens d'armes*; *Gens de conseil*; *Gens sacerdotal*) and non-citizens (*Cultivateurs de terre*; *Gens de mestier*; *marchans*), BNF, M Fr 9106, fols. 243v–244r. Permission BNF. The duke of Orléans, brother of Charles V, ordered this copy in the 1390s.[26]

[26] My thanks to Dr. Guy Lurie for alerting me to this illustration.

marked the unequivocal beginning of permanent, and unvoted, taxation in France. The monarchy would claim the aides had been approved in 1360, just as it would later claim that because the *taille* voted in 1439 paid for the *compagnies d'ordonnance* (standing royal army), and the army obviously continued to exist, there was no further need to vote the *taille*. The Estates General of 1484 disagreed, and it got the monarchy to agree to a two-year grant of taxation, with the promise of further grants at Estates meeting in 1486. They did not meet again until 1560.

Artisan guilds wanted a share of power, and the town elites often – as at Abbeville in the 1380s – sought royal authorization for freezing out guild participation in governance. By the late fifteenth century, in the meeting of 1468 and, especially, 1484, the Estates General had become a mechanism to consult Oresme's Aristotelian citizens: those who ruled the kingdom at the local level. The deputies from 1484 onward came from three basic groups: bishops, abbots, priors, and cathedral canons for the clergy; *baillis* and military commanders for the nobility; royal judicial officers and a smattering of municipal officials and *avocats* for the Third Estate. Rulers calling representative assemblies, like Jeanne d'Auvergne, de facto regent of Burgundy for her son Philippe in the mid-1350s, specified in their letters that towns should send two or three of their "most capable and most notable persons" to the assembly, in this case the Estates of Burgundy.[27] The 1484 Estates, however, marked one dramatic shift: all deputies had to be chosen by a local assembly. Individuals, like bishops, who had received personal invitations to attend – as was true in most provincial estates and at the Estates General of 1468 – no longer got them, and the deputies specifically rejected the claims of bishops who sought to attend without having been chosen by local bodies.

The lowest-level meetings theoretically involved all male heads of households in rural parishes (or small clusters of parishes, in a castellany), and a wide variety of citizens in the towns: we have records of town "general assemblies" involving hundreds of people meeting about important issues (especially defense and taxation). Bailiwick assemblies held between 1500 and 1520 codified local customary laws; these assemblies often had hundreds of participants, mainly judges and lawyers. Similar assemblies held in the 1570s proved to be even larger.[28] The regional meetings, held at the chief town of the bailiwick, differed considerably: royal judges and lawyers formed the overwhelming majority of those present to draw up the Third's bailiwick *cahier* and to elect the deputy or

---

[27] Petit, *Histoire des ducs de Bourgogne*, IX (Paris, 1905), 90, citing convocation letters for the 1357 meeting.

[28] We rarely have full lists of participants below the bailiwick level: I have seen no evidence of women present, prior to the Estates General, where royal women sat in prominent positions and other elite women sat in the galleries. Female nobles could [and did] send *procureurs* to represent them in provincial assemblies.

two sent to the Estates General. In most cases the judicial elite kept tight control over the selection, often choosing the bailiwick's chief judge (*lieutenant général*) as their deputy: after all, who could be more "notable?"

The local and regional leadership of these men helped spread the phrase "bien de la chose publique," which took over political discourse not just at the national level but in municipalities in the parts of the kingdom represented at the Estates of Languedoïl in the late 1350s and 1360s. The local usage through-out the region represented at the Estates General of Languedoïl, to which we can add Brittany and Burgundy – neither of which sent deputies – illustrates, in my view, the close connection of the spread of this vocabulary to the meetings held in 1356–1358 in Paris.[29]

Some outlying regions – Flanders, Dauphiné, much of Langue d'Oc – retained the old vocabulary of "rights, liberties, franchises, usages, and customs," to defend their version of the "civitas"; Flanders and Dauphiné switched over in the begin-ning of the fifteenth century.[30] Border regions had reason to be reticent to get into this discourse. The town records of Bergerac, which passed back and forth between the kings of England and France during the Hundred Years' War, avoided any mention of the larger "chose publique"; in July 1379, back in French hands, they told a local noble that they had taken an "oath of loyalty to the king of France, our lord [*nostre sire*]," and they would keep it to the extent of their power. They emphasized, however, that they had been faithful to the king of England, when they had been his subjects, a suitably cagey response given that the city had just [1377] changed hands.[31] They also used the simple term "nostre sire" common in the southwest for the king of England in his territories; in other parts of France, the standard phrase for the king was "our sovereign lord" [*nostre souverain seigneur*].[32]

---

[29] Charles of Blois, whom the king of France recognized as duke of Brittany, was the head of the order of the nobility at the Estates Generals of October 1356 and February–March 1357, and John II's second wife, Jeanne de Boulogne, then ruled Burgundy on behalf of her son by a first marriage, duke Philippe de Rouvres.

[30] "droits, libertés, franchises, usages, coutumes." The king added the term "privileges"; see Chapter 1. Langue d'Oc refers to the broad southern region, with seven core seneschalsies; Languedoc is the later province of that name, containing the three seneschalsies of Toulouse, Beaucaire, and Carcassonne. Convocation letters used two distinctions: Languedoïl/Langue d'Oc and *droit coutumier/droit écrit* [customary/written law]. On the late spread to Dauphiné, see G. Lurie, "Citizenship in Later Medieval France, c. 1370–c. 1480," Ph.D thesis, 2013, Georgetown University. I became aware of A. J. Vanderjagt, *Qui Sa Vertu Anoblist: The Concepts of Noblesse and "Chose Publicque" in Burgundian Political Thought*. (Groningen: J. Miélot and Co., 1981) only after I had finished the manuscript, but his work contains many fine Burgundian examples of this vocabulary from the fifteenth century.

[31] G. Charrier, *Les Jurades de la ville de Bergerac* (Bergerac, 1892), v. I, 54: "nos aven fach sagramen de fialtat al rey de Franssa." In the Midi, "Franssa" meant the region north of the Loire.

[32] E. Audoin, *Recueil de Documents concernant la Commune et la Ville de Poitiers* (Poitiers, 1928), II, 261, for a rare example in 1373 letters of Jean de Berry about collecting a tax. Details below, Chapter 5.

Municipal deliberations of many towns enable us to see this vocabulary at work in local politics from the fifteenth century onward. In additional to the constant reference to the "bien de la chose publique," we see the phrase "bien public" [public good] becoming more prominent in the fifteenth century.[33] Its most famous usage, to describe the War of the Public Good (*Guerre du Bien Public*, 1465), reveals a defining moment in the reign of Louis XI, a rare French king who systematically questioned the commonwealth element of his monarchy. In the sixteenth century, in certain towns – especially those with a sovereign court or an important bailiwick court, the term "respublique" began to appear, in part because legal elites played a larger role in municipal governance, and they were the agents of change from "chose publique" to "respublique."

For the term "respublique" I have followed the choice of translators like Richard Knolles, who rendered Jean Bodin's *Six Livres de la République* as the *Six Bookes of the Commonweale* (1606). This commonwealth ideology took multiple forms, not simply among different polities – kingdoms, principalities, composite monarchies, dynastic agglomerates – but *within* those polities. Throughout the period in question here, five of the six original lay peerage fiefs of the Crown of France – what everyone called the "membres" (limbs) of the "corps politique" (body politic) – maintained their representative institutions. As late as the Estates General of 1588, the lone exception, the county of Champagne, agitated for the restoration of its estates.[34] The first [1297] two long-lasting new peerages – the duchy of Brittany and the county of Artois – also kept estates, until 1789.[35] Other major fiefs, like Auvergne, long maintained their estates, as did later additions to the lands of the king of France, like Dauphiné and the county of Provence.[36]

I.1   The Language [*langage*] of Politics

Citizen : Citoien est celui qui a puissance de communiquer en aucun temps en princey consiliatif ou judicatif ; ce est a dire qui peut aucune foiz avoir vois et aucune auctorite es conseulz ou es jugemens de la cite ou de partie de elle

---

[33] The phrase occurs in some fourteenth-century texts, but far less often than in later times.

[34] Lalourcé and Duval, *Recueil*, IX, 120. This "Champagne" consisted of the bailiwicks of Troyes, Sens, Provins, Chaumont, Vitry-le-François, and Meaux. The other five original lay peerages were the duchies of Aquitaine, Burgundy, and Normandy, and the counties of Flanders and Toulouse.

[35] The third peerage created in 1297, the county of Anjou, had local estates in the fourteenth and early fifteenth century. Louis XI inherited it, as an individual, in 1481.

[36] J. R. Major, *Representatives Government in Early Modern France* (New Haven and London: Yale UP, 1980). Neither Provence nor Dauphiné were part of the medieval kingdom of France.

Monarchy: Monarchie est la policie ou le princey que tient un seul. Et sunt.
ii. especes generales de monarchie; une est royalme et l'autre est tyrannie.

Tyranny: Premierement, ce est un seul qui tient le princey et la monarchie a son propre profit et contre le bien publique.

Kingdom: tout un royalme ou un pais est une grande cité, qui contient plusieurs cités partiels

Definitions from: Nicole Oresme, *Le livre de Politiques d'Aristote*.[37]

Charles V, the "Wise," sponsored a broad program of translations of Classical texts in the 1370s. Christine de Pizan, who popularized Charles' sobriquet, claimed that he deliberately focused his translation program – more than thirty Classical texts – on politics.[38] Nicole Oresme, who translated Aristotle's *Politics* and *Ethics* from the Latin versions created by William of Moerbeke in the 1270s, wrote in his proem to the latter that Charles knew Latin, but not the scholarly language of Aristotle's works, "so the King wished, for the common good (*bien commun*), to have them translated into French, so that he and his counselors and other powerful people could better understand them."[39] Oresme praised this characteristic of "affection and love of the *bien public*, which is the best [attribute] there could be in a prince and in his councilors, after the love of God."[40] The claim taken up by Aristotle's sixteenth-century translator Louis Le Roy that politics end, "which is the sovereign human good," encompasses all other goals, resonated in the France of the 1370s.[41]

The obsession with the combination of practical and theoretical can be dated back to the 1350s, when catastrophic events overtook the young Valois

---

[37] Nicole Oresme, *Le livre de Politiques d'Aristote*, ed. A. Menut, *Transactions of the American Philosophical Society*, new series, v. 60 (Philadelphia, PA: APS, 1970). http://gallica.bnf.fr/ark:/12148/btv1b84516069/ holds the two copies made for Louis, duke of Orléans, in the 1390s.

[38] C. de Pizan, *Livre des fais et bonnes meurs du saige roy Charles V* (1404), ed. S. Solente (Paris, 1936–1940), 2 vols.

[39] Oresme, *Ethique d'Aristote* [Paris, 1488], "Le roy a voulu pour le bien commun les faire translater en francois affin que il et ses conseilliers et autres les puissent mieulx entendre mesmement ethiques et politiques" [image 9 on Gallica, no folios #s.]

[40] Oresme, *Ethique*, image 9 on *Gallica*. "affeccion et amour au bien publique, qui est la meilleur qui puisse estre en prince et en ses conseilliers, après l'amour de Dieu." See also C. Sherman, *Imaging Aristotle: Verbal and Visual Representation in Fourteenth-Century France* (Berkeley: University of California Press, 1995), 37–38. Prior to 1500, the standard spelling was "publicque" or "publique", but I will use the modern standard "public" for the masculine modifier; it became common in the sixteenth century. Thus "bien public" but "chose publique" will be used throughout.

[41] Le Roy, *Politiques d'Aristote*, introduction, image 11 online, "comprenant en sa fin, qui est le souverain bien humain, les fins de toutes" [les disciplines]. Le Roy lamented, in his dedication to Henry III, that "la Politique, qui est la plus digne, plus utile & necessaire de toutes, estre demourée en arriere."

dynasty. The political rhetoric developed in the aftermath of King John II's capture at Poitiers became the language of politics in France for the next two centuries, in part because of Charles V's patronage of these translations. Charles adopted some of their key terminology in his ordinances, establishing a template followed by his successors for nearly 200 years. In the monarchical commonwealth created by Charles V, scholars and artists praised the king for creating a "new Athens"; the same milieu three centuries later called Louis XIV's France a "New Rome."

Oresme's revolutionary claim that "All of a kingdom or a *pays* is a large *cité*," defined the kingdom as a political community similar to a Roman *civitas*: that parallel – *polis-civitas-cité* – remained in place until the end of the sixteenth century, when French political rhetoric abandoned the commonwealth for the State.[42] The commonwealth, as Cicero said, in a definition universally used in the period discussed here, was a "collection of citizens living under a common law" and seeking the common good.[43] A State, as Paul Pellisson put it to the Académie Française in 1652, was "a collection of men" living under a common ruler. A century after Pellisson, Anne-Robert Turgot called a State "an assemblage of men [people] reunited under a single government."[44]

---

[42] "*Cité*" most commonly referred to an episcopal city, but almost all of them had been a Roman *civitas*, chief town of a *pagus*, so the term *cité* as a translation of *civitas* had a civil, not ecclesiastical origin. Oresme thus drew together the *res publica*, whose political form might be considered unclear, and the civitas, a political and social unit: many of these units called themselves a "*universitas/université*," to emphasize this common bond. Marsiglio of Padua specifically considered Italian polities to be a form of *civitas*, not *res publica*: J. Canning, *Ideas of Power in the Late Middle Ages, 1296–1417* (Cambridge: CUP, 2011), 86. The members of the *civitas* were, by definition, free men, all the more reason why in the earliest assemblies the third order was the "good towns," not the amorphous category "tiers état." Provincial estates continued the practice of towns only (and often specific towns) as the third order.

[43] In Latin, "bonum commune," in French, "bien commun" or, rarely, "commun bien": some documents spoke of the "bien de la ville" or the "bien du pays," the latter was fairly common in the municipal records of Poitiers. René Favreau has published these deliberations, starting from 1412, in three volumes: in the first of the three volumes, *Poitiers, de Jean de Berry à Charles VII. Registres des délibérations du corps de ville* (Poitiers: Société des Antiquitaires de l'Ouest, 2014), we see deputies going to the Estates of Poitou (1412) for the "profit of the pays" or for the "bien du pais [1413] (pp. 27 and 36). In 1421, it was again "le bien du pays", while in 1422 it was "le bien et profit du pais." In 1423 (172), their deputy had to act on matters related to "le bien du roy et du peuple." The first mention of the "bien de la chose publique" came in 1440 (273) when Alain Moisonne, student in the faculty of medicine, argued he should be exempt from the *taille* because he served the "bien de la chose publique": the council agreed. In 1461, at the Estates of Poitou, their deputy let them know the body had acted for "le bien universel du pais." [Favreau, *Poitiers (. . .) registres des délibérations du corps de ville*, 157].

[44] "un assemblage d'hommes réunis sous un seul gouvernement." A.-R. Turgot, *Œuvres*, I, 440. "Hommes" meant "humans" in the broader social context, but men only in the political one of public participation. Women from elite groups participated in politics, but

If we want to distinguish "men" from "citizens," we must ask: what made you a citizen, and who were the citizens? All other issues aside, a citizen was, by definition, a free man, associated with other free men. In the period covered here, the definition of the citizen came from Aristotle, by way of Nicole Oresme's 1373 French translation: those who had "authority" and "voice" in the *civitas/cité*, either in its courts or its councils.[45] The actual identity of these people varied somewhat from Oresme's distinctions among the six groups noted above. His "citizens" of the kingdom-as-*cité* would be joined by the town magistrates and officials, drawn not only from the world of the law, but from two groups Oresme had excluded: merchants and, at the local level, guild officers. The king regularly consulted the general, rather than local citizens, but, in effect, royal legislation even reached out to the latter. The eighteenth-century jurist and historian Gabriel Henri Gaillard offered a clear description to the Académie Française in 1767, in his speech praising King Charles V:[46]

> We must not forget a constant custom from which Charles never distanced himself, which depicts his character. Did he wish to issue a statute about jurisprudence? He assembled Magistrates. Was it a question of Commerce? He called great Merchants. Was it a question of Military Ordinances? He consulted the Warriors. He illuminated himself always with the lights of others and decided by his own.

These meetings brought together the highest echelons of society – princes of the blood, prelates, leading judges and administrators – and supposed experts drawn from the relevant group. The legislation created after the periodic meetings held to discuss coinage reform, for example, always made a point of emphasizing the participation of merchants who were "expert" in such matters. Guild statutes invariably began as documents generated by the guild itself: the guild would then move up to the town council, thence to the royal government for the unique legitimacy offered by royal letters. Many of these statutes listed the names of all guild members present at the assembly that created the rules.[47]

---

rarely as speaking or voting members in public fora. That such women felt themselves to be citizens comes through most clearly in Christine de Pizan's *Cité des Dames* (1405), invariably translated into English as the *Book of the City of Ladies*, which entirely misses her deliberate political assertion of female citizenship. Female guilds, like the *harangères* or the silk spinners, could submit grievances to a town assembly, just like male ones, and they, too, had royally issued statutes.

[45] As Oresme's wording makes clear, citizen meant those eligible [*peut ... avoir*].

[46] G. H. Gaillard, *Éloge de Charles V, roi de France* (Paris, 1767), 29–30. Gaillard won the oratory prize of the Académie in 1767 for this speech.

[47] On the many systems of guild regulation, see J. P. Leguay, *Vivre en ville au moyen âge* (Plouédern: Éditions Gisserot, 2006), ch. 5. Thierry's documents on both Amiens and Abbeville contain many examples. AM Dijon, GG 1–3, contain guild statutes from the fourteenth to eighteenth centuries.

Fourteenth-century people perfectly understood Oresme's term *civitas/cité*: the political society of their walled town, or, more broadly, of their *pays*, their region. Oresme's remarkable innovation, claiming the kingdom was merely a *civitas* writ large, undergirded Charles V's political enterprise: creating a unified kingdom built upon the commonwealth's citizens. French elites had faced several fourteenth-century crises that called into question the unity principle: the succession to Louis X in 1316; the accession of Philip VI in 1328; negotiations with Edward III and Charles the Bad of Navarre in 1355–1360; the perennial Flemish question; and the ongoing problems of apanages, for younger sons, and dowries, for royal daughters. The consensus opinion, whether in the succession crisis of 1316–1317 or in the legislation on apanages, was that the kingdom of France had to remain united: no individual king had the **right** to dismember it.

The kingdom, as a *cité*, was a self-governing community, with its own group of citizens; the "partial" *cités* of which it consisted were also self-governing communities, on the local level, with their citizens. This second, larger group of citizens did not have to be – and, in Oresme's eyes, was not – coterminous with the restricted group of citizens who constituted the *cité* of the kingdom as a whole. This dissonance created significant problems, particularly between 1356 and 1422: the groups who were local but not national citizens looked askance at "representative" bodies that imposed taxes to which, in their view, they had not properly consented. Virtually every municipal government consulted a "general assembly" of some kind before creating new taxes or raising the rates of the existing ones. From the Étienne Marcel episode of 1356–1358 to the Maillotins of 1382 to the Parisian massacres of the 1410's, town elites – Oresme's non-citizens – often violently demanded the defense of the "bien de la chose publique": in the end, the merchants and artisans largely failed in this broader reach for a share of national political power, but they retained considerable local power. Pirenne long ago argued that rural governance remained patriarchal, while urban governance had become fraternal in the Low Countries; the contrast holds up in many French towns, and medieval French representative bodies assumed that lords – lay and ecclesiastical – represented the peasantry, while the deputies of the "bonnes villes" protected urban interests only. In a sense, the urban elites got what they most wanted from the king: control of the local **form** of taxation. The inhabitants of the most powerful French cities, like Paris, Rouen, Reims, or Lyon, also got exemption from the *tailles*, not only for their holdings in town, but for those in the countryside worked by "servants."[48]

The assemblies called by kings included those we call Estates General, a misleading generic label.[49] Philip IV and his sons called massive meetings,

---

[48] If the owner rented to a farmer, the farmer had to pay the *taille*. This distinction obviously lent itself to fraud; rural areas near such cities long protested this exemption.

[49] J. R. Major, in his many works on representative bodies, argued that the 1560 meeting was the first real Estates General; the meetings prior to 1560, even of 1576, had a variety of

involving hundreds of urban deputies, usually gathered in two separate venues: Languedoïl and Langue d'Oc. After the 1350s, in the north, the "Estates General" were an institution that allowed the government to consult the local officials – royal, ecclesiastical, noble, and municipal – who ruled the country on an everyday basis. They were **not** primarily a representative assembly designed to hear from constituencies of any kind, whether individual or corporate. From 1560 onward, in contrast, the Estates Generals combined this previous function with an expectation that they would present to the king the just grievances of his subjects.[50] The king and his council strongly insisted on this new function, and regularly chastised local officials who did not sufficiently seek out and incorporate popular grievances into the cahiers.[51] The combination of the new purpose of the Estates Generals of 1560–1588 and the tumultuous, massive meetings about customary law redaction in the 1570s created a democratic political impetus that was deeply frightening to the Parlementaire milieu, from which the king drew so many central administrators.[52] Unsurprisingly, Catholic elites hurled the "democracy" charge against Protestants: "democracy," in their Aristotelian vocabulary, was one of the three corrupted forms of government.[53]

The "respublique françoyse" was a monarchy, in which these various assemblies provided elements of aristocracy and, in some cases, of "popular government." Whether it was the France of Charles V or that of Louis XIV, political elites thought of themselves as citizens, urban bourgeoisie in particularly invariably so described themselves.[54] Even Jacques-Bénigne Bossuet, in his supposed

configurations that make the generic "Estates General" a problematic term. The usual royal term was "les gens des trois estatz de nostre royaume" [the men of the three estates of our kingdom]. Some major provinces did not send deputies to assemblies prior to 1484 (Brittany only in 1560).

[50] Deputies in 1484 brought local grievances. The Burgundian example provided in P. Pélicier, "Voyages des deputes de Bourgogne à Blois (1483)," *Bibliothèque de l'École de Chartes* 47 (1886): 357–369: 365–367.

[51] In towns, the royal government insisted that the council place a locked trunk, with a slot on top, in the town hall: inhabitants of the town could (and did) deposit anonymous suggestions in this trunk. The council usually appointed two or three notables to read these suggestions and make a report about them. The central government chastised towns that failed to make such a trunk available, or that tried to limit the hours when it would be accessible, as was the case in Paris in 1576.

[52] BNF, M Fr 16,624, fols. 6–22: meeting of the estates of the city, prévôté, and viscounty of Paris in 1588, with deputies from nearly 300 parishes, most of which sent two representatives.

[53] H. Daussy, *Le parti Huguenot* (Geneva: Droz, 2014), 494–505, on the particularly important role of the controversy about the writings of Jean Morély, which touched off a Protestant debate about the balance among the three elements – monarchical, aristocratic, popular – of legitimate government.

[54] C. Le Mao, ed., *Chronique du Bordelais au crepuscule du Grand Siècle : Le Mémorial de Savignac* (Bordeaux: PU of Bordeaux, 2004), reveals the "citizen" mentality of a Parlementaire of Bordeaux in the years around 1700.

defense of louisquatorzien absolutism, repeatedly talked about citizens: he assured readers that Jesus and the Apostles were "bons citoyens" (good citizens) of their patrie![55] The deputies in these many regional and local assemblies, as well as those elected to run town governments, spoke the language of politics. The monarchy had to communicate with them, and negotiate with them, in a language they could understand and respect. As Philippe-Joseph Salazar put it, in his preface for Jacques Amyot's *Projet de l'éloquence royale*: "The word of the Prince must not only be true and beautiful, it must also be efficacious."[56]

For the fourteenth century, in particular, the English word "language" creates a theoretical confusion, with respect to Pierre Bourdieu's distinction between "*langue*" and "*langage*." "Langue" means the actual language: Serge Lusignan has provided a compelling and detailed study of the French monarchy's shift from Latin to French in the fourteenth century.[57] Those shifts remind us of how personal political power could be: Philip VI, notorious for his ignorance of Latin, shifted to French; his son, John II, whom Philip criticized for being too learned, shifted back to Latin; John's son, Charles V, although he knew some Latin, clearly preferred French, and shifted back again. In this respect, England and France followed similar paths, with the vernacular taking over the language of politics, even while sharing ground with Latin in the realm of political philosophy. The greater role of French in political theory comes through clearly in the works of Christine de Pizan, whose importance to the language of practical politics is only now achieving the recognition it deserves.[58]

"Langage" carries the sense of a specialized vocabulary, one often known only to specialists, and, furthermore, one that often contradicts the generally received meaning of a given word in everyday language: in our own day, the contrast between scholarly, especially scientific use of the word "theory" and the popular meaning is one of the most troubling examples. The vocabulary discussed here often began as a specialized "langage" of those involved in

---

[55] J.-B. Bossuet, *Politics Drawn from the Very Words of Holy Scripture*, trans. P. Riley (Cambridge: CUP, 1990), 27ff: book I, article VI (de l'amour de la patrie), propositions 2 and 3. In proposition 2, we read of Jesus that "On le reconnoissoit pour bon citoyen" and that he always remained "faithful" [fidèle] to his patrie; he thus inspired the same in his apostles – proposition 3 tells us "The apostles, and the first faithful, were always good citizens." The original 1709 [posthumous] edition is online at Gallica. http://gallica.bnf.fr /ark:/12148/bpt6k103256m/f1.image Bossuet wrote this text in the 1680s.

[56] Cited in R. Roy, "L'institution oratoire du Prince ou le savoir au service du bien dire," *Renaissance et Réforme* 31, n. 4 (2008), online : http://jps.library.utoronto.ca/index.php /renref/article/view/9151/6115

[57] S. Lusignan, *La langue des rois au Moyen Âge. Le français en France et en Angleterre* (Paris: PUF, 2004).

[58] T. Adams, *Christine de Pizan and the Fight for France* (State College, PA: Penn State University Press, 2014), and F. Autrand, *Christine de Pizan. Une femme en politique* (Paris: Fayard, 2009), and several others have opened up new avenues of research on Christine de Pizan and politics.

political life and, especially, in the law, but it had to function in the larger universe of communication: Benoît Lethenet, in his study of Macon, neatly captures the process in the title of his ninth chapter, "Receive and Transmit."[59] Kings, princes, estates, town governments, and orators had to use a terminology that made sense to their audience, and they communicated through interlocutors. For the king, that meant bishops for the clergy, *baillis* for the nobles, lieutenants generals (chief judges) of the bailiwicks, and town governments. The rural population often received information both through the judicial chain of command and from its priests.

In the sixteenth century, a new term became popular with the Parlementaires and, later, the nobility: the "respublique françoyse." Town governments started to use the term "respublique," but did so often to refer to the town itself rather than to the kingdom.[60] Jean Bodin's *Six Livres de la République* (1576), often misleadingly read as a text about "absolute monarchy," in fact sought to describe and analyze the monarchical commonwealth, just as its title implies.[61] Yet practical developments had pushed the monarchy in directions that made the old commonwealth increasingly anachronistic as an organizing device. Francis I had taken two key steps in undermining this commonwealth: the Concordat of Bologna (1516), which replaced episcopal election by royal nomination, and the legalized venality of office (1522), which eliminated the nominal system of election to judgeships in the Parlements. Eudes de Mézeray, royal historiographer of Louis XIV, claimed the mastermind of this pernicious step was chancellor Antoine du Prat:[62]

> [du Prat] died [. . .] much tormented by the remorse of his conscience
> [. . .] for not having observed Laws other than those of his proper interests,
> and the passion of the Sovereign. It was he who removed the election to

---

[59] B. Lethenet, "'Comment l'on doit se gouverner': La ville, la guerre et le pouvoir. Macon (vers 1380–vers 1422)," Ph.D. thesis, Université de Strasbourg, 2012, ch. 9.

[60] Neatly captured in the title of O. Carpi's *La république imaginaire. Amiens pendant les troubles de Religion* (Paris: Belin, 2005). The vocabulary of "republic" had a long history in southern towns like Arles.

[61] That later writers used Bodin's arguments to justify the "monarchie absolue" is certainly true; seventeenth-century political theorists in France and the Empire, above all, viewed Bodin as a key theorist of such a system. On the latter, see R. von Friedeburg, "The Reception of Bodin in the Holy Roman Empire and the Making of the Territorial State," in *The Reception of Bodin*, ed. H. Lloyd (Leiden: Brill, 2013), 293–322.

[62] E. de Mézeray, *Abrégé chronologique de l'histoire de France* (Amsterdam, 1740), III, 144. [du Prat] mourut [. . .] fort tourmenté des remords de sa conscience, comme ses soupirs & ses paroles le firent connoître, pour n'avoir point observé d'autres Loix (lui qui étoit grand Jurisconsulte) que ses intérêts propres, & la passion du Souverain. C'est lui qui a ôté les élections des Benefices & les privileges à plusieurs Eglises; qui a introduit la vénalité des Charges de Judicatures; qui a appris en France à faire hardiment toutes sortes d'impositions; qui a divisé l'intérêt du Roi d'avec le bien public". Jouanna, *Le pouvoir absolu*, 316, speaks of the "authoritarianism" of Francis I and Henry II.

benefices and the privileges of several Churches; who introduced the venality of judicial office; who taught France to boldly levy all sorts of taxes, who divided the interest of the King from the *bien public*.

That elites objected strongly to both policies is obvious from the records of meetings from 1484 to 1576. At the Estates General of 1484, the general *cahier* had demanded the election of virtually every judge and royal attorney in France.[63] The Estates' spokesman, Jean de Rély, and his fellow deputies also demanded regular meetings of the Estates General and insisted that a representative assembly had to vote all taxation. Rély was the king's almoner, and later an important councilor of Charles VIII, so hardly someone hostile to royal authority. The Estates General of Orléans (December 1560–January 1561) repeated most of these demands, particularly those related to election of bishops, abbots, and royal judges.[64]

Kings nominally respected the taxation principle at the provincial level, in large parts of the kingdom. As noted above, they always argued that the *taille* relied on a vote at the Estates General of 1439. At the Estates General of 1484, the deputies from Normandy and the members of the royal council got in a heated debate about precisely this point: the Normans insisted their oath to defend the "interests of the people" meant they had to oppose the continuation of the *taille* – a tax that brought "servitude" and "damage" – when the "commonwealth was not in danger."[65] Here again Francis I innovated: he created a tax on walled towns, to pay for the infantry, without any pretense of a vote by an assembly. In time, this tax became known as the levy for the 50,000 infantry: one of the great successes of urban elites was that this tax disappeared in the fourth quarter of the sixteenth century, never to return.[66] Local and regional assemblies continued to wield considerable power in the great pays d'États, until 1789.[67] They had

---

[63] Masselin, *Journal*, appendix, 682, *cahier* of the Estates.

[64] The occasional procès-verbal of an "election" makes it clear that most of the time it was cooptation, but in some cases an array of candidates presented themselves and the scattered vote totals indicate a real election, within the limited group of electors. The documents for elections in Blois in 1576 and 1614, for example, make it clear that the rural delegates – almost all of whom were local court judges – had instructions to vote for the lieutenant general; only in Blois and one or two other large towns did delegates dare to support someone else. In the city, prévôté, and viscounty of Paris in 1588, in contrast, eighteen candidates received votes, and the *prévôt des marchands*, Michel Marteau, master of accounts, narrowly defeated [139–105] the lieutenant *particulier* of the prévôté, Me Mathias de La Bruyère. [BNF, M Fr 16264, fols. 6-22]. AM Blois, BB 5 (1576) and 17 (1614).

[65] Masselin, *Journal*, 418–421, which is unfortunately his Latin version of debates held in French. The phrase "reipublicæ majori periculo" almost surely was "chose publique" in the French.

[66] As Robert Knecht has pointed out in his many fine works on Francis I and the sixteenth-century monarchy, Francis I and Henry II had a strong case to make about the unfairness of urban exemptions from the *tailles*.

[67] Marie-Laure Leguay, *Les états provinciaux dans la construction de l'État moderne* (Geneva: Droz, 2001); François-Xavier Emmanuelli, "L'administration provinciale des

particularly wide powers in determining **how** the money would be raised, an issue of vital importance because it enabled the wealthiest to shield their forms of wealth.

De Rély had also played a major role in the 1461 defense of the Pragmatic Sanction, whose full restoration was a key goal in 1484 and in 1560.[68] The first article of the Ordinance of Orléans, produced in response to the Estates General of 1560, specifically called for the election of bishops, by their cathedral chapters and two dozen local lay notables, half of them noble. Later meetings of both provincial and general estates continued to insist on the implementation of article 1. When the Estates General of 1576 asked Henry III to implement this **royal** legislation, he ridiculed their demand in a meeting with bishops whom he mockingly reminded would be unlikely to hold their sees if he and his brother had restored the Pragmatic Sanction. As Mark Greengrass has carefully documented, the reform agenda built on commonwealth principles foundered precisely in the period 1576–1583.[69]

The Estates General of 1560–1561 provide a perfect ending point, in part because of the publication of so many of the key commonwealth texts by Vincent Sertenas, a royal printer with close ties to chancellor Michel de l'Hospital. In 1560–1561, Sertenas printed the Parlement's 1461 defense of the Pragmatic Sanction, Jean Gerson's 1405 sermon *Vivat rex*, and the cahier of the Estates General of 1484, including de Rély's speech.[70] These texts, along with Oresme's glossary and the political writings of Christine de Pizan and Philippe de Mezière's *Songe du Vieil Pélerin* (1388), formed the canon of monarchical commonwealth ideology.[71] The tradition had its heroes – not just Gerson, but men like Jean de Saint-Romain, the *avocat général* of the Parlement of Paris who fought Louis XI's assault on the Pragmatic Sanction, and the members of the Juvénal des Ursins family.

États de Provence (XVIe–XVIIIe siècles). Bilan provisoire," *Provence Historique* (2010), now accessible online at: https://liame.revues.org/129

[68] The Pragmatic Sanction of Bourges (1438), issued by Charles VII, mandated election of archbishops, bishops, abbots, and priors.

[69] M. Greengrass, *Governing Passions: Peace and Reform in the French Kingdom* (Oxford: OUP, 2007).

[70] Gerson's role in both as a conciliarist and as a key figure in the commonwealth political tradition had much to do with the connection between debates in the Church, between councils and the Pope, and those in French lay society about royal power, on which, see Lange, *First French Reformation*.

[71] Évrard de Trémaugon's *Songe du Vergier* (1378) had a major impact on Gerson and Christine de Pizan, and so might be added to this list, but later writers and orators rarely cited him. In the sixteenth century, Guillaume Budé's treatise on coinage, *De Asse et partibus eius* (1515 and a French summary, ordered by Francis I, of 1522), had a major impact: see L.-A. Sanchi, "Humanistes et antiquaires. Le *De Asse* de Guillaume Budé," *Anabases* 16 (2012), http://anabases.revues.org/3977; DOI: 10.4000/anabases.3977.

Their model king was Christine de Pizan's Charles V, the "Wise."[72] The Charles VII of the post-1435 period came in for high praise, too: he had, in fact, issued many edicts enshrining election, which usually meant selection by the local elite's members of the given profession – cathedral chapters for bishops; subaltern judges and perhaps some *avocats* for judges. Louis XII regularly convened assemblies, although not an official Estates General, and he remained proverbial both for his low level of taxation and for his reputation as "le père du peuple," an image the royal government peddled hard in the late sixteenth century and after.[73] As part of the shift to the "bien de l'Estat" model, the central monarchy moved away from the old metaphor of the king as the head of the "body politic," and toward this new metaphor of the king as the father of his people.[74] At the national level, the assemblies of members of that body politic – Estates General in 1560, 1561, 1576, 1588, 1593 (Leaguer), and 1614; Assemblies of Notables in 1558, 1560, 1566, 1575, 1583 [first use of the actual term], 1596, 1617, and 1626 – simply ceased.[75]

Political ideas have meaning, in an immediate sense, only in an actual political context, in an actual '*rapport des forces*', or balance of power(s). In a highly personalized political system, like that of monarchical France, the '*crédit*' of the king himself played a fundamental role in determining the meaning of political terms: Charles V had a lot more credibility than his feckless father or his mentally unstable son. Their contemporaries had fundamentally different views of Henry III and Henry IV. Political speech acts appealed to different audiences, often directly targeting interest groups. Because different political configurations favored different interest groups, we must begin our analysis of both the given moment's system and of its political discourse with a detailed deconstruction of the people, the interests, and interest groups at play. We need to start treating the

---

[72] His subjects called him Charles the Rich, because of his many taxes and healthy treasury.

[73] Many sixteenth- and seventeenth-century sources refer to the assembly Louis XII convened in 1506, to break off his daughter's Claude's engagement to Charles of Ghent (later Emperor Charles V) and to affiance her to the future Francis I, as an Estates General, but no formal convocation process took place. The king invited specific people and towns.

[74] That no one took literally this metaphor is obvious from the speeches given in 1614 to the then thirteen-year-old Louis XIII. C. Cuttica, *Sir Robert Filmer (1588-1653) and the Patriotic Monarch: Patriarchalism in Seventeenth-Century Political Thought* (Manchester: Manchester UP, 2012), shows the same evolution in England.

[75] The French clergy continued to meet in a general assembly every five years and voted money to the king; the monarchy called a meeting of the Estates General in 1649, postponed it to 1651, but then never convened it. Local meetings did take place, and we have a few surviving local cahiers. D. Le Page and J. Loiseau, *Pouvoir royal et institutions dans la France moderne* (Paris: Armand Colin, 2019), 42–43 provide a convenient chart, and add a meeting of the expanded royal council in 1625. They do not include the important Moulins meeting of 1566. Earlier meetings would include at least two called by Louis XII in 1498–1499, about currency, 1506 (about breaking Claude de France's engagement to the future Emperor Charles V), and meetings called by Francis I to discuss peace treaties with the Emperor.

political actors as politicians who were speaking and acting to achieve specific ends and using a given political rhetoric to achieve their goals, rather than to make far-reaching philosophical statements about the nature of the political community.

I.2   A Socio-Political History of Political Ideas

In my opinion, the cause is that the learned men [*gens sçavans*] who have decorated it a little by their writings, have entirely left the handling of affairs, to give themselves completely over to inquiry of the truth, making contemplation their supreme felicity. And those called to offices [*charges*], and public administrations, do not usually have great learning, or, if they do, lack the leisure to write, such that the learned [*doctes*] leaving negotiation, and the negotiators study, this science, which is imperfect without learning [*sçavoir*] and experience together, has remained, as I said, behind.

Loys Le Roy, *Politiques d'Aristote* (Paris: A. Drouart, 1599), author's preface.[76]

How does my approach here differ from that of others? Like Louis Le Roy, I begin with the question: how do political ideas and political practice intersect? The political reality sets the agenda of what problem needs to be solved. The great scholars of political theory and language have established several different contexts for the problem solvers. The foundational works of Quentin Skinner, John Pocock, and Marc Fumaroli came out in a five-year period (1975–1980), forever changing the way historians look at the history of political theory and practice.[77]

Scholars of French royalist discourse, which emphasized the king's broad prerogative, have not given sufficient attention to the fact that specific interest groups often picked up a language of royal "pleine puissance" or even "puissance absolue" if they had the king on their side. The most obvious example of this phenomenon came in 1576, at the Estates General of Blois, when the clergy tried to convince the king to use his "puissance absolue" to force acceptance of the decrees of the Council of Trent. Those same ecclesiastics violently objected to the idea that the same "puissance absolue" could be used to force them to sell their properties to help pay the king's debts: the two lay orders had agreed on precisely this course of action in 1560–1561, and local assemblies continued to call for the measure long afterwards.

By looking at the practical political interests of different groups, we can see more clearly the accurate meaning of their political rhetoric. Just as in our

---

[76] Edition revised by F. Morel, based on the 1576 expanded edition. Accessible on Gallica: http://gallica.bnf.fr/ark:/12148/bpt6k52144c/f10.image Gallica now has the 1576 edition online: https://gallica.bnf.fr/ark:/12148/bpt6k8707808j/

[77] Q. Skinner, *Foundations of Modern Political Thought* (Cambridge: CUP, 1978), 2 vols.; J. Pocock, *The Machiavellian Moment* (Princeton, NJ: Princeton UP, 1975); M. Fumaroli, *L'âge de l'éloquence* (Paris and Geneva: Droz, 1980).

own day, some of that rhetoric was bunkum – code words aimed at one's constituents – and we need to understand the political purpose of such language, rather than simply viewing it as the childish ranting of reactionary nobles or simple-minded common folk.[78] The two forces – the commonwealth's advocates and the centralizing royalists – struggled for centuries, and the pendulum swung back and forth. We have imposed an order on this struggle based on some dubious premises, above all on the premise that because centralizing forces won out in the seventeenth century, they had the upper hand in earlier times.

The danger of our traditional approach to political theory and political rhetoric is that we tend to read the latter simply as a derivative of the former: I will argue here that the relationship was symbiotic, and that practical political reality had more to do with such rhetorical choices than did France's intellectual heritage, from which a broad vocabulary could be drawn. The king – using his "puissance absolue" – could and did simply ignore inconvenient precedents to get what he wanted, a process that accelerated considerably in the sixteenth century. Little wonder that elites sought a political discourse, and practice, that would put limits on royal action.[79]

In looking at the transition away from the monarchical commonwealth, however, we must make the distinction between means and ends. With respect to the Church, the sixteenth-century *cahiers* presented a remarkably consistent set of demands: physical residence by benefice holders; a limit of one benefice per person; professional competency (including the requirement that, for example, a bishop actually be a priest); French nationality; moral rectitude among the clergy; and various other reforms. They prefaced articles with these specific demands, the general point being that the king needed to restore the Pragmatic Sanction.[80] In the seventeenth century, Henry IV and Louis XIII, abetting a clergy reformed after the Council of Trent, enacted most of the reforms: that is, they achieved the ends, but by different means. The practical reforms in the Church were an example of effective royal action on an issue of great importance to many French people, but action taken within the

---

[78] B. Rosenwein, *Emotional Communities in the Early Middle Ages* (Ithaca: Cornell UP, 2006), for a critique of old views of the role of emotions in medieval society.

[79] Contemporary readers might consider that American presidents, for one, have regularly used "executive orders" in the last two decades to do things manifestly in violation of the US Constitution, as understood by those who wrote it. The prosecution of mass-scale wars, without benefit of an actual Congressional declaration of war, is also an obvious violation both of the actual Constitution and, even more egregiously, the spirit behind it. James Madison's notes on the debates in Philadelphia could not be clearer on this point.

[80] These *cahiers* – even those from hardline Catholic local assemblies – often demanded election of parish priests by the parishioners, too. Lange, *First French Reformation*, on the royalist use of arguments similar to those of Popes struggling to gain the upper hand over Church councils.

framework of the emerging royal State, not by means of reforms resuscitating the monarchical commonwealth.

As with the Church, so, too, in secular matters: the king's unique authority to sanction action – for example the universally recognized principle that the king had to approve any tax, levied by anyone – meant provincial estates would appeal to the king to prevent levies by his armies, carried out without letters from him, while simultaneously claiming that the king could raise taxes in their province only with **their** approval. We can see the obvious shift caused by the permanent taxation created (de facto) in 1360 (and 1383): the Norman Charter (1314) cited the need for the king to inform and to consult Normans before taxing them, but it says nothing about consent. Fifteenth-century agreements, like those with the Burgundians (1477), in contrast, specifically recognized the right to vote taxation.[81] The massive financial demands of the Wars of Religion drove French towns to ever expanded taxation, all of which required royal approval. The contrasting legal status between *deniers patrimoniaux* – immemorial taxes, automatically included in a king's initial renewal of a town's rights, liberties, and privileges – and *deniers d'octroi* – new taxes, for which the town had to seek periodic royal permission to continue – profoundly increased royal leverage on French towns, as Henry IV would make clear.[82]

Rather than seek out the "genesis of the early modern State" [*genèse de l'État moderne*], as Jean-Philippe Genet has called it, I seek instead to understand the political system of late medieval and Renaissance France on its own terms. That many of the basic elements of the early modern monarchical State took root in this period – permanent taxation, a standing army, an ever-expanding royal officialdom – is beyond question, but I seek to analyze the developments of the France of Charles V or Charles VII outside the framework of a dubious construct like the "absolutism" of Louis XIV.[83] The key change – creation of permanent taxation by 1383 – brought together the political and economic dimensions of the *chose publique*, and provided an ideal common ground for development of that political vocabulary.

How does one research such an issue? All books begin with assumptions, and mine are drawn from my own upbringing as the child of professional

---

[81] Louis XI's letters specifically stated that "no aids or subsidies" would be levied in Burgundy unless they had been "accorded, consented, and granted by the said men of the three Estates."

[82] A. Finlay-Crosswhite, *Henry IV and the Towns* (Cambridge: CUP, 2000).

[83] Genet has edited a series of volumes of papers given at several conferences on this theme. I benefitted greatly from conversations with him at a conference on State Formation in Medieval and Early Modern Europe, held in Bergen, Norway in 2012. B. Bove, *Le temps de la Guerre de Cent Ans, 1328–1453* (Paris: Belin, 2009), 537–539, has some perceptive remarks about Genet's project. My own *State in Early Modern France* (Cambridge: CUP, 2nd ed., 2009), makes clear the connection between medieval and Renaissance developments and the early modern State.

politicians. French politicians – and throughout this book I will think of them as **politicians** – of the fourteenth or sixteenth centuries worked within functioning political systems. Politicians from each interest group sought to achieve their ends, in part, by crafting a system that would benefit their group's members. The monarchical commonwealth system that functioned from the 1360s through the 1570s gave control of local governance to a coalition drawn from many groups: clergy, military nobles, merchants, bourgeois, guild members, lawyers, judges, notaries, financial officials, even, in the villages, some of the peasants. The coalition varied from town to town and from province to province, and its members regularly fought internal political battles to achieve local dominance: the more powerful groups – merchants, clergy, legal men, and nobles – regularly sought royal intervention on their group, or even individual behalf. Direct royal intervention in municipal politics had far more often to do with a response to a local request for support than to some effort to expand royal prerogative. Royal demands for money invariably led to negotiations, and walled towns regularly got to keep a share of the money for their military preparedness.[84]

Traditional intellectual history, focused internally on its texts, can help us identify which texts these late medieval and Renaissance writers, orators, and political actors cited. We can certainly see the influence of an Aristotle on royal officials like Jean Juvénal des Ursins, but one could say as much of his influence on a provincial royal officer or town magistrate. When speakers and writers cited their sources, tracing such influence is relatively simple, but often they did not: in some cases, they surely felt their assumed audience knew the source, so they had no need to cite the obvious. Traditional intellectual history leaves aside many important questions, among which we might single out the issue of choice: why choose a given Classical author, why again the given work, and why a third time the given passage? Anyone who has read sixteenth-century French speeches knows that orators repeated endlessly the same stories from the same Classical authors, and often chose the same biblical passages.[85]

Skinner created a context of other texts, beyond the canon of great works, in which we can see how a political actor *could* think about a problem, that is, what

---

[84] CAF, #13079, for example, shows Lyon getting permission to raise a new tax on hooved animals entering the city; the king allowed them to use part of the proceeds to pay their share of the infantry tax on walled towns and part for the upkeep of their walls. Narbonne obtained an exemption from the infantry tax in 1560, on the grounds that the costs of maintaining the soldiers manning its walls exceeded what it would have paid for the infantry tax. G. Moynès, *Inventaire des archives communales antérieur à 1790, série AA* (Narbonne, 1877), 187.

[85] Descimon and Cosandey, *L'absolutisme en France*, has a particularly fine presentation of the influence of neo-stoicism in France. M. Houllemare, *Politiques de la parole. Le parlement de Paris au XVIᵉ siècle* (Geneva: Droz, 2011), is indispensable on the discourse of the Parlement of Paris.

system of analytical thought one could use to frame a solution in coherent, systematic language.[86] Pocock focused more on specific language and rhetoric: actors had to choose given words, and use given rhetorical strategies. Fumaroli's analysis demonstrated how French political actors moved from a rhetoric rooted in Cicero to one based on Tacitus, that is, in the perspective examined here, from a commonwealth to an imperial register. Ciceronian rhetoric fitted neatly into the politics of the monarchical commonwealth; Tacitus better suited the royal State.[87]

Many scholars, working in traditional political theory, have tracked down the intellectual roots of such ideas, or within their contemporaneous political dialogues. In the revival of interest in forms of "republicanism," however, Skinner and others have largely excluded France, because of its supposed "absolutist" outcome.[88] One of the key texts in setting the Anglophone world's view of the French monarchy, Sir John Fortescue's famous distinction between *dominium regale* (in France) and *dominium politicum et regale* (in England), did indeed present an accurate contrast in the time of Louis XI, when Sir John was in France. Louis XI pushed the limits of royal power to the extreme and offered justifications well outside the commonwealth discourse that was dominant during the period examined here. Yet Louis XI's violations of accepted French norms sparked both opposition and opprobrium, and his successors restored several key elements of Charles VII's monarchical commonwealth.

I seek to place political ideas "in context" in a way that goes beyond locating them within what are now the dual approaches to intellectual history: their place in the ongoing dialogue with the dead that always justifies a given political order; and the context of their rhetorical and textual moment. We must situate political ideas in their political context, and, more broadly, in the constellation of power relations of their own day. In a sense, I follow here the obverse of the *Begriffsgeschichte* approach initiated by Reinhard Koselleck and followed up by scholars such as Janet Coleman: they look at the social reality through the lens of a concept, or perhaps we might say, along with Skinner, at the expression of a concept; I look at the concept, and its expression, through the lens of social and political reality.

Koselleck writes: "Without common concepts, there is no society, and above all, no political field of action." I am trying to find the intersecting genealogies of

---

[86] See L. Febvre *Le Problème de l'incroyance au XVIᵉ siècle* (Paris, 1941), which deals extensively with the problem of *what* it was possible to think at a given moment; I would say the Cambridge School adds to his insights the issue of *how* it was possible to think.

[87] Tacitus was the only Classical author to use the term *res publica* to mean a form of government contrasted to monarchy, so the shift to the rhetoric of Tacitus was helpful for Europeans to shift the meaning of *res publica* from legitimate form of government to non-monarchical government.

[88] Q. Skinner and R. Van Gelderen, eds., *Republicanism: A Shared European Heritage* (Cambridge: CUP, 2002), 2 vols. The concept of a single "republican" heritage is problematic, for reasons clearly laid out by David Wootton in his review of these volumes: *English Historical Review* 120, n. 485 (2005): 135–139.

several related concepts, the various *langages*, traditions of political discourse (and utterance of such discourse, in performance) and the words attached to them, but to situate my analysis at all times within practical politics.[89] As John Watts has pointed out about fifteenth-century writers on politics, "an increasing number had acquired their learning in the course of political and administrative careers." He rightly emphasizes "the growing sense on the part of politicians that they needed to communicate with a broad cross-section of society in order to justify public action or to guide public behaviour."[90]

Koselleck argues that words have autonomous power, "without whose use human actions and passions could hardly be experienced, and certainly not made intelligible to others."[91] That strikes me as overstatement – we might ponder the similar power of visual images – but I am more interested in his tripartite division of social and political concepts: 1) 'traditional' ones, like Aristotelian categories, that apply in a vast array of situations; 2) conceptual false cognates, if you will, that is, specific words that persist, but whose meaning undergoes fundamental change;[92] and 3) neologisms related to "a specific social or political circumstances." I think all three of these factors were at work in the period covered here.

With respect to the first factor, I agree with Janet Coleman:[93] "concepts from the past are not universal or transhistorical; they have a history but not on their own. Their history is due to there having been re-thought, reconsidered and rendered intelligible and therefore changed by historically-situated thinkers, and we are simply the latest in the queue." Again, agreeing with Coleman, I reject the implication that binaries are the motor of change in meaning; not only did given words have multiple meanings, but we are dealing with a group of words, none of which defined precisely what everyone was trying to describe, but each of which caught some part of its essence. Governments, representative bodies, and political writers and orators deliberately played with these ambiguities in terms like kingdom, nation, *patrie, bien public, res publica, estat, dominium, imperium, potestas-pouvoir-puissance (puissance absolue), auctoritas (autorité royale),* king/monarch, *république, chose publique.*

---

[89] For a fascinating sense of the many "languages" of sixteenth and seventeenth-century political discourse, see A. Pagden, ed., *The Languages of Political Discourse in Early-Modern Europe* (Cambridge: CUP, 1987).

[90] J. Watts, *The Making of Polities: Europe, 1300–1500* (Cambridge: CUP, 2009), 381.

[91] R. Koselleck, *Futures Past: On the Semantics of Historical Time*, trans. K. Tribe (Cambridge, MA: MIT Press, 1985), 74, both quotations.

[92] J. Coleman, "El concepto de república. Continuidad mítica y continuidad real," *Res Publica* 15 (1) (2005), for a nice presentation of the problems with respect to the term "res publica."

[93] J. Coleman, "The Practical Uses of Begriffsgeschichte," 30, consulted at http://www.jyu.fi /yhtfil/redescriptions/Yearbook%201999/Coleman%20J%201999.pdf

The chronological framework of this study comes from two major shifts in French political discourse:

1) In the 1350s, when the vocabulary of the "bien de la chose publique" and "bien public" became the normative discourse of political life.
2) In the late sixteenth century, when commonwealth discourse gave way to one built around the "good of the State," a process I have examined in detail in a second book.

The chapters follow developments chronologically, beginning with the fundamental shift in the 1350s, on through the reign of Henry II. I make one exception to that procedure, in Chapter 5, on the special case of the towns.

Examining and analyzing the language of politics requires research from the ground up: in what follows, I will look at the language used in town council meetings, in local estates, in regional estates, in the Estates General, in correspondence, in speeches, and in royal laws and edicts. I will cross-reference that language with the contemporaneous texts in political theory.

The minutes of the dozen full, and more numerous partial, municipal council deliberations I have consulted provide a key source about this language.[94] The documents generated for the Estates Generals of 1560 and 1561 provide an excellent presentation of mainstream commonwealth ideology, at a point at which elites hoped to "restore" a political system based on its principles. I will pick up the story of how and why they failed in *From Monarchical Commonwealth to Royal State, 1561–1651.*

---

[94] Municipal deliberations everywhere focus on quotidian reality: the water supply, military matters, loans and taxes, etc. Anyone who has ever attended a committee meeting knows that the minutes are not a verbatim record. For an introduction to this subject, see the invaluable C. Fargeix, *Les élites lyonnaises du XVe siècle au miroir de leur langage* (Paris: De Boccard, 2007); the 2005 thesis on which the book is based is available online. On published deliberations, see the excellent bibliography in N. Murphy, *Ceremonial Entries, Municipal Liberties and the Negotiations of Power in Valois France 1328–1589* (Leiden: Brill, 2016).

1

La chose publique de nostre royaume

From the late thirteenth century onward, Philip IV and Edward I of England sought greater resources from their subjects to carry on wars. They convened assemblies of the most powerful members of their societies: archbishops, bishops, abbots, and cathedral chapters; members of the royal family, aristocrats, and leading nobles; merchants and legal men from the "good towns" [walled]. Some of the assemblies called by Philip IV and Philip V had representatives from scores of towns, many of them scarcely more than *bourgs*.[1] The mid-fourteenth-century meetings involved far fewer towns, and, with one exception, met in two regional assemblies: Languedoïl and Langue d'Oc.[2] In the north, these assemblies primarily consisted of deputies from demesne holdings of the king and his immediate family.

Such assemblies took place all over Europe, and they shared many key characteristics, such as the recognition of the authority of a given prince to call the assembly, the creation of normative places and times of convocation, and the establishment of powers of representation for those called to the assembly. Michel Hébert stresses these assemblies as places of negotiation, but they were also places used for publicity – for making known a given princely policy that affected all – and for implementation: the deputies often came from the ranks of local officers who would have to carry out the policy in question.[3]

At the same time that the men invited to the general assemblies constituted a civic society,[4] as a social fact, scholars and lawyers alike sought theoretical

---

[1] Philip V convoked over 100 towns to the March 1317 southern assembly at Bourges. A "town" [*ville*] had walls; a *bourg*, in common parlance, did not. Royal legislation used the term "villes closes."

[2] Southern assemblies sometimes included regions like Poitou or Berry. Périgord, Quercy, Bigorre, Agenois, and Rouergue passed into the hands of Edward III via the Treaty of Calais, so they did not contribute to John II's ransom: Devic and Vaissette, *Histoire de Languedoc*, IV, 308.

[3] M. Hébert, *Parlementer. Assemblées représentatives et échange politique en Europe occidentale à la fin du Moyen Âge* (Paris: De Boccard, 2014), 1.

[4] The political community of citizens theoretically excluded women; in practice, some of them participated.

justifications for collective actions. The rise of Aristotelianism, solidified by William of Moerbeke's translation (c. 1270) of *The Politics* into Latin, deeply affected European political theories of the time, as we can easily see in the writings of Thomas Aquinas, Dante, Marsiglio of Padua, Giles of Rome, Guillaume Durand and his eponymous nephew, William of Ockham, and many others.[5] In France, one trail ran from Ockham to his student Jean Buridan, on to Buridan's younger colleague Nicole Oresme, thence to Oresme's acolytes like Jean Gerson.[6] In the second half of the fourteenth century, the Collège de Navarre – founded by Jeanne de Navarre in 1305 – would play a fundamental role in the rise of a specifically French ideology of the "public good," in part because of Oresme's central role in creating that ideology.[7]

Jeanne de Navarre, wife of Philip IV, in founding her Collège, relied on two figures deeply implicated in the critical dynastic events of 1314–1318: Raoul des Presles and Gilles I Aycelin.[8] They founded this institution specifically to train royal officials in the liberal arts, **not** in the law or medicine, but the "royal" element of the Collège remained more rhetorical than real prior to the reign of Charles V. From his reign forward, the Collège de Navarre became and long remained the intellectual nexus of commonwealth ideology.

In the split between scholars and lawyers that Jacques Krynen has so rightly emphasized at the French Court from the late fourteenth century, the Collège de Navarre trained the scholarly wing.[9] Alumni of the Collège in key roles included Jean Gerson, Jean de Montreuil, Nicolas de Clamanges, Michel Creney (preceptor of Charles VI), and Pierre d'Ailly.[10] That elite encountered,

---

[5] Krynen, *L'empire du roi*; C. Fasolt, *Council and Hierarchy: The Political Thought of William Durant the Younger* (Cambridge; New York: CUP, 1991) and *Past Sense – Studies in Medieval and Early Modern European History* (Leiden: Brill, 2014); J. Ryan, *The Apostolic Conciliarism of Jean Gerson* (Oxford and NY: OUP, 2012); and M. Randall, *The Gargantuan Polity : On the Individual and the Community in the French Renaissance* (Toronto: UT Press, 2009).

[6] Buridan belonged to the Picard "nation" and Oresme to the Norman one, so Oresme was not his student.

[7] N. Gorochov, *Le Collège de Navarre, de sa fondation (1305) au début du XVe siècle (1418). Histoire de l'institution, de sa vie intellectuelle et de son recrutement* (Paris: Honoré Champion, 1997), says that Buridan was not a member of the Collège's faculty.

[8] Gorochov, *Collège de Navarre*. On the Aycelin family, J. Strayer, *The Reign of Philip the Fair* (Princeton, NJ: Princeton UP, 1980). Gilles became chancellor under Philip V; his eponymous nephew was also chancellor, and a chief negotiator between John II and Edward III. Charles V mandated (1373) that the royal confessor would have final say on admissions to the Collège.

[9] In addition to his broader works, see J. Krynen, "Les légistes 'idiots politiques'. Sur l'hostilité des théologiens à l'égard des juristes, en France, au temps de Charles V," in *Théologie et droit dans la science politique de L'État moderne* (Rome: Mélanges de l'École Française de Rome, 1991): 171–198.

[10] Autrand, *Christine de Pizan*, 121. When Jean sans Peur's forces seized Paris in 1418, they sacked the Collège and murdered some of its key figures, like Jean de Montreuil, whom they associated with the Armagnac party.

in the highest ranks of royal officialdom, Krynen's conflicting legal elite, educated at Orléans (civil) and Paris (canon).[11] The Collège's former students long played a major role in monarchical administration: Cardinal Richelieu offers a seventeenth-century example.[12]

Philippe de Beaumanoir, a royal *bailli* from Clermont-en-Beauvaisis, in his extremely influential *Customs of the Beauvaisis* (1283), shows how such principles affected practical politics: in his list of ten virtues a *bailli* must possess, he began with "sapience," the virtue that enables all the others, and only then turned to "the love of God." Yet Beaumanoir also shows us the limits: he may have given primacy to practical reason, but he knew little or nothing of Aristotle's political categories. His famous description of the corrupted town governments of northern France, in which he (rightly) claimed the rich excluded the poor and middling and passed the administration from one family member to another, makes no mention of the obvious term, oligarchy, because it did not yet exist in French.[13] The process took place in a world bristling with paradoxes, which they embraced. In periods of contested power relations in particular, the participants often prefer ambiguity, both practical and legal.[14]

We need go no further than Giles of Rome to seek evidence of apparent contradiction.[15] Although his *De ecclesiastica potestate* provided justification for Boniface VIII's power grab, Giles' *De regimine principum* (1279), written for the young prince soon to become Philip IV, became a fundamental text in the education of generations of French [and other] kings. Philip III had Henri de Gauchi create a French translation and abridgement (1282), and a certain "Guillaume" created for Guillaum de Beles Voies, "citoyen" and royal judge at Orléans, a full French translation in 1330.[16] Noëlle-Laetitia Perret and others

---

[11] Many students from Orléans attended either Bologna or Padua. Buridan attended the Collège de Lemoine and remained a Master of Arts, not a theologian.

[12] All three principals of the War of the League – Henry, duke of Guise, Henry III, and Henry IV – attended classes there together. Throughout the text, readers will notice the remarkably high number of former students of the Collège de Navarre among the *dramatis personnæ*.

[13] Beaumanoir, *Coustumes*, II, 267. Oresme's 1373 glossary is the first known French usage of "olygarchie."

[14] On the dangers of such "simplification," see Jouanna, *Le pouvoir absolu*, 14.

[15] On Giles of Rome, see Blythe, *Ideal Government*, ch. 4; Krynen, *L'empire du roi*; and K. Pennington, *The Prince and the Law, 1200–1600: Sovereignty and Rights in the Western Legal Tradition* (Berkeley: University of California Press, 1993). The 1502 Venice printing of *De regimine* is available at: https://archive.org/details/hin-wel-all-00000256-001 On image 16–17, in the proem, Giles is discussing hereditary monarchy, and specifically the succession of the later Philip IV to his father, Philip III: "nullum uiolentum cons[is]tet esse perpetuu[m]." The fourteenth-century manuscript version at the BNF-Arsenal (M. 744) reads "violentu[m] ce[] p[er]petuum fere via nat[ur]alia" in the context of lineal succession. More than 500 manuscript copies of *De regimine* survive.

[16] N.-L. Perret, *Les traductions françaises du De regimine principum de Gilles de Rome: Parcours matériel, culturel et intellectuel d'un discours sur l'éducation* (Leiden: Brill, 2011),

have emphasized the aristocratic ownership of most of the surviving manuscripts of Giles' work, either in Latin or in translation, yet this full French translation belonged to a royal judge, and the town government of Poitiers demanded, in June 1453, that Me Denis Dusserre return "a volume named Giles of Rome" that he had borrowed from the University's library.[17] Dusserre regularly served as Poitier's main lawyer: in 1461, they charged him with writing up their proposals to Louis XI, who was supposed to make an official royal entry, which he subsequently cancelled.[18] Anyone dealing with a French king from Charles V onward was well advised to be familiar with Giles' arguments, because Charles VI, Charles VII, and Louis XI had all read the work as part of their education into the responsibilities of kingship.[19]

Charles V commissioned a translation in 1372 (Besançon Manuscrit 434): this unknown translator clearly had access to Guillaume's 1330 version but did not simply recopy it. Charles owned four Latin copies of *De regimine*, but this work was clearly part of his extensive translation campaign of 1370–1373. He signed books for which he had a special affection – Oresme's translation of the *Ethics*, the *Songe du Vergier*, and both the Latin and this French version of *De regimine*.[20] "En ce livre roman sont conteneus pluseurs notables et bons livres et est a nous Charles le Ve de notre nom roy de France et fimes escrire et parfere l'an M CCC. LXXII. Charles."[21]

Its opening words stated that:[22]

68–71, and the review by Silvère Menegaldo in *Cahiers de Recherches Médiévales et Humanistes* (2011): http://journals.openedition.org/crm/12686 Gauchi's version was published by S. P. Molenaer, *Li Livres du Gouvernement des Rois* (New York: Macmillan, 1899). https://archive.org/details/lilivresdugouver00colorich/page/n7

[17] Favreau, ed., *Poitiers (…) registres des délibérations du corps de ville*, II, 59. See C. Briggs, *Giles of Rome's De Regimine Principum. Reading and Writing Politics at Court and University, ca 1275 – ca 1525* (Cambridge: CUP, 1999), ch. 5, on the use of Giles as a university textbook from the early fourteenth century at Paris.

[18] Favreau, ed., *Poitiers (…) registres des délibérations du corps de ville*, II, 164.

[19] Briggs, *Reading and Writing Politics*, 50, mentions that key figures of what I am calling commonwealth ideology – Gerson, Christine de Pizan, and Philippe de Mezières – all drew material from Giles.

[20] Perret, *Les traductions*, 75, citing Leopold Delisle's work on inventories of the royal library. See below, ch. 3.

[21] Perret, *Les traductions*, 72.

[22] Gallica, municipal library of Besançon, Manuscript 434, f. 103r. Gallica gives the compilation date of this group of manuscripts (*"Traités philosophiques et moraux"*) as 1372, and misleadingly says they are in Latin. It **must** be searched by this title. Buridan paraphrased Giles, arguing that tyrant is not a prince because he relies on violence, which is not natural. Giles' debt to Aquinas on this point is clear. "Or dit aussi le ph[il]osophe que chose qui est violent et p[ar] force n'est point p[er]petuel, ne ne puet longuement durer. Mais ce est p[er]petuel et dure longuement qui est selonc nature. Donc q[ui] veult la seignourie faire durer no[n] pas et pou de temps un an ou a la vie – mais p[er]petuelme[n]t si se estudie que son gouvernem[en]t ne soit par viole[n]t mais soit selonc nature. Lequel ne puet estre naturel se il n'est selonc raison." The Latin of *De regimine* differs

the philosopher [Aristotle] said that something done by force and violence is not perpetual and cannot last long. But that which is according to nature is perpetual and can last long. Thus he who wishes to make his lordship [*seignoirie*] last [can do so] by studying that his governing not be violent but by nature. [Government] can only be natural if it is according to reason.

De regimine, in Latin and in French translations, belonged to many royal family libraries, including those of such key women as Clémence of Hungary (second wife of Louis X) and Blanche of Navarre (second wife of Philip VI). In the fifteenth century, Jean Gerson – preceptor to the Dauphin – would insist it should be the basic text for educating all heirs to the throne.[23]

The various authorities – Pope, Emperor, king of France – each developed the usage of a vocabulary of political supremacy. French royal documents, starting at least in 1297, made regular use of the Latin phrase "plenitudo potestatis" already used by the Pope to define the range of his power: French charters used "pleine puissance."[24] For French royal lawyers, the king of France, just like the Pope or the Emperor, had the power to act without reference to an earthly superior: he was, in the phrase promulgated by Philip IV's lawyers, and made popular under Charles V, "emperor in his own kingdom."[25]

French legists, both in the secular and the ecclesiastical dimension, fiercely defended the **king of France's** "puissance absolue," which we must not confuse with the power of the specific, living king.[26] All of these texts – whether Giles of Rome's *De regimine*, or Beaumanoir's *Customs*, or Oresme's translations of Aristotle – agreed with the fictional Arthur of Chrestien de Troyes: the king

considerably in detail, if not in the general sentiment. The opening phrases, about the young Philip, are relatively close, and the text moves on to a discussion of "violence," but does not here delve into Aristotle.

[23] Briggs, *Reading and Writing Politics;* Jean Gerson wrote [c. 1410] a treatise on educating Dauphins of France [initially for Louis, duke of Guyenne, who died in 1415], in which he recommended Aristotle's *Ethics* and *Politics,* and Giles of Rome. His friend Jean Majoris would later be the tutor of Louis XI. A. Thomas, *Jean Gerson et l'éducation des dauphins de France* (Paris, 1930).

[24] O. Guillot, A. Rigaudière, and Y. Sassier, *Pouvoirs et institutions dans la France médiévale. T. 2, Des temps féodaux aux temps de l'État* (Paris: Armand Colin, 1994, 1999), 110. The papal adoption of this concept owed much to the Frenchman Guillaume Durand the Elder. K. Pennington, *Popes and Bishops. The Papal Monarchy in the Twelfth and Thirteenth Centuries* (Philadelphia: University of Pennsylvania Press, 1984), emphasizes the permanence of this concept from Innocent III onward; Fasolt, *Council and Hierarchy,* 67, on Durand's influence.

[25] On the debt of secular debates to disputes about papal authority, see the summary assessment of Pennington, *The Prince and the Law, 1200–1600.*

[26] J. Canning, *Ideas of Power,* ch. 1, which focuses not on power, as I am defining it here, but on "legitimate power, that is, authority." (11) French kings did not make law based on *puissance absolue,* but on their "science certaine, pleine puissance et autorité royale."

had to "govern according to the statutes and laws and ordinances left to him," as Oresme put it. Beaumanoir preferred a different phrasing: the king "is held to guard and to have guarded the customs of his kingdom."[27]

Thirteenth-century French kings sought to claim broader regalian rights, on matters such as coinage, taxation, and jurisdiction.[28] With respect to serfs, the king sought to establish limited rights, above all the right to tax.[29] As for jurisdiction, Beaumanoir emphasized that any fief over which the king of France had "ressort," was, by definition, in the kingdom: "all *ressort* in the kingdom is held of the king, in fief or *arrière-fief.*"[30] Royal ordinances – and the Parlement of Paris – emphasized "ressort" in almost all cases.[31]

Unlike "souveraineté" [for the Latin "superior"], *ressort* rarely appeared in the plural: the king held multiple sovereignties, but only one *ressort* within the kingdom.[32] The charters of the town of Abbeville show the mayor and *échevins* recognized [1320] the "ressort" and "souveraineté" of the count of Ponthieu, except in cases in which the count [Edward II of England] had a lawsuit against the town government, in which case the king of France, or his Parlement, had *ressort.*[33]

---

[27] Cited in S. Petit-Renaud, "Le roi, les légistes et le parlement de Paris aux XIVe et XVe siècles: contradictions dans la perception du pouvoir de 'faire loy' ?", *Cahiers de recherches médiévales et humanistes*, 7 (2000), consulted online, April 2011. Religious belief reinforced this principle (see below). Oresme here followed closely the arguments of Jean Buridan, *Quæstiones super octo libros politicorum Aristotelis* (Paris: Jean Petit, 1524), particularly his questions to Book III of Aristotle. Available on Gallica.

[28] W. C. Jordan, "Jews, Regalian Rights, and the Constitution of Medieval France," *AJS Review*, 23, n. 1 (1998): 1–16, and *The French Monarchy and the Jews* (Philadelphia: University of Pennsylvania Press, 1989), calls the king of France's efforts to assert his unique jurisdiction over Jews a radical departure in royal praxis.

[29] J. Vallejo, "Power Hierarchies in Medieval Political Juridical Thought: An Essay in Reinterpretation," in *Ius Commune* (1992), accessed through academia.edu, follows Pietro Costa, *Iurisdictio. Semantica del potere politico nella pubblicistica medievale (1100-1433)* (Milan, 1969), in his rightful emphasis on jurisdiction (*ressort*, in French), and the "judicial vision of political power" (Vallejo, 5) in this period.

[30] Beaumanoir, a royal judge, specifically ties this principle to the right of appeal to the king in case of false judgment. Beaumanoir, *Coutûmes*, I, 163.

[31] Beaumanoir oversimplified here; he likely referred to fiefs having rights of justice, because as a royal *bailli* he would have had a vested interest in the principle that the judgments of such courts could be appealed to a royal one. In real life, that principle took centuries to establish.

[32] "*Ressorts*" could appear when referring to multiple territories, each of which would have a "*ressort.*" In the kingdom of France, the king and his Parlement claimed to have *ressort* over everyone. Dauphant, *Royaume des quatre rivières*, shows how limited the Parlement's writ could be, but also how it expanded over time. Aristotle was, in one of the French versions of the proem to Giles of Rome, "the sovereign philosopher," a typical use of the term.

[33] Thierry, *Recueil des monuments inédits de l'histoire du Tiers Etat [. . .] Abbeville*, IV, 108.

The regalian right of pardon provided the main manifestation of "ressort"; in most documents, the king coupled the words "jurisdiction" and "ressort" to cover both his right (and that of Parlement) to hear appeals and his right, his alone, to issue letters of remission and pardons. Kings sometimes specifically granted feudatories, such as the dukes of Brittany or Burgundy, the right to pardon; in both cases, the duke/duchess would use regalian powers – coining money, issuing pardons – to demonstrate a level of independent action. Ducal rulers in Burgundy and Brittany regularly issued their own coins and both levied taxes voted by local estates, without benefit of specific royal letters, although the monarchy always covered its tracks by calling their ability to do so a grant from the king.[34]

By the fifteenth century, as in the Treaty of Arras (1435), the word "ressort" meant both sorts of jurisdiction: the operative words had become "ressort et souveraineté du Roy et de sa court de parlement," which were reserved, in separate articles, for the counties of Macon and Auxerre, granted as fiefs to Philip of Burgundy and his heirs, female or male.[35] The duke got the right to nominate all officers, but they received royal letters of "commission and institution" and acted in the king's name. Philip and his "heir" [singular] were also granted [art. 16] all the tax revenues for the county of Auxerre: *gabelles*, taxes on wine and other goods, *tailles*, *fouages*, and all other "aides." Article 29 specifically mandated that Philip had to recognize, in written documents and orally, Charles VII as his "souverain seigneur," without in any way prejudicing the exemptions from homage, *ressort*, and *souveraineté* he personally had been granted in the treaty, with respect to the person of Charles VII. Those exemptions did not apply to **either** of their successors, so that Philip would owe – and did perform – homage to Louis XI in 1461. Charles the Bold in Burgundy even insisted his subjects call him their "souverain seigneur."[36]

Philip IV's disastrous efforts to debase his coinage, in the name of the "common good," both emphasized a key regalian right (minting money), and recognized the civic society's right to a say in the matter.[37] The many assemblies called by Philip IV, his sons, and the first two Valois kings often focused on coinage issues: the royal perspective that coinage was proprietary, so that the king had a right to profit from it, conflicted sharply with the perspective of his subjects that sound coinage underpinned what from the 1350s onward they called the "chose publique," so that it was a public not a particular matter. This philosophical conflict over coinage led directly to the

---

[34] B. Schnerb, *L'état bourguignon* (Paris: Perrin, 2005).
[35] Cosneau, *Grandes Traités*, 131, art. 11 of the Treaty of Arras.
[36] Garnier, ed., *Correspondance de la mairie de Dijon*, I, contains multiple examples.
[37] Many of the pennies (*deniers*) were minted by local lords: J. Belmon, "La monnaie de Rodez: la mort d'un monnayage seigneurial (vers 1270–1340)," *Revue numismatique* 6 (2003): 355–418. Philip and his sons did make significant progress in reducing the number of seigneurial mints.

adoption of the "bien de la chose publique" vocabulary in the 1350s. Coinage issues long remained a central issue for representative assemblies: in 1484, the Third Estate's grievances began with articles on coinage, and even the meeting of 1576 took up currency matters.[38]

By virtue of being a legitimate king, as Giles of Rome had pointed out to Prince Philip, the king of France had to rule according to law and reason, the highest combination of which was God's law.[39] The coronation ceremony itself made that clear: the king took an oath, which God's law mandated that he observe. He swore to protect the privileges of the French church, prevent evildoing, render justice, and show clemency. From Charles V's coronation (1364) onward French people also believed the king swore to be an inviolable custodian of the French crown (*corone francie*) and not to transfer or alienate either the Crown or any of its rights or properties.[40] The principle appeared, loosely, in a 1318 edict of Philip V about rescinding the "excessive" alienations of royal rights, lands, and prerogatives that had taken place since the death of Saint Louis (1270), but Charles V would issue the key legislation touching on this vital point in the rules he laid down for apanages, which from his time forward reverted to the Crown, absent a legitimate son (or grandson, in case of predecease of the son).

While French kings emphasized their legitimacy as monarchs, they also emphasized their special relationship to the Church. The canonization of Louis IX (1297) transformed the French monarchy's image. The Christian king had to live according to God's law: from the late fourteenth century onward, the king of France, as the papally recognized *rex Christianissimus*, had even more

---

[38] J. B. Henneman, *Royal Taxation in Fourteenth-Century France: The Development of War Financing, 1322–1356* (Princeton, NJ: Princeton UP, 1971) and *Royal Taxation in Fourteen-Century France: The Captivity and Ransom of John II, 1356–1370* (Philadelphia: Transactions of the American Philosophical Society, 1976). The *Charte aux Normands* begins with two articles about sound money, and the other provincial charter movements of 1314–1315 also did. After completing the manuscript, I became aware of Adam Woodhouse's article in *Speculum* 92, n. 1 (2017): "'Who Owns the Money?' Currency, Property, and Popular Sovereignty in Nicole Oresme's *De Moneta*"; I do not really agree about the popular sovereignty element he attributes to Oresme ["one of the most radically populist works of medieval political thought"], but I certainly agree – as will become apparent – that Oresme emphasizes the rights of the political community with respect to coinage.

[39] E. Grant, *God & Reason in the Middle Ages* (Cambridge: CUP, 2001), speaks of the "new professionalism" produced by universities by the end of the twelfth century. Grant emphasizes the importance of reason, particularly Aristotelian logic, in changing medieval society in the twelfth and thirteenth centuries. "Civil and canon law were transformed ... [into] disciplines where reason was systematically applied to laws that were now intended to be universal in scope, while also attempting to meet the needs of the new merchant class and guilds ..." (81–82).

[40] G. Leyte, *Domaine et domanialité publique dans la France medieval (XIIe - XVe siècles)* (Strasbourg: Presses Universitaires de Strasbourg), part II, ch. 2.

pressure to rule according to God's law, reason, and justice.[41] In the well-ordered Christian kingdom, these three elements were inseparable. Christine de Pizan, in founding her community of female citizens, the *Cité des Dames*, relied precisely on three "*dames*": Reason, Rightfulness (*Droicture*), and Justice. In her *Book of Peace*, Christine de Pizan began with praise to God, for having granted peace. She listed God's attributes, among which were that He was "our good pastor, very just judge, our wise master, our very powerful supporter (*aideur*), our helpful physician, our clear light."[42] The third part of her book would explain to the young Dauphin (Louis, duke of Guyenne, then about fifteen) how to "well govern the people and the chose publicque."[43]

Charles V began his 1374 ordinance on the royal wardship/*tutelle* (should he die without an adult heir) making precisely the point that kings must set an example:[44]

> Kings, who by their sense, honest life and good government, must give to their subjects form and example of life, all the more so as God has given them greater authority and seigneury

Charles V here glossed the 1372 French translation of Giles of Rome, which argued that the king needed to use his reason to restrain his passions, and then those of others. The Besançon manuscript attributes to Aristotle the sentiment that "he who wishes to govern his seigneury according to the passions and by will alone is not a natural seigneur but a serf by nature."[45] Throughout the

---

[41] John of Salisbury, in *Policraticus*: "A commonwealth, according to Plutarch, is a certain body which is endowed with life by the benefit of divine favor, which acts at the prompting of the highest equity, and is ruled by what may be called the moderating power of reason." The title *rex Christianissimus* came into informal use around 1400 but achieved official recognition only under Louis XI. J. Krynen, "Rex Christianissimus: A medieval theme at the roots of French absolutism," *History and Anthropology* (1989), which, in my view, offers an anachronistic analysis.

[42] BNF, M Fr 1182, f. 5v.

[43] BNF, M Fr 1182, f. 3v, "bien gouverner le peuple et la chose publicque". Her image of the king as pastor offers an early example of one of the key attributes leading to the later governmentality, analyzed by M. Foucault, *Security, Territory, Population: Lectures at the Collège de France, 1977–1978*, trans. G. Burchell (New York: Picador, 2007). The French original was published by Éditions du Seuil in 2004.

[44] *Ordonnances*, VI, 49. Archbishop Hincmar of Reims made this point in a letter to Louis III in 882. French customary law often divided responsibility between the widow and the senior male member of the deceased husband's family, leading to innumerable lawsuits.

[45] Gallica, municipal library of Besançon, Manuscript 434, f. 103r "c'il qui veult seignourie gouverner selo[n]c les passions et de volente tant seulem[en]t n'est pas seigneur naturel ains serf par nature." In the Besançon manuscript, the translation of "de l'enseigne-ment des princes" precedes "le livre du gouvernement des roys et des princes," which starts on f. 103r. Jean Golein translated this text: Équipe Golein, "Remarques sur la traduction de Jean Golein du 'De Informacione principum," *Neuphilologische Mitteilungen* 95, n. 1 (1994): 19–30, which the Golein group of researchers identify as a separate late thirteenth-century text, and not, as catalogues claim, a version of *De regimine*.

period here, political discourse took as a given that reason had to constrain simple will, lest it be governed by appetite.

The gendered dichotomy male:rational/female:emotional meant the greater emphasis on reason controlling emotion and appetite – an emphasis powerfully reinforced by Humanism – had practical implications for the many women who played key roles in French politics. One particularly active line of political women ran from Jeanne de Penthièvre, who claimed the duchy of Brittany from her uncle (Duke Jean III), to her daughter, Marie de Blois, to Marie's daughter-in-law, Yolande of Aragon, to her daughter, Marie d'Anjou. Jeanne led one of the two sides in the Breton civil war – Jeanne of Flanders, wife of Jean de Montfort, who claimed succession through his father, Duke Arthur II, led the other – and her daughter Marie, left a widow with a two-year-old son [Louis II d'Anjou], had to defend the family's political and economic interests for decades.[46] Yolande, mother-in-law of Charles VII, led one of the factions at his court and almost certainly provided the key sponsorship for Joan of Arc. All these women had great reputations as patrons of learning: Yolande passed this trait to her son, René d'Anjou, who was both a patron and poet. Whether it was the women directing the "war of the two Jeannes" [Penthièvre and Flanders], the fiscal wizardry of Marie de Blois, or the political acumen of Yolande d'Aragon, their contemporaries invariably insisted on their "male" qualities being "unusual" in a woman.[47]

This term "seigneur naturel," soon inverted (*naturel seigneur*) became one of the most important new elements of French royal discourse in the second half of the fourteenth century, precisely because the monarchy drew on this connection between "nature" and "justice." The monarchy thus built on the premise of Giles of Rome and Jean Buridan: "natural" polities rested on justice, not on violence. Speakers from the foureenth century to the early seventeenth

---

[46] The Breton succession, like the successions to the throne of France (1316), to the county of Artois (1316), to the duchy of Burgundy (1360), revolved around gender. Jean de Montfort was the son of duke Arthur's second wife; by his first marriage, Arthur had three sons, the eldest of whom, Jean III, succeeded him as duke. The second son, Guy, predeceased his brother, and left as heir a daughter, Jeanne de Penthièvre. Philip VI recognized her claim, and that of her husband, Charles of Blois, Philip's nephew. Edward III recognized Jean de Montfort, who died in 1345, leaving his wife, Jeanne of Flanders, to lead their party. Charles spent nine years in an English prison and died at the 1364 Battle of Auray.

[47] Z. Rohr, *Yolande of Aragon (1381–1442). Family and Power* (Houndmills: Palgrave, 2016); M. Kekewich, *The Good King: René of Anjou and Fifteenth Century Europe* (Houndmills: Palgrave, 2008); T. Adams, *The Life and Afterlife of Isabeau of Bavaria* (Baltimore: Johns Hopkins UP, 2010); E. Maëlan Graham-Goering, "Negotiating princely power in late medieval France: Jeanne de Penthièvre, duchess of Brittany (c. 1325–1384)," Ph.D. thesis, University of York, 2014. My thanks to Dr. Graham-Goering for sharing her thesis, which has recently been published by CUP (2020), *Princely Power in Late Medieval France: Jeanne de Penthièvre and the War for Brittany.* Jeanne de Penthièvre's great-granddaughter, Jeanne de Laval, was René d'Anjou's second wife. They had no children.

century invariably reminded kings/listeners of Aristotle's point that a kingdom without justice is simply brigandage.[48]

Oresme's definition of the kingdom as a *cité* operated another dramatic definitional shift: if we look at the assemblies discussing the kingship in July 1316 and in 1328, we can see why. Beaumanoir focused on the relationship between fiefs and the kingdom, which consisted of the fiefs held by the king's vassals (and sub-vassals). In July 1316, when Philip of Poitiers convoked an assembly to discuss the succession of Louis X, and in 1328, when Philip of Valois convoked an assembly to rule on the succession of Charles IV, the chronicles say that they summoned **barons**, among whose number we would have to place the six ecclesiastical peers.[49] The composition of these two assemblies, specifically called to deal with the succession to the dignity [*dignitas*] of the king of France, indicates that contemporaries thought of the kingdom precisely as the collection of fiefs, and the king as the highest lord (*souverain seigneur*), holding a high office [*dignitas*].[50] In contrast to the assembly of February 1317, when chronicles cite the presence of bourgeois of Paris, or those of March 1317, when deputies arrived from more than thirty towns, no evidence survives of townsmen at the assemblies of either July 1316 or 1328.[51] During the crisis of the late 1350s, when King John II was a prisoner in England, the assemblies called by the regent, Charles (later Charles V), included urban deputies, who by then had a say in the fate of the kingdom. In 1328, elites, including royal lawyers, believed the kingdom of France was a collection of fiefs; in 1359, those same groups held that the kingdom of France was a commonwealth of citizens. In both cases, however, the assemblies agreed on the fundamental principle that the kingdom of France could not be divided.

---

[48] Pennington, *The Prince and the Law*, has a detailed discussion of the role of natural law in emerging royalist [and papalist] discourse. The Florentine Agnolo Pandolfini, in 1411, argued that justice alone keeps the poor, so more numerous, from devouring the rich. "Quia si iusticia cessaret, omnia periclitarentur." Cited in G. Brucker, *The Civic World of Renaissance Florence* (Princeton, NJ: Princeton UP, 1977), 330. Florentine political ideas deeply influenced French discourse in the early fifteenth century (see Chapter 3). The connection of reason and justice to political legitimacy could be found in innumerable Classical and Christian sources.

[49] In 1316, the bishop-peers included Robert de Courtenay (Reims), a member of the royal family. The *Chronique des quatre premiers Valois*, ed. S. Luce (Paris, 1862), 1, says that Philip seized the kingdom of France with the "accord and will of the princes of the said kingdom."

[50] P. Lehugeur, *Histoire de Philippe le Long* (Paris, 1897), 37, cites the presence in 1316 of Mahaut d'Artois and Blanche de Bretagne, daughter of Duke Jean II of Brittany, and widow of Philip, count of Artois.

[51] Dauphant, *Royaume*, Map 44, illustrates the names of towns called to three assemblies of towns called for early 1316 by Louis X. Philip V called thirty-two large southern towns to meet at Bourges in March 1317. C. H. Taylor, "Assemblies of French Towns in 1316," *Speculum* XIV, n. 3 (1939): 275–299.

From 1356 onward "la chose publique" (*res publica*) became the term for the political society corresponding to the kingdom, in the regions tied to the Estates General of Languedoïl, among which we may place Brittany, due to the role of Charles of Blois, the Valois-recognized duke. "La chose publique" described both a civic society, the one made up of its citizens, and a civil society, all those born in the kingdom (the *regnicoles*, those who were *de regni*, in Philip IV's usage) and all its legitimate inhabitants (those who were *in regno*). Its political citizens had a special duty to those not of "sufficient reason" to rule themselves: women, children, and, in the eyeås of most of the elite, those who worked with their hands. In the body politic image in which artisans and peasants were the legs and the feet, the cleric in Évraud de Trémaugon's *Songe du Vergier* (1378), simply asked whether one wished the head or the feet to make decisions for the body. On into the seventeenth century, elites would regularly insist that "gens mécaniques" should have no part in political decision making.[52]

This local citizenship and the political system built upon it had several characteristics worthy of note:

- In the countryside, nobles holding rights of high justice invariably referred to their peasants as their "subjects."[53]
- In a town, local rules usually defined a "droit de bourgeoisie."[54] By the fourteenth century, this designation – the legal rights and privileges of a "bourgeois" of the town – had been extended to all permanent legal inhabitants, but not to transients.
- Residents who were *regnicoles* had legal citizenship – the protection of the town's laws and privileges – but not political citizenship.
- Municipal politics, and thus systems of representation, often focused on groups – nobles, clergy, merchants, guilds, residents of a district – and not on individuals.[55]

---

[52] Christine de Pizan's many political writings make clear her concerns about such people making political decisions: her contemporaries looked to the urban revolts of the 1380s and the Cabochien Uprising of 1413 as examples of the nefarious consequences of popular political participation.

[53] *Choix des pièces inédites relatives au règne de Charles VI*, 80–81: documents XL and XLI offer examples.

[54] A concept similar to the "freedom of the town" in England: P. Withington, *The Politics of Commonwealth. Citizens and Freemen in Early Modern England* (Cambridge: CUP, 2005). Hébert, *Parlementer*, ch. 7, on the remarkably diverse methods of selecting local deputies throughout Europe.

[55] Rouen's city government lay in the hands of the "100 Peers," the families with the sole right to hold office; in Dijon, however, even ordinary *vignerons* could vote. The Crown regularly changed such rules in the aftermath of revolts. The rules for Paris, laid down by the king in 1554, basically excluded "gens mécaniques" and set up a political framework tied to geography, but not solely determined by it. M. Demonet and R. Descimon, "L'exercise politique de la bourgeoisie: les assemblées de Ville de Paris de 1528 à 1679,"

- Great lords, lay and ecclesiastical, still controlled major towns.[56]

The traditional vocabulary of the municipal layer of this system appeared in their royal charters, which granted or conceded (*concedimus*) "customs and liberties" (*consuetudines et libertates*) to the citizens (*civium Rothomagi*, the citizens of Rouen, to quote from one of the most widely copied charters).[57] At Rouen, as in so many cases, any adult male who had lived in the city for a year and a day had to take an oath to the city, in front of the aldermen (*échevins*), and then became a citizen (*bourgeois*), subject to the town's jurisdiction (*ban*). Those failing to do so could be clapped in irons, and, if recalcitrant, forced to leave the town.

In the fourteenth century, three changes took place in this vocabulary. First, the monarchy regularly added a new term: privileges. The renewal of the "franchises, liberties, usages and customs" of Macon in 1346, gave way to charters like that of Angoulême, issued by Charles V in 1372, which granted them "privileges, franchises, and liberties."[58] This new word – "privileges" – long proved contentious: citizens invariably referred to their "droits, libertés et franchises"; the king might use some or all of these terms in his reply, but added "privileges," a term that became standard two-way usage in many towns in the fifteenth century: some towns held out until the late sixteenth century. When the future Charles V came to Normandy in 1350, to be instituted as duke, the Norman spokesman, the canon Simon Baudry, presented to Charles "the franchises and the liberties of Normandy"; he asked Charles "to guard and have guarded them well and truly, the which he well and willingly swore."[59] Godefroy de Harcourt supposedly brought the original copy of the Charte aux Normands with him: he told Charles, "my natural lord, here is the charter of the Normans. In the form that is contained within it, if you are pleased to swear and keep it, I am completely ready to do homage to you."[60] Harcourt here

---

in C. Dolan, ed., *Les pratiques politiques dans les villes françaises d'Ancien Régime* (Rennes: PUR, 2018), 113–163.

[56] The duke of Brittany was direct lord of twenty-five of the sixty walled towns in his duchy: the other lords including the Laval (8), Rohan (7), and Rieux (4) families, and the high clergy (6). J.-P. Leguay, *Vivre dans les villes bretonnes au Moyen Age* (Rennes: PUR, 2009), 194–195.

[57] Towns in the Southwest, like Saint-Jean d'Angély, copied the Rouen system.

[58] Macon: *Ordonnances*, II, 348. Angoulême: *Ordonnances*, V, 677. G. Marlot, *Histoire de la ville, cité et université de Reims*, t. IV (Reims, 1846), IV, 62, royal letters of December 1345 about the new tax of 4d/l, which was not to prejudice the city's "privileges, liberties, and franchises" nor to imply the king had obtained a new right [*droict nouvel*]. On citizenship, see G. Lurie, "Citizenship in late medieval Champagne: the towns of Châlons, Reims, and Troyes, 1417 – c. 1435," *French Historical Studies* 38, n. 3 (2015): 365–390.

[59] F. Michel, ed., *Chronique des abbés de Saint-Ouen de Rouen* (Rouen, 1840), 89.

[60] *Chronique des quatre premiers Valois*, 34. "Mon seigneur naturel, vecy la charter des Normans. En la fourme qu'il est contenu dedens s'il vous plaist à jurer et tenir, je suy tout prest de vous faire hommaige." He was the uncle of Jean de Harcourt, executed at Rouen;

repeated a demand he had made in 1337, to Philip VI, who sought money from the Estates of Normandy, to fight Edward III. Harcourt insisted that the king "maintain them in their liberties and franchises," as laid out in the Charter. Philip and his son John, then duke of Normandy, had sworn to uphold the Charter, but then levied new, unvoted taxes and issued "feeble money." To the Normans, the "strong money of Saint Louis" was one of their liberties.[61] Harcourt refused to allow the taxes to be collected on his lands and fled to England when the king sent troops to do so.

This episode ties together the larger concern of civil society for sound money, with the personal quarrels of the powerful. Harcourt's quarrel with Philip VI and then John II had much to do with the preeminence of the Melun family at Court: they had intermarried, and gained the inheritance of, the house of Tancarville, which had engaged in a private war against the Harcourt in 1300. Through marriages and royal service, the Melun had gained the upper hand in Normandy: John II made Tancarville a county, and Jean II de Melun, through marriage to Jeanne Crespin, became hereditary constable of Normandy, adding to his office as grand chamberlain of the king. Jean II's brother, Guillaume, was archbishop of Sens, thus metropolitan of Paris.[62] Jean II de Melun's second wife was Isabelle d'Antoign, mother of Charles de La Cerda, whose murder by the Navarre family (1/1354) precipitated a fatal rupture between John II and Charles of Navarre, and Navarre's ally, the Harcourt family. Godefroy de Harcourt may have cited the "liberties and franchises" enshrined in the Charte aux Normands to defend his position, but it would be folly to ignore the deeply personal grievances involving the Valois, the Navarre-Évreux family, and the Melun and Harcourt clans in Normandy.[63]

In the urban perspective, the king recognized the legitimacy of rights, liberties, usages, and customs; he **granted** privileges. What the king granted, he had every right to take away; any attempt to abrogate liberties and customs,

---

the *Chronique* claims he tried to warn Jean to get away, but that Robert de Lorris prevented Jean's escape. Harcourt refused to turn over the original, which he returned to the abbey of Notre Dame; he urged Charles to have a copy made and to take the oath to uphold it. Harcourt left without doing homage.

[61] *Chronique des quatre premiers Valois*, 5–9. Harcourt helped lead the English army at Crécy. His brother Jean died on the French side; sources of the time claim Godefroy was so shaken by his brother's death that he immediately switched allegiances.

[62] Guillaume and Jean II were both captured at Poitiers.

[63] In Latin, the charter reads "libertates, usus & consuetudines antiquas" and begins with Louis X lamenting the prejudice done to Normans "contra patriæ solitam consuetudinem, contra jura, & libertates eorum." No version of it mentions "privileges," but the eighteenth-century editor of the *Ordonnances*, in his title for the document, refers to Louis X confirming the "privileges" of the Normans, a fine example of the vocabulary shift. *Ordonnances* I, 588 ff. French translations used the phrase "contre la coustume du pays & contre les droits et franchises d'icelui."

however, was certain to undermine the political system. Princely entries into towns show the elaborate ritual of exchange: the town officials would meet the prince/king **outside** the town. They would offer him the keys to the city; he would promise to uphold their rights, liberties, usages (and, of course, sneak in "privileges"). Only **after** he had done so, did he enter the town, invariably after returning the keys to the municipal officers, with instructions to maintain order in the town in his (or her) name.[64]

The documents related to the transfer of Dauphiné to young Prince Charles, in 1349–1350, offer an ideal example of the vocabulary common at that precise moment.[65] Young Charles promised, in a document drawn up by French royal lawyers, to protect the "privileges, liberties, franchises, and immunities" of the inhabitants of Dauphiné. Just prior to the transfer, the last independent Dauphin, Humbert II, had issued a clear statement of the "liberties, franchises, graces, concessions, declarations, and privileges" of his subjects. One notices the word order: Humbert adds "privileges" at the end; Charles puts it in first place. Humbert's declaration then laid out the "usages, customs, liberties, and privileges" in a series of articles, which treated matters like military service obligations, the levying of taxes, and the promise of "moneta certa & durabilis." Only this article (XI) on sure and durable coinage mentioned the "utilitate patriæ."

The actual act of donation between the living, from Humbert II to Charles, stated that Humbert "thought of the utility of our commonwealth" [*pensata nostræ reipublicæ utilitate*] in taking his action.[66] The Estates of Dauphiné ratified the agreement prior to Charles actually taking possession. They mentioned that Charles would receive the sceptre and ring of the Dauphin of Viennois, and would henceforth have the rights, nobilities, vassals and homages, and high and low jurisdictions attached to Humbert's lands and seigneuries.[67] The young prince promised to make no "novations" in existing agreements [*convenances*]. The Estates' document does not use the word "privileges." In the list of those who would take the oath of loyalty to Charles, the Estates made specific reference to nobles and town officials and inhabitants, but then reverted to "other subjects."

A second vocabulary shift applied to this litany of terms: in the central areas of the kingdom and in Brittany, documents like charters shifted in the late 1350s to add the phrase "bien de la chose publique." The phrase burst into prominence in Paris in 1356–1357, during the Estates General of Languedoïl, and appears to have become important in towns like Reims in 1358–1359. In

[64] Details in Murphy, *Ceremonial Entries*.

[65] J.-P. Valbonnais, *Mémoires pour servir à l'histoire de Dauphiné* (Grenoble, 1711), 669, for Charles' oath; 639ff for Humbert II's charter. Article XI made specific reference to the fineness of the alloy.

[66] Valbonnais, *Mémoires*, 649. He later mentioned the "felicis regiminis nostræ Reipublicæ"

[67] Valbonnais, *Mémoires*, 658–659.

the southwest, places like Bergerac, Bordeaux, Poitiers, and Saint-Jean d'Angély avoided this vocabulary and typically used the phrase "the king, our *sire*," rather than "souverain seigneur." In the 1360s and 1370s, this locution made a great deal of sense, because the king of England, as duke of Guyenne or lord [*Dominus*] of Aquitaine – the latter the title to which he had right according to the 1360 Treaty of Calais – was not their "souverain seigneur": much safer to call him, "le roy nostre sire" and to use the same term with respect to Charles V, when he retook cities like La Rochelle (1372), Poitiers (1372), and Bergerac (1377).[68]

Third, local practice in the towns led to significant social and political conflicts as urban elites sought to discourage democratization. In the early fourteenth century, the royal documents invariably contrasted citizens and inhabitants. By the 1350s, the matter was far less clear. The June 1351 levy of an aide in bailiwick of Amiens had been approved by a meeting of "prelates, barons, other nobles, & *civibus bonarum villarum*" [citizens of walled towns] from the bailiwick of Amiens and other places in the kingdom. Next door, in the Vermandois and Beauvaisis, a local assembly of prelates, cathedral chapters, other ecclesiastics, nobles, "*communes*" (self-governing towns), aldermen, and other men (*autres gens*) of the towns had voted the local tax. "Autres gens" were not at all the same as "*civibus*"; more and more of the documents suggest that broader social groups participated in the political process. After all, they had to pay too, and the principle of *quod omnes tangit* (all those most concerned with the topic had to discuss it) applied to them.[69] The local assemblies who chose deputies to the Estates General, in contrast to the central body, **did** contain large numbers of merchants and, in some towns, representatives of major guilds.[70] In 1351, the king convoked an assembly of Norman "towns" to vote on a new tax: 163 deputies from 63 "towns" participated. The presence of so many villages show that at the bailiwick level ploughmen could participate.[71] Most towns had a small oligarchic council running the city, but a much larger assembly that had to vote on vital issues, like new taxation. Conflict between the mercantile elite running the former and the artisans

---

[68] The English captured Bergerac in 1345; they received La Rochelle and Poitiers as a result of the Treaty of Calais. Poor Bergerac passed from English to French back to English and back to French between 1372 and 1377. The English recaptured it in 1435, lost it back to the French in 1442, retook it, and lost it again in 1450. In the second period, Henry VI claimed to be king of France, so the legal situation differed from that of the 1370s.

[69] *Ordonnances*, III, lxxiii–lxxv gives the details of a tax strike in Forez over this principle.

[70] On rapidly changing social dynamics, see D. Barthélemy, *La société dans le comté de Vendôme: de l'an mil au XIVe siècle* (Paris: Fayard, 1992).

[71] A. Coville, *États de Normandie: leurs origines et leur développement au XIVe siècle* (Paris, 1894), 264ff gives the list of "towns" that participated in fourteenth-century meetings. The bailiwick of Rouen had 25, Gisors 10, Caux 27, Caen 9, and Cotentin 8. The suffix "ville" is common for Norman villages.

numerically dominating the latter broke out all over France, and Europe, in the late fourteenth century.[72]

1.1 The "bien de la chose publique"

What was the right term for the larger political community? The pre-eminent thirteenth-century professor of law at the University of Orléans, Jacques de Révigny, whose work provided the basis for fourteenth-century instruction in law, made the distinction between the res publica clericorum and the res publica laicorum, so trained lawyers working for the central administration formed their fundamental ideas about the government of the kingdom precisely within the framework of the "res publica."[73] A theoretical justification of the unity view existed, the Practica Aurea Libellorum of Pierre Jacobi, composed between 1311 and 1331, widely used in his own time, and renowned among sixteenth-century French jurists in its 1492 French printed translation. Jacobi uses the term "res publica totius regni" (the commonwealth of the whole kingdom): he regularly writes of necessitas rei publicæ and utilitas res publicæ.[74] In the transfer of Dauphiné, Humbert II used the terms res publica and patria to refer to Dauphiné, and the Norman Charter spoke of the Norman "patria," translated into French as "pays," so clearly not meaning the kingdom as a whole. With respect to usage by John II and Charles V, the key figures surely included a former student and professor at Orléans, Pierre de la Forest, chancellor of France in the 1350s and one of Charles' chief advisors during his

---

[72] Les établissements de Rouen, ed. A. Giry (Paris: BEC, 1883–1885), t. 2, pp. 56ff, confirmation of charter of Rouen by Philip Augustus, 1207, article 6. On the thirteenth-century roots in Italian towns: E. Crouzet-Pavan, Enfers et paradis. L'Italie de Dante et de Giotto (Paris: Albin Michel, 2001), ch. 5 and 6. On the Florentine 1378 revolt of the Ciompi, see Il Tumulto dei Ciompi: un momento di storia fiorentina ed europea (Florence: Olschki, 1981); J. Najemy, "'Audiant omnes artes': Corporate Origins of the Ciompi Revolution," as its title suggests, stresses the corporate nature of politics. A. Stella, La révolte des Ciompi: Les hommes, les lieux, le travail (Paris: EHESS, 1993), shows the remarkable social and economic divisions **among** and even within the textile workers' different trades. Brucker, The Civic World of Renaissance Florence, emphasizes the shift to an elitist politics c. 1400.

[73] K. Bezemer, "The Law School of Orleans as School of Public Administration," Tijdschrift voor Rechtsgeschienedis (1998): 247–278. On Durand's role, Fasolt, Council and Hierarchy.

[74] A. Rigaudière, Penser et construire l'État au Moyen Age (Paris; CHEFF, 2003), ch. XI. As Rigaudière points out, twelfth- and thirteenth-century writers had extensively mulled over the terms regnum and civitas. Kempshall, Common Good, rightly insists that the emphasis on the "common good" over the "public utility" often implied the superiority of the spiritual power, the Church, over the temporal one, because the "life of virtue," in a Christian community, was, by definition, within the purview of the former. By Charles V's time, I would argue such was no longer the case.

regency, and Robert le Coq, bishop of Laon, who also attended Orléans, and the so-called legal reformers of Charles V's time, like the Dormans brothers.[75]

Fourteenth-century political actors were not quite sure what term to use, in part because political discourse was shifting from Latin to French, at least in the *langue d'oïl*: Serge Lusignan shows that ninety-one percent of Philip VI's acts for that region were in French after 1330 (as against only four percent of Philip IV's acts). John II returned to Latin, ninety-eight percent of all royal acts of the chancery, but Charles V restored French. Henceforth, the king would use Latin only for letters of nobility and legitimacy, for towns with consulates, and for most acts related to the Church.[76] The shift from Latin to French reflected to a large degree a desire for a political vocabulary better suited to the reality of French politics circa 1370 – that is, to a politics in which people who did not read Latin played important roles. Oresme, in the proem to his translation of the *Ethics*, had made precisely that point about the king's counselors.

The king would invariably refer to "nous et nostre royaume" or to "us and the Crown of France." King John II's 1358 letters to "the mayor, échevins, bourgeois, inhabitants, and all the commune of the town of St-Omer," about the "treason" of the local *bailli*, spelled out the usual royal formula:[77]

> The sire of Beaulo, our liege man and subject and our sworn *bailli* of the bailiwick of our said town of St-Omer, has made himself and makes himself our enemy and put himself in rebellion against us and our kingdom [. . . allied with Charles of Navarre . . .] going against his faith, loyalty, and oath, and incurring the crime of lèse-majesté and treason notoriously against us and the crown of France.

This formula left a key gap: the kingdom and its political society were not coterminous. The composer Guillaume de Machaut, in his motet 22, likely written after Reims resisted an English siege (1359–1360), wrote: "Plange! Regni respublica" (Weep, commonwealth of the kingdom!).[78]

---

[75] Nephew of a bishop of Le Mans, de la Forest supposedly got his license at twelve and was a doctor of both canon and civil law. "The light of his brilliance shining even into the inner reaches of John's house" (Du Chesne). John, then duke of Normandy, made him chancellor of Normandy, later of France.

[76] Lusignan, *La langue des rois au Moyen Âge*.

[77] Pagart d'Hermansart, *Histoire du bailliage de St-Omer, 1193–1790* (St. Omer, 1898), II, 365. "se est rendu et fait nostre ennemy et mis en rébellion contre nous et nostre royaume [. . .] en venant contre sa foy, loyauté et serrement, et en encourant crime de lèse majesté et trayson notoirement contre nous et la couronne de France."

[78] A. Walters Robertson, *Guillaume de Machaut and Reims. Context and Meaning in his Musical Works* (Cambridge: CUP, 2002), gives two different translations on p. 202 (Weep! You, commonwealth of the kingdom) and in an appendix that gives the Latin text and her translation of it (cited in the text above).

De Machaut here uses the same language as the mayor and *jurés* of Noyon, writing to the town government of Reims on behalf of an assembly of twenty-four northern towns, which had met with major members of the clergy and some leading nobles, to draw up grievances (above all about troop pillaging) to present to the regent. They asked the Rémois to join them at an assembly to be held on September 1, 1359 at Compiègne, and urged them to include local clergy in their town assembly: "This matter and all the facts regard each one, and all of the 'chose publique.'"[79] The "treaties" of alliance between Reims and Rethel and Châlons-en-Champagne in 1358, in contrast, had spoken of the "honor of God, the profit, guard, and surety of all the kingdom of our lord [*sire*] the king" and then of the "enemies of the kingdom"; they made no mention of the *chose publique*.[80] Yet the town government of Reims, in late 1358, used the new vocabulary in writing to the Dauphin to seek his support to force ecclesiastics to pay their share of "the aide of the king, of the kingdom and of all the chose publique, as is done in the other bonnes villes."[81]

These documents offer a hint as to the critical vocabulary shift taking place in the crisis years 1356–1360. The 1356 Estates of Languedoïl, meeting after John II's capture, had referred to the need to act for the "honor of God, the profit and deliverance of the king, for the kingdom, for Monsieur the duke [Charles], and 'la chose publique.'" The *Chronique des quatre premiers Valois*, likely written in Rouen at the end of the fourteenth century, shows a general familiarity with this wording: the author tells us that Le Coq said that the "three estates of the kingdom, the estate of the Church, the estate of the nobles, and the estate of the bourgeois" offered Charles advice "on the state of the bien commun and the deliverance of the king your father, our true and sovereign seigneur."[82] The *Chronique* offers another telling detail: "the above said estates deliberated that there should be strong money in your lands of Normandy and Dauphiné and in the kingdom of the king your father." If the duke minted

---

[79] Varin, *Archives administratives*, III, 144, letter of August 22, 1359: "les en prions comme la chose et tous li fais regarde un chacun, et toute la chose publique."

[80] Varin, *Correspondance administrative*, t. III, 123ff, document DCXCIV (Rethel); Marlot, *Histoire de Reims*, IV, 626, document XXIV (Châlons). "Ad l'oneur de Dieu, et au proffit, garde, et seureté de tout le royaue du roy notre sire, de M. le régent." And later, "afin de résister plus puissamment contre les ennemis dudit royaume."

[81] Varin, *Archives administratives*, III, 116, note, quoting from the seventeenth-century compiler Rogier, who was citing documents no longer in existence in Varin's time. "l'ayde du roy, du royaume et de toute la chose publicque, comme il se faisoit aux aultres bonnes villes." Charles, as Regent, was regulating this dispute between the clergy and the town government in September 1358.

[82] *Chronique des quatre premiers Valois*, 58–59. "les trois estats du royaume, l'estat de l'eglise, l'estat des nobles et l'estat des bourgoiz ont eu adviz sur l'estat du bien commun et de la deliverance du roy vostre pere, nostre droit et souverain seigneur." The chronicler comments on these proposals, in a classic statement of the gap between good intentions and results, "Bon commencement ourent, mais mal finerent."

strong money, they would pay for the support of 30,000 men-at-arms. He goes so far as to say that the estates, "on their own authority," minted sound money, of good alloy.[83] In 1357, when, under pressure from the Parisians, Charles had to criticize certain royal councilors, he accused them of acting not for the profit of "*la chose publique* but for their *profit singulier* and that of their friends," a contrast that became proverbial in political discourse.[84]

Kings seemed reticent to use a term other than kingdom. In French, *res publica* appeared most often in royal documents as "la chose publique de nostre royaume." Anne Robertson suggests that, after the king's capture at Poitiers, "In the absence of the ruler, the concept of 'commonwealth of the kingdom' was all that remained, especially in view of the fact that the young Duke of Normandy had not yet found his voice." Robertson emphasizes that Charles, as Dauphin, in his grand *arrêt* of 1363 spoke often of the *res publica*, as in the royal takeover of the defense of the city of Reims, on the grounds that "the power of the people, by their own wish and assent, was thereafter transferred to the prince or emperor for the better ordering of the common-wealth" (*reipublice*).[85]

The key shift, however, took place in Paris between 1356 and 1358. Charles did not initiate this change, which seems to have taken over political discourse in the aftermath of speeches given by Robert le Coq, drawing on the ideas of Oresme and Buridan, in November 1356 and March 1357. The vocabulary of the "*bien de la chose publique*" became standard political speech in the period between the meeting of the Estates General of Languedoïl in October 1356 and the coronation of Charles V in 1364. Le Coq's choice of "chose publique," a purely vernacular translation of *res publica*, rather than "*respublique*," a more learned possible choice, tells us how important it was to find a language that could achieve political ends with the audience of citizens – in that case, many urban deputies almost certainly unfamiliar with Latin. Let us examine that process in detail.

1.2   The Crisis of 1356–1358 and the New Vocabulary of Politics

The small elite at the core of the French government in 1356 included families from the high Parisian bourgeoisie, the titled nobility, and branches of the royal house. Just as John II, his son-in-law Charles of Navarre, and Edward III contested the inheritance of Philip IV, so, too, the brothers-in-law Robert de Lorris and Étienne Marcel contested the inheritance of their father-in-law,

---

[83] No such minting took place in 1356; in fact, the Estates protested – and got withdrawn – the new silver coins, of weak money, being produced while the Dauphin was visiting his uncle Emperor Charles IV in Metz.

[84] Isambert, IV, 775–780.

[85] Robertson, *Guillaume de Machaut and Reims*, 212. Robertson translates *reipublice* as "state."

Pierre des Essarts, and the Harcourt and Melun families jousted in Normandy. These family quarrels had a decisive impact on the events of 1356–1358. Charles of Navarre failed in his attempt to claim the French throne; Navarre's ally, Marcel, lost his life as a direct result of his inheritance quarrel. These events took place at a time in which it was far from obvious that the kingdom of France would remain a coherent entity: both Charles of Navarre and Edward III made it clear they would settle for portions of the kingdom they believed belonged to them. John II suspected his son Charles, the last real duke of Normandy, of wanting to establish an unacceptable level of independence in that vital province – claimed as well both by Edward and, in part, by Charles of Navarre.[86]

Before looking at the key meetings of October 1356 and March 1357, however, we need to re-examine the nature of assemblies at that time, so we can get a clear sense of precisely who was using this new vocabulary. The term "Estates General" is certainly misleading because the term implies broad, implicitly universal geographic participation within the two regions: not so. The collection of great fiefs within the kingdom of France belonged mainly to members of the royal family, who had both personal and collective interests. Without the permission of the duke of Burgundy or duke of Brittany, no Burgundian or Breton deputies would go to an "Estates General.[87] The counties of Artois and Flanders did not send general delegations, although some major towns (Lille, Arras, Douai, Tournai) came to certain meetings.[88] If the king of France wanted money from the county of Artois, he had to ask the local estates for it.[89]

The same principle held even with the new, smaller peerage fiefs. The county of Évreux, which belonged to Charles of Navarre, and that of Alençon, held by John II's cousin, did not send deputies to the "Estates of Normandy." Even within the five Norman bailiwicks at the Estates of 1352, representatives of the duke of Orléans (John's brother), for the county of Beaumont-le-Roger, and of the king of Navarre, for his county of Longueville, declared that they could not

---

[86] Navarre inherited the county of Évreux from his father, Philip, nephew of Philip IV. Charles' brother, Philip, inherited the counties of Longueville; by agreement with John II, Charles obtained Beaumont-le-Roger, Pont-Audemer, and most of the Cotentin peninsula.

[87] Houses like the Montfort line in Brittany, the Bourbons, the dukes of Burgundy (both Capetian and Valois), the dukes of Anjou and of Orléans [in successive lines], all descended in the male line from kings of France and were in the line of succession to the throne throughout this period.

[88] Tournai long remained a royal enclave in the north, and regularly participated; it housed a royal mint.

[89] *Ordonnances*, IV, 589, grant of August 1365, for the "great desire and affection they have to Us, and to the bien commun de nostre royaume," is a typical example. Lille cut its own deal on the ransom aides (*Ordonnances*, III, 504), paying 3,000 gold florins over six years to be exempt from the aides created in 1360.

approve the tax voted by the Estates because they did not have the permission of their lords to do so. This tactic, claiming that one needed the permission of one's lord (including the king) before taking a given action, provided an ironclad excuse for a wide range of resistance, from towns seeking to avoid paying royal taxation in the fourteenth century to Burgundian serfs refusing to borrow money to pay royal direct taxes in the mid-seventeenth century.

We have a list of the thirty-six towns[90] who got a copy of the actions taken at the December 1355 meeting of the Estates of Languedoïl: from outside the regions of Paris, Champagne, and the north, deputies came only from the Seine valley in Normandy (Rouen, Harfleur, Honfleur), the main Loire towns (Angers, Tours, Saumur, Chinon, Orléans), Bourges, Poitiers, La Rochelle, Limoges, and Lyon.[91] The absence of Norman deputies from the Estates General of Languedoïl led to Navarre and his allies, the Harcourt family, organizing effective Norman resistance to the levying of these taxes.[92] John II viewed this refusal, in a duchy nominally in the authority of his oldest son, Charles, duke of Normandy, as the final insult, after Navarre's murder of John's favorite, Charles d'Espagne.[93] John stormed into the dinner party of his son, Charles of Navarre, and Jean V de Harcourt at Rouen. He had Jean V de Harcourt decapitated the next day (April 6, 1356), without trial. This episode led to civil war in Normandy.[94] (See Illustration 1.1.) As the *Chronique des quatre premiers Valois* put it, "greatly was king John blamed for the murder of the said seigneurs and great [due to it] was the malevolence of the nobles and of his people, especially those of Normandy."[95]

---

[90] In addition to those listed in the text: Amiens, Doullens, Montdidier, St-Quentin, Laon, Beauvais, Senlis, Compiègne, Vertus, Louvres, Corbeil, Troyes, Provins, Mélun, Meaux, Sens, Montlhéry, Chartres, Joigny, Pontoise, and Poissy – all towns within the royal demesne. The helpful map and list in Burgière and Revel, eds., *Histoire de France*, 138–139, contains minor inconsistencies.

[91] No deputies from the Auvergne were present, but the Estates of the Auvergne soon approved the new taxes, with the proviso that they collect and spend the money. In October 1356, six deputies from the Auvergne were present, and the local estates voted taxes on the clergy, nobility, and commoners. Secousse, "Préface," *Ordonnances* III.

[92] Peasants, too, resisted these new taxes and the frequent requisition of food, forage, and animals. B. Chevalier, ed., *Les pays de la Loire moyenne dans le Trésor des chartes* (Paris: Archives nationales, 1993), #275, in March 1361, for example, gives remission to Guillaume des Barres, chevalier, who murdered four armed peasants resisting royal requisition orders. #276 gave him remission for other "acts of war."

[93] Charles de la Cerda was the great-great-grandson of Louis IX. John was close to Charles and named him Constable in 1350, after executing Constable Raoul, count of Eu. Charles of Navarre objected to la Cerda receiving the county of Angoulême.

[94] Coville, *États de Normandie*, 79–80. Charles apparently felt mortified at his father seizing and executing one of his guests; he later pardoned Harcourt and restored most of his possessions to the count's son, Jean VI de Harcourt, who married Charles' sister-in-law.

[95] *Chronique des quatre premiers Valois*, 157.

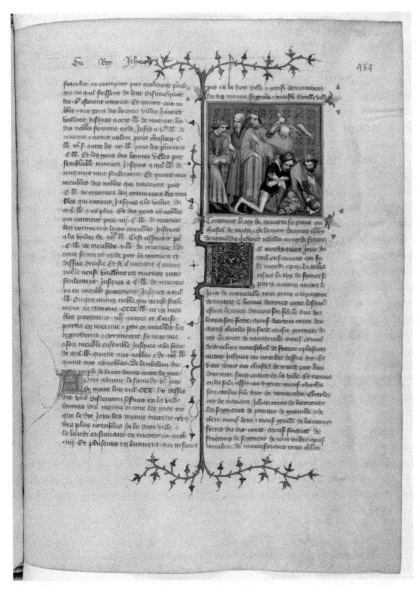

Illustration 1.1   Execution of Norman nobles, 1356: *Grandes Chroniques de France,* M Fr 2608, fol. 454r. Permission BNF

The town deputies for the December 1355 meeting came only from the royal demesne, from areas controlled by the Dauphin Charles, by the king's brother Philippe, duke of Orléans, by the king's sons Louis (count of Anjou), Jean (count of Poitou), and Philip (count of Touraine), by the king's wife (Jeanne d'Auvergne), and from towns under royal safeguard like Limoges and Lyon. In contrast with the earlier assemblies, such as that of February 1317 in Paris, we see the disappearance of almost all Norman towns, those from Artois and southern Flanders, and Burgundy.[96] The list also excludes Blois, and parts of central France, like the Auvergne, that often did send deputies to the northern estates. As Raymond Cazelles pointed out, "the great fiefs did not consider themselves concerned by the Estates General."[97]

The March 1356 meeting had virtually no one from Normandy. Three other documents from 1356 to 1358 add nine more towns known to have participated to some degree: Reims, Châlons-en-Champagne, Abbeville, Noyon, Tournai, Douai, Lille, Arras, and Auxerre.[98] If we take the three lists combined, we get forty-five towns, but by October 1356, Limoges, Poitiers, La Rochelle, and the four Loire towns joined the Normans among the missing. Aside from the metropolitan *cités* – Reims, Lyon, Bourges, and Rouen – towns outside the immediate region of Paris and of areas north and east in close connection with Paris had disappeared.[99] In an immediate sense, the vocabulary of the "bien de la chose publique" took root precisely in the geographic regions represented at the Estates of Languedoïl, with Brittany added in. Charles of Blois, Valois-recognized duke of Brittany, led the Second Estate, while Jean de Craon, archbishop of Reims, led the clergy.

Aside from Craon, three other archbishops played important roles in 1356–1357: Guillaume de Melun (archbishop of Sens); Pierre de la Forest (Rouen), chancellor of France; and Raymond Saquet (Lyon). Saquet, a former councilor of the Parlement whom Cazelles identifies as pro-Navarre, attended the October 1356 meeting, but stayed in Lyon after that; Innocent VI used him as one of his three legates to Paris in 1358. De la Forest was a target of the Estates, but after he became a cardinal in December 1356, and stepped down as chancellor, he conveniently left for Bordeaux, to return the seals to John II (Jan. 1357).

---

[96] Northern towns present in 1317 but absent in 1355–1356 included: Calais (in 1355, an English possession), St-Omer, Aire, and Thérouanne. From Normandy, no deputies came from Dieppe, Caen, Coutances, Avranches, Évreux, Verneuil, Bayeux, and Lisieux – Charles of Navarre controlled most of these towns. Dijon and Autun attended in 1317, but not in the 1350s. Langres, site of a peerage bishopric, was missing in 1355; Macon attended in 1317, but might have gone to the southern assembly in 1355.

[97] R. Cazelles, *Société politique, noblesse et royauté sous Jean II et Charles V* (Geneva: Droz, 1982), 208. The absence of the town of Blois is striking: Louis III, count of Blois, was a close relative of Gaucher de Châtillon, spokesman of the nobility at the Estates.

[98] Étienne Marcel also wrote to Ghent, Ypres, Courtrai, and Bruges.

[99] The seat of an archbishopric was always under royal safeguard. A. Collas, "Aperçu sur le clergé du diocèse de Tours au XIVe siècle," *Annales de Bretagne* 87 (1980): 612–613.

Guillaume de Melun was one of the three dominant royal councilors of the early 1350s, closely associated with John II's failed effort at reform. Melun's mother, Jeanne de Tancarville, brought not only her family's estates, but its quarrel with the Harcourt, complicated by the fact that the Melun family, with its ties to Enguerrand de Marigny, were clients of the house of Navarre. Philippe de Melun, uncle of Guillaume, and archbishop of Sens from 1338 to 1345,[100] was even chancellor of Navarre and its governor. Guillaume and his brother Jean, count of Tancarville, were captured at Poitiers, but obtained quick release; he participated in royal councils of the fall of 1356, but then went to Bordeaux, where he was part of the French team negotiating the truce of March 1357. The other negotiators included his brother Jean, Simon de Bucy, de la Forest, and Robert de Lorris – that is, in the case of the final three, precisely the men the Estates General of Languedoïl demanded be removed from royal office in October 1356, after the Poitiers disaster. When the Melun brothers, and their brother-in-law, Jean d'Artois, count of Eu, returned to Paris in early April, hostile public reception forced them to flee.[101]

The Melun brothers spent a good part of the next two years in prison in England, their large ransoms (48,000 écus for Guillaume alone) unpaid.[102] When John II stood surety for the brothers, they returned to France: the Dauphin stayed in the archbishop's *hôtel* in Paris in 1360, while Jean II de Melun acted as one of the two main French negotiators at Brétigny. When the negotiators sent the draft treaty back to Paris, the Dauphin heard it read in Guillaume de Melun's *hôtel*, by the royal lawyer Jean des Mares, whom we will encounter in key episodes later. As for the other archbishops, the only one regularly to attend the royal council in 1357 was Jean de Craon, who was very active from March through May, during and immediately after the time of the renewed "Estates General" of Languedoïl.[103]

The regional and local assemblies played as important a role as the "national" ones in the 1350s: in terms of collecting taxes, they played

---

[100] Another uncle had been archbishop of Sens from 1315 to 1329. Philippe de Melun seems to have fallen out with Jeanne de Navarre, and thus lost his position in 1345. This split may explain the Navarre-Melun division of 1356.

[101] Jean d'Artois, count of Eu, son of the Robert III d'Artois who caused so many problems in 1313–1317, as a direct, male-line descendant of Louis VIII, was in the line of succession. He married Isabelle de Melun, half-sister of Guillaume and Jean, in 1352; he had received (1351) the county of Eu, confiscated from Constable Raoul de Brienne, who had been executed (without trial) for treason in 1350. Like his brother and brother-in-law, he had been captured at Poitiers. King John II was Jean d'Artois's first cousin.

[102] John II finally made payments for both brothers in 1360. Cazelles, *Société politique Jean II*, 372–373.

[103] Cazelles, *Société politique Jean II*, 265: Craon attended four meetings of the royal council in March, ten in April, three in May, none in June.

a greater role. Unsurprisingly, given the long *civitas* tradition of the southern towns, the earliest evidence of the "public good" vocabulary appears in the south at the 1343 estates of the seneschalsy of Carcassonne, which agreed to levy a sales tax of 1.66% in return for the restoration of the "strong money" of Saint Louis: the king said he restored it "for the good of the republic of all our subjects" [*pro bono republicæ omnium subditorum nostrorum*].[104] The "republic" in question was not France, but the Langue d'Oc.[105] Three years later, the count of Armagnac, the king's lieutenant, again used the term "pro bono publico" with respect to the discussions about coinage at the Estates of Langue d'Oc, but the letters for the local assembly in the seneschalsy of Carcassonne spoke only of the king's desire to "govern and nourish his people in tranquility and freedom (*franchise*)" and the convocation letters for Estates Generals of Langue d'Oc did not use commonwealth vocabulary.

In April 1356, meeting simultaneously with the "Estates General" held at Paris, the southern assembly acted for "republican and private honor and utility."[106] We see here a more traditional term, utility, and the distinction between personal [private/individual/particular] and public that would play so large a role in the northern assemblies. Oddly enough, the southern assemblies, despite the strong *civitas* tradition in their urban governments, moved away from the discourse of the public good or "chose publique." It played virtually no role in their discussions after 1356; they preferred the language of "liberties, rights, and freedoms," which held sway everywhere in the south and, until the fifteenth century, in Flanders.[107] In the north, the tumultuous events of 1355–1358 brought the use of the discourse of the public good into the mainstream of French political life.

The process began, in many ways, with the meetings of the Estates General of Languedoïl in November 1355 and March 1356, in Paris. John II convinced

---

[104] Devic et Vaissette, *Histoire de Languedoc*, VII, *Preuves*, 470; in their discussion of this assembly, Devic and Vaissette suggest that the "third estate" dominated it (VII, 194ff). The king did not share the Estates' sentiments: in January 1347, in letters sent to the seneschal of Beaucaire, he claimed that he alone had the right to mint and to determine the value of the currency in money of account (*Ordonnances*, II, 254).

[105] The consuls of Saint-Flour still used the old locution "went into France" for crossing the Loire River. *Registres consulaires de Saint-Flour (1376–1405)*, ed. M. Boudet (Paris and Riom: Champion; Jouvet, 1900).

[106] Devic et Vaissette, *Histoire de Languedoc*, VII, *Preuves*, document LII (495ff): "ad ipsius honorem utilitatem que reipublicæ et privatæ." Further along the king specifies "reipublicæ Linguæ Occitanæ" as the region of his son Charles' commission, and Jean, count of Armagnac, royal lieutenant, in 1357 (499) referred as well to the "patriæ" and the "regimine et statu Linguæ Occitanæ."

[107] *Ordonnances*, III, 99ff has the text of the ordinance. Cazelles, *Société politique Jean II*, 235, rightly points out the revolutionary implications of this assertion. Devic and Vaissette, *Histoire de Languedoc*, VII, *Preuves*, 507, for Jean de Berry's 1359 letters calling an assembly for the defense of the *patria* of the kingdom of Linguæ Occitanæ.

the November 1355 Estates to vote a tax package [3.33% on sales other than land; a *gabelle* on salt] to be collected and overseen by commissioners named by the Estates; in March, after finding out that the taxes voted in November were insufficient (and wildly unpopular), the new assembly created a tax on incomes and capital, including the income of clergy and nobles.[108] Matteo Villani tells us both that John promised, in return for the taxes, to issue sound gold and silver coinage, and that the sales tax was so unpopular that merchants abandoned France, and many towns refused to receive the royal officials charged with the collection.[109]

This shift in the tax mix incontestably responded to urban demands: the introduction of sales taxes invariably touched off urban revolts, whether at Rouen in the 1290's, Arras in 1356, or throughout the kingdom, in 1380–1382. The urban victory on the tax issue makes one suspect that the assembly included a substantial number of deputies from the world of commerce.[110] In Normandy, Jean V de Harcourt reportedly stated that "By God's blood, the blood of God, this King is a bad man, and is not a good King," during the February 1356 meeting of the Estates of Normandy that approved the collection of the sale tax and *gabelle* in Normandy.[111]

The three spokesmen for the Estates were Jean de Craon, his cousin, Gauthier de Brienne, constable of France, and Étienne Marcel, merchants' provost of Paris. The terms of this grant showed the usual effort by elites to share real power. The Estates named three supervisors from each order to oversee the collection and to make sure that money got spent only on troops, and to the extent possible, on local troops: each "*cité*" was to have one overseer from each order, a receiver, and a clerk. All officials were to answer to assemblies.[112] These provisions resembled those followed in local assemblies

---

[108] Isambert, *Recueil général*, IV, 734ff. At Arras, on 6-8 March 1356, a rebellion of the poor against the sales taxes killed twenty of the leading citizens; Marshal Audenham, in reprisal, beheaded twenty "leaders" of the rebellion, and imprisoned eighty more. The Estates of the Auvergne approved the fifteen percent tax on income of clergy and nobles, and hearth tax on free and serf hearths, with the latter paying half rate.

[109] M. Villani, *Cronica di Matteo Villani*, ed. F. Dragomanni, 2 vols. (Florence, 1846), II, 191–192.

[110] The harsh comments about popular political participation in Buridan's *Quæstiones* and Oresme's exclusion of merchants and artisan masters from full political citizenship both have their roots in the broad participation of such men in the assemblies of 1356–1358, in my view. For that reason, I have a different reading of *De Moneta* than Woodhouse, "Who Owns the Money?" Oresme was speaking on behalf of the right of the "citizens" as against the prince, but his later writings make clear his suspicion of too broad a definition of citizen.

[111] R. Delachenal, *Histoire de Charles V*, I (Paris: A. Picard, 1909–1931), 139.

[112] The December 1355 ordinance had the same clauses about control by the Estates, but they had voted a sales tax and a *gabelle* on salt. In that ordinance, John cited the "clamour de nostre peuple, & de noz subgiez" about currency fluctuations, and promised to maintain sound money henceforth, even as he decried the ill effects of "tres fort

of the 1340s and 1350s, such as the estates in Normandy, the Auvergne, and in Vermandois.[113]

The assemblies of November-December 1355 and March 1356 showed a marked suspicion of those running the royal finances.[114] One of the primary grievances, particularly of the merchants, was incessant manipulation of the coinage: quite apart from legal manipulation of the ratio of money of account (*livres*) to actual coins, Philip VI, John, II and the Dauphin Charles reminted almost all of the kingdom's coinage in 1349 and 1355, and large parts of it in 1356, 1357, and 1359.[115] Philip VI had stated (January 1347) unequivocally that the right to issue ordinances about coinage belonged solely to the "royal majesty," but the tradition of the king supervising the coinage on behalf of the community remained strong. Philip IV's lawyers had admitted as much in 1309: contesting the right of the count of Nevers to debase coinage, they insisted that the king alone had the right to "debase and reduce coinage" as a "royal right," but he could only do so "in one case, necessity," and could not convert it into "special profit," but only do it for the "profit and defense of the common."[116] The charters granted to the Normans and Burgundians in 1315 had both made a return to the sound money of Saint Louis one of the main demands, and Louis X promised them both to return to the sound money of good alloy, and further promised that neither he nor his successors would debase the coinage again. Coinage, which brought together the political and economic elements of the "chose publique," proved to be the key issue in the birth of the new rhetoric of politics.

Monnoye" during the war. [*Ordonnances*, III, 26–27]. The follow-up ordinance of May 26, 1356 gave serfs ("taillables haut & bas à volonté") a fifty percent reduction, but specified that nobles and clergy (if not paying the tenth voted in December 1355) had to pay. He further stipulated that copies with "our authetical seals" would be given to each "Ville" to give faith (*foy*) as if they were the "true Original." [p. 55]

[113] Henneman, *Royal Taxation* and *The Captivity and Ransom of John II*. Ordonnances, II, 393, on Norman taxes.

[114] Philip VI and John II had each created commissions to "reform" finances and minting.

[115] The royal treasury accounts show a minting profit in 1349 that implies re-minting of about 53,000kg of silver. The 1355 re-minting involved 27,700 kg of silver; from 1356–1358, the mints produced a steady average of just over 18,000 kg, dropping to about 15,000 kg in 1359 and 1360. In the entire reign of Charles V (1364–1380), in contrast, the mints produced only 11,000 kg of silver. Gold coin output peaked between 1360 and 1365, mainly new *écus* for John's ransom, but the average amount of 1355–1359 – 1500 kg – was about equal in value to the silver coinage. H. Miskimin, "L'or, l'argent, la guerre dans la France médiévale," *Annales. Histoire, Sciences Sociales* (Jan.–Feb. 1985): 171–184. Henneman, *The Development of War Financing*, 331–344, argues that the nobles, in particular, wanted "strong" money, to preserve their incomes. The re-mintings of 1349 and 1355 responded in part to their demand.

[116] S. Piron, "Monnaie et majesté royale dans la France du XIVe siècle," *Annales. Histoire, Sciences Sociales* 51, n. 2 (1996): 325–354. Buridan and Oresme also took this position.

Poitiers transformed the French political scene because so much of the military and political leadership was either killed or, like John II, taken prisoner.[117] The two discredited adolescents who straggled into Paris on September 29 – duke Charles, and John II's young brother, Philippe, duke of Orléans – did not provide much legitimacy or real leadership.[118] The main leadership group left intact in October 1356 was the legal men – chancellor Pierre de la Forest, former chancellor Guillaume Flote (seigneur de Revel), First President of the Parlement Simon de Bucy, and future chancellor Pierre d'Orgemont – and the financiers. With the assistance of a few major nobles, such as Charles of Blois, and ecclesiastics like Jean de Craon, they surely made the key decisions.[119] Unsurprisingly, the Estates demanded the ouster of la Forest, Bucy, Flote, Bucy, and d'Orgemont, whom they held responsible for the catastrophe, "the worst ever to befall the kingdom of France."

On the day the Dauphin Charles got back to Paris, he and the royal council called a meeting of the northern Estates, for October 15, 1356, at Paris, and a similar meeting, for the Langue d'Oc, at Toulouse. The Paris meeting was a vast gathering of 800 deputies, of whom 400 came from the towns: given fourteenth-century logistics, almost all of these urban deputies had to have come from towns near Paris, although we know that at least six deputies came from the distant Auvergne.[120] The nobles and clergymen, like the urban deputies, on the "commission" created by the Estates came overwhelmingly from Champagne, Picardy, and other regions in the north and northeast: many of them were open partisans of Charles, king of Navarre, who was then in prison. Navarre hoped to become king of France, or at least to regain his mother's lost fiefs, above all Champagne, and to consolidate his hold on Normandy.[121]

The slight evidence we have about the urban deputies implies a strong presence of the world of commerce and production. The March 1356 meeting not only overturned the sales tax; they voted a fifteen percent levy on noble and clergy incomes and a hearth tax on lay commoners, without the customary

---

[117] Cazelles, Société politique, noblesse et royauté sous Jean II et Charles V, 230, for a list of dead and captured.

[118] The chronicles disagree about Charles' behavior, but all agree that Philippe's cowardly flight played a major role in the French defeat. Villani, Cronica di Matteo Villani, II, 182ff, says 5,000 knights fled with them.

[119] Charles of Blois took the place of his deceased relative Gauthier de Châtillon as spokesman of the nobility. Craon and Marcel remained the spokesmen of the other two orders.

[120] Dauphant, Royaume, map 5, indicates that a message could reach Limoges or Clermont in six days, Lyon in eight. John II's second wife, Jeanne d'Auvergne, ruling Burgundy on behalf of her son, duke Philippe de Rouvre, then a minor, clearly coordinated her actions with those of the Dauphin.

[121] Normandy then produced roughly twenty-five percent of French tax revenue.

distinction between urban and rural hearths.[122] The October 1356 delegation from Soissons included Regnaud, *cabaretier*, and Jean Tatini, draper, both "citizens" of Soissons. When they returned to Soissons, some of their fellow citizens maltreated them – Regnaud received fourteen separate wounds – as punishment for their intemperate remarks about royal councilors, "made under the pretext of the 'bonum publicum.'"[123] In 1363, the documents from Reims indicate that the Estates of Languedoïl meeting at Amiens in December had voted a hearth tax to pay for troops because the aides created in 1360 for the ransom meant "the merchants of the kingdom are burdened, and commerce reduced throughout the kingdom [. . .] so we are advised that a double tax or any surtax would not be good." The deputies chose a hearth tax; on the advice of the Regent Charles, the assembly ruled that 100 urban hearths would pay the same as 150 rural ones.[124]

The "pretext of the public good" takes us to the heart of our interest in the meetings of 1356 to 1358. If we are to pick one moment for the decisive entry of the "la chose publique" into the evolving political discourse of the French monarchy, it would be this meeting of the Estates of Languedoïl in October 1356, and the follow-up sessions of February–March 1357.[125] The proposed commissioners of the October 1356 Estates were to take an oath in front of the Dauphin that they would act for the good government of the kingdom "and of la chose publique," and not for their "singular profit or for their friends."

Jean Buridan's likely key role as a representative to the Estates in 1356, make his *Quæstiones* an intriguing look at the arguments in play.[126] He begins the *Quæstiones* on Aristotle's *Politics* with a clear statement that the common good must be preferred over the particular good: Buridan takes this characteristic to be the essence of any legitimate polity [*policia*]. No manuscript of Buridan's

---

[122] In both north and south, the final tax distinguished between serfs – "*taillables*" – and free men: serfs paid one-half the tax levied on free people. In Normandy, the early hearth taxes levied one man-at-arms per seventy urban hearths, and one per 100 rural ones. Ordonnances, III, 24, note (c).

[123] Secousse, *Charles de Navarre*, v. III, xlviii, note * At least four of the eighteen urban deputies on the commission of October 1356 were lawyers and four others masters of theology. The three Parisians were merchants.

[124] Varin, *Archives administratives*, III, 274ff. The tax called for a levy of 3 francs/hearth, with a range from 1 franc – "which is not even a penny a day" – to 9 francs for the wealthiest. They made the urban/rural distinction because in many dioceses the countryside had been ruined by troops.

[125] Insofar as I can tell, he issued only letters recalling the deputies for the February–March 1357 meeting.

[126] Buridan's *Quæstiones* on Aristotle's *Politics* may have a direct connection to these events. Oresme and Buridan had financial responsibilities within the university, so they had practical experience. Buridan regularly uses the term "*bonum commune.*" J. Kaye, *Economy and Nature in the Fourteenth Century: Money, Market Exchange, and the Emergence of Scientific Thought* (Cambridge: CUP, 1998), 30–31.

work survives, but he constantly refers to issues at play in 1356–1358, like currency reform and the need to limit political decision making to a more aristocratic element, in the Aristotelian sense of the word.

The single person most responsible within the Estates for the prominent reference to the "chose publique" appears to have been Robert Le Coq, trained in both canon and customary law (at Orléans), and former *avocat* for John II.[127] Le Coq delivered two key speeches: on November 3, to a rump final session of the Estates that opened on October 17, 1356, which the Dauphin seems to have prorogued on November 2;[128] and on March 3, 1357, to the deputies of the Estates in full session, with the Dauphin in attendance. The Dauphin sent letters recalling the Estates on January 25, 1357, to meet in Paris on February 5: once again, the short notice meant that only those very close to Paris, or deputies already present, could attend. A small group, led by Marcel, visited Charles when he got back to Paris; they continued to fight about the manipulation of the coinage. The deputies seem to have held just a brief meeting, and then gone back to meet with their local constituents. They returned once more, in early March, claiming the propositions they had sent back had been "read and approved by those of the *pays*, men of the Church as well as nobles, bourgeois of the good towns, and others."[129] The uprising at Arras suggests that the artisans blamed the wealthy [the GCF calls them the "gros", the big ones] for the Estates' inability to replace the sales tax with a levy on incomes.[130]

The *procès-verbal* of the October meeting, which exists in a copy prepared by the royal librarian in 1647, shows that Charles and the royal council immediately lost control. Le Coq's speech of November 3 raised the issue of a Pope removing a tyrannical king. In a famous anecdote, one of his friends supposedly kicked him after this intemperate remark, and Le Coq corrected himself: he meant to say that the Pope had deposed a king (the last Merovingian) at the **request** of the three Estates. The accusation against Le Coq, probably prepared by royal council officials in October-November 1356,

---

[127] Douët-d'Arcq, "Acte d'accusation contre Robert le Coq, évêque de Laon," *BEC*, v. 2 (1841): 350–388. A. Funk, "Robert Le Coq and Etienne Marcel," *Speculum*, vol. 19, no. 4 (Oct. 1944): 470–487. Le Coq had been an avocat at the Parlement, then replaced Pierre de la Forest as Philip VI's *avocat* there. In 1347, he became chancellor of John, duke of Normandy (John II). Under John II, he held positions as a master of requests, as royal chamberlain, as *avocat du roi*, and a president of the Parlement.

[128] This session did not meet in the hall of the Parlement, as the official ones had done, but at the convent of the Cordeliers, on the Left Bank, close to the Sorbonne, far from the regular sites of royal political power.

[129] The Estates in October had suggested just such a course of action: BNF, Dupuy 646; citation here from f. 66v. Numbers in parenthesis below are the folio numbers of this document. Isambert, *Recueil*, IV, 771ff has the text.

[130] There were also disturbances in Norman towns. Viard, ed., *Chronique de Jean II et Charles V*, I, 62.

cites this phrase as proof that he was disloyal to King John, the Crown, and the Dauphin.[131]

He reprised many of his main points in a speech given to the full Estates, the Dauphin present, in March 1357. (See Illustration 1.2.) In November, on behalf of the deputies, he had proposed that eighty of their number be a commission, which would swear on the Holy Gospels to act for "honor of God and profit of the King our lord (*sire*) of his deliverance, of the crown of France, of monsieur the duke, and *la chose publique.*" He criticized certain royal councilors, who had at heart only their "singular [*particulier*] interest" not "fear of God and the honor of king and profit of the kingdom." These men had not looked out for the "public profit and utility." (45) Reprising these themes in March, Le Coq demanded, on behalf of the Estates, not simply the dismissal and investigation of the eight councilors mentioned in November, but of twenty-two men in all. The Estates further demanded a purge of the Parlement and of the Chamber of Accounts, as well as a temporary suspension of all royal officials (this last not approved by the Dauphin). The Dauphin, as lieutenant of King John, removed the twenty-two men and issued letters criticizing counselors who did not think of "*la chose publique* but of their singular profit and that of their friends."[132] The deputies, from October through March, consistently claimed that they acted for the "profit of *la chose publique.*" Their constituents, like the good citizens of Soissons, were fully aware of their claim to have done so.

1.3   Buridan, Oresme, and Le Coq: The Rhetorical Triumph of the *chose publique*

Let us stop for a moment to consider these extraordinary events, in terms of the main actors and their war of words. The use of the term "bonum publicum," as at Soissons, was not unprecedented – the southerners used the phrase in a discussion of coinage in 1343 or 1346 – but it was unusual. The massive ordinance on the privileges and rights of mint workers, issued by Philip VI in 1337 and re-issued by John II in 1350, illustrates the connection of money to the public good, even though neither king used the phrase in that document. Its absence, unusual in an ordinance on coinage after 1361, was common prior to 1356. The great police ordinance issued by Jean II in 1350, made no mention of the "bien public" or "chose publique," with respect to a subject for which those terms would become obligatory by the 1360s.[133] Philip VI used the standard terminology when he renewed the privileges of the fairs of

---

[131] BNF, Dupuy 646, fols. 51v and ff.; Douët d'Arcq, "Acte d'accusation."
[132] Isambert, *Recueil*, IV, 814–15, March 3, 1357.
[133] *Ordonnances*, II, 339 (minters) and 350 (police).

Illustration 1.2   Robert Le Coq addresses the Estates General of Languedoïl, March 3, 1357, at the Palais du Parlement; the accused officials look on in fear: BNF, M Français 2813, *Grandes Chroniques de France* fol. 402v. Permission BNF

Champagne and Brie in 1349: the "good, honor, and profit of our Kingdom, and *du commun* of all *pays*, as they say."[134] Le Coq's verbal assault on the royal government, in the name of the "chose publique," seems to have been the turning point in the shift to this vocabulary, and it had a direct connection to a topic widely believed to belong to the collective citizenry: the coinage.

Unsurprisingly, the royal government, which defended the king's right to control the coinage for his own benefit,[135] took slowly to the discourse of the "chose publique." When the Dauphin regained control, after the murder of Marcel on July 31, 1358 and the execution of key allies the next day, he continued to manipulate the currency. He issued a blizzard of edicts about coinage in late 1358 and 1359: these edicts do not refer to the "bien public" or the "chose publique," but instead speak of the "profit and *bien* of the kingdom" or the "*bien* and profit of all the common people," as he put it on August 5, 1358.[136] The ordinance on coinage of October 30, 1358 made it clear that the Dauphin thought of the revenue from coinage as part of the royal "demesne."[137] Even so, the Dauphin could not ignore the "common people's" views: after issuing letters about minting new coins at Paris in November 1358, three months later he had to back down, due to popular resistance: he had heard people were unhappy with new coins, "and We, who do not wish in any manner to give displeasure to the said people," therefore would limit the issue of the new coins to the 700 *l.p.* worth already produced.[138] In December 1360, in the act that created the aides for his ransom, John II re-established sound money, wanting to act "in the praise of and for the pleasure of God. And for the profit and *bien commun* of all the people of our kingdom."[139]

---

[134] *Ordonnances*, II, 319.

[135] Letters sent to the seneschalsy of Beaucaire in 1346: *Ordonnances*, II, 254. See R. Cazelles, "Quelques réflexions à propos des mutations de la monnaie royale française (1295–1360)," *Le Moyen Age* (1966) and Henneman, *The Development of War Financing*.

[136] *Ordonnances*, III, 242ff.

[137] *Ordonnances*, III, 266.

[138] *Ordonnances*, III, 308. In Dijon, a crowd set fire to churches and sacked the office of the royal official in charge of the aides in 1359; at Châtillon-sur-Seine, a crowd murdered the royal provost charged with collection the taxes. Petit, *Ducs de Bourgogne*, IX, cites local sources that the bishop of Langres, Guillaume de Poitiers, urged his officers to prevent the levy of these taxes. The repression at Dijon included the burning of Adeline the hatmaker and the execution of Laurent, the painter [149]. Villani mentions the Dijon riots (II, 210) as a rising by the poor (*populo minute*) against the better (*maggiori*) and richest (*piu ricchi*) citizens (*cittadini*).

[139] *Ordonnances*, III, 439–40. Delachenal, *Charles V*, v. II, 265, sees the hand of Oresme in the monetary policy. E. Bridrey, *La théorie de la monnaie au XIVe siècle. Nicole Oresme* (Paris, 1906), 12, claims that for twenty-five years (1356–1380) the French government followed Oresme's theories, but the evidence suggests that prior to November 1359, when we know he was a "secrétaire du roi," he was one voice among many, and that only from December 1360 did Oresme's ideas take over.

This phrase came from Nicole Oresme's treatise, *De moneta*, which stressed that money existed "for the common utility" [*pro utilitate communi*] or "is greatly useful and necessary for the good of the public community" [*est moult utile et necessaire pour le bien de la communaulté publicque*],[140] as he put it in the French version he created, "petit traicté de la premiere invention des monnoies," which exists in two manuscripts at the Bibliothèque Nationale de France.[141] Oresme expressed the hope that his work "could profit princes, subjects, even all of the chose publicque." [*quod principibus et suiectis, ymo toti rei publice, proficiat in futurum/ aux princes, aux subgectz, voire et à toute la chose publicque, puisse profiter*] In the French version, Oresme continued his proem: he claimed merchants now bargained longer over the value of coins than over the value of the merchandise being sold, to the total confusion of the "universal good of his [the prince's] kingdom and *pays.*"

The prince put his image on the money for the "common utility" [*utilité commune/utilitate communi*] and not because the money belonged to him [*non tamen ipse est dominus seu proprietaries monete/ Il ne s'ensine pas que celluy seigneur et prince soit et doibve estre proprietaire et seigneur de la monnoie courant en sa principaulté et seigneurie*]. Money "belonged to the community and singular persons" [*a la communaulté et aux personnes singuliers/ communitatis et singularium personarum*]: he cited Aristotle and Cicero as authorities on this point.[142] Here in Chapter 6 we read about money's use to pay the "tribute" to the one who "fights and combats for the chose publique and for the defense of the kingdom and public utility."[143] Money was public, and the prince, as the "most public of individuals and with the greatest authority" [*personne la plus publicque et de plus grande auctorité/ magis publica et maioris auctoritatis*], therefore had a special responsibility for it, not property rights to it.[144]

And what about Le Coq, who was he, and why did he use the vocabulary of the public good? Why did the Estates focus so much on the contrast between "singular" or "particular" interest and the good of the "chose publique?" The work of Noël Valois and Raymond Cazelles enables us to see precisely the "singular" interest of the key players in this "pièce de théâtre." As Valois rightly

---

[140] De Moneta *of Nicholas Oresme*, trans. C. Johnson (London, 1956; Auburn, AL, 2009), ch. VI, 10–11, the prince coins money "pro utilitate communi."

[141] H. Omont, *Catalogue général des manuscrits français* (Paris, 1902), II, 213. M Français 23926 (sixteenth-century copy) and 23927 (fifteenth-century text). L. Wolowski published an edition of the former: *Traictie des la première invention des monnoies de Nicole Oresme* (Paris, 1864). The original is also available on Gallica. M Fr 23,927 later belonged to the de Thou family, who sold it to Cardinal Richelieu.

[142] Oresme, *De moneta*, ch. VI, 9–11; BNF, M Fr 23926, fols. 12r–13v.

[143] BNF, M Fr 23926, f. 13r. In the Latin, "qui pro re publica militabat"; the "kingdom" phrase is an addition to the French text.

[144] BNF, M Fr 23296, f. 12r [Wolowski, xix]; Oresme, *De moneta*, 10.

said, the grievances of the Estates combined genuine desire for reform of the kingdom – hardly surprising considering what contemporaries considered to be an unprecedented disaster – and personal vendetta.

Le Coq's disgrace generated a highly unusual document that helps us understand his ideas: a list of the manuscripts he owned, which were confiscated by the government. Le Coq owned seventy-six manuscripts, mainly in law; the two booksellers estimated the value at 354 *l.p.* Aside from law books like the *Digest*, we see our old friend Giles of Rome, *De regimine principum* (at 50 *s*, one of the most expensive of the "books"). Le Coq owned several works of theology and philosophy, from Boethius' *Consolations* to commentaries of the *Sentences* of Peter Lombard. He had a copy of Barthélemy l'Anglais' *Liber de proprietatibus rerum* [70 *s*], a work soon to be rendered into French by one of Charles V's scholars, Jean de Corbuchon. One manuscript carried the title of extracts of the books of "Tullius" (Cicero) and Le Coq owned Augustine's *De Perfectione Iustitiae Hominis* and Aquinas on the *Ethics* of Aristotle.[145] Cicero, Aristotle, Augustine, Aquinas, Gilles of Rome, Barthélemy l'Anglais – Le Coq got the rhetorical universe for his political ideas from familiar sources.[146]

Yet he surely turned as well to a new source, Nicole Oresme's *De Moneta*, likely written at precisely this moment.[147] Oresme picked up on principles enumerated in Philip VI's 1337 renewal of the privileges of the mint workers, reissued by John II in November 1350. The said minters had been created, the ordinance tells us, for the "common profit of all the people, because without money the world cannot be well governed, nor is it possible to do just equality to each of what is his."[148] This last point springs right out of Aristotle, a connection that soon

---

[145] He had commentaries on the *Sentences* by both Jean de Galles and Aquinas. R Delachenal, "La bibliothèque d'un avocat au XIVe siècle," *Nouvelle revue historique de droit français et étranger* (1887): 524–537.

[146] M. Keys, *Aquinas, Aristotle and the Promise of the Common Good* (Cambridge: CUP, 2006) and Kempshall, *Common Good* explain the special importance of Aquinas' commentary on Aristotle for the rise of the "common good" as a unifying theme of fourteenth-century political theory. The library of Blanche de Navarre, widow of Philip VI, contained many of the same books: M. Keane, *Material Culture and Queenship in Fourteenth-Century France: The Testament of Blanche of Navarre* (Leiden: Brill, 2016). Léopold Deslisle, *Testament de Blanche de Navarre, reine de France* (Paris: SHF, 1885) item 207, for example, is a book of "government of princes according to theology" [Giles of Rome], bound with a chess manual, given to Louis II, duke of Bourbon, brother-in-law of Charles V and key councilor of Charles VI.

[147] Oresme's specific criticism of the *gabelle* on salt, and his failure to mention the king's capture, seem to situate the text between December 1355 and September 1356. The consonance of vocabulary of the coinage edict of December 1355 and of *De moneta*, and the prominence of the coinage manipulation debate in spring 1356, also suggest a composition in that period. His discussion of currency reveals a strong nominalist background.

[148] *Ordonnances*, II, 339–340: "pour le commun proufit de tout le peuple, car sans monoie ne pourroit le monde bonnement estre gouverné, ne faire droite égaulté à chascun de ce qui est sien." Princes like the duke of Brittany simply copied royal language in their

became fundamental in the royal shift to the vocabulary of the public good. The royal ordinances on money in 1358–1359 used a variation of Oresme's precise phrase: the "profit of all the common people" or, in some cases, spoke of the "common profit and good" or the "profit and good of all the people."[149]

The public outrage about coinage manipulation, and its connection to "la chose publique," and the obvious profits made by those in charge of the minting, was absolutely genuine: Oresme touched a nerve. His Aristotelian argument that the currency belonged to the commonwealth helped make commonwealth language part of mainstream political discourse. Buridan may have played a similar role, given that his *Questiones* on the *Politics* included comments denouncing currency manipulation. Question 11 to Book 1 asked whether it was licit in a well-ordered polity [*policia bena recta*] to manipulate the currency. The first response stated it was illicit to do so if it led to "seditions," which was certainly the case in France in the 1350s. The second response claimed it was illicit if it was done for a particular good, rather than the *bonum commune*. Manipulating currency for the "utility of the lord" was noxious. Buridan concluded that "in no case is mutation of currency licit for private individual gain." These positions agree entirely with the arguments Oresme made in *De moneta*. Given that both men had financial responsibilities within the University of Paris, and that, as Bridrey has suggested, they probably belonged to the University's actual delegation to the assembly, we can be virtually certain that they set forth, as the University's official position, the idea that currency belonged to the *bonum commune*.

Oresme's claim that the stamp on a coin was merely the issuing authority's attestation to the fineness of the alloy in the coin, so that the institution of fixed value coins was a matter of the community's good [*pro bono communitatis*], and not of seigneurial profit [*non tamen ipse est dominus seu proprietarius monete currentis in suo principatu*], found ready takers among French elites.[150] Buridan admitted that the prince alone could change the value of the coinage, but he was to do so only on the advice of "all who govern the polity."[151] Oresme

ordinances, such as Jean V of Brittany's 1420 renewal of the "liberties, franchises and exemptions" of the minters of Nantes and Rennes : they had been given these "privileges" for the "proffit commun de tout l'universel peuple, à ouvrer et faire monnoye, pour ce que entierement le monde ne pouvoit bonnement estre gouverné, ne droicte esgalité à un chascun de ce que est sien estre faicte." *Lettres et mandements de Jean V*, #1444.

149 *Ordonnances*, III, 321 (February 1359, for Langue d'Oc), 343 (May 1359), both use the "all the people" phrase.

150 The prince stamped the coins for the common utility (*utilitate commune*): ch. 5–6. In chapter 7, he adds that "moneta igitur non est solius principus," money does not belong to the prince alone. He cites Aristotle and Cicero as his authorities on this point. Oresme, *De Moneta*.

151 "capitut ibi princeps non per uno homine solum, pro omnibus qui habent policiam regere." Buridan's next sentence states unequivocally that in no case can mutation of the coinage be licit if done for private gain.

was unequivocal: any prince who manipulated the currency for his own "vile" profit was a tyrant, because his profit was the community's loss (ch. XV). Carried to the extreme, as it would inevitably be in time in Oresme's view, because of human greed, it was "*perfecta tyrannis*." A prince changing the value of his money is "detestable," for he should not call gold, what is not gold, and a pound, what is not a pound: "woe unto them that call evil good and good evil." {*I Kings* xiv, 27 and *Isaiah* v, 20}[152] Oresme's point about calling things by their proper name would be repeated endlessly in later speeches, including Jean Gerson's 1405 sermon *Vivat rex*, one of the fundamental texts of commonwealth ideology.

Given the obvious influence of Oresme's ideas on the Estates General of Languedoïl of December 1355, and on the coinage policy and theories of the estates from October 1356 through March 1357, there can be little doubt that Le Coq took his public good vocabulary right out of Oresme's arguments about coinage as a "necessary" part of the public good, belonging to all the citizens. Émile Bridrey's suggestion that Oresme was likely one of the two "masters of divinity" identified as accompanying the Parisian delegation to the Estates, and advising their commission, gets striking confirmation from the consonant language of Le Coq's speeches and Oresme's arguments with respect to coinage.[153] In the February 1357 meeting, the procès-verbal identifies these two masters as among the official orators for the Estates. Given Oresme's promotion to grand master of the Collège of Navarre in October 1356, it is entirely possible he was even one of these orators.

Oresme's arguments bring forward many of Aristotle's key points. A king, he tells us, prefers the public utility to his own; a **tyrant** prefers "proprium commodum." A kingdom or a *res publica* is like a human body (*Politics*, V).[154] Those claiming that to deny coinage is a prince's right are not denying his

---

[152] French orators regularly used this biblical verse. Buridan, *Quaestiones*, Book I, question 11, argued that if coinage were not made of rare material, and of stated weight and value, then it was not legitimate (*recte*). Like Oresme and the king, Buridan believed "money is necessary in the polity." The prince could modify the coinage only in cases – such as inaccurate weight – mandated by public necessity or the utility of the commonwealth [*utilitatem reipublice*].

[153] E. Bridrey, *La théorie de la monnaie*, 476–477; on 467, he calls the University of Paris' role in the reform movement a "virtuous conspiracy for the *bien public*" led by Oresme and Jean Buridan. Oresme was grand master of the Collège de Navarre in 1356. Buridan was actively involved from 1356–1358 in a jurisdictional dispute between the Picard and English "nations" at the university. Charles of Navarre had extensive Picard support, and one must wonder about Buridan's relationship to Navarre's faction in 1357–1358. Buridan was not a master of divinity, so if that description is accurate, he cannot be the second person.

[154] Oresme draw here upon the body politic of John of Salisbury's *Policraticus*. The *Avis au roy* (c. 1347–1350) contains an image of the body politic, with the parts identified: Morgan Library, Ms 456, f. 5r, image on the Morgan's website. The *Avis* does not use the "chose publique" vocabulary. See Chapter 3, below.

majesty or power, and those so accusing them are *"rei publice proditores"* [traitors to the republic]. Moneychangers, "bankers" [*mercatores monete*], and dealers in bullion – i.e., precisely the people criticized by Le Coq – were unwanted by the *res publica*. Both the Dauphin (in 1359) and John II (when he returned) issued new legislation regulating the money changers. Money belonged to the community [*moneta sit communitatis*] and existed for the utility and good of the "civil community" and the "necessity" of the *"rei publice."* In the *Accusation* against Le Coq, the author claimed that witnesses "worthy of faith" had said that Le Coq claimed John II was unworthy to be king, was of tainted blood: just as would be the case at the time of the assassinations of Henry III and Henry IV, the legitimacy of violent resistance to a "tyrant," as opposed to a king, undergirded royal foes. Jean V de Harcourt and, if the *Chronique des quatre premiers Valois* is to be believed, the nobles and people of Normandy took a similarly negative view of King John.

Like Oresme, the deputies wondered who could trust a prince who would alter the weight of silver in his coins, without changing their official value? John II's August 1356 edict, changing the number of coins struck per mark of bullion, contributed mightily to the discontent of the fall of 1356: Marcel and the Parisians got it rescinded in December 1356, by Louis, duke of Anjou, the young prince acting for his father during the Dauphin's absence.[155] Oresme cited Solomon, Deuteronomy, and Cicero against modifying measures or changing the alloy of coins without changing their face value. Given that John had taken precisely that step in August, Le Coq's defense of the "chose publique" and his attack against the very men responsible for the currency had powerful resonance. The mint-making profits of Jean Poilevilain and the Braque brothers surely fell within the objections of Buridan and Oresme to coinage modification carried out for private gain.[156]

The Dauphin, in his letters of remission for Parisians, after the fall of Marcel, admitted as much: poor Guillaume le Fèvre, a fish seller, had, like many Parisians, been misled by Marcel and his allies, whom they believed wanted to ransom the king and serve the *"le bien public."* King John's general letters of remission for Paris made the same claim: some had sought to remove Paris

---

[155] In chapter 9, Oresme warns of the "scandal and murmuring" among the people if the money is altered. Later, he states specifically that a *gabelle* on salt is unjust and that setting an unfair price for coins is tyranny. He cites *Isaiah* x, 1, and its curse on princes who issue "unrighteous decrees." Buridan, in his first objection to modifying currency, cites modifications that lead to sedition; the coincidence between this objection and the events of December 1356 strongly suggests that Buridan was writing precisely in this moment or soon after.

[156] Parisians called the objectionable pennies "poillevillains" after Jean, master of the mint from 1359. The Braque brothers – Nicolas, maître d'hôtel du roi, and Aumary, treasurer of France – were involved in many sleazy deals and covered up some of their malfeasance through authorized murders: R. Cazelles, "Mouvements révolutionaires au milieu du XIV siècle," *Revue Historique*, 229 (1962): 279–312.

from John's "government and Seigneury," and those doing so "feigned by their great malice that they did it for a good end for the *bien public*." The king claims that, inspired by the Holy Spirit, Parisians saw through the ruse, overthrew Marcel, and so acquitted their loyalty to John II, Charles, and the Crown of France.[157]

The leadership of the Estates split in the summer of 1357. Jean de Craon, who mysteriously lurks in the background of many key events of the period 1356–1371, went over to the side of the Dauphin. He had close family ties to the powerful Châtillon family; in December 1359, those ties enabled the royal chamberlain Gaucher de Châtillon to mediate a compromise between Craon and the town government of Reims, which suspected the archbishop of treasonous ties to his "relative," Edward III.[158] Craon seems to have played a critical role in the events of the summer of 1357 in Paris, because of his shift to the Dauphin's party. He later crowned Charles V and participated in the special session of the Parlement of Paris that stripped Edward III of his rights in Aquitaine in 1369; in 1371, he baptized the king's son, Louis. One aspect of his beliefs deserves mention: contemporaries held him to be a major proponent of strong money, an issue that lay at the heart of the new use of the vocabulary of commonwealth.

Given Craon's reputation as a proponent of sound money, can we see at this moment a shift of the sound money group, led politically by Craon but intellectually by Oresme and Buridan, moving away from the hardliners like Marcel and Le Coq?[159] The pro-royal Estates meeting at Compiègne in February 1358 – a meeting surely attended by Craon – kept many of the key elements of the Estates' policies of 1357, such as direct control of receipt and disbursement of taxes, and an emphasis on sound money.[160] Desperate for revenue in 1358–1359, Charles went back to the bad old ways, but the return of peace ushered in an era of unprecedented monetary stability, built on a royalist

---

[157] Secousse, *Recueil des pièces*, 87ff., reproduces the letters. The Dauphin made the same argument when, in 1359, he restored the offices (and lost wages and pensions) of the officers excluded in 1357. (*Ordonnances*, III, 28 May 1359.) John's letter spoke of the "fausses paroles, inducions et prédicacions" and "autres voies malicieuses et décevables, à vous traire" and they "feissent à bon fin pour le bien publique."

[158] Edward III and Jean de Craon both descended from Isabelle de la Marche. A. W. Robinson, *Guillaume Machault and Reims: Context and Meaning in his Musical Works* (Cambridge: Cambridge University Press, 2002), 210–211. Varin, *Archives administratives*, III, documents DCCIII, DCCXIX, etc. At one point, Craon, pike in hand, and his armed retainers faced off with the "common people"; Châtillon stepped between the parties and restored order. Marlot, *Histoire de Reims*, t. IV, 79, n. 1.

[159] Le Coq, as bishop of Laon, was in the ecclesiastical province of Reims, so Craon was his direct superior.

[160] Picot, *États-Généraux*, I, 160, rightly emphasizes that the Compiègne assembly took a harder line on coinage than even Marcel and the Parisians.

version of Oresme's ideas, expressed in the ordinance creating the ransom aids in December 1360.[161]

1.4   Public Good and Private Revenge

Those using commonwealth vocabulary invariably blended personal agendas with legitimate defense of the public good. Le Coq put this vocabulary to work to advance his personal agenda, and, to some degree, that of Charles of Navarre. The October assembly, both in its delegation and through the mouth of Le Coq on November 3, voiced strong grievances against chancellor Pierre de la Forest, First President Simon de Bucy, and the six most powerful financial officials, starting with Nicolas Braque, *maitre d'hôtel du roi*, and his brother Aumary, *trésorier de France*. Noel de Valois called them "the veritable type of the odious minter," stopping at nothing – including murder – to hide their malfeasance.[162] Yet Nicolas Braque remained in Charles's good graces for decades: he was among the group of France's "wisest men" – along with Simon de Bucy, Pierre d'Orgemont, and Jean des Mares – chosen to judge the merits of the Armagnac appeal of 1368–1369, which set in motion Charles V's confiscation of Guyenne.[163] In the 1370s, he was one of the French negotiators at Bruges.

The other men singled out included Enguerrand du Petit Celier, *trésorier de France*; Bernart Fermant, *trésorier de France*; Jean Chauveau, war treasurer;[164] and Jean Poilevilain.[165] Poilevilain, who was married to Étienne Marcel's cousin, Agnès, spent "a long time" in prison under Philip VI, for both civil and criminal charges, later dropped, in part because of entreaties from those of the king's "lineage."[166] When the

---

[161] Piron, "Monnaie et majesté royale dans la France du XIVe siècle," rightly points out that these ordinances do **not** accept Oresme's idea of the community's right, but they do use his vocabulary.

[162] N. de Valois, "Notes sur la révolution parisienne de 1356–1358: la revanche des frères Braque," *Bulletin de la société historiques de Paris et d'Ile-de-France* X (1883): 100–126. Mint investigator Michel de Saint-Germain, brought to the Châtelet, on their orders, was drowned in the Seine, without trial. John II's letters of remission stated that the Dauphin told him the murder took place at his orders, for "just cause." Braque lent Charles 2,000 *moutons d'or* for his urgent trip to Metz in November 1356.

[163] Delachenal, *Charles V*, v. IV, 138–139. The group included the Dormans brother and Jean des Mares.

[164] R. Cazelles, "Mouvements révolutionaires," 279–312, shows that the three men most commonly present at council meetings in 1353–1356 were in fact Bucy, Forest, and Jean Chauveau's brother, Regnaud, bishop of Châlons-en-Champagne; Regnaud had been killed at Poitiers, reportedly by an irate peasant, so he was beyond Le Coq's reach. Le Coq fought with all three.

[165] Cazelles, "Quelques réflexions," 83–105; 251–278. Marcel had been involved in silver coinage up to 1352

[166] Shortly after his release, Poilevilain became "sovereign master" of the mint: J. Viard, *Documents parisiens du règne de Philippe de Valois*, 2 vols (P, 1899, 1902). #

Dauphin created a *gabelle* on salt in 1359, among those he consulted were Poilevilain, Simon de Bucy, and Jean des Mares.[167] Complaints about these men mixed the genuine public outrage about the dilapidation of the kingdom's finances and the constant manipulation of the coinage, with private score settling by Étienne Marcel, against Robert de Lorris.[168] As for Le Coq, he had a longstanding quarrel with Bucy – Le Coq's brother received a royal pardon for murdering one of Bucy's clerks on the president's own doorstep in 1352 – and had contested the bishopric of Laon with Regnaud Chauveau, Jean's brother: the royal emissary arguing Regnaud's case to the Pope had been none other than Bucy himself.[169] The political upheaval in Paris in the 1350s owed as much to a family quarrel between Lorris and Marcel and to the rivalry of Le Coq and the Bucy-Chauveau-la Forest alliance, as it did to the family quarrel of John II, Charles of Navarre, and Edward III.[170] When Marcel fell murdered in the streets of Paris, those leading the assault were his wife's relatives: Martin and Pepin des Essarts, Jean de Charny, and Jean Maillart.[171]

What did Parisians make of this carnage in the streets, and the impunity of those tied to the financial elite? In the grand ordinance of March 3, 1357, the Dauphin specifically stated that he would no longer grant remission for "murder or dismemberment [. . .] perpetrated with ill intent and by deliberation, or for rape of women [. . .] or for burning of churches or other places by ill intent."[172]

CCCLXXXIV. Marcel's father-in-law, Pierre des Essarts, was Poilevilain's partner in the 1340s.

[167] *Ordonnances*, III, 358. By April 1359, Poilevilain oversaw all French minting: *Ordonnances*, III, 335. Unable to provide sufficient gold to mint the coins for John's ransom, he lost favor.

[168] Viard, *Documents*, #CCCLXXV, blanket letters of remission [1346] for Lorris, to protect him from the charge that he had "defrauded and exploited" Philip VI and young duke John by taking "excessive gifts" from the latter, without the king's knowledge.

[169] Viard, *Documents*, CCCXLVIII, CCCLIV, royal pardons for murders committed by Petit-Celier's brother. The first pardon comes from John, then only duke of Normandy, a highly unusual situation.

[170] See R. Cazelles, "Étienne Marcel au sein de la haute bourgeoisie d'affaires," *Journal des Savants* 1, n. 1 (1963): 413–427 and *Société politique*, 196ff on Lorris and Marcel; and "La Jacquerie fut-elle un mouvement paysan?" *Comptes rendus des séances de l'Académie des Inscriptions et Belles-Lettres*, 122, n. 3 (1978): 654–666, points out the obvious collaboration of various town governments and the Jacques, in terms of their chosen targets, usually tied to Lorris, des Essarts, et al. F. Autrand, *Charles V* (Paris: Fayard, 1994), 87, on the innovative presence of specialists on the royal council. On intermarriages among the Parisian elite, see B. Bove, *Dominer la ville. Prévôts des marchands et échevins parisiens de 1260 à 1350* (Paris, 2004).

[171] Cazelle, "Étienne Marcel," on the tangled genealogy of all the principals, who were cousins, brothers-in-law, nephews, etc. In the 1360s, in a fitting example of how these families found ways to reconcile, Robert le Coq's nephew, Jean, married Maillart's daughter Jacqueline.

[172] *Ordonnances*, III, 128. See ch. 1 of C. Gauvard, *"De grace especial" Crime, état et société en France à la fin du Moyen Age* (Paris: PU Sorbonne, 1991, 2010).

The Estates meeting at Compiègne in 1358, supposedly under the control of the Dauphin and the nobility, got the Dauphin to agree (articles 11 and 13), to end abuse of letters of remissions, issued by the king, queen, Dauphin, constable, captains, "and others who claim to have that power," for unspecified crimes.[173]

In spring 1358, when the Dauphin had left Paris and called a meeting of Estates of Languedoïl to meet at Compiègne, we can see how the nature of political discourse had shifted. The historiography cites the domination of the nobility at this assembly, and their hostility to the Parisians – Le Coq, who came to the meeting, apparently fled for his life – but that assertion is contradicted by the actions taken by the assembly.[174] Quite apart from their demand about the abuse of royal pardons, the deputies followed many of the same principles as their predecessors of 1357, perhaps because key early reformers, like Jean de Craon, pushed the original agenda. They relied on a direct tax, not a sales tax; they insisted that qualified men-at-arms from towns had to be accepted into the army; they wanted reformers to look into the conduct of royal officers and that of the mints; they maintained local control of receipt and disbursement of money; they insisted on the local creation of three-member commissions to counsel military captains, who were forbidden to spend tax money without the unanimous consent of the commissioners.[175]

The Dauphin's rehabilitation (May 28, 1359) of the twenty-two officers further reveals the extent to which political discourse had changed. He first claimed that the Estates of March 1357 had many deputies "innocent and of good faith" who naively believed the leaders, who had claimed to be acting for deliverance of king and honor and *bon estat* of king, Dauphin, and the whole kingdom. These leaders turned out to be "traitors and conspirators against the Majesty of king and Dauphin, honor and *bien* of Crown and kingdom of France." These officers – Bucy, Forest, Braque, d'Orgemont, Poilevilain – had been dispossessed not for "good intention nor for the *bien* of justice, but by ill courage, by hatred, envy and unjust and angry vengeance." The procedure had not followed any order of Law (*Droit*) or Custom. The Dauphin took the decision to rehabilitate the counselors after great and full deliberation, with

---

[173] *Ordonnances*, III, 219ff. Chevalier, ed., *Les pays de la Loire moyenne*, shows that one document after another (JJ 80–235) is a letter of remission, often for a murder: #2, for Jean Florat, a day laborer, #3 for the Munier brothers.

[174] Picot, *États-Généraux*, I, 77, cites a passage in the GCF, in which the discontent of Parisians about the shift to Compiègne contrasts with the "great joy" of those of other towns. Picot does not stress any sort of "noble domination," but instead the deep loyalty of the assembly to Charles. B. Bove, *Le temps de la Guerre de Cent Ans, 1328–1453* (Paris: Belin, 2009), 107, oddly refers to the Compiègne meeting as an assembly of nobles, but otherwise his chapters III and IV offer a superior introduction to the events of the period, with some particularly spectacular illustrations.

[175] *Ordonnances*, III, 319ff. The changes they made – separate categories for hearths in towns and for free and serf country dwellers – reflected social reality and were in line with standard local practice.

the Grand Conseil, in the chamber of Parlement, with men of his lineage, dukes, counts, barons, prelates and other churchmen, nobles and townsmen of the kingdom in great number. He had acted not at the urging of anyone, but from "pure and noble office to which it belongs to recall and correct both our acts and those of others." To highlight the public nature of his action, he sent notification to the Pope, the College of Cardinals, the Emperor, all prelates, nobles, and good towns, especially those where confiscation had been publicized.[176]

The royal government thus accepted the distinction between "singular" profit and some sort of public or common profit: they turned Le Coq's accusation on its head, saying that he, not the counselors, had acted out of hatred and envy, the most personal of motives. A thousand kilometers away, in Florence, Matteo Villani knew about the importance of this distinction in French polities. He tells us that the Dauphin revealed secret letters from Charles of Navarre, which showed that Navarre "sought more his singular profit than the common good."[177]

---

[176] *Ordonnances*, III, 345ff, 28 May 1359.
[177] *Cronica di Matteo Villani*, II, 123, "più a singulare profitto che a comune bene."

2

Political Vocabulary in Action

2.1   King and Commonwealth: The Treaty of Calais

Charles V inherited a much-truncated kingdom of France. In the process of regaining the provinces lost by his father, he also created the prototype of the monarchical commonwealth that remained the political ideal of most French elites for the next two centuries. John II and Edward III had created the truncated France when they signed the Treaty of Calais, on October 24, 1360.[1] (See Illustration 2.1.) This document differed significantly from the earlier draft, known as the Treaty of Brétigny: well-informed contemporaries, like the Florentine chronicler Matteo Villani, certainly knew the difference. For the Brétigny version, Villani says Edward III would not owe service to the king of France for Ponthieu and Guyenne, and that legal cases in those lands would not be subject to appeal to Paris.[2] With respect to the final, Calais version, Villani rightly emphasizes the fundamental point that John II and "the Dauphin" did not give up sovereignty [*sovranità*] or ressort [*risorto*]. He tells us that Edward III, while he agreed to stop using the title king of France, did not surrender his legal claim to the kingdom, **because** John had refused to relinquish sovereignty and *ressort* in the cities, castles, and lands handed over to Edward.[3]

The Treaty of Calais' clauses defined the French monarchy as a Capetian-Valois family corporation **and** as a commonwealth.[4] Jurisdictional boundaries,

---

[1]   Representatives of the Dauphin and of the Prince of Wales signed the preliminary Treaty of Brétigny on May 8, 1360; the two **kings** signed a slightly, but vitally different document at Calais. See Cosneau, *Grandes traités*, 36. Evrard de Trémaugon, *Le Songe du Vergier*, ch. 146, strongly emphasizes the differences in the two treaties.

[2]   *Chronique de Jean le Bel*, ed. J. Viard and E. Déprez (Paris, 1905), II, 314, describes the Brétigny version, not that of Calais. He also wrongly says (316) that the king of England had to give up his right (*droit*) to be king. The pro-French *Chronique normande* (153) confirms Edward III would get Ponthieu and Guyenne without having to do homage for either, or being in the *ressort* of the king of France for these lands, but it is discussing the Brétigny text.

[3]   Villani, *Cronica*, II, 325–328. Gauvard, *De grace especial*, 63 describes royal letters of remission as "a regalian act, par excellence."

[4]   "Corporation" here in the modern sense of a family company, not in the medieval technical sense of the term: everyone in this vast family kept careful tabs on the territorial

such as those between the Empire and the kingdom of France, remained fluid, and the practical reach of the king's authority, that is, the real kingdom, as Léonard Dauphant has brilliantly demonstrated, ebbed and flowed.[5] Places like Brittany or the Bourbonnais had little to no connection to the Parlement in Paris, and vast regions of the center and southwest remained outside the normal sphere of action both of the Parlement and of the king as the source of legal pardons.[6] Quite apart from the changing boundaries of the practical kingdom, principalities moved in and out of direct French royal possession with bewildering complexity because kings from Louis VI (d. 1137) to Charles VI (d. 1422) had so many surviving sons, and, from Louis VIII (d. 1228) onward, created so many apanages for their younger sons.[7]

The distinction between royal demesne and kingdom remained fundamental well into early modern times; the remarkable Rizzi-Zannoni *Atlas historique de la France Ancienne et Moderne*, produced under Louis XV, carefully presented, for each reign, separate maps of the kingdom and of the royal demesne. The printer, Desnos, even produced a separate volume of the latter, to show the gradual absorption of the great fiefs by the Crown as holder of them in demesne.[8] The events of the middle of the fourteenth century made it essential for John II and Charles V to lay out rules related both for the kingdom of France and for the royal demesne. An original peerage fief like the county of Flanders – a "member" of the body politic – could have a mixed relationship to the Crown and its institutions. Kings led armies into Flanders in support of

---

acquisitions of even distant relatives, because they might, at some future point, claim them as an inheritance. Aristocratic families followed a similar pattern, as the "eternal" lawsuits about some inheritances by collateral lines make clear. The Angevins had claims to Provence, Naples, Aragon, Hungary, Poland, Lorraine, and various other smaller principalities: that branch of the family fought wars in southern Italy, Spain, Provence, and Lorraine to push these claims.

[5] Philip IV's commission on the boundaries of the seneschalsy of Beaucaire: *Ordonnances*, XII, 357. Dauphant, *Le royaume des quatre rivières*, maps 13a–13d.

[6] G. Dupont-Ferrier, *Les officiers royaux des bailliages et sénéchaussées* (Paris: Émile Bouillon, 1902), pointed out the monarchy's lack of an administrative map of the kingdom at the end of the fifteenth century.

[7] Louis VI's younger sons, Robert of Dreux and Peter of Courtenay, sired long-lasting male lineages. Dreux's direct male descendants ended with François II, duke of Brittany, in 1488; a branch of Courtenay's family lasted until the mid-eighteenth century. In 1328, even allowing only descent through males, eight separate lines existed. In 1380, princes from the royal family held Brittany, most of the Loire Valley, Alençon, Berry, Burgundy, Nevers, Artois, Eu, Flanders (after 1384), and the Bourbon lands of the center (Forez, Beaujolais, Bourbonnais, Auvergne). The male lines of the Montagu and Portuguese branches of the Capetian House of Burgundy, descended from King Robert II (d. 1031), lasted until 1471 and 1383.

[8] See the discussion in W. Goffart, *Historical Atlases: The First Three Hundred Years, 1570–1870* (Chicago and London: University of Chicago Press, 2003), 162–168. He dates the original Paris: Desnos, 1764.

their vassal, the count, and the Parlement of Paris ruled on the succession to the county of Flanders in 1323, yet Flanders did not send deputies to meetings of the Estates General of Languedoïl. Artois voted separate taxes and collectively did not attend those Estates, yet five northern towns – Arras, Douai, Lille, St-Omer, and Tournai – were among the twenty who had to send hostages to England as part of the Treaty of Calais.[9]

Few if any Flemish appeals showed up in Paris in the late fourteenth century, perhaps due to the creation of the *Audience du comte*, and the *souverain bailli* (1369), which marked a clear step toward judicial independence.[10] Following the principles laid down in Beaumanoir, judicial independence meant political independence. The Treaty of Arras (1435) between Philip the Good of Burgundy and Charles VII reintegrated the duke's French lands into the kingdom; within months of the Treaty, ducal officials complained to Charles VII about the Parlement's interference in Flanders and Burgundy.[11] Dauphant's maps show the renewed use of the Parlement of Paris by litigants both in Flanders and in Burgundy in 1454–1455 and 1464–1465.[12]

Edward III wanted a document that extended beyond an agreement with John II and his son Charles. Not content with their promises, Edward insisted that John's brother, his three younger sons, his cousins, and "others of his close lineage" swear to the treaty: many did so at Calais. In return for John's release, Edward took (or kept) as hostages: the king's brother, Philippe d'Orléans; his son, Louis d'Anjou; other apanaged royal princes; and many of the great nobles, some of whom had been captured at Poitiers. Edward here took a normal step, recognizing that the monarchy was a collective, family

---

[9] Tournai remained a loyal royal outpost until taken by the English in 1519. Briefly reunited to France, it passed to Emperor Charles V in 1521. Tournai's mint produced the royal currency for the surrounding region. *Ordonnances*, V, 82, Estates of Artois in 1367, one of many examples of voting the annual sum for the king and the "bien commun de nostre royaume."

[10] Dauphant, *Royaume*, maps 13a–b. Philip the Bold, duke of Burgundy, and count of Flanders (through his wife), regularly levied taxes in both Burgundy and Flanders with the consent of local estates; he did not seek the king's specific permission, but various royal documents had granted taxing authority to dukes of Burgundy. The Treaty of Arras gave Philip the Good the right to keep all tax revenues in the counties of Auxerre, Bar-sur-Seine, and Macon.

[11] R. Vaughn, *Philip the Good* (Woodbridge: Boydell, 1970, reprinted edition of 2002), 114.

[12] Dauphant, *Royaume*, maps 13c–d. Charles the Bold would transform the Great Council of Mechelen into a "Parlement" in 1473, but under local pressure, especially from her lands outside the kingdom of France, his daughter Mary abolished it. Her son, Philip, recreated the Great Council in 1504, but avoided the word "Parlement," surely because his son, Charles, had just been affianced to Claude of France [b. 1499]. W. Blockmans, W. Prevenier, eds., *The Promised Lands. The Low Countries under Burgundian Rule, 1369–1530*, trans. E. Fackelman (Philadelphia: University of Pennsylvania Press, 1999), 190–191. Dauphant, *Royaume*, map 14a, shows that appeals from Flanders had virtually ceased by then.

possession: he got all the members of the Board of Directors to sign, and took hostages not simply from the king's immediate, but from their shared extended family.[13]

But Edward did not stop there; he also insisted that the "twelve peers" of France witness the treaty. Members of the extended royal family held other, newer lay peerages, such as the duchies of Anjou, Bourbon, Brittany, and Orléans, and the county of Étampes: some of them, or a close relative, also swore to the treaty at Calais.[14] Two members of the Châtillon family, the counts of Blois and of Saint-Pol, took the oath, as did the deadly Norman rivals, the counts of Harcourt and Tancarville (Melun). Charles, king of Navarre, held the county-peerage of Evreux; he signed a separate treaty with John II on October 24.

Edward III recognized the commonwealth aspect of the French polity by insisting that John have dukes, counts, barons, great landowners ("*grands terriers*"), and all royal officers, at the moment of their institution, swear to the treaty. He further insisted that the mayors, *échevins*, aldermen, consuls, and all town governments of the kingdom swear to it. Taking no chances, Edward demanded hostages (the "wealthiest men") from Paris (four) and nineteen other towns (two each): all were either royal towns or lying in fiefs held by members of the immediate royal family.[15] These hostages served in rotation; men continued to take their turns as hostages as late as 1369, when the new hostages for Lyon and Caen arrived.[16]

His contemporaries fully understood this approach. Evrard de Trémaugon, writing in the 1370s to justify Charles V's interpretation of the Treaty of Calais, placed a fascinating argument in the mouth of his clerical debater. Speaking of the 1360 treaties, he claimed:[17]

---

[13] Medieval charters and treaties everywhere in Europe regularly included the names of key witnesses and often had their seals attached to the document. John and Edward shared as great-grandfather King Philip III.

[14] The two claimants to the duchy of Brittany, Charles de Blois and Jean de Montfort [the later duke Jean IV, not his father], seem to have held talks at Calais in September–October 1360, under the aegis of the two kings. A. de la Borderie, *Histoire de la Bretagne*, t. III (Paris and Rennes, 1894), 564.

[15] In addition to Paris, the five northern towns cited above, and four archbishoprics (by law, under royal protection) in Lyon, Rouen, Tours, and Bourges, the towns were, from the royal demesne: Toulouse, Reims, Châlons, Troyes, Compiègne, Amiens, and Beauvais; and from fiefs held by the immediate royal family: Orléans, Chartres, and Caen. See, by way of comparison, a map of fifteenth-century royal towns in Dauphant, *Le royaume*, carte 46.

[16] Rymer, *Foedera*, III, 871. Towns often dragged their feet. Many of the first group of hostages died of plague.

[17] *Le Songe du Vergier*, ch. 145: "car ledit traittié fut fait du consentement de ses pers de France, & des plus grands & des plus notables de son royaulme, de son lignaige & de son peuple, comme il appert: car des plus notables de son lignaige & des bourgeoys de

because the said treaty was made with the consent of the peers of France, and of the greatest and most notable people of his kingdom, of his lineage, and of his people, as it appears [from the treaty]: because the most notable of his lineage and the bourgeois of each cité of his kingdom went to England to be held as hostages until the said treaty was fully accomplished and completed, point by point.

The cleric then claimed that the participation of these men meant that the king and the people had agreed to give up sovereignty and *ressort*, which, he claimed, they had the right to do. The knight protested several elements of this interpretation – above all the idea that *ressort* and sovereignty had been given away – but he did not object to the principle that the peers, notables, and people of France had approved the treaty. He did object, in contrast, to the idea that anyone other than the king could have the right to renounce sovereignty and *ressort*, and then further rejected the idea that even the king could do so, because the individual king – John II – could not diminish the powers of the king of France.

Edward III took seriously these oaths. At English urging, John wrote to the seneschal of Toulouse in February 1361, reminding him that the king had promised to have not only his relatives, but prelates, dukes, counts, barons, other great landlords, royal officers, and officials of town governments all swear. The seneschal was supposed to have seen to it, but he had not, "to the grand peril and inconvenience of our kingdom, our subjects, and the *chose publique*."[18] Edward thus made the Treaty with four distinct groups: 1) the king and his immediate heir(s); 2) the Capetian-Valois family corporation; 3) the leading members of the lay and ecclesiastical elite; and 4) the representatives, the citizens, of the commonwealth of the kingdom of France.

John's letters to the local authorities in Poitou, for the handover of authority in the summer of 1361, made clear that he had signed the Treaty upon "the counsel and consent" of several of those of "our blood and lineage, prelates of the holy church, dukes and counts, both peers of France and others, clerics and men of the church, of barons, knights, and other nobles, bourgeois, and other wise men of our kingdom." These letters, too, reserved "sovereignty and final ressort," until the renunciations were made.[19] The mayor of Poitiers, in agreeing to obey the king of England, asked Chandos to confirm their

---

chascune cité de son royaulme alerent en Angleterre pour tenir hostaige jusques a tant que ledit traittié fut de point en point tout accomply & entériné."

[18] Delachenal, *Chronique*, III, 84. We have no evidence anyone followed up on these letters.
[19] *Procès-verbal de déliverance à Jean Chandos*, ed. A. Bardonnet (Niort, s.d.), letters of August 13, 1361 [13] and letters of July 27, 1361 [16]: "sauf et reserve a nous, la souverainete et darrenier resort, jusques lez renunciacions soient faictes." Delachenal, *Charles V*, II, 334, points out that the letters for La Rochelle, the county of Guines, and Calais – all drawn up in October 1360, do not make this restriction, but all the later missives do so. *Chandos* does not have the La Rochelle documents, which are found in

"privileges, rights, franchises, ancient usages, and liberties," which Chandos confirmed on behalf of Edward.[20] The following day, at the oath-taking ceremony, the mayor, clergy, nobles, and principal bourgeois had to swear loyalty to Edward, and not to recognize "another seigneur or sovereign." The mayor, twelve échevins, and thirteen "jurés" listed by name swore on the Gospels; the crowd simply raised their hands and swore.

The Treaty of Calais went beyond a simple agreement between two kings because of Edward III's insistence that the key members make it binding on the commonwealth both through oath and through hostages, and because John clearly specified to all, in the documents authorizing local handover of power to the English, that he had acted with the "advice and consent" of the citizens of the commonwealth. After the Treaty, John and Charles V quickly moved to tie permanently and irrevocably their key fiefs – their four peerage fiefs first among them – to the Crown of France, the royal demesne, and the kingdom of France. By 1369, when Charles V began to overturn the Calais settlement, he and his father had covered the kingdom with a mass of fiefs and towns permanently united to the Crown, and with ecclesiastical and urban letters of royal safeguard: holders of such letters, even in an apanage, remained under the direct jurisdiction of the king.[21] After 1369, Charles invariably took the step of issuing a letter of permanent liaison to the Crown for each major town and fief he regained. At his death in 1380, a dense network of legal connections bound much of the kingdom of France into a single entity.

2.2   The Royal Commonwealth of Charles V

Charles V made immediate use of the phrase "bien de la chose publique" in his public acts. In April 1364, acting as lieutenant of his father, he issued letters raising the "salaire" of the fish wholesalers of Paris, acting on their behalf, for their trade, and for the profit of "la chose publique." The current system reduced the supply of fish, "to the great prejudice and damage of the bien de la chose publique." Charles, wishing to act for the "bien commun" ordered his officials to investigate the matter and raise the "salaire" of the supplicants.[22]

Rymer, III-2, 674–675. John's emissary, Jean de Melun, count of Tancarville, brought official letters.

[20] *Chandos*, 21. The document lists thousands of men, by name, in various towns. In the separate list of nobles swearing "foyauté," Ysabeau d'Avaugour, viscountess of Thouars, was a rare female noble who took the oath for herself, rather than sending a procureur.

[21] Letters of royal safeguard in the period 1300–1350 primarily covered churches or abbeys of royal foundation.

[22] *Ordonnances*, IV, 417. April 23, 1364. Charles was already king by this time, yet the letters describe him as acting for his father; they mention the need to create a royal seal as the reason for the anomaly. He issued brief letters on April 17 ordering all royal officers to continue in their duties, and sealed them with his private seal, which he had used prior to coming into the "government." Charles was using the royal seal by May 1, 1364.

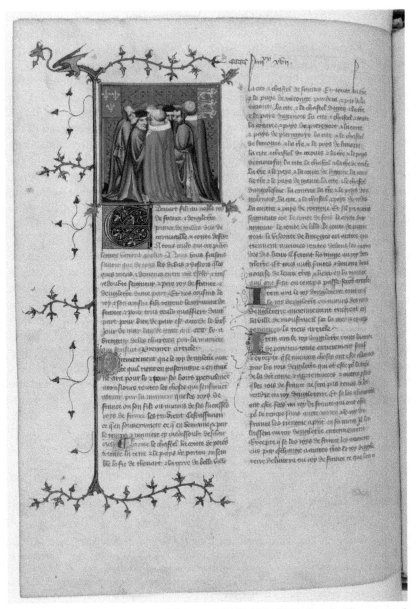

Illustration 2.1   Negotiations at Calais, 1360: BNF, M Fr 2608, *Grandes Chroniques de France*, fol. 483v. Permission BNF

Five days later, in virtually his first act as king, Charles V confirmed the officers of the Parlement, stressing his solicitude for the care of the "Commonwealth's health" [*Reipublice saluti*]. The [Latin] letters consistently used the term *res publica*, emphasizing his concern for the Justice of the Republic.[23]

In July 1364, Charles extended for two years the privilege of bourgeois of Paris to remain exempt from having their goods seized (by royal soldiers or households of the royal family), he cited the city's regular willingness to aid his father "in all his necessities, and in others touching the bien commun of the Kingdom."[24] In 1365, when the municipal government of Tournai asked him for permission to sell certain properties to provide for the upkeep of the orphans in its care, he acted to defend "our said Town and its bien public [*nostredicte Ville & du bien publique d'icelle*]." He acted in favor of the said orphans "and for the bien public of it our Town."[25] Letters in Latin, like those for the butchers of Bourges, spoke of the "Republic."[26]

Charles V used the unified "chose publique" concept in most of his legislation. His regulation of the apanage process in the 1360s and 1370s entailed the revocation of all grants of "Nobilities and Seigneuries, *rentes* and revenues from the royal demesne and *propre* heritage of the Kingdom and Crown of France." As François Autrand has said, these policies show the extent to which Charles conceived of the kingdom as "quasi-federal."[27] The Crown's "Hautesses et Noblesses" had been greatly reduced by such grants.[28] Charles V made the reversion clause normative in all apanage grants. John II had already issued letters patent in November 1361 permanently codifying a law of his father that attached the duchies of Burgundy and Normandy, and the counties of Champagne and Toulouse to the Crown.[29] As the royalist lawyer

---

[23] *Ordonnances*, IV, 418, April 28, 1364. "Inter ceteras nostre sollicitudinis curas, quibus Reipublice saluti, ac nostrorum commoditatibus inclinamur." John had died in England on April 8, and news reached Paris on April 16. The first act of Charles V dates from April 17. The word "saluti" referred both to health and to salvation; for at least another two centuries, in French-language royal documents "salut" regularly, and deliberately, implied both. Letters for the Parlement, for ecclesiastics, and even for many towns – especially in the south – still used Latin.

[24] *Ordonnances*, IV, 462–463, July 12, 1364.

[25] *Ordonnances*, IV, 594. Letters regulating a dispute between the bailiwick court and the drapers of Troyes in May 1360 (*Ordonnances*, III, 410–411), spoke of the "assemblies, unions, monopolies and conspiracies against the said seigneurs [the judges] and the bien publique." A year later the new royally sanctioned statutes of the drapers spoke of the lack of such rules being to the great "damage of the common people and the chose publique." [*Ordonnances*, III, 511].

[26] *Ordonnances*, III, 394, insisting that their assemblies not be conspiratorial, nor "Reipublice detrimentum redoubtet."

[27] Autrand, *Charles V*, 525.

[28] *Ordonnances*, IV, 466–467, July 1364.

[29] John had so stated in the edict granting Burgundy to his son Philip in 1361. He promulgated a specific edict on these fiefs in November 1361, *Ordonnances*, IV, 212.

Anseau Choquart put it, "The kingdom must remain united without any dismemberment or excessive dividing up (*partage*)."[30] John II's letters bound him and all his successors; starting with Charles, all of them would have to swear to keep these fiefs united to the Crown at the coronation (when receiving the royal insignia). The *Coronation Book of Charles V* cites the new oath he took to protect Crown rights; this oath had never previously been part of the ceremony, and, in fact, may not have been an actual part of Charles' coronation. Many sources make reference to this oath in later centuries, but we cannot be certain if any king between Charles VI and Henry III uttered the phrase; we know Henry IV did not.[31] French elites, however, universally **believed** that kings from Charles V did take this oath, and kings made constant reference to having done so.

This principle extended far beyond the six original lay peerages: during the reigns of John II and Charles V an unending stream of towns, lordships, and even villages demanded royal charters recognizing them as permanently attached to the royal demesne and, often, to either the "kingdom of France" or "our kingdom." St-James-de-Beuvron's letters had the usual formula: "without division, transfer or separation ... from Us, from our own demesne, Sovereignty, Jurisdiction, obedience and Seigneurie in all cases and in all the things, rights and Sovereignties that our Predecessors and Us [had from all ancient times]."[32]

Charles V systematically made each of the lost provinces he regained into permanent parts of the royal demesne. For the town of Abbeville and the county of Ponthieu, he cited the "honor, state and perpetual profit of Us and our Kingdom" and promised never to allow the town of Abbeville and county of Ponthieu to leave "our hands or the royal demesne of Us and the Crown of

---

[30] C. Taylor, *Chivalry and the Ideals of Knighthood in France during the Hundred Years War* (Cambridge: CUP, 2013), 30, says that Choquart's humiliating defeat at the hands of Petrarch, at a debate in Avignon, convinced Charles V of the need to improve greatly French erudition. Petrarch had ridiculed Choquart's clumsy Latin and famously implied that only Italians had real command of the Classical language. Taylor suggests that the two institutions leading the French push into Humanism were the Collège de Navarre, particularly Oresme, and the group of notary-secretaries around the king, that is, in Krynen's terms, the scholars and the lawyers.

[31] R. Jackson, *Vive le Roi! A History of the French Coronation from Charles V to Charles X* (Chapel Hill: University of North Carolina Press, 1984), has a long discussion of this issue. Text in R. Jackson, ed., *Ordines Coronationis Franciae*, v. II (Philadelphia: University of Pennsylvania Press, 1995, 2000), 476; in n. 47, Jackson reveals that this phrase was added by the scribe, who erased the segment of the oath based on earlier *ordines*. Jackson argues that the change was certainly not in a different hand and was perhaps implemented for the ceremony.

[32] *Ordonnances*, III, 490 (April 1362). Saint-James was a small fortress on the border between Normandy and Brittany. The use of the term "choses" (things) has obvious connections to "la chose publique." The Latin letters for Pontoise, in May 1359, promised to keep the town in the "supreme jurisdiction and ressort" of the king. *Ordonnances*, IV, 198.

France"; the rights of Justice, and the bourgeois and inhabitants of the town and county, were to remain perpetually under the direct jurisdiction of the king. In the south, he gave letters to unite Montauban to the Crown demesne; the "*civitatem*" (*cité*) submitted itself to his obedience, recognizing that he was their "Superiorem Dominium" (i.e., souverain seigneur); he accepted for the "perpetual utility of our kingdom." The letters for the city of Limoges spoke of "the immense utility that will come to Us and the commonwealth [*rei publice*] of our Kingdom; they had submitted to him because of "the *souveraineté* that we have in the duchy of Guyenne" and they recognized him as their "souverain seigneur."[33]

The words "souveraineté" and "souverain" had shifting meanings by the time of Charles V. Documents still used the traditional "souverain" for the Latin "superior"; Beaumanoir had explicitly stated that every baron was "sovereign" in his barony, and he takes the king to be "sovereign" over all others precisely because he was the highest seigneur, not because of any connection to some abstract principle of Roman law, like *imperium* or *maiestas*.[34] Many texts, including Charles V's instructions to his negotiators in the 1370s, used the plural form. Apanaged princes consistently referred to their "sovereignties," while the king insisted that he maintained his "ressort" and "sovereignty" within the area of their apanages.[35] John II, in his October 1361 ban on private war, spoke of the "wound to Us and our Seigneury and Sovereignty" and the damage to the kingdom and its subjects.[36] Many documents referred to "jurisdiction(s) et ressort," but some now used the combination "ressort et souveraineté." The duke of Brittany, in particular, tried to stay out of this language, touching off

---

[33] *Ordonnances*, V, 175 (Abbeville), 268 (Montauban), 439 and 443 (Limoges). Barbey, *Être roi*, 139, traces the use of this phrase to *Le Songe du Vergier*, but these texts show it had already taken root. Barbey is certainly right that *Le Songe du Vergier* played a key role in its wider dissemination.

[34] Beaumanoir, *Coustumes*, II, 22–23.

[35] Francesco Maiolo, *Medieval Sovereignty. Marsilius of Padua and Bartolus of Saxoferrato* (Delft: Eburon, 2007), 285–287, makes the clear distinction between the post-Bodinian notion of sovereignty (as manifested in the nineteenth-century nation-state) and medieval ideas of "sovereignty." I completely agree that medieval writers and actors had a clear sense of the highest power (*potestas*) in a given area (precisely the area of *iurisdictio* or *ressort*), and further agree that *iurisdictio* and sovereignty were not co-terminous (see Maiolo's ch. 5). In France, everyone accepted the principle that the king was the ultimate source of secular legitimacy. On *cas royaux*, see the discussion in Guillot, Rigaudière, and Sassier, *Pouvoirs et institutions dans la France médiévale. T. 2.*, 210–213. See *Ordonnances*, VI, 96, for the February 1375 edict issued about the precise rights the king reserved in the apanage granted to his brother, Jean, duke of Berry: *foy, hommages, ressort, souverainetés*, cathedrals and churches/abbeys of royal foundation. The old, Beaumanoir usage remained current: in a royal ruling about a court case in Rouen in 1380–1388, the document refers to the location of the crime – the archbishop's palace – as "a place sovereign and free."

[36] *Ordonnances*, III, 525 (October 3, 1361): "lesion de Nous et nostre Seigneurie et Souveraineté."

extended disputes that eventually led Charles V to confiscate the duchy. Guillaume de Saint-André, secretary of Duke Jean II, in his rhymed *Histoire de Jean IV*, made clear the Breton understanding of their duke's special status, outside the realm of liege homage: "And had minted new coins/Very very good and very very beautiful/Because by his right he can do it/In his *pais* is Prince and Mayor."[37] [Et fist faire monnoye nouvelles/Moult trés-bonne & moult trés-belle,/ Car de son droit le povoit faire;/ En son païs est Prince & Maire]

The Breton emissaries to the king laid out clearly the duke's claim to "Regalie Regni," on the grounds that the duke of Brittany "is in possession of Royal rights" and neither he nor his predecessors had ever recognized a "Souveraint."[38] Ancient Breton kings had passed on to the counts and dukes royal rights, "like coinage." The duchy had a general "Parlement de Bretagne" [meaning the Estates], which had met for such a long time that no living man had memory of the contrary.[39] The duke called "Prelates, Barons, and others of the capable [*suffisans*] of the *pays* of Brittany, which is and demonstrates Royal act [*fait Royal*]."[40] Moreover, the *pays* of Brittany was governed by "Customs, & law of this *pays*, without regard to the laws and customs of other *pays*." Disputes over the customs and laws were settle by the prince, the prelates, the barons, and the common [estate] of the said *pays*"; these assemblies also voted subsidies. The duke held the *régale* of the nine bishoprics and *ressort* of them all, for secular cases; the bishops owed him a loyalty oath. All these things belong to "the Prince of Brittany and his Body politic."[41] Yet these same

---

[37] Dom Morice, *Preuves*, II, 382. A few lines above, Saint-André takes pains to say that the duke of Brittany is not "subject" to the king, as duke. The actual duke, Jean IV, admitted he was subject to the king of France for other holdings. In his letters to his brother Louis, duke of Anjou, whom he had named to be his lieutenant after the confiscation, Charles V claimed that duke Jean IV had done liege homage and that because he had acted against his "faith, his oath, and homage" the duchy had been taken into royal hands, by mean of an arrêt of "our sovereign Court of Parlement, garnished with the Peers of our Kingdom, and several Prelates, Barons & other nobles, and several other wise people." [Morice, *Preuves*, II, 414]

[38] Dom Morice does not give the date, but it surely comes from 1379–1380, when the Estates of Brittany defended the rights of the "duke of Brittany," as against those of Jean IV himself, then stripped of the duchy for having allied with the English.

[39] The Parlement/Estates had a special small commission that acted as an appellate court. Jean V tried to create a permanent tribunal in 1424, but an actual "Parlement" had to wait until 1484. J.-P. Leguay and H. Martin, *Fastes et malheurs de la Bretagne ducale* (Rennes: Éditions Ouest-France, 1997), 190–191.

[40] In a 1384 agreement with the bishop and town of St-Malo, Jean IV specifically referred to his "Royal and Ducal rights" and insisted their emissary, on his knees, call him their Souverain Seigneur and use the term "Majesté," in seeking his pardon, by "grace especial," that is, using the precise term kings of France used in their royal pardons. Dom Morice, *Preuves*, II, 466.

[41] Morice, *Preuves*, II, 458. The messengers, sent on behalf of the Estates, to support the rights of the duke, were the bishop of Tréguier, Jean de Rochefort, sieur de Rieux, Raoul

deputies admitted that the king had to be satisfied only with "his ressort in sign of Sovereignty," by which they referred to appeals to Paris for false judgment. One need hardly point out that the king of France did not accept the broader philosophical claims, but he had to respect the various facts on the ground: the duke did mint money, issue laws, guarantee customs, hold Estates, issue pardons, and empower a court of appeal. Kings of France had a different perspective: Louis XI, in accepting the homage of duke François II in the 1460s, made sure to indicate that he had given the duke *permission* to do all these things.

"Souveraineté" [*sovranità*, for Villani] in the Calais Treaty, and the utilization of this term, in conjuction with ressort, in the dispossession of Edward III in 1369–1370, or of Jean IV of Brittany in 1379, shows that it had now taken on a meaning distinct from the one given by Beaumanoir. Tying together sovereignty and *ressort* made this emerging usage into something specifically royal, although the "puissance absolue" [independent power] associated with it referred to lack of subordination to the Emperor and the Pope. The evolution to a Bodinian meaning of sovereignty took nearly two centuries.

The Treaty of Calais had granted to Edward III all the "honors, obediences, homages, liege homages, vassals, fiefs, services, recognitions, oaths, jurisdictions ... seigneuries, and '*souverainetés*'" of the king of France in the lands shifted to him. The first draft of the treaty, the May 8, 1359 version known as the Treaty of London, ceded all the old Angevin territories, including Normandy and Anjou, renounced homage, *ressort*, and any form of sovereignty.[42] Little wonder that Charles and an assembly like an Estates General of Languedoïl, meeting in Paris in late May 1359, quickly rejected these terms. Jean le Bel says the barons and deputies from the towns rejected the terms as too onerous for France, not wishing to "consent that the noble kingdom of France should be thus reduced and divided by the said treaty."[43]

The following year, the Treaty of Brétigny began with the statement that in the lands turned over to Edward, he would get what had been held as demesne, as demesne, and what had been held as fief, as fief. All vassals in these lands were to do homage to Edward, and to owe service to him. In article VII, the list of items turned over to Edward included both "ressorts" and "sovereignties." In article XI, *ressorts* and sovereignties have disappeared. The final, Calais

de Caradeuc, doctor in both laws, Alain Chauvet, and Mᵉ Guillaume de Saint-André, Jean IV's secretary.

[42] Rymer, *Foedera*, III, art. 11 of the Treaty of London. John also renounced sovereignty and *ressort* over Flanders and Brittany.

[43] The Melun brothers and marshal Audreham – whose foolish counsel at Poitiers led to the disaster and to his own capture – brought the terms to Paris. *Chronicle de Jean le Bel*, II, 289: "que à consentir que le noble royaume de France fust ainsy amendry et departi par laddite paix." Villani's first description [ch. 98] of a proposed treaty is, in fact, the 1359 Treaty of London, which alone had clauses about Normandy passing over to the English.

version of the treaty made specific mention of the "renunciations" the two sides had to make in 1361, without which the Treaty would be null and void.

In his *Songe du Vergier*, Evrard de Trémaugon insisted on the difference between the two treaties: Brétigny had only been a draft, so that the new clauses in the Calais treaty – which he claimed specifically reserved sovereignty and *ressort* for John – were the ones that mattered.[44] The delegates of the two kings never exchanged those renunciations; Charles cited the failure of the English to carry out renunciations as grounds for insisting he still had *ressort* in Guyenne. Edward III claimed that Charles V had broken his word with respect to French renunciations, so that Edward would now reclaim his right to the French Crown.[45] No longer would he style himself "Dominus" (the term used for Ireland) of Aquitaine; he again became "king of England and of France."

Charles V's grant of money to the sieur d'Albret in 1368 pounced on the key word, *ressort*. Albret got the grant so long as he continued to be "an adherent to the appeals made against Edward, eldest son of Edward of England, by our cousin of Armagnac and many other nobles, because of the *ressort* and sovereignty of the duchy of Guyenne," thus recognizing the king of France as his "sovereign [i.e., highest] seigneur because of the said *ressort*."[46]

Charles claimed to act on behalf of some of his vassals, who objected to a hearth tax voted to the Prince of Wales (duke of Aquitaine) by an assembly in 1368. The first two vassals to come forward were Jean, count of Armagnac (April 1368) and Arnaud Amanieu, the sire d'Albret (September), but about 900 others joined them after an organized campaign.[47] They all claimed the tax had been created without their consent, a violation of their "liberties and franchises." The French claimed that no king of France, or prior ruler of Aquitaine, had ever done such a thing. The thirty-five-man council of April told the king he had to hear the appeal, because he had *ressort*, and "he had to do for them what a sovereign seigneur must do for his subject." [*leur devoit faire ce que souverain seigneur doit faire à son subjet*][48]

---

[44] *Le Songe du Vergier*, ch. 146: "Mais il est certain que quant la possession des villes & des chasteaulx fut délivrée par le roy de France ou par ses depputez par lettres publicques et patentes au roy d'Angleterre ou à ses depputez ou procureurs, esdictes lettres patentes ou publiques le roy de France reservoit la souveraineté & le ressort [...] aussi quant on les livroit, protestèrent ilz qu'ilz ne renonceroient pas à la souveraineté & ressort du roy de France."

[45] Rymer, *Foedera*, III, 874, letter to the Black Prince. Edward had agreed to pursue his claim through legal channels. Emperor Charles V would do the same in the sixteenth century, with respect to his claim to the duchy of Burgundy.

[46] *Mandements de Charles V*, 561, cited in Lavisse, *Le pouvoir royal sous Charles V*, 4.

[47] Charles V cemented the loyalty of Amanieu by marrying him to his wife's sister, Margaret of Bourbon. Charles' brother Jean, duke of Berry, was the son-in-law of the count of Armagnac.

[48] R. Delachenal, *Chronique des règnes de Jean II et de Charles V*, IV (Paris, 1910, 1916), document XVII, 123ff, instructions to royal deputies to the negotiations of 1372.

D'Albret, Armagnac, and the counts of Périgord and of Comminges had, in fact, protested in 1360 that the king of France had no right to remove them from his suzerainty, that is, to transfer their homage and final *ressort*, without their accord.[49] In his instructions to his negotiators of 1372, Charles V said that he had specifically noted that he reserved sovereignty and *ressort*, in the letters sent to Armagnac and d'Albret telling them to do homage to the Black Prince. Louis de Mâle, count of Flanders, made precisely the same argument about possible alienations of homage by fief holders in the immediate suzerainty of Yolande of Flanders, during her negotiations with Charles V in 1372: Yolande could not transfer the homage of her vassals to Charles V without the vassals' consent and could not transfer her fiefs held of Louis de Mâle without his consent.[50] Evrard de Trémaugon, in his *Songe du Vergier*, defending the position of the king of France with respect to "Guyenne," made the same point:

> they [the king of France's subjects from Guyenne] protested that it was not their intention that the sovereignty and *ressort* would in any way be transported to the king of England. Thus the sovereignty and *ressort* remained with the king of France as he who was true and sovereign seigneur for so long that there is no memory of the contrary.

In another passage, Trémaugon traced the connection back to Charlemagne.[51]

No individual king had the right to give away the Crown's *ressort* in any region or town. Beaumanoir had clearly stated the principle that so long as the county of Poitiers or duchy of Guyenne or any fief remained within the kingdom of France, by definition, it **had** to be within the *ressort* of the king of France and, by extension, of his Parlement. Charles V made precisely this argument to the Parlement of Paris, only too willing, for its own reasons, to agree, in 1369.[52] Charles had first written to some of the most famous jurists in Europe, at leading Italian universities. John of Legnano, who taught law at Bologna, on behalf of himself and of three other Bologna faculty – Jerome Andree, Gaspar Calderinni, and Nicolas Zanasiis – stated clearly that the king of France could not be deprived of "auctoritate," and, more specifically, "iuris superioritatis vel ressorti." Their first two conclusions were: 1) "*iura superioritatis et ultimo ressorti* were owed to the lord king of the Franks" and 2) that

---

[49] The lord could not unilaterally change the terms of liege homage; Edward III's insistence on fief holders swearing to the Treaty thus dealt specifically with that legal issue.

[50] M. Bubenick, "À propos d'une correspondance inédite de Charles V et de Louis de Mâle: étapes, moyens et enjeux d'une négociation politique," *Revue Historique* n. 1, (2003): 3–42.

[51] *Songe du Vergier*, ch. 145 and 146. Krynen, *L'empire du Roi*, and Barbey, *Être Roi*, both have extensive discussions of the importance of Trémaugon.

[52] Dauphant, *Le royaume des quatre rivières*, shows how limited was the area sending appeals to the Parlement in this time, so that the court would have been particularly anxious to assert its *ressort*.

the prince could not be deprived (*privavit*) of these "iurium."[53] Charles V took the position throughout the negotiations in the 1370s that no king of France had the right to surrender "souverainetés et ressort."

Nor was this clause in any way unique to the case of Edward III's fiefs: the special letters given to Charles V's brother Louis, promising him the apanage of Touraine should Charles have a son, reserved for the king the "homage, sovereignty, and *ressort* of our court of Parlement," as well as the "sovereignty in fealty" of the archbishop of Tours and the abbot of St-Martin of Tours. The royal *bailli* retained the king's "souveraineté et ressort." The cases that had to be tried by the *bailli* included lèse-majesté in the first degree, infractions against the king's safeguard, counterfeiting, and "notable" carrying of arms (defined as a company of men-at-arms, fully equipped).[54]

In 1376, when English and French envoys discussed a treaty in Bruges, Charles V sent a special envoy, Jean Le Fèvre, abbot of St-Vaast, to explain to the English why the king did not have the **right** to renounce "sovereignty and *ressort*" even in the reduced territory to be kept by the English.[55]

> The first reason is that the King at his origin and consecration swore in the presence of his people not to alienate the rights of his crown. And the greatest of the principal rights of his crown are his *ressorts*, homages and sovereignties; had he done the contrary, he would have been a perjurer and, by consequence, infamous, and would not be worthy to be King.

The credential cited a maxim of Roman law : "Quia infamibus non porte dig[nita]tum."[56] The second reason cited in the credential is that the matter touched the right of the people and *pays* of the duchy of Guyenne (and others) to whom the kind "had to administer reason and justice in cases of sovereignty as their King, and it would be a great injustice to fail them in it . . . Saying that

---

[53] *Camden Miscellany*, vol. XIX (Third Series, v. LXX) (London: Royal Historical Society, 1952), contains two fundamental articles, with documents. The text of the two opinions is found in the first article by P. Chaplais, "Some Documents Regarding Fulfilment and interpretation of the Treaty of Brétigny, 1361–1369," Camden Miscellany, vol. XIX (Third Series, v. LXX) (London Royal Historical Society, 1952); Legnano's opinion is found on 70–78. Legnano was so famous that Chaucer refers to him simply as "Lynyan," a philosopher as well known as the poet Petrarch, in the tale of Griselde. See: J. McCall, "Chaucer and John of Legnano," *Speculum* 40, n. 3 (July, 1965): 484–489.

[54] *Ordonnances*, VI, 428–429.

[55] Le Fèvre studied law at Paris and Orléans, that is, both canon and civil law; he later became bishop of Chartres and chancellor of the duke of Anjou. The consonance of these letters and of Evrard de Trémaugon's arguments make it obvious they were part of a coherent publicity campaign.

[56] Perjury was one of the crimes that carried infamy and rendered one unworthy of public office. This issue of being unworthy to be king came up multiple times: Le Coq raised it against John II; Charles V's lawyers used it here; and Charles VI and his rump Parlement literally declared his son, Charles, unworthy to be king, in 1420, on the grounds of his complicity in the murder of Jean sans Peur.

he would not be worthy [digne] to be called King if he did not do justice."[57] The royal government later came to recognize the dangerous implications of this position and abandoned it, certainly by the late fifteenth century, after the War of the Bien Public.

The letters about ressort in Aquitaine all antedated the confiscation of Edward's gains from Brétigny-Calais. In the May 14, 1370 letters confiscating lands granted to Edward III and Edward, Black Prince, by the treaty, Charles V accuses them of trying to usurp "Superioritatis et Ressorti nostrorum" (our superior lordship and final jurisdiction) and later speaks of "scandal and irreparable danger to Us and the whole commonwealth of our kingdom."[58] The various letters make clear the desire to establish legal permanence for the kingdom of France and the royal demesne. In them, Charles V makes it "impossible" ever again to give away Aquitaine, Normandy, Abbeville, and the countless other towns and fiefs that had obtained the letters.

These efforts, admirable in the abstract, immediately faced one of the most difficult moments for any monarchy: a royal minority. Scarcely more than a decade later, an even greater catastrophe befell France, when its young king, Charles VI, had his first fit of madness en route to punishing a recalcitrant vassal on the Breton border. For the next thirty years, France's political system pivoted around a man afflicted with intermittent, regular bouts of madness. No time could have been more propitious for the solidification of the ideology of commonwealth.

The process carried out in the 1370s involved a remarkably complex production of Bourdieu's legitimate and legitimizing political language helping to create a specific vision of a political unit.[59] Charles V took over a kingdom in disarray, not simply in geographic boundaries and dynastic legitimacy, but in linguistic and intellectual chaos, too. He brought all these ordering processes together, in action and in multiple forms of discourse. As Jean Corbechon put it in the introduction to his translation of the Liber de proprietatibus rerum of Barthélemy l'Anglais, "according to the truth of divine and human Scriptures, among all the human perfections that a royal heart must desire, the desire for sapience must by reason hold the first place. The cause is that the nobility of royal heart must sovereignly and firstly desire to well and honorably and justly

---

[57] All three quotations are from E. Perroy, "The Anglo-French Negotiations at Bruges, 1374–1377," in Camden Miscellany, v. XIX, 57. "La premiere si est que le Roy en sa nouuelleté et consecration jura en la presence de son peuple non aliener les drois de sa couronne. Et les plus grans et plus principalx droiz de sa couronne sont ses ressors, hommages et souverainetéz ; pour quoy, se il faisoit le contraire, il seroit parjur et par consequent infames et ne seroit digne d'estre Roy."

[58] Ordonnances, VI, 508ff: "scandala et irreparabilia pericula Nobis ac toti reipublice regni nostri."

[59] P. Bourdieu, "La production et la reproduction de la langue légitime," in Langage et Pouvoir symbolique (Paris: Seuil, 2001).

reign and govern the subjects."[60] Corbechon then praised Charles V's creation of the royal library:

> Good hearted prince, it's the desire for sapience that God has very firmly [. . .] rooted in your heart since your childhood, as it appears manifestly in the great and copious multitude of books of various sciences that you have assembled [. . .], from which books you can draw out the profound water of sapience, at the will of your vivid understanding, to spread it in councils and in judgments, to the profit of the people whom God has committed to you to govern.[61]

Charles V reunited the kingdom, gaining back the lost provinces using first the weapon of legitimizing language (the word *ressort*) and then military success. Charles V had Parlement, and the great men of the kingdom, agree that the legitimate meaning of the term "Kingdom of France" carried with it the corollary that the king of France **had** to hold *ressort* in all areas within the kingdom of France. Jean Juvénal des Ursins, in his "Audite celi" (1435), summarized the key points – that neither John II nor his son could have alienated "ressort et souverainneté et hommaige lige," that these rights could not be detached from the person of the king, and that no king, in any kingdom, **could** be king unless he held *ressort*, sovereignty, and liege homage.[62]

Charles V emphasized the commonwealth element of the kingdom of France, in part because, as chancellor Michel de l'Hospital would tell the Estates General in 1560, the citizens of that commonwealth, in 1328, had chosen his grandfather as king, so his own dynastic legitimacy had immediate ties to the legitimacy of the commonwealth.[63] He sponsored the translation of key texts of political philosophy, such as those of Aristotle and John of Salisbury. The translators, men such as Corbechon, Denis Foulechat, Nicole Oresme, and Raoul de Presles, operated a reciprocal legitimization process. Oresme held a doctorate in theology from the Western European Christian world's most important religion faculty, the University of Paris; de Presle studied law at Orléans: these institutions provided intellectual legitimacy,

---

[60] Robert Le Coq owned a copy of L'Anglais' treatise, as did Blanche de Navarre and Jean, duke of Berry.

[61] Reproduced in B. Ribémont, "Jean Corbechon, un traducteur encyclopédiste au XIVe siècle," *Cahiers de recherches médiévales* [Online], 6 | 1999. URL: http://crm.revues.org /932. Corbechon cites Solomon, "who asked God to give him science and sapience by which he could justly govern his people," Cicero, who said that "knowledge [*savoir*] is a royal work," and Seneca, who "said it is a golden age when wise men govern." The BNF has an outstanding online presentation on Charles V's library: http://classes.bnf.fr/ren dezvous/pdf/fiche_livre3.pdf

[62] J. Juvénal des Ursins, "Audite celi," in *Écrits Politiques de Jean Juvénal des Ursins*, ed. P. S. Lewis (Paris: Klincksieck, 1978), I, 207.

[63] Only fief holders seem to have participated in the assembly of 1328, so the application of the concept "commonwealth" to that decision was an anachronism (deliberate, I believe).

similar to that provided today by a top university.[64] Their own legitimacy received further recognition from the king's patronage: generous pensions, religious benefices, and royal offices.

Using language provided by these texts – in some cases neologisms from them, Charles V and his lawyers reorganized the royal financial administration in 1372–1373, forever altering the structure of French government. In January 1383, when Charles VI and the princes returned from their triumph at Roosebeke, the royal lawyers again issued legislation mandating royal officials – *élus*, receivers – at the local level of the tax administration, to be accountable to the generals of finance in Paris. The legislation specifically excluded this financial apparatus from the overview of the Parlement.[65] Pintoin claims to have had intimate knowledge of their debates:[66]

> Since the time of the late king Charles until today they had been paid, contrary to former usages, without the consent of the people [*sine populari consensus*]. Nonetheless, some proposed, not only to reestablish them, but to make them a part of the royal demesne [*merum dominium*] .... Others, seeing more clearly, judging the future by the past, fearing that his unheard-of innovation would lead to a general rebellion in the kingdom; they counseled to remain on the ordinary path

The *fouages/tailles* would be levied irregularly for the next fifty years, becoming permanent in 1439, but the "aides" [sales taxes and *gabelle* on salt] remained permanent. Urban taxpayers, as they made obvious by their many uprisings, resented this favoritism shown to rural dwellers, protected by their noble and ecclesiastical lords. This permanent financial administration, with annual taxes not requiring any vote by an assembly, did mark a significant advance in royal power. The Norman deputies to the Estates General of 1484 specifically objected to the fact that, "by grave corruption," the aides and *gabelle* had, like the royal demesne, become "eternal." The royal councilors present demanded to know if the Normans believed subjects could be permitted to refuse to contribute for the "necessitities of the commonwealth."[67]

---

[64] Corbechon also attended the University of Paris in theology; Foulechat, a Franciscan in Paris from 1363 to 1369, was condemned for heresy by the Sorbonne in 1363, for his attacks on the wealth of the Church. He retracted in 1365. C. Brucker, ed., *Denis Foulechat, Le Policratique de Jean de Salisbury (1372), livres I–III* (Geneva: Droz, 1994), quotation on 22–23. Des Presles was the natural son of the Raoul de Presles who helped found the Collège de Navarre.

[65] *Ordonnances*, VI, 705, ordinance regulating the powers of the *généraux-conseillers*.

[66] Pintoin, *Chronique*, 243. Choisy, *Histoire de Charles VI*, 69, in his version of Pintoin, adds the phrase, after "consent of the peoples," "which from all times has been required to make the levy."

[67] Masselin, *Journal*, 418–421, in his Latin translation of the French original: *reipublicæ necessitatibus satis*.

French historians, in particular, have viewed these practices as an effort to make the king **the** unifying element of the French polity. Charles V's lawyers certainly pursued that goal, but his philosophers – Oresme, Corbechon, et al. – pursued a different one: a political unity built around the commonwealth and the Crown of France. The lawyers and philosophers agreed on this second element – the Crown, which gave them a common ground on which to build. Yet the lawyers had a second vocation, perhaps best described by Donald Kelley, speaking about their sixteenth-century successors: they were "a unique lay class analogous to the clergy, a sort of secular intellectual corporation whose vocation was the analysis and regulation of human relations – the cure, in a sense, not of souls but of citizens. They were devotees not of 'sacred' but of 'civil science'. "[68] The traditional historiographical emphasis **only** on the king makes no sense in light of the political reality of the late fourteenth and early fifteenth centuries. Central administrators like the Jouvénal des Ursins family prided themselves on their joint service to the king and to the "chose publique." The two often worked together, but they contained an inherent tension, which finally split them apart in the second half of the sixteenth century.

The two outside claimants to the throne of the middle of the fourteenth century – Edward III of England and Charles of Navarre – happily settled for pieces of the kingdom, so we should not underestimate the threat to its unity. The intermittent madness of Charles VI could hardly have been reassuring to French elites concerned with unity, even before the civil war touched off by the murder of the duke of Orléans (1407). In the end, Charles VI signed away the kingdom to Henry V of England and his heirs. French elites sought to create a political unity distinct from the king himself, even as they developed a king-centered royalist discourse.

2.3 Founder of the Monarchical Commonwealth: Charles V, the Wise

> Among the kings of France, sire, the one is called by excellence, the Wise, like Charles V; another is called Great, like Charles the first, saint Charlemagne; the other is called by excellence the Strong, like the king Clovis.
>
> Jean de Rély, at the Estates General, 1484.

The reputation of Charles V, "the Wise," weighed heavily on later developments. French kings carefully managed not only their personal image, but that of the Crown: starting with Charles V, they deployed a new set of philosophical principles to justify those images. As Anne-Marie Lecoq has argued in her book on Francis I and monarchical symbolism, "From Charles V, the royal figure had not ceased to be reinforced in the [realm of the] imaginary, by

---

[68] D. Kelley, *The Beginning of Ideology* (Cambridge: CUP, 1981) 185.

means of words, images, and ceremonies."[69] Charles V created an extensive propaganda apparatus, whose most famous outputs are the illustrated *Grandes Chroniques de France*, at the intersection of the written and the visual, and Evrard de Trémaugon's *Songe du Vergier*. We must also associate these texts with the new vocabulary of royal ordinances issued from 1372 to 1374, and with the simultaneous appearance of translations of Aristotle, Augustine, and John of Salisbury, all funded by Charles V.[70]

Evrard de Trémaugon's work had an enormous subsequent influence, as is obvious from how heavily those like Jean Gerson borrowed from him. Trémaugon emphasized that Charles had reconquered Guyenne and parts of Picardy and Normandy, and that he had sometimes captured in a week what Charlemagne had besieged for seven years. That *Song of Roland* reference was as clear as it could be: "no one not Roland or Arthur or Olivier had done more by feats of arms than you have had done in your time by your sense, your prudence, and your holy piety."[71]

For centuries after his death, Charles V remained a key figure in the pantheon of French kings. In the 1570s, in a memoir prepared for the king, a royal councilor listed them: "Charlemagne, St. Louis, from whom you are descended, Sire, Charles the Wise, Louis (XII) surnamed the 'Father of the People,' Francis I, and several other of your predecessors." The councilor praised them for taking good counsel, and thus being well served; "from which they took the high formulary of a life whose good odor has come down even to us, and will never leave the memory of men."[72] Leaving aside the relatively recent kings – Francis and Louis XII – Charles V was in pretty fast company: Charlemagne and Saint Louis. We might think as well of the three sobriquets: "the great"; "saint"; "the wise." Einhard, writing shortly after Charlemagne's death, called his biography the *Vita Karoli Magni Imperatoris*, establishing for all time that Charles as great.[73] The

---

[69] A.-M. Lecoq, *François Ier imaginaire: Symbolisme et politique à l'aube de la Renaissance* (Paris: Macula, 1987), 18–19; see also G. Sabatier, *Le Prince et les Arts. Stratégies figuratives et monarchie française de la Renaissance aux Lumières* (Paris: Champ Vallon, 2010) and A. Ellenius, ed., *Iconography, Propaganda, and Legitimation* (Oxford and NY: OUP, 1999).

[70] Krynen, *L'empire du roi*, 110–124, lays out the internal quarrel between the lawyers responsible for the ordinances and the scholars, like Oresme.

[71] *Songe du Vergier*, 6. "ne die nul que oncques Roland Artus ne Olivier feissent plus du mestier d'armes que tu as fait faire de ton temps par ton sens, par ta prudence & par ta sainte priere."

[72] BNF, Mss Fr 4875, fol. 31ff, remonstrance on disorders in justice, not dated. Internal evidence suggests the author might have been Pomponne de Bellièvre, who began royal service in 1554, writing to Charles IX in early 1572.

[73] J. Favier, *Charlemagne* (Paris: Fayard, 1999), ch. XXI, "Charles le Grand," points out the ambiguity of Einhard's title; in 840, Walafrid Strabon got rid of the ambiguity in his *Karoli Magni Vita*.

sobriquets of Charlemagne and Louis IX (canonized in 1297) had long since passed into permanence; the two men were transcendent European figures.

Charles V, "le saige roy," was an altogether different matter. As in Charlemagne's case, an early biographer added the adjective: Christine de Pizan, in a text ordered by Charles' brother Philip, duke of Burgundy, used the title, *Le livre des fais et des bonnes meurs du saige roy Charles V*.[74] She perhaps borrowed the term from Oresme's preface to his translation of the *Ethics*, in which he wrote: "our good King Charles could be called Charles great in wisdom."[75] Charles V needed that second element, his "good habits" if you will, because his deeds (*fais*) as an individual were few. Christine de Pizan did not shy away from the fact but embraced it: she stated unequivocally that Charles had re-conquered his kingdom from the English by means of his wisdom, not his personal force. In the eighteenth century, Villaret, in his history of France, would write that "The reign of this monarch, unfortunately of too short a duration, goes to prove how much the superiority of enlightenment wins out over an excess of courage."[76]

Where Charlemagne took his title from the greatness of his "*prouece*" [knightly prowess], Charles V, for his virtue and wisdom, would be forever called "the Wise." Christine de Pizan would later suggest that "the good (*bien*) of understanding is the sovereign of goods, because all the others obey it, whence it is that wise men are naturally the seigneurs of others, and those who lack in this engine are naturally serfs."[77] Alfred Coville, in the great Lavisse *Histoire de France* (v. IV), memorably summed up Charles : "He was in his time a redoubtable enemy, more for his subtlety, his lawyerly chicaneries, his secret ways, than for his strength, which was nonetheless real."[78]

---

[74] Philip died just before she finished, so she actually delivered it to Jean, duke of Berry.

[75] "nostre bon roy Charles puet estre dit Charles grant en sagesce": A. Menut, ed., Maistre Nicole Oresme, *Le Livre de Ethiques d'Aristote* (NY, 1940), 100.

[76] Villaret, *Histoire de France*, t. X, 2, (1776).

[77] Christine de Pizan, *Le livre des fais et des bonnes meurs du saige roy Charles V*, ch. LXIII. "Tout ainsy que le bien de l'entendement est le souverain des biens, car à luy tous autres obéyssent, parquoi naturellement les hommes sages soyent seigneurs des autres, et ceulx qui defaillent d'engin soyent naturellement serfs." Besançon Manuscrit 434 has precisely this same comparison to a serf. She here glosses Aristotle's argument about natural slavery, as well as Giles of Rome and Oresme. She would have known Oresme from her childhood, when he was an important opponent of her father, who was both Charles V's doctor and his astrologer: Oresme ridiculed astrology.

[78] Cited in Autrand, *Charles V*, 52; Coville, *Les premiers Valois et les débuts de la Guerre de Cent Ans* (Paris, 1902), t. IV of the *Histoire de France* edited by E. Lavisse, 190. Mézeray, *Histoire*, II, 496, says the Charles was often found at the Parlement and was known as the "praticien" and the "avocat." He begins his section on Charles by noting that courage without prudence is worthless.

Speakers would often add a few other kings – Philip Augustus; Philip the Fair; sometimes even Clovis or another Merovingian – but the holy trinity of Charlemagne, Saint Louis, and Charles the Wise held pride of rhetorical place. Let us listen to Jean de Rély, spokesman for the Estates, responding to the chancellor, at Tours in 1484. After singling out Charlemagne, Clovis, and Charles V, he said of the latter: "of whom it was said that he never bloodied his sword, and yet he recovered his kingdom and reigned all his life in peace and in justice."[79] The good king always reigned with justice and, circumstances permitting, in peace. De Rély's speech was a cardinal document of the French commonwealth tradition, and his remarks about Charles V cemented that king's place in it.[80]

We might pose three questions: 1) In what way was Charles V, "the Wise?" 2) How deeply rooted in his own time was this image of Charles? 3) How did Charles V reshape the French monarchy, not simply in practice but in theory? Charles sponsored an outpouring of learning in Paris in the 1360s and 1370s. He extensively associated with such leading scholars as Oresme and de Presles; his propaganda machine made sure to publicize the king's special patronage of their efforts. Charles prided himself on turning his capital into a new Athens, a description that grateful scholars were only too happy to popularize. We might consider one of his most far-reaching (if initially ill-adopted) reforms: the standardization of time in Paris, in 1370. Charles' own palace clock – a mechanical one, striking equal hours – henceforth was to be the standard for all time, and clocks, in Paris.[81]

Charles V's key ordinances often made specific reference to fundamental philosophical points. His patronage of translations of political treatises, such as Aristotle's *Politics*, had a publicly proclaimed practical purpose, made obvious by miniatures in his *Grandes Chroniques* such as the one showing him reading Foulechat's translation of John of Salisbury's *Policratique*, or the similar images placed in the front of the translations.[82]

---

[79] K. Langdon Forhan, *The Political Theory of Christine de Pizan* (Burlington, VT: Ashgate, 2002); Adams, *Christine de Pizan,* reads de Pizan's extensive political writings within the political context of her own time.

[80] Several of Christine de Pizan's other works, like *Le livre de la paix*, contain frequent positive references to Charles V.

[81] Charles was also a devotee of astrology: as Charles Jourdain points out, Charles' library had more works on astrology than any other topic: *Nicole Oresme et les astrologues de la court de Charles V* (Paris, 1875), 10.

[82] BNF, M Fr 24,287, f. 1. Charles reads a Latin passage from the Bible, "Beatus vir qui in sapientia morabitur, et qui in justicia sua meditabitur" [*Ecclesiasticus/Sirach*, xiv, 20–22]. In the King James Version, it is verse 20, "Blessed is the man that doth meditate good things in wisdom, and that reasoneth of holy things by his understanding." The term "*sapientia*" places the emphasis on reasoned wisdom, not wisdom gained by practical experience (*prudentia*), the central consideration in Charles V's translation program.

Charles V brought together the key elements of making manifest royal power: Jews, coinage, taxation, jurisdiction, and lawmaking. As regent he had allowed the Jews back into the kingdom (for a price) and made the count of Étampes protector of all Jews in Languedoïl.[83] Existing courts predictably fought this limitation on their jurisdiction; as king, Charles reconfirmed Jews' right to stay in the kingdom and Étampes' monopoly, and warned the judges that resistance was "in contempt of our letters." He warned those who persisted that they "would displease Us."[84]

Charles V simultaneously emphasized, in royal propaganda, the image of the just king as *princeps*. He commissioned the so-called scepter of Charlemagne, and then made sure it appeared in many of the miniatures that bear his likeness, such as the one of him receiving the scepter at his coronation, in the official coronation book.[85] (See Illustration 2.2.) This scepter long remained important in ceremony and symbol: in his speech to Louis XIII, after his coronation in 1613, Achille de Harlay, First President of the Parlement of Paris, opened with a comment on its meaning: "Sire ... the royal scepter is presented to you, to be held in your right hand, so as to teach you that God gave you royal power to defend your subjects from oppression and to oppose yourself by force to the evil intentions of enemies of your state."[86] The king then received the "hand of justice," in his left hand, "to represent to you that good Kings reign by justice, and that without justice Kingdoms are no longer Kingdoms Kings are no longer Kings, exchanging the beautiful name of King for other odious names; Justice is the firm column on

---

[83] King John issued letters confirming this appointment. Louis, count of Etampes, son of Charles of Evreux, was the great-grandson of Philip III.

[84] *Ordonnances*, IV, 438, May 1364, and 496, October 1364. In 1378, the Jews of Languedoïl "lent" the king 20,000 francs and paid a weekly gift of 200 francs, in return for exemption from the traditional taxes of Jews. *Ordonnances*, VI, 339.

[85] E. S. Dewick, *The Coronation Book of Charles V of France* (London: Henry Bradshaw Society, 1899), copy of British Library manuscript. Charles also encouraged the cult of "Saint" Charlemagne, although the recent work of scholars like Matthew Gabriele has brought to light how powerful was that cult already in the eleventh century. *The Charlemagne Legend in Medieval Latin Texts*, ed. M. Gabriele and W. Purkis (Cambridge: Brewer, 2016) and Gabriele's monograph, *An Empire of Memory: The Legend of Charlemagne, The Franks and Jerusalem before the First Crusade* (Oxford: OUP, 2011).

[86] BNF Arsenal, Ms 4058, f. 136v. "Sire apres plusieurs prieres que l'esglise en vostre sacre pour vostre prosperité le sceptre royal vous sera presenté pour le tenir en la main droicte qui vous sera un enseignement que dieu vous donne une puissance royalle pour deffandre vos subiectz de l'oppression et vous opposer par force aux mauvaises intantions des ennemis de vostre estat. [. . .] main de justice en la main senestre pour vous representer que les bons Roys regnent par la justice que sans la justice les Royaumes ne plus Royaumes les Roys ne sont plus Roys eschangent ce beau nom de Roy en autres noms odieux, la Justice est la ferme colonne d'un estat, et seulle peult asseurer les bons et faire craindre les mauvais."

which rests a state, which alone can reassure the good and make the evil fear."
This terminology mixes the new state, with the old "kingdom," a usage taken
directly from Oresme's glossary of political terms, at the end of his translation
of *The Politics*.[87] Charles VIII, after his death, lay in state with the scepter in his
right hand and the hand of justice in his left.[88]

The lawyers in Charles V's entourage take us into the different intellectual
world of the law schools, especially those of Orléans and Montpellier. Pierre de
la Forest, a famous Orléans professor, served as one of Charles' chief advisors
in the late 1350s. The king's Council, with its many lawyers, naturally emphasized the importance of a legal education to good government: Philip VI, in his
1337 letters for the University of Orléans, noted that the children of dukes,
counts, princes, barons, bourgeois, merchants, and those of other estates,
"from all nations," came to Orléans to be "introduced to the science of Civil
and Canon Laws, necessary and profitable for a government of rightness and
reason."[89]

Charles developed a unique relationship to the position of chancellor. From
his chancellors, the brothers Jean and Guillaume de Dormans, and Pierre
d'Orgemont, we have the first evidence of an oath of office and the introduction of the practice of electing the chancellor at a meeting of members of the
Parlement, Chamber of Accounts, and Grand Conseil (then not a royal court
but a body including the great princes and nobles, and prelates). In 1371, when
Jean de Dormans stepped down after becoming a cardinal, a body of 200 men
elected his brother Guillaume. They both died soon after, and the king held
another election, this time with 130 votes: each person, the king included,
stepped up and gave his vote, hand on the Scriptures: Pierre d'Orgemont got
105 votes and received the seals after taking the following oath:[90]

> You swear to the King our Sire, that you will well and loyally serve and
> counsel him to the honor and profit of him, of his Kingdom, in the face of

---

[87] D. Russo, "Les modes de représentation du pouvoir en europe dans l'iconographie du
XIVe siècle," in *Représentation, Pouvoir et Royauté à la fin du Moyen Âge*, ed. J. Blanchard
(Paris: Picard, 1995), 177–198, offers some insightful comparisons between Charles V and
his uncle, Emperor Charles IV.

[88] *Ordonnance faict par messire Pierre d'Urfé pour l'enterrement du roi Charles VIII* (Paris,
1498). D'Urfé, *grand écuyer de France*, says that all arrangements were approved by the
first chamberlain, Louis II de la Trémoïlle, in consultation with the other royal chamberlains, so the presence of these two symbols was not some sort of personal whim on
d'Urfé's part. D'Urfé's account unfortunately does not say if the symbols were removed
before the closing of the casket.

[89] Ordonnances, II, 476: "le gouvernement de droiture et raison."

[90] Du Chesne, *Chancelliers*, 370–371. The chancellor had to promise to return presents
previously given to him by others unless he had the king's permission to keep them. The
practice of electing the chancellor lasted until 1413, when a group of ninety electors that
included the king and the dukes of Berry and Burgundy chose Henry de Marle; Marle died
during the riots of 1418. Du Chesne gives no evidence of any later elections of chancellors.

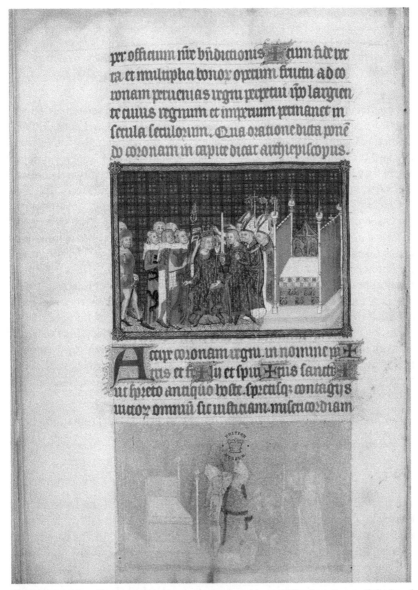

Illustration 2.2 Charles V being vested with the scepter of Charlemagne and the hand of justice at his coronation: Coronation Book of Charles V of France, British Library, Cotton MS Tiberius B. viii/2, fol. 59v. permission BL

all, and against all: That you will guard his Patrimony, and the profit of *la chose publique* of his Kingdom to your power; that you will serve no other Master, or Lord [Seigneur] than him, nor take robes, presents, pensions or profit from any Lord or Lady whomsoever [. . .] and thus swear you on the Holy Scriptures of God that you touch. The which Messire Pierre responded: Thus I swear, my most redoubted Lord [*Seigneur*]

We might contrast this oath with the one given to *baillis* and seneschals, which stressed first the obligation to do justice to all subjects, rich and poor, in their district, but then shifted entirely to obligations to the "droit du Roy": they were to guard the "droit du Roy" and "his secrets," and to seek to restore royal rights where they had been alienated or lost. If unable to restore a right on their own, they were to contact the king, his Council, or the Chamber of Accounts.[91]

Charles V's publicists similarly emphasized that the French royal banner, the Oriflamme, had been passed down from Charlemagne, as Jean Golein put it, "as a sign of perpetual empire."[92] The knight who was to bear the Oriflamme had to take an oath, in which he swore to hold and "govern" the Oriflamme for the "honor and profit of him [the king] and his kingdom." The Oriflamme rarely appeared in battle, perhaps because the French lost it at least four times between 1302 and 1415. After a brilliant success like Roosebeke, however, chronicles reported its miraculous effects: when unfurled at Roosebeke, the dark sky immediately vanished, replaced by a brilliant clear blue. Several eyewitnesses told Froissart they saw a white dove circle the king's army several times, and then land on one of his banners, a sure sign, they believed, of the coming victory.[93]

2.4   Monarchy and the Public Good: Oresme and Trémaugon

Monarchy is the polity or the princedom held by one alone. And there are two general types of monarchy: one is kingdom and the other is tyranny.

N. Oresme, "Glossary" to Aristotle's *Politics*, 1373.

The dual independence from Emperor and Pope provided the basis for the French king's claim of what sixteenth-century writers often called "puissance absolue," that is, "independent power."[94] (See Illustration 2.3.) The coronation oath bound the king to render justice. Kings iterated that promise, and, after

---

[91] Sécousse, editor of the *Ordonnances*, suggests that this final clause indicates that the Chamber itself created the oath; *baillis* and seneschals took their oath in the Chamber.

[92] Sherman, *Imaging Aristotle*, 10, gives specific examples. In his own hand, Charles says he ordered the book's production, and signs his note.

[93] Froissart, *Chroniques*, II, chap. CXCVI–CXCVII. Other chronicles repeat this story.

[94] Even the miniaturists of the *Grandes Chroniques*, however, could not ignore the fact that the Emperor, and he alone, wore a closed crown, as they rightly showed in their images of Emperor Charles IV and King Charles V.

Illustration 2.3   *Songe du Vergier*, 1378, Charles V between the spiritual (his right) and secular powers, represented by two queens and by the cleric and knight who debate in the text: BL, Royal Manuscript 19 C IV, frontispiece. Permission BL

Charles V, the one to preserve the rights and properties of the Crown in other documents, especially at large public meetings. As Dauphin in 1357, Charles had promised the Estates General of Languedoïl that he would not alienate any of the royal demesne or dignities or freedoms of the Crown, and he repeated those sentiments in his ordinances about the succession and a potential regency.[95]

Charles V insisted that his brother, Louis, duke of Anjou, as designated regent, make a similar promise: he would guard and defend "the demesne, the nobilities, the rights and seigneuries of this kingdom, against all living men, without alienating or suffering to be alienated in any possible manner nor for any possible cause, color, or occasion that there might be."[96] Louis had further to swear to protect the "good, honor & profit of our eldest Son our heir and successor, and of all the *bien public* of the kingdom." The *Grandes Chroniques* report a large council of great men in 1375 telling the king he could not "surrender any of his sovereign rights or powers without breaching his coronation oath, and thus imperiling his honor and his soul."[97] In the early fifteenth century, Jean Juvenal des Ursins would specifically advise the king that he was only usufructer of the kingdom.

King John II had recognized the special status of the demesne in 1360, in the edict by which he ratified acts (naming of officers, gifts, etc.) taken by Charles during the king's captivity: he specifically excluded all gifts of the "demesne of the Kingdom and of the Crown of France, which we might revoke and repeal." He did not surrender his royal prerogative over such land and rights, however, because he reserved the right to order "as it seems best to us" what should be done with them.[98] When Charles reaffirmed (July 24, 1364) his father's edict rescinding all grants of royal demesnes and rights executed since 1314, he excluded only grants to the Church and to his three brothers, for the "upkeep of their Estate." In those letters, Charles referred to "the nobilities and seigneuries, rents and revenues, which are of the royal Demesne and private [*proppre*] inheritance of the Kingdom and Crown of France," taking his father's edict one step closer to the understanding of the demesne as something beyond the control of any single person.

We have abundant evidence that the kings took seriously their obligation to protect these "rights," and above all to keep their oath about preserving the Crown and its appurtenances intact.[99] Here we see contradiction; they saw

---

[95] He promised not to alienate "highnesses, dignities, franchises" or demesnes. *Ordonnances*, III, 140, cited in Leyte, *Domaine*, 336. John II, in his treaties with Edward III, had alienated such attributes of the Crown.

[96] *Ordonnances*, VI, 47.

[97] Delachenal, *Chronique*, II, 176–77: "que il ne povoit ne devoit laissier aucune chose de ses ressors et souverainnetez, et, se il le faisoit, ce seroit contre son sairement et son honneur, et ou detriment de son ame."

[98] *Ordonnances*, III, October 14, 1360. John also rescinded all grants of royal demesnes since Philip IV.

[99] Medieval and early modern texts often refer to the "parole de roi," the king's word of honor, as a guarantor of unimpeachable integrity. Hincmar's 882 *De ordine palatii*, addressed to Louis III, clearly set forth all these moral obligations; the arguments changed little after his day. Hincmar, not coincidentally, in his *Life of St. Remigius*, invented the Holy Phial story. Sixteenth-century sources sometimes refer to "parole publique" to mean a promise made by the king and/or his government.

none. If God, by definition, must act according to reason, so that His laws must follow the dictates of reason (a proposition brought front and center into medieval theology by the efforts to integrate the teachings of Aristotle into mainstream Christian thought),[100] then so, too, should the king, instituted by God, anointed by holy oil of chrism (in the French case, oil miraculously generated within the Holy Ampoule at Reims), be bound by God's law and reason. Here we see the obvious and intimate connection with the commonwealth (*res publica*, or general *cité*, to use Oresme's term), which was the precise word for a polity ruled by reason and justice.

The king, by virtue of being a king, and by sworn promise to God in his coronation oath, must rule according to reason and justice. Oresme's glossary of terms for his *Politiques* reveals the contemporaneous meaning of these terms, in which "kingdom" was the legitimate form of monarchy, and tyranny the illegitimate one. He completes the circle through his definition of tyrant: "First of all, it is one person who holds the princedom and the monarchy for his own profit and against the public good."[101] From the start, French definitions of tyrant thus focused on his actions against the public good.

In 1378, Charles V ordered a translation, the *Songe du Vergier*, of the work *Somnium viridarii*, composed between 1374 and 1376, by Évrard de Trémaugnon, a master of requests of the royal household who held degrees in canon and civil law.[102] The *Somnium* brought together texts from the royal-papal dispute going back to the 1297 *Disputacio inter militem et clericum*, and included references to Marsiglio of Padua, William of Ockham, and others. Jacques Krynen calls the *Songe* simultaneously "a treatise of public law [*droit*] and a manual of governance," that is, precisely the summation of the two tracks followed here.[103] The *Songe du Vergier* bears out Patrick Arabeyre's comment, in his review of Schnerb-Lièvre's edition of the *Somnium*, that "French political science was without doubt born in the last quarter of the 14th century at the court of Charles the Wise." Viewing the efforts of Charles V as mainly "the construction of the notion of royal and state sovereignty," however, makes

---

[100] Grant, *God & Reason*, ch. 6, points out that Peter Lombard's *Sentences*, which emphasize God's rationality, was the textbook on theology at Paris from the late twelfth century until the end of the seventeenth century. Krynen, *L'empire du roi*, on the application of this point in France. In Paris, Aquinas and William of Ockham played a key role in establishing the principle; Ockham's teaching established the foundation of what became the Collège de Navarre.

[101] Oresme, *Politiques*, 373, glossary. Oresme carefully includes the odd word "princey," in order to emphasize that the king is also "*princeps*." "Premierement, ce est un seul qui tient le princey et la monarchie a son propre profit et contre le bien publique."

[102] M. Schnerb-Lièvre, ed., *Le Songe du Vergier* (Paris: CNRS, 1982), 2 vols. and *Somnium viridarii* (Paris: CNRS, 1996). Schnerb-Lièvre argues that the *Somnium* existed merely to provide a text for translation into French. The *Songe du Vergier* greatly expands upon the *Somnium*.

[103] Krynen, *L'empire du roi*.

little sense.[104] Trémaugon certainly did seek to establish Charles V's "sovereignty" in the 1378 meaning of the term, but that meaning was by no means incompatible with "la chose publique," a term used by Trémaugon, Oresme, and Philippe de Mezières for the political community.

Trémaugon's "new" disputation between a knight and a cleric about the respective powers of secular rulers (the Emperor and the king of France) as against those of the Pope begins with the cleric claiming that Popes have, in fact, deposed rulers, such as a king of France. He cites the example of Pope Zachary, whom he claims deposed Childeric III, the last Merovingian, in favor of Pepin the Short, founder of the Pippinid/Carolingian monarchy. The knight replies that the cleric has chosen the wrong word: Zachary did not "depose" Childeric; the "barons and council of France" would never have accepted such an action. Trémaugon here reprises the story used by Robert le Coq in November 1356. The knight gives his own version of the story: "Pepin king of France sent his messengers to Zachary the Pope to ask him whom he would counsel would best be king, one who for the profit and common good (*bien commun*) of the kingdom sustains great torments and labors or one who is lazy and does not take any labors for the "chose publicque" ... to which Zachary replied that he would best be called king who defended the kingdom and "la chose publicque."[105] Royal apologists for kings from Charles VI through Henry III invariably claimed that the king, like Pepin, was acting on behalf of the "chose publique," that is, acting as a legitimate monarch, not a tyrant. In the royal copy of the *Songe du Vergier*, the scribe notes that "les clers ne pueut user de prescripcion contre le salut de la chose publicque" [clergy cannot use exemption against the salvation of the chose publique] when the knight insists – as town governments everywhere did – that clergy have to contribute to taxes for the defense of the chose publique, while the cleric insists that clergy have "liberty and franchise" from paying *tailles* and subventions. On the next page, we read the note that kings cannot give privileges to clerics "against the chose publique."[106]

Charles V carried out a dual offensive: one was spearheaded by lawyers, like Trémaugon, d'Orgemont, and Dormans; the other was led by intellectuals, above all Oresme. The lawyers sought to make the commonwealth (*chose publique*) and the Crown coterminous in the eyes of their contemporaries. By making the Crown, not the king, coterminous with the commonwealth, the lawyers thus made the bodies they dominated, above all the Parlement, the

---

[104] *Annales E.S.C.* 50, n. 3 (1995), reviews by P. Arabeyre (614–615) and by Alain Boureau (of Autrand's biography *Charles V*, in which he rejects her federalism argument), 613–614. His phrase is "souveraineté royale et étatique"; I object particularly to the term "étatique" in its usual meaning.

[105] *Le Songe du Vergier*, 1491 edition, on Gallica, images 50–51. This example played a prominent role in disputes about royal and papal power under Henry IV, too.

[106] Royal Manuscript 19 C IV, f. 15v.

institutional focus of the common weal. Oresme takes us into the realm of what Bourdieu calls official language:[107]

> This language is the one which, within the territorial limits of that unit, imposes itself on the whole population as the only legitimate language, especially in situations that are characterized in French as more *officielle* [...]. Produced by authors who have the authority to write, fixed and codified by grammarians and teachers who are also charged with the task of inculcating its master, the language is a code, in the sense of a cipher enabling equivalences to be established between sounds and meanings, but also in the sense of a system of norms regulating linguistic practices.

For two centuries afterwards, written texts were festooned with direct quotations from Oresme's glossary. As late as 1576, in his *Remonstrances aux Estats pour la Paix*, Philippe Duplessis-Mornay would write: "All this kingdom is only one Cité."[108] Oresme's remarkable collection of neologisms made it possible for all the citizens of the French commonwealth to speak a common political language.[109]

These authors created a vocabulary sanctioned by the king and those around him. Thus, Foulechat's translation of the Latin "cives" [citizens] into the French "peuple" fitted into contemporaneous conflation of the terms "bourgeois" or "citoyens" and "habitans." The royal re-production of Oresme's legitimate language in many royal ordinances and edicts simultaneously provided a new layer of legitimacy for those laws and for the authors cited in so authoritative a text because they made it clear that Charles V accepted Oresme's neologisms as legitimate speech: Oresme's definitions thus became the *langage* of politics. Louis Le Roy's new translation of Aristotle arrived at precisely the moment (1576) when political discourse in French moved away from Oresme's normative meanings.

The crisis of the first third of the fifteenth century accelerated many of these developments. Jacques Krynen and Jean Barbey have rightly emphasized the consolidation of key elements of royalist ideology. Krynen highlights the contribution of Évrard de Trémaugon's *Songe du Vergier*, with its emphasis on the king of France as emperor in his own kingdom, and as the source of public law. Trémaugon certainly did focus on the king's independence from the Emperor – hardly surprising in a text handed to Charles V on the eve of Emperor Charles IV's visit in 1378 – but the royal librarian, in a margin note to

---

[107] P. Bourdieu, "The Production and Reproduction of Legitimate Language," in *Language and Symbolic Power*, ed. J. Thompson, trans. G. Raymond and M. Adamson (Cambridge, MA: Harvard UP, 1993), 45.

[108] "Tout ce royaume n'est qu'une Cité, qu'une maison, qu'un corps, qui n'a qu'un Roy, un Père de famille, un chef, qui se ruine, se brusle, se meurt tout ensemble." P. Duplessis-Mornay *Remonstrance aux Estats pour la Paix* (1576), 56.

[109] Later writers often adopted Foulechat's French translations of key terms in John of Salisbury.

Charles V's own copy of the *Songe,* annotated a passage that, in his words, explains "how the Pope must not have knowledge of what touches on the temporal justice of the king."[110] The marginal note to folio 19v emphasizes the knight's point that the kingdom of France can be called an "empire" and the king of France an "emperor." Between Philip IV and Charles V, the king of France effectively claimed both the *plenitudo potestatis* of the Pope and the *imperium* of the Emperor, within the boundaries of the kingdom of France: little wonder that the king's advocate general, Jean Le Maître, claimed in 1499 that the king of France had more "authority in his kingdom than the Emperor does in his Empire." Yet actual practice tells a different story. Rather than viewing the use of the title *"rex Christianissimus"* as the root of "absolutism," we are far better off reading political developments in the perspective of their own time, and not as precursors to some future political system. (See Illustration 2.4.)

Barbey has restored the centrality of Jean de Terrevermeille's 1419 *Tractatus de iure futuri successoris legitimi in regiis hereditatibus,* with its emphasis on Salic Law and on the legal foundation of royal succession.[111] We can contrast Terrevermeille's writings with the statement by Charles V, in a letter to the town government of Montpellier in 1364, that he had succeeded to the throne by "droite paternelle," as if it were simply a piece of ordinary property.[112] Even in 1381, in letters about the apanage of Orléans, the operative phrase was that the duchy remained attached to the Crown as "patrimonial" property. Terrevermeille offered a coherent statement of principles already implicit in Charles V's legislation; the regular usage of "la chose publique" and, to a lesser degree, "bien public," and the series of letters tying towns and provinces

[110] Trémaugon studied with John of Legnano, his "master." The *Songe du Vergier,* a text widely distributed among the royal family (the dukes of Burgundy, for example, owned a copy), also provides two chapters on Brétigny and Aquitaine. Charles V's copy is British Library Royal Manuscript 19 C IV: www.bl.uk/manuscripts/Viewer.aspx?ref=royal_ms_19_c_iv_fs001rf. 37r, the scribe notes in the margin that "prelates and other clerics be subject to the king"; on 63v, he emphasizes that the Pope had no *"seigneurie"* over temporal matters over the king of France.

[111] Krynen, *L'empire du roi;* Barbey, *Être roi* and *La fonction royale. Essence et légitimité d'après les Tractatus de Jean de Terrevermeille* (Paris: Nouvelles éditions latines, 1983). Jean de Montreuil had emphasized the Salic Law in the first decade of the fifteenth century; Terrevermeille created a far more comprehensive synthesis built on it. See also Nicole Pons, *L'Honneur de la Couronne de France: Quatre libelles contre les Anglais (vers 1419 - vers 1429)* (Paris: SHF, 1990). R. Giesey, "The Juristic basis of dynastic right to the French throne," *Transactions of the American Philosophical Society,* new series, v. 51, n. 5 (1961): 3–47, also gives importance to Terrevermeille (12–17), and to his insistence that the "people" - thus the Estates of the "realm and of the republic" - by means of law, and not the king regulated the succession.

[112] Delachenal, *Charles V,* III, 546, *pièce justicative* IV, letter of April 26, 1364. Montpellier had not been part of the kingdom of France, but of that of Majorca, whose king sold it to his French colleague.

Illustration 2.4 *Traicté des vertus* of Blanche of Navarre, made for Philip IV: BL M 54180, fol. 91v. Permission BL

irrevocably to the Crown made evident the distinction between a piece of property inherited by "paternal right" and a "dignité."

In the fifteenth century, Jean Juvénal des Ursins argued precisely that the Crown was a *dignité*, that is an office exercised for the common benefit, and that as a public office it transferred by law, not by simple inheritance.[113] Again and again in his writings and speeches, Juvénal des Ursins says the king acts for "la chose publique": for example, the just king spends the tax revenues for the needs of "la chose publique." The conflict of lawyers and scholars in Charles V's entourage notwithstanding, the two groups often worked together in developing a theory that moved the kingdom outside the jurisdiction of individual kings and into that of a larger collective identity, either Crown (lawyers) or commonwealth (scholars).[114] We see the combination in Philippe de Mezières *Songe du vieil pelerin* (1388), which relies on the terms "la chose publique" and "bien public."[115]

Ideas such as the Salic Law and the king's independent lawmaking authority certainly do lie at the heart of royalist ideology as it developed over the coming centuries, but we must distinguish between their later implications, in profoundly different practical settings, and their meaning within the commonwealth mentality, and political and institutional instability, of 1400. Both the written sources of the time, say a text like Jean Gerson's *Vivat rex* sermon of 1405 [see Chapter 3], and its institutional practices show the extent to which ruling elites conceptualized France as a commonwealth. We make a fundamental misreading when we fetishize the royal preoccupation with phrases that emphasize subjection and humble redress.[116]

---

[113] Once again, if we look back to Robert Le Coq, he had argued, so the *Accusation* said, that John II was not "digne" of being king, surely a deliberate choice of a word so closely related to *dignité*.

[114] Juvénal des Ursins, in "Audite celi," has a long discussion of how the king has no right to strip his heir of royal rights: he argues that a king could strip his son of hereditary right to the throne only for "just, holy, and reasonable cause," at a meeting of the Three Estates, holding a "lit de justice," with the peers present, and by means of a fair and open trial. Earlier he had summarized the main point: "et ne peut quiconcques est mon roy preiudicier a son heritier ou successeur, ne alyener ou transporter le royaulme en aultre main que celle ou elle doyt venir par succession hereditale." [186] Juvénal des Ursins relied heavily on Gerson and on Alain Chartier.

[115] Modern critical edition by G. W. Coopland, *Philippe de Mézières, Le Songe du Vieil Pelerin* (Cambridge: CUP, 1969) 2 vols.

[116] J. Krynen, *Idéal du prince et pouvoir royal en France à la fin du Moyen Age (1380–1440): étude de la littératue politique du temps* (Paris: A. and J. Picard, 1981), overemphasizes the subjection vocabulary, in my view. See the outstanding presentation by A. Rigaudière, "Un grand moment pour l'histoire du droit constitutionnel français: 1374–1409," *Journal des Savants* (2012): 281–370, which has a list of key ordinances in an annex. Although we might perhaps disagree on the use of l'État as a concept in this period, I strongly support his emphasis on the reality of a late medieval monarchical constitution – what I view as the practical constitution of the monarchical commonwealth.

If we move beyond the simple language, into the broader processes of which it formed a part – the "utterances," as literary scholars would call them – we can see how the ordering of such utterances reflected a specific hierarchical view of the world. When the king, or a prince such as the duke of Burgundy, renewed the privileges of a given town, he would always begin by saying that the townsmen had to take their oath of fealty to their "seigneur et prince" rendering "vraie et pleniere obeisance" [true and complete obedience], as Jean sans Peur put it in renewing the "privileges, franchises, libertés, coustumes, usaiges et drois" of Ghent in 1405.[117] The subjects first swear fealty, then get the **freely** given privileges, liberties, rights, etc., which are specified as being precisely those granted by previous counts of Flanders to the good town of Ghent. The ordinance specifically says the full enumeration of those rights and privileges will await verification by the count's chancellor and other experts, who will consult the previous charters. In 1629, Louis XIII caused an uproar in Dijon when he refused to confirm the city's privileges and rights because neither his keeper of the seals nor his secretaries were then with him, so he felt the proper document could not be created. The city had to wait several months for the document, a fitting climax to what was a catastrophic royal entry.[118]

The wording and the ordering of actions – here the verbal expressions, above all the oath, being explicit utterances, located in time and space, not just in language itself – implies the free action of the prince, yet the universal understanding of the men of Ghent would be that the count, however "free" in the gesture of granting the charter, **had** to do so in order to reassert his legitimacy as prince. Just as the obedience of the Gantois had to be "vraie," so, too, the reciprocal "bienfait" of the prince had to be true to traditional forms. These exchanges took place **outside** the town gate and involved the handing over to the prince of the keys to the town, which were then returned immediately to the mayor. The prince then entered the city. The duke of Brittany, for example, went through precisely this ceremony on his first entry into the capital city of Rennes.[119]

The language of fealty, of mutual obligation, and of the "bien public" remained central to the idea of the kingdom of France of provincial nobles, of town elites, and of the judicial hierarchy until the Wars of Religion.[120]

---

[117] J.-M. Cauchies, *Ordonnances de Jean sans Peur 1405–1419 Recueil des ordonnances des Pays-Bas, 1ᵉ section, T 3* (Brussels: Ministère de Justice, 2001), 10.

[118] M. Holt, *The Politics of Wine in Early Modern France* (Cambridge: CUP, 2018), 288–308. A year after this fiasco, the Lanterlu rebellion broke out: outraged Dijonnais carried portraits of Louis XIII into the street to deface (a crime of lèse-majesté), while simultaneously parading behind portraits of, and singing praises to, his father.

[119] Murphy, *Ceremonial entries,* provides multiple examples.

[120] V. Shearer, "A good deed is never forgotten: crédit and mutual exchange in seventeenth-century France," Ph.D. thesis, 2005, Georgetown University, shows the centrality of reciprocity to social relations and cultural norms.

Krynen's tension between lawyers (like Trémaugon) and scholars comes out clearly in a text like Gerson's *Vivat rex*, which castigates lawyers as a threat to the commonwealth, just as Trémaugon and Foulechat, in their writings, stress the importance of "jurists" in the creation of good governing practice. On a practical level, we can see the conflict play out in many a *civitas*: "men of law" (*gens de justice*) regularly sought to use princely authority to take control of town governments from merchants, as at Ypres in the 1430s. The desertion of the lawyers in the last third of the sixteenth century marked the end of the commonwealth.

Charles V had promulgated fundamental laws that unequivocally gave preeminence to the Crown over the king, to the king's "civil body" [Gerson] over his temporal one. The Crown was the essence of the commonwealth; the institutions that protected the Crown's rights, like the Parlement, and the individuals who made up its body ["members"], the princes of the blood and the peers, collectively protected it against the excesses of one individual.[121] The fiasco of Calais-Brétigny, when King John had so clearly violated the Crown's rights, taught French elites that the individual king had to be restrained by the "puissance absolue" of the Crown. Gerson, in his *Vivat Rex* sermon, repeatedly stated that the king's "civil life," which is permanent, is more important than his temporary, corporal life, "because it derives by legitimate succession of the Royal line, and is more to be loved than the first, just as the *bien commun* is worth more than the individual [*propre*] one."[122]

The French could turn to Italian cities for a vocabulary of the commonwealth: unsurprisingly, the Italian city republics of the fourteenth century had often had the same conflict between lawyers and scholars as came out in France in the 1370s.[123] The European vocabulary of the "common good" began mainly in Italian and other Mediterranean towns; Charles V's innovation was to use it to describe a large kingdom, rather than a traditional *civitas*. His theoretician Oresme had used precisely that word – *civitas/cité* – to describe the kingdom as a whole. That shift, making the **kingdom** into a *civitas*, was the fundamental change implemented by Charles V, and theorized by Oresme. Before we emphasize too much the reliance of fifteenth-century French authors like Jean de Montreuil and Alain Chartier on Italian authors like Coluccio Salutati, we must remember that French political

---

[121] During his quarrel with Philip of Burgundy, Louis d'Orléans, in his meeting with a delegation from the University of Paris, at Mélun, told them that the University [which was pro-Burgundy] should not interfere in reform of the kingdom, because many "estrangers" were part of the University. Reform should be carried out, he told them, by "those of royal blood and the Grand Conseil."

[122] Jean Gerson, *Vivat Rex* (Paris, 1561), 8–8v.

[123] Crouzet-Pavan, *Enfers et paradis*, on the evolution of polities in thirteenth-century Italy. *Origini dello Stato. Processi di formazione statale in Italia fra medioevo ed età moderna* (Bologna: Società editrice il Mulino, 1994) has a range of interesting essays on key issues.

discourse had already developed the idea of a "bien de la chose publique" for the kingdom between 1356 and 1380, well before anyone in France was familiar with Salutati's writings. Salutati did not offer them a new idea, but better arguments to support the public good theme.[124] He and other Humanists surely had a fundamental influence in the adoption, by the legal elite above all, of "respublique" in the place of the vernacular "chose publique." That usage remained rarified for over a century, but in the sixteenth century it would gradually supplant, among both judges and nobles, a term that had so plebian an origin.

---

[124] Jean de Montreuil went to Italy in 1384, as part of a French contingent sent to help Louis d'Anjou push his claim to Sicily. Montreuil met Salutati, who introduced him to Petrarch and Boccaccio's writings. Montreuil was the secretary of chancellor Miles de Dormans, so he would have had opportunity to introduce Italian ideas into the highest levels of the French government.

3

Murder, Justice, and *la chose publique* in an Age of Madness

First, in all that they do, they look to the chose publique, and put behind them their particular good and profit. Second, that the chose publique, of which they have the government, the body of which they are the heads, and the subjects are the members; in such manner that, if any of the members are wounded, the pain moves to the head. And to come to my point, I consider that this kingdom of Christian France is a body of which our sovereign lord [*seigneur*] is the head; and the members are the subjects.

Me Guillaume Saignet, spokesman of Louis II, duke of Anjou, "king" of Sicily, and Charles, duke of Orléans, to the warring princes, Vernon, July 1413.[1]

Guillaume Saignet, judge of Nîmes, in his speech to the assembled warring princes of 1413, in the aftermath of the Cabochien uprising in Paris, laid out the image of the commonwealth as a body politic, of which the king was the head, the princes were the eyes, and the people the "members." Other writers – such as Marsiglio of Padua – had offered a secular body politic, but the royalist, secular version used in fifteenth-century France came from Christine de Pizan. Marsiglio, in contrast, would seem to be the main inspiration for the endless use of medical body politic metaphors common in the fifteenth and sixteenth centuries in France.

Saignet's use of a purely secular metaphor of the body politic indicates he drew this image from Christine de Pizan, rather than from John of Salisbury,

---

[1] Jean Le Févre, *Chroniques*, ed. F. Morand (Paris: Renouard, 1876), I, 89–91. "Premiers, que en tout ce que ilz feront, ilz ayent le regard à la chose publicque, en délaissant, et mectant derrière leur bien particulier et prouffit. Secondement, que la chose publicque, dont ilz ont le gouvernement, représente un corps dont ilz sont les chiefs, et les subgectz sont les menbres; en telle manière que, se aucuns des menbres sont bleschiés, il en descende douleur au chief. Et pour venir à mon propos, je considère ce royaume de France chrestien estre ung coprs duquel nostre souverain seigneur est le chief; et les menbres sont ses subgetz." Louis II, duke of Anjou, was the nephew of Charles V. He married Yolande of Aragon; their daughter, Marie (b. 1404), married Charles VII six months before he became king, in 1422. A. Coville, *Les cabochiens et l'ordonnance de 1413* (Paris: Hachette, 1888), 343–344, offers a scathing critique of the speech.

because she had laicized John's metaphor by removing the clergy as a separate element (the soul) of the body politic.[2] Christine de Pizan and her friend, Jean Gerson, produced texts in the first decade of the fifteenth century that would broaden and strengthen the foundations of monarchical commonwealth ideology. Gerson and Christine de Pizan relied, in part, on Évrard de Trémaugon, who, in turn, referred to Marsiglio of Padua, whose own body politic discussions clearly affected French discourse. They did so in an environment in which political actors of all kinds had turned to the "bien de la chose publique" vocabulary to justify their positions, and in which that vocabulary had become normative in most "good towns" in the kingdom of France, both in discussions of the economy and of politics.[3] In this chapter, we will look first at the general climate of political rhetoric, then at specific works of Christine de Pizan and Gerson.

Saignet spoke right after Charles VI had recovered from one of his bouts of madness, which had coincided with the Parisian uprising of May 1413, during which several prominent royal officials had lost their lives, and the king and queen had been humiliated by the crowd. Saignet began with the "chose publique" precisely because the "head" of the body politic was a madman. The warring factions traded control of the mad king. Charles VI himself could hardly provide an effective unifying mechanism; moreover, as he would demonstrate with the Treaty of Troyes (1420), allowing one man to make law about the unity and inheritance of the kingdom was spectacularly ill-advised in a realm ruled by a madman.

Charles VI's wife, Isabeau of Bavaria, acted in his name, with support of various princes, especially from his younger brother, Louis of Orléans.[4] His

---

[2] T. Adams, "The political significance of Christine de Pizan's Third Estate in the *Livre du corps de policie*," *J. of Medieval History* 35, n. 4 (2009): 385–398 and *Christine de Pizan*. S. Rigby, "The Body Politic in the Social and Political Thought of Christine de Pizan: Reciprocity, Hierarchy and Political Authority," *Cahiers de recherches médiévales et humanists* [On line], *Études christiniennes*, URL: http://crm.revues.org/12965 Christine started this work as a primer for Louis, duke of Guyenne, the Dauphin of 1404. Two early "chapters" discuss the proper education of a young prince. Marsiglio's medical training, and the connection between medical metaphors and political bodies, has come under considerable recent scholarly scrutiny. See the suggestive essays by T. Shogimen, "Medicine and the Body Politic in Marsilius of Padua," in *A Companion to Marsilius of Padua*, ed. G. Moreno-Riaño and C. Nederman (Leiden: Brill, 2012): 117–138 and J. Kaye, "Equalization in the Body and the Body Politic: From Galen to Marsilius of Padua," *Mélanges de l'École française de Rome – Moyen Âge* 125, n. 2 (2013), online, http://mefrm .revues.org/1252. C. Nederman, *Community and Consent: The Secular Political Theory of Marsiglio of Padua's Defensor Pacis* (London: Rowman and Littlefield, 1995), 133–135 on the medical element. Marsiglio located the direction of the body in the heart, consisting of the political leaders; French writers, unsurprisingly, specifically placed the king as its head, and director.

[3] The southwestern towns remained an exception to common usage of this term.

[4] On the much-vilified Isabeau, see the important revisions of Adams, *Isabeau of Bavaria*.

uncles, the dukes of Burgundy and Berry, had episodic control of him. After Jean sans Peur succeeded his father, Philippe le Hardi, as duke of Burgundy (1407), he had Louis d'Orléans murdered in Paris, touching off a civil war that lasted for two generations. The Orléans (Armagnac) and Burgundy factions traded control of the mad king: Charles VI would strip the party out of power of their lands and offices, only to restore them when the tables were turned. How could such a man be the head of a stable political order? Quite obviously, he could not, and Saignet's speech, together with innumerable other documents of the period, show the efforts of French elites to make the "chose publique," the monarchical commonwealth, the unifying principle of their political order. The princely manifestos of the early fifteenth century all used the terminology of "la chose publique": it had become the standard language of politics. The September 1410 letter of the princes to Parlement uses the standard phrasing, heavily redolent of the words of the 1356 Estates General of Languedoïl: "the honor of the King, his justice and the state of the Kingdom and of *la chose publique* have been trampled underfoot and deeply wounded."[5]

The vocabulary got exemplary usage in January 1418, when Isabeau's commission for Louis II of Chalon-Arlay to hold the "intendance souveraine" of Languedoc, Auvergne, and Guyenne, began with the statement that Charles VI had given her the government and administration of this kingdom. She acted for the[6]

> good of Monseigneur [the king], the conservation of his Lordship [*seigneurie*] and the repair and maintenance, and for the bien de la chose publique of this said Kingdom, which for a long time has been much desolated by the guilt and evilness of some men of small estate, who by their authority have undertaken the government.

Their actions, "under the guise and shadow of bad and damned government," had led to many evils – to violence, pillaging, the destruction of the royal demesne, and the desolation of the poor people. They had levied excessive *tailles*, loans, tenths and "other charges and unsupportable servitudes" for their "singular profit, without having in any way profited the bien public of this said Kingdom." Their bad government had led to the loss of Normandy and Guyenne to the English.[7] These evil men held her son, the Dauphin

---

[5] L. Douët d'Arcq, ed., *Choix des pièces inédites relatives au règne de Charles VI* (Paris, 1864), I, 327: "l'onneur du Roy, sa justice et l'estat du Royaume et de la chose publique estoient foulez et bléciez."

[6] "le bien de Monseigneur, la conservation de sa Seigneurie & la reparation & substentaton, & pour le bien de la chose publique de cedit Royaume, qui par longue espace de temps a esté moult desolée par la coulpe & mauvaistié d'aucunes gens de petit estat, qui de leur auctorité ont entreprins le gouvernement" [*Choix*, I, 186].

[7] Guillaume Besse, *Recueil de diverses pieces servant à l'histoire du roy Charles VI* (Paris, 1660), 185–195: "mis à leur profit singulier, sans avoir aucunement proffité au bien publique de cedit Royaume." [187] Besse, a lawyer in Carcassonne, reproduced the copy

[Charles], as their "prisoner." Isabeau herself, in January 1418, was a virtual prisoner of the real sponsor of this text, Jean sans Peur, who made sure to praise his own disinterested efforts for France.

Commonwealth principles provided the vocabulary of the French monarchy's legitimizing *langage*, but they often faced practical difficulties. Less than a month after Charles V's death, his brother, the duke of Anjou, acting as regent, called (October 1–2) a meeting of peers, princes, prelates, and barons, in conjunction with the Parlement and other chief officers, to approve premature legal majority for Charles VI. Jean des Mares, *avocat du roi* at the Parlement, speaking for the regent, argued that even though the king was a minor, being only eleven, nonetheless, for the "bien de la chose publique" and the "good government of the kingdom" and to keep peace among his uncles, Charles should be crowned as soon as possible. Des Mares made the extraordinary argument that "no matter what law or ordinance had been made in the past, it could be altered or changed to avoid greater difficulties [*inconvenians*]."[8]

Louis d'Anjou forced chancellor Pierre d'Orgemont to step down on October 1, 1380, at a meeting of the Grand Conseil, which "elected" Miles de Dormans, the duke of Anjou's own chancellor, as chancellor of France: d'Orgemont took Dormans' office as president of the Chamber of Accounts.[9] This action, a new king creating a new chancellor, illustrates the fragility of the distinction king-Crown in 1380. John II, in 1350, took the unusual step of retaining his father's chancellor, Pierre de la Forest; Charles V followed that precedent in 1364, keeping Jean de Dormans. The contrast with the actions of kings from Philip III through Philip VI, who all brought in a new chancellor, could not have been clearer, and clearly reflected a new attitude toward the position of chancellor. The change in 1380 could cite precedent before 1350, but French political society had by then largely accepted the idea that the

---

in the registers of that city's seneschal. Louis II de Chalon-Arlay, soon to become Prince of Orange, was a client of Jean sans Peur. Jean and Louis' father, Jean, Prince of Orange (*de jure uxoris*), are listed on the document as part of the royal council that took this decision.

8 "J. Juvénal des Ursins," *Histoire de Charles VI, roi de France* (Paris, 1841), 324. I have used quotation marks for Juvénal des Ursins because Peter Lewis has raised fundamental doubts about whether Juvénal des Ursins wrote this text: "L'Histoire de Charles VI attribué à Jean Juvénal des Ursins: pour une édition nouvelle," *Comptes-rendus de l'Académie des Inscriptions et des Belles-Lettres* 140, n. 2 (1996): 565–569. "Inconvenians" carries a much stronger connotation than the tepid English "inconveniences."

9 F. Du Chesne, *Histoire des chancelliers de France et des gardes des sçeaux de France* (Paris, 1686), 385–386. The elections of chancellors, First Presidents, and other judges often seem to have been perfectly legitimate, but princes did intervene to manipulate the outcome in some cases, such as this one. Nicolas de Baye, the *greffier* of the Parlement, provides fascinating detail on the August 1413 elections of the chancellor and of the Fourth President *à mortier* of the Parlement: when the duke of Guyenne's (Charles VI's oldest son) candidate for Fourth President finished third, with fourteen votes (the leading candidates had seventeen and fifteen, respectively), Guyenne and other princes added their votes *ex post facto* to shift the selection to Guyenne's candidate, Jean de Vailly.

chancellor was a Crown, not a royal officer. When Louis XI removed his father's chancellor, in 1461, he outraged the political society of his time, and laid the foundation for the War of the Public Good (1465).[10]

The day after he stepped down, d'Orgemont argued to the meeting that the late king's letters on legal majority had to be respected: the sources of the time state that many at the October 2 assembly sided with d'Orgemont, who was, by the terms of Charles V's will, the late king's testamentary executor.[11] Jean des Mares, arguing for immediate coronation, spoke on behalf of the duke of Anjou, whereas d'Orgemont, arguing for respect of Charles V's will, spoke for Burgundy and the others, who had been given oversight of the long-term preservation of Crown property and rights.[12] Philip, duke of Burgundy, came away from this meeting bearing a considerable grudge against des Mares. Pintoin says des Mares added to Burgundy's "hatred" of him in a speech after Charles VI's coronation, when the avocat praised excessively the wisdom and action of Louis d'Anjou, and said nothing about the dukes of Berry, Bourbon, and, most critically, Burgundy.[13]

Anjou wanted the young prince crowned in order to have complete legal control of that property, within the limits to which he had sworn in 1375.[14] A chronicle of Rouen states that Anjou did seize the entire royal treasury, amounting to 17 million *francs*: the sum is an exaggeration, but such a rumor

---

[10] The rule of "inamovibilité" dated legally only to Henry III's ordinance of April 3, 1582, the first edict to establish the official list of "grand officiers de la Couronne," and their preeminence. On institutional rules for the later monarchy, B. Barbiche, *Les institutions de la monarchie française à l'époque moderne* (Paris: PUF, 2000, 2012). Philippe de Commynes contrasted Louis XI's behavior with the wisdom of Louis XII in 1498: "he did not change any pensions for that year [...] He removed few offices, and said that he wished to keep every man in his full possessions and estate; and all that was *bien seant*." [*Mémoires*, II, 596.]

[11] "Jouvenal des Ursins", *Histoire de Charles VI*, 323–324, has a detailed presentation of the meeting and of the sharp division among the princes. Bellaguet, trans., *Chronique de Saint-Denis*, 9–13, confirms this conflict. The chronicler – Michel Pintoin – claims to reproduce the actual speeches of des Mares and d'Orgemont. When des Mares speaks of the "reipublice utilitati," Bellaguet translates it as "bien de l'État." In the opening passages of d'Orgemont's speech, Bellaguet turns both "regnum" and "reipublice" into "État."

[12] Whether noble or peasant, successions often followed a division of the *tutelle* (immediate care, given to the widow, if alive) and *curatelle* (long-term preservation of the property, usually given to the senior patrilineal male). J. Bart, *Histoire du droit privé de la chute de l'Empire romain au XIXe siècle* (Paris: Montchrestien, 2009, 2nd ed), 308–312, emphasizes the key developments of the fourteenth century in the evolution of such practices. Charles V's wife, Jeanne de Bourbon, died in 1378, so there was no widow.

[13] *Chronique de Saint-Denis*, 42–43, "odii ac invidic", despite his "Ciceronian" [*tulliana*] rhetoric.

[14] Anjou had sworn to respect Charles V's ordinances on age: the text of his oath can be found in Devic and Vaissette, *Histoire de Languedoc*, IV, *Preuves*, 326–327. As a crowned king, Charles VI had legal authority over laws issued in his name, which allowed each of his uncles to lobby him for their purposes, thus reducing Anjou's freedom of action.

helps explain why his contemporaries called Charles V, the "Rich."[15] Charles VI got his crown on November 4, a month before his twelfth birthday.[16] We do not have much popular testimony about kingship and coronation, but what testimony we do have, such as Jeanne d'Arc's insistence on calling Charles VII, "monseigneur le dauphin" prior to his coronation, suggests the ordinary people tied full kingship to the coronation ceremony.[17] Right after Charles VI's coronation, the princes rushed back to Paris, and, building on the institutional ambiguity of the time, tied the opening session of the Parlement, which began its main term on November 11 each year,[18] to a new assembly of the great men of the commonwealth: "princes, prelates, and barons" held in Parlement, as the registers of the Parlement put it.[19] A legal case in Sens in March 1381, about a disturbance there in November 1380, reveals that the local officials believed this first meeting to have been a council of the members of the royal family; in contrast, the court case makes reference to letters sent to Sens (and other places) asking that deputies come to Paris for a meeting of the "three estates of the *pays* of Languedoil" held starting on January 3, 1381, if the Sens documents can be believed.[20]

---

[15] A. Héron, ed. *Deux chroniques de Rouen* (Rouen: Lestringant; Paris: Picard, 1900), 74–75. The *Chroniques de France* says Anjou seized the treasure, worth 18,000 "lyons" [lion d'or, a coin minted by Philip VI]. Pintoin claims they found treasures worth 15,000 *écus d'or* [*Chroniques de Saint-Denis*, 29]. Froissart speaks of the "innumerable" jewels owned by Charles V, seized by Anjou.

[16] Des Mares cited the precedent of Saint Louis (IX), crowned at age twelve. The English followed this precedent: the duke of Bedford had the ten-year-old Henry VI crowned king of France at Paris in December 1431.

[17] N. Grévy-Pons, "Propagande et sentiment national pendant le règne de Charles VI : L'exemple de Jean de Montreuil," *Francia - Forschungen zur westeuropäischen Geschichte*, vol. 8 (1980): 127–146. Marc Bloch long ago made this argument in *Les rois thaumaturges* (Paris, 1924). Legal kingship, however, began right away, as royal acts make clear. Giesey, "Juristic Right," 7, points out the barons recognized Philip III as king prior to his coronation in 1270.

[18] G. Ducoudray, *Les origines du Parlement de Paris et la justice au XIIIe et XIVe siècle* (Paris, 1902), 55–56. L. Mirot, *Les insurrections urbaines au début du règne de Charles VI* (Paris, 1907), 26, n. 5, argues that the royal party skirted all large towns between Reims and Paris to avoid urban discontent that might force the young king into abolishing the aides.

[19] Isambert, VI, 538–539, also gives a list of the main princes and prelates in attendance. Mirot, *Insurrections urbaines*, ch. III, insists the November 1380 meeting was an Estates General of Languedoïl. Parisian bourgeois notables certainly participated, as did deputies from some nearby towns. C. Radding, "The Estates of Normandy and the Revolts in the Towns at the beginning of the reign of Charles VI," *Speculum* 47 (1972): 79–90, on the genuinely popular nature of these revolts.

[20] *Oeuvres de Froissart*, XVIII, 557. The meeting of those of the "blood" of the king, on the Thursday after Saint Martin's Day (which, in 1380, meant the next day, November 12), abolished the "aides" in the areas in which they existed. See Coville, *Les États de Normandie au XIVe siècle,* and Du Chesne, *Histoire des chancelliers,* 386.

Charles VI, in the ordinance issued following up the meeting, refers to the "general assembly of men of the clergy, nobles, bourgeois, and inhabitants of the good towns of Languedoïl" that he had convoked at Paris. Letters sent to Reims in March use the unusual phrase, the "men of the clergy, nobles, bourgeois and inhabitants of the good towns of our kingdom of Languedoïl,"[21] while those sent to Mantes in July use the normative phrase "the assembly of the three estates of our kingdom held at Paris."[22] The kingdom in question was surely not France: we have no evidence of deputies from the larger Langue d'Oc, nor, naturally, from Flanders, nor from Brittany, nor Burgundy.[23] The duke of Anjou, then regent, noted that the Parlement had offered counsel on its suggestions and "corrected" the agreement reached by the "king" (then twelve) and the assembly.[24] The princes clearly used every institution they could to gain legitimacy for their actions: the *Chronicle of Saint-Denis* says that Anjou called no fewer than seven extraordinary assemblies of the great men of the kingdom in 1381. Moreover, the royal government followed a practice typical of many town governments: convene the small body first, in November, and then call a "general" assembly to approve the prospective course of action, in January.

The January "general meeting of the three estates" in Paris decided to call meetings of local and provincial estates to vote new subsidies: that very act by the small town government in Sens led to a riot in March 1381, led by a rich merchant draper and "citizen of Sens," Jean Chasserat. He claimed the small council had violated standard practice by failing to sound the town bell and to assemble the largest possible group of citizens: according to Chasserat, the meeting had had only twenty men present. When he heard the rumor that this tiny assembly had approved a sales tax of ten percent (*2s/l*), he went immediately to the home of the lieutenant of the *bailli*, interrupting him at table. Chasserat claims he was polite; the lieutenant and other witnesses claim he swore ("by God's Blood!") and had assembled a large crowd at the butchers' street. The lieutenant, fearing for his life, sounded the bell and called an assembly.[25] The royal prosecutor claimed Chasserat had "offended the king in several ways" and demanded that he pay the staggering fine of 40,000 *l.p.*

---

[21] Varin, *Archives administratives de Reims*, III, document DCCCLIX.

[22] *Ordonnances*, VI, 606.

[23] Quite aside from the Estates General of Langue d'Oc and of Burgundy, the four members – Bruges, Ghent, Ypres, and the small towns (known as the Franc de Bruges) – met under the aegis of the Count of Flanders, and the Estates of Brittany met under the authority of their duke, not of the king. By agreement between Charles V and his brother, Philip, duke of Burgundy, the duke kept all taxes levied in Burgundy. In both Flanders and Brittany, the king of France did not directly levy taxes, nor did he get any of the revenue.

[24] Maugis, *Parlement*, I, 524.

[25] *Oeuvres de Froissart*, XVIII, 557. See also the discussion in G. Lurie, "French Citizenship and the Uprisings of 1380–1383," *The Medieval Chronicle* X (2015): 119–140.

The February 1382 Maillotins riot in Paris had the same origin: a small group, meeting at the Châtelet, stealthily pushed through the "approval" of the new taxes there. The population rose up against these "illegitimate" taxes: the king later pardoned most of the rioters, but he drowned the ringleaders. We might see such disturbances as a good example of the dangers inherent in the divided system of citizenship: general bodies, like the Estates General of Languedoïl, included virtually no one outside the governing elite. The leading merchants, who played so important a role in town governments, now had a liminal status in the general meetings: aside from participating in assemblies related to coinage, the extent of their presence in other meetings – including those voting on new forms of taxation – seems to have been limited from the 1360s onward. Men like Jean Jouvenel des Ursins, who headed Paris' government from 1388 to 1412, belonged to the world of the law: he worked his way up from being the king's *avocat* to a judgeship in the Parlement: one son became chancellor, and another archbishop of Reims.[26] Local and regional estates included a broad range of social groups, and merchants – often in conflict with guilds – dominated the town governments. This larger group of local citizens rejected the legitimacy of taxation to which it had not consented, as became obvious from the riots in Rouen, Paris, and elsewhere in 1380 and again in 1382.

The very day of Charles V's death (September 16, 1380) letters went out to every major town in the kingdom, and soon even to the rural *bourgs*, where the priest cried it from the church's doorstep, that the dying king had abolished all hearth taxes as a final gesture of pity for his people. Urban populations took a very dim view of the abolition of the *fouage* – paid mainly by rural dwellers – and the continuation of the indirect taxes, especially the five percent on sales, paid mainly by townspeople. Urban artisans seized the opportunity to claim the abolition applied to ALL taxes, including the indirect levies (*aides*) that fell much more heavily on the towns. At the same moment as the meeting of the "great assembly," the new chancellor (Miles de Dormans) had to give a speech to an angry crowd in Paris, announcing that the government would indeed abolish all levies: the regent issued the letters on November 16.[27] Michel Pintoin's *Chronicle of Saint-Denis* says that Dormans asked the people of Paris to stop their "commotions," and spoke to them on the theme: "novus rex, nova lex, novum Gaudium," that is, the new king meant a new law.[28]

---

[26] His grandfather was a draper at Troyes.

[27] *Ordonnances*, VI, 527. Lurie, "Uprisings of 1380–83,"; Radding, "The Estates of Normandy," and Mirot, *Insurrections urbaines*, which points out that only the *Chronique de Saint-Denis* mentions Dormans speaking to a crowd in this way; Mirot argues that the chancellor probably spoke to a delegation of Parisian notables, known to have petitioned the king and Anjou for the abolition of the aides.

[28] *Chronique de Saint-Denis*, 20–23. Dormans here aligns himself with royal lawyers such as Évrard de Trémaugnon. His use of the term "gaudium" [joy] surely resonated with those who believed the days of paying taxes had ended.

Moreover, Pintoin's *Chronicle* emphasizes the considerable grievances of French townsmen at their tax burden and their desire to be "nursed by the hope of liberty." The people wanted to be free from the "yoke of subsidies" [*jugum subsidiorum*]; a *mégissier* (leather worker) protested that Parisians wanted to curb the excessive cupidity of the lords [*cessabit dominorum excrescens cupiditas*]. Did the citizens not know, he asked, in what contempt the lords held them? Dormans, replying for the duke of Anjou, tried to reassure them, but the former merchants' provost, Jean Caldoë the younger – egged on by the crowd – told Dormans they would all "rather die than lose their ancient liberties." Dormans promised the next day to abolish the taxes, but the crowd sacked the tax offices, threw the money into the street, tore up the registers, and then turned on the Jews, some of whom were involved in the tax collecting.[29] Pintoin tells us that "this audacious spirit of revolt gained not only the Rouennais but all the people of France" [*totus populus Francie*]: in fact, tax resistance had begun in Languedoc, in 1379, picked up in Rouen in February 1381, and then spread to Paris and other towns.[30] As Bernard Guenée has written, speaking of the passions of this time – France against England; Burgundy against Orléans; poor against rich – hatred was "an essential given of political life."[31] Anjou became regent; the three other princes – Berry, Burgundy, and Bourbon – got the authorization to raise the child king.

The Parisians celebrated the end of the aides by pillaging the Jews on the rue des Juifs.[32] The royal letters mentioned the heavy burden placed on subjects by all the taxes for the wars, and carefully insisted that despite all their woes and difficulties, they had "voluntarily paid the said *Aides*, like our good and obedient subjects." This phrase sums up beautifully the continuing dialogue between the two conceptions: it emphasizes "good and obedient subjects," along the lines of the lawyers' royalist discourse, but it says they paid

---

[29] *Chronique de Saint-Denis*, 42–53. Caldoë had been merchant's provost from 1364–1371; in 1381, the provost was Jean Fleury, who fled in terror, given that the crowds had already sacked the houses of several municipal officials. Caldoë's eponymous father had succeeded Étienne Marcel at the head of Paris' government; Charles V allowed the senior Caldoë to be godfather to his son, Jean, born in 1363 (he died in 1366). On these events, see B. Bove, "Alliance ou défiance? Les ambiguïtés de la politique des Capétiens envers leur capitale, XIIe–XVIIe siècles, " Publications de la Sorbonne (2005): https://halshs .archives-ouvertes.fr/halshs-00640418/document

[30] *Chronique de Saint-Denis*, 128ff. Pintoin further explains that the revolts in the Flemish towns and in England encouraged this rebellious spirit in France. He claims (134–135) to have been an eyewitness to events in London and to have seen the people kick the head of Archbishop of Canterbury, Simon Cadbury, through the streets.

[31] B. Guenée, *L'opinion publique à la fin du Moyen Âge d'après la chronique du religieux de Saint-Denis* (Paris: Perrin, 2002), 65.

[32] The anti-tax disturbances in other towns invariably included pillaging of the local Jews, as in Rouen. Men-at-arms coming from Paris to Mantes pillaged Jews there, too. Charles VI expelled all the Jews in France in 1394, although the Jewish community of Montpellier, for one, remained. See Lurie, "Citizenship," ch. 2.

"voluntarily," that is, in the manner of free men, of citizens in a commonwealth. The chronicles insist that the Parisians accused those seeking to restore indirect taxes of being "enemies of the commonwealth."[33]

The king had not abolished taxation, only taxes created since Philip IV, to pay for wars; moreover, the abolition of taxes only nominally applied to Langue d'Oc, where estates immediately voted new levies, or Artois, whose estates continued their regular, annual levies.[34] Moreover, we know contemporaries viewed such "irrevocable" actions as far from certain: as soon as Charles V died, one group after another, from the *arbeletiers* of Rouen to the inhabitants of the viscounty of Turenne or the town of Abbeville, insisted on renewal of its privileges, above all its exemption from taxation. Towns and villages in Langue d'Oc demanded letters about reduction of their hearth counts, on the well-founded assumption that hearth taxes would continue to be levied, as they were in Langue d'Oc, and, starting in 1382, in Languedoïl.

We get some sense of the independence of meetings of estates from the situation in Langue d'Oc: when the duke of Anjou convinced Charles VI to name the duke of Berry as governor of Langue d'Oc, the previous governor, the count of Foix, held a meeting of estates at Toulouse, who demanded that Foix be retained. The *Chronicle of Saint-Denis* says the young king was so outraged that he came to the abbey to have the Oriflamme blest, intending to lead an army to Toulouse, but that the duke of Burgundy talked him out of it, due to the more serious troubles in Flanders.[35] Resistance to taxation in Langue d'Oc led to open revolt at Nîmes, where the town militia fought a battle with Berry's men-at-arms: after his victory, Berry carried out brutal repression in the city. At Amiens, Charles VI's letters of July 1385 revoked the right of the "mayors of the banners" of the guilds and the "men of common and small estate" to participate in the election of the mayor and *échevins*, on the grounds that they had perpetrated (in 1381–1382) a rebellion "against the royal majesty and the bien de la chose publique."[36]

In February 1382, a tax increase in Normandy led to the Harelle uprising in Rouen. The rioters pillaged public buildings, destroyed records, paraded the

---

[33] Lurie, "Citizenship," 50; they specifically targeted des Mares with this label. *Chronique de Saint-Denis*, 130, has them call those proposing taxes as "hostes reipublice," enemies of the commonwealth (again, the French on 131 calls them "ennemis de l'État").

[34] The Estates of Normandy also voted a hearth tax in 1381, to pay for troops, for the king's glorious accession, and for his "estate." They successfully insisted on regaining control of the collection and disbursement. Saint-Flour and surrounding regions assessed (January 1381) and collected (April) a *taille* to pay for the English to abandon Carlat: the Estates of the Auvergne had allocated 50,000 *l*. *Registres consulaires de Saint-Flour*, 107ff.

[35] Berry had a reputation for cupidity from his tenure in Poitiers: R. Favreau, *La ville de Poitiers à la fin du Moyen Age. Un capital régional* (Poitiers: MSA Ouest, 1977–1978), 2 vols.

[36] Janvier, *Livre d'or de la municipalité amienoise* (Amiens, 1892), 337.

town charter around the city, and forced the archbishop, Guillaume de Lestrange, to renounce his lordship over the city. Arnaud de Corbie, First President of the Parlement, and soon (1388) to be chancellor, explained to a new meeting of the Estates General of Languedoïl at Compiègne (March 1382) how the king needed money for war and for "son estat"[37]: "and it is not possible to conduct '*la chose publique*' without the *aides*." The Maillotins revolt broke out in Paris a few days later, and many other cities had similar revolts.[38] The king and his uncles marched on Rouen, hanged about a dozen men, fined both Rouen and Paris large amounts, but failed to get the towns to pay new taxes. The Normans voted new taxes the following month, and, in theory, kept control of the money.

These urban events illustrated the contentious nature of citizenship in the monarchical commonwealth. Oresme's text had clearly eliminated merchants and artisans from political citizenship at the level of the kingdom, but these two groups agitated strongly for greater input, particularly with respect to the tax system. They surely resented an outcome in which the taxes that fell on peasants – and hence hurt the income of noble landowners – were abolished, whereas the taxes that fell mainly on urban dwellers remained in place. The dénouement of the crisis took place in Flanders, where Charles VI's victory at Roosebeke (November 1382) gave the royal government a free hand to deal with the recalcitrant French towns. The *Chronicle of St-Denis* reported that the young king was particularly outraged to find that some Parisians had corresponded with the rebels of Courtrai, proposing an alliance.[39]

Pierre Cauchon, an apostolic notary at Rouen, considered Roosebeke to have been essential for the survival of both the kingdom and the social order: "if the Flemings had had the day for them, all nobility and gentility, clergy and rich bourgeois and men of name and estate would have been '*rués jus*,' and governed by scum and worthless men." Cauchon believed von Artevelde and his men intended to divide up the kingdom of France, with von Artevelde becoming "king of Paris."[40] Cauchon was hardly alone in this social conflict theory of political events. The Parisian government, let us recall, had written in July 1358

---

[37] "Estat" here means his establishment, or household. Letters cited in Du Chesne, *Chancelliers*, 371ff.

[38] *Choix des pièces inédites rélatives au règne de Charles VI*, 20, the carpenter Gervais de Grengies of St-Quentin explains he had gone to the "commotion" there in May 1381 because such assemblies were so uncommon. Mirot, *Insurrections urbaines* (20-21), points out, however, that St-Quentin had an anti-tax riot on October 9, 1380; most of the other northern towns – Compiègne, Amiens, Laon – had such resistance, often supported, as at Laon, by the town government. See Lurie, "Uprisings of 1380–1383." Pintoin [130–133] calls the idea that taxes could be abolished "ridiculous" in the eyes of prudent men.

[39] Pintoin, *Chronique*, 230–233; Juvenal des Ursins, *Charles VI*, 342, on the king's displeasure with the "very bad and seditious" letters written by the Parisians to the Flemings.

[40] Cauchon, *Chronique*, 172.

to town governments in the north, presenting a noble-commoner class warfare interpretation of that crisis. They told the town council of Ypres (July 11) that evil councilors had convinced the Regent Charles (V) to desire the "universal destruction of us, of the men of the good towns and all the countryside." When Meaux surrendered to him in good faith, the nobles destroyed "the cité and all the citizens." Nobles, without distinction of guilt or innocence, of good or bad, murdered, robbed, burned towns, killed "bonnes gens" without pity or mercy, "corrupted maidens, and raped wives in front of their husbands." The Parisians cited the good recommendations made by the meeting of the Estates General in Paris: among those recommendations was that "the great alienations of the patrimony of the kingdom to unworthy [*indignes*] persons" be revoked, and the properties be incorporated into the patrimony again.[41] Froissart, like Cauchon and the Parisians, took the class conflict line: "and everyone in the communities [the towns] said that the Gantois were good men and that they valiantly stood up for their freedoms [*franchises*], for which they had to be loved and honored by all people."[42] Froissart claims the duke of Berry told the young king that the Gantois wished to be masters of all, and to put an end to all nobility. Both Froissart and the *Chronicle of Saint-Denis* stress the extreme hatred between the two sides.

When the army returned to the capital, the king insisted on marching through the battered down gate of St-Denis, with three "battles" of men-at-arms in full dress. He refused to listen to a welcoming speech from the Merchant's Provost and ordered the immediate arrest and execution of the leaders of the Maillotins. The *Chronicle* reports that soldiers hanged some of them from the windows of their houses; 300 men met their deaths. The king had the leaders decapitated on the place de Grève, in front of the town hall. He ordered each household in Paris to send at least one member, bare-headed in sign of submission, to the square in front of the palace, where Pierre d'Orgemont read, in Charles VI's name, a long bill of particulars spelling out the misdeeds of the Parisians, but also offering them pardon, on certain conditions – not least of them heavy fines. The king used this money to reward those who had marched to Flanders with him and to pay off officials for their back-due salaries.[43] Me Jean de Romilly lost two rural manors in the bailiwick of Melun: one of the happy recipients was Nicolas Braque, one of the royal officials targeted by the Estates Generals of 1356–1357.[44]

One of those so punished was none other than Jean des Mares, whose eloquence allowed Charles VI to be crowned at age eleven. The dukes of Burgundy and Berry got revenge on des Mares by blaming him for the

[41] Delachenal, *Charles V*, t. II, pièce justificative, # XXXVI.
[42] Froissart, *Chroniques*, II, ch. CXXVIII.
[43] Mirot, *Insurrections urbaines*, 194–195.
[44] Mirot, *Insurrections urbaines*, 187, n. 1.

seditions; des Mares received no civil trial. Both the *Chroniques de France* and Froissart claim des Mares spoke to the massive crowd, demanding, to no avail, that his accusers show themselves and prove the charges against him. Asked to demand pardon from the king, he refused, saying that he had honorably served the three previous kings, and would ask pardon only of God. Charles V had in fact ennobled Jean des Mares in 1366 for those services: ironically, the letters stated that it was right to allow entry into the nobility of "those who have rendered and render still services to the king, in his affairs, in those of the kingdom and of la chose publique."[45] His execution took place "to the great displeasure of many notable worthy men, from relatives of the king to nobles to the people." Froissart expresses his astonishment at the execution of so honorable, loyal, and distinguished a royal servant: "the greatest part of the people cried for him."[46] Pintoin praises des Mares but suggests he might have urged the Parisians to arm themselves in 1382, for protection. Des Mares, who was then seventy and who had to be carried around the city on a litter, had been at the center of affairs for decades: as an *avocat* he pleaded, in 1359, for the arrest of Robert le Coq and other allies of Charles of Navarre; he had personally read the treaty of Brétigny to John II and was part of the council of seventeen men who discussed it; later, he would be one of the group of royal counselors who ruled, in 1368, that the treaty of Calais should be considered *caduc*.

The detailed account of Nicolas de Bosc, bishop of Bayeux, one of the French delegation to the peace negotiations with the English, at Boulogne in 1376, makes clear how important it was to the French negotiators that the representatives of the allies of the two sides not include delegates from Ghent, whose presence, they argued, would detract from the "honor, profit, and good example" of the negotiations, and worried about the "peril" that might result. In short, they wanted to make sure that rebellious urban subjects would not be recognized as legitimate participants in an international treaty negotiation.[47] We need not accept the premise of a planned general massacre of nobles, but from Étienne Marcel and the Parisians in 1356 through the aftermath of Roosebeke in 1382–1383, urban mercantile elites made an unprecedented attempt to share kingdom-wide political power.[48] They lost.

---

[45] Cited in F. Autrand, "Noblesse ancienne et nouvelle noblesse dans le service de l'Etat en France: les tensions du début du XVe siècle," in *Gererchie economiche e gerarchie sociali secoli XII–XVIII* (Florence, 1990), 611.

[46] A quarter century later, des Mares' children got permission to bury his body in a chapel he had founded at Ste-Catherine du Val des Écoliers' church, provided they did so without ceremony. Des Mares and the others executed after the Maillotins rebellion had been secretly buried in the church's cemetery. *Choix de pièces inédites relatives au règne de Charles VI*, v. 1, piece CXXVIII.

[47] "Voyage de Nicolas de Bosc," in *Voyage littéraire de deux religieux bénédictins de la Congrégation de Saint-Maur*, ed. E. Martène and U. Durand (Paris, 1724), 332.

[48] At least one of the Parisians executed in 1383, Nicolas Le Flament, had been pardoned in 1358 for supporting Marcel. Both Marcel and Philippe von Artevelde came from patrician

The contrast between the core lands of the French monarchy, which had adopted the vocabulary of "le bien de la chose publique" by 1380 at the latest, and outlying regions like Flanders[49], Dauphiné or Guyenne, remained true into the early fifteenth century. Among the princes, some documents preserved the old vocabulary, even in the 1380s. When the dukes of Brittany, Burgundy, and Bourbon made a treaty among themselves, taking care to specify that they excluded any hostility against the duke of Anjou (by then known as the king of Sicily), they claimed to be guarding "the good, honor, seigneuries, liberties, rights, heritages and profits" of the king. Twenty years later, when Isabeau of Bavaria allied with the dukes of Orléans and Berry, they agreed to act for "needs and affairs of the king, his kingdom, and *la chose publique* of the kingdom."[50] Under the influence of his father-in-law, Jean sans Peur, the young Dauphin, Louis, duke of Guyenne, issued a manifesto saying that the 1413 violation of his hôtel [in Paris] and imprisonment of his "favorites" were done with his consent and for the bien de la chose publique." Two years later, after the Agincourt fiasco, Jean sans Peur issued a manifesto against the Armagnacs, "men of small estate and unknown, who immersed themselves in the government of the chose publique."[51] How had the Armagnacs damaged the *chose publique*? They had kept Jean sans Peur away from the king, ruined the kingdom by borrowing huge sums, led the army to disaster at Agincourt, and tried to poison the Dauphin, Jean, duke of Touraine.

The princes of the blood had a very powerful sense that they were the "members" of the body politic, and that they, above all others, had a responsibility to preserve it, if the king could not. This metaphor made perfect sense in a culture in which the "house" took precedence over the individual: for them, the king, as head of the family (and its corporate self)

---

families. Crouzet-Pavan, *Enfers et paradis*, ch. 5, offers helpful cautions about the term *popolo* in thirteenth- and fourteenth-century Italian cities; her warnings apply as well to analyses of French municipal governments of the time.

[49] The famous 1296 agreement establishing the rights of Ghent's municipality stuck to liberties, rights, etc. Bi-lingual text in C.-L. Diericx, *Mémoires Les Lois, les Coutumes et les Privilèges des Gantois* (Ghent, 1818), v. II, 193ff. Guild statutes in this region spoke of the common utility, and of liberties, franchises, and privileges. No text in Diericx's collection uses the term "chose publique." In Flanders, three languages were involved – guild privileges in Ghent or Bruges were in Netherlandish: Walter Prevenier has made available online a clear summary on this issue: "La Flandre au Moyen Âge: Un pays de trilinguisme administrative," https://biblio.ugent.be/publication/382887/file/581689.pdf

[50] Douët-d'Arcq, *Choix des pièces inédites*, pieces XXVII and CXX. In a 1402 agreement, Isabella and the princes referred to the "honor of God" and of the king, and to the "honor and rights of the Crown." (#CII). Lurie, "Citizenship," ch. 5, contains many examples of their use of the term.

[51] AM Dijon, AA 12, I, pieces 7bis and 8. Jean of Touraine was married to Jean sans Peur's niece, Jacqueline. Jean of Touraine's sister, Marguerite, raised the boy in Hainaut. Philip the Bold had Jean and Jacqueline betrothed as infants; they married in 1415, soon after she turned fourteen. John died suddenly on April 5, 1417; Burgundian sources claimed he was poisoned.

was the head of the body politic, of which they were the "members" (as in body parts). Charles V had expressed these same sentiments in a letter to Jean IV of Brittany in 1372. The *avocat* Moulinet, speaking at the lit de justice for the lèse-majesté trial of Charles of Navarre (May 2, 1386), claimed that those who "commit felony against their seigneur" forfeited their goods to him, and that a vassal was completely "denatured to be against himself" in acting against a prince such as the King, "who is the head of *la chose publique* in his Kingdom."[52] The king as head of the "chose publique," however, went far beyond the extended royal family.

Louis, duke of Orléans, reacting to the "kidnapping" of the Dauphin by the duke of Burgundy in 1405, denounced this wounding of the king's lordship [*seigneurie*] and the estate of the queen, and claimed that "We all of his blood, and especially those who are closest to my said seigneur and to the crown must and are held to see to these matters," that is, to the defense of the Crown's power, lordship, and honor.[53] Despite this term's absence in his alliance with the other princes, Philip of Burgundy was an early proponent of usage of the concept. His letters establishing the Chartreux of Dijon in March 1385 mentioned that their prayers would serve for the "salvation of souls, for prosperity and for the good estate of the bien public." Philip commissioned Christine de Pizan to write her biography of Charles V: he died before she could present it to him. Her prefatory tribute to Philip's memory emphasized his lifelong commitment to "le bien public."[54]

3.1   Female Citizens: Christine de Pizan

Political citizenship in the larger commonwealth excluded most members of society. Christine de Pizan reminds us that, as a theoretical construct, civic society – the political community of citizens – excluded women.[55] In practice, some women did participate: queens like Isabeau played vital political roles during royal minorities or when the adult king was incapacitated, like Charles VI, and aristocratic women participated in practical politics. Pintoin lamented the death of Marguerite of France, daughter of Philip V, dowager countess of Flanders: he claims she had several times prevented her son, count Louis de Mâle, from allying with the English by making public reproaches of him as

---

[52] BNF Arsenal, M Français 2831, fol. 165: "ceux qui commettent felonnie contre leur seigneur luy sont acquis car le vassal si desnature d'estre contre luy mesmement contre tel prince que le Roy qui est chef de la chose publique en son Royaume."
[53] Douët-d'Arcq, *Choix des pièces inédites*, # CXIX.
[54] Denis Godefroy, ed., J. Chartier, *Histoire de Charles VII* (Paris, 1661), 366.
[55] Her political writings, prominent in the fifteenth and sixteenth centuries, fell by the wayside, except for R. Thomassy, *Essai sur les écrits politiques de Christine de Pisan* (Paris, 1838). He points out (iii) that the great seventeenth-century bibliophile Gabriel Naudé highly praised her *Livre de la Paix*.

a degenerate son, unworthy [*indigne*] of his inheritance. Pintoin claimed that Marguerite had personally prevented the marriage of Louis' heir, Marguerite of Flanders, with the duke of Lancaster; Marguerite instead married Philip of Burgundy, bringing both Flanders and Artois into the French royal family.[56]

Blanche de Navarre, widow of Philip VI, participated in the council held after Charles V's death, to discuss the regency. The early modern historian, the abbé de Choisy, in his *History of Charles VI*, says that "her age and her virtue gave her much *crédit* under the reign of Charles V," and the *Grandes Chroniques de France* emphasize visually her intercession, and that of her aunt Jeanne d'Évreux [widow of Charles IV], in the pardoning of her brother Charles, for the murder of the constable Charles d'Espagne.[57] Blanche's inventory after death survives, so we know something of the contents of her library: she left to Louis, duke of Bourbon, her copy of "our book of gouvernement des princes selon theologie" bound with a book on chess. Her book on the "gouvernement des princes selon philosofie, et le fist frère Gilles l'Augustin" [Giles of Rome] went to Robert Cresserel, a monk, "companion of our confessor"; Louis, duke of Orléans, got her sumptuously illuminated "somme le roi" [a treatise on morality composed for prince Philip in 1279, by "brother Laurent"] that had belonged to Philip IV. Blanche may well have admired "Master Honoré's" illumination, for example, of the four cardinal virtues – Prudence, Moderation (*Attrempance*), Force, and Justice – all of which involve women. In the illustration of "Prudence" we see a king reading in the company of three women, who are also reading.[58] (See Illustration 2.4) Female political agency ran in a direct line from Jeanne de Penthièvre to Yolande of Aragon, mother-in-law of Charles VII.[59]

[56] *Chronique de Saint-Denis*, 156–159.

[57] F.-T. de Choisy, *Histoire de Charles VI* (Paris, 1695), 6. Blanche was the daughter of the Jeanne de France dispossessed in 1316. Choisy is best known for his memoirs as a transvestite in Louis XIV's France. For the image of the pardon, see BNF, M Fr 2813, f. 395.

[58] www.bl.uk/IllImages/BLStudio/big/Add54180/add_ms_54180_f091v.jpg A second copy of the "La somme le roi" went to a woman in her household. M. Keane, *Material Culture and Queenship*; L. Delisle, *Testament de Blanche de Navarre reine de France* (Paris, 1885). Her manuscript collection consisted primarily of religious texts, and she left dozens of small legacies to religious houses. One of her most prized objects was the psalter of Saint Louis, passed by him to his daughter Agnès, duchess of Burgundy, by Agnès to her daughter Jeanne, Queen of Navarre, thence to her son-in-law Philip VI, who graciously gave it to his wife, Blanche. She left it to her "son," Philip, duke of Burgundy [Philip VI's grandson, by his first wife], to be keep in his "line." [Delisle, 29-30). See the analysis of her bequests in B. Buettner, "Le système des objets dans le testament de Blanche de Navarre," *Clio. Femmes, Genres, Histoire* 19. (2004): http://journals.openedition.org/clio/644

[59] M. Gaude-Ferragu, *La Reine au Moyen Âge. Le pouvoir au féminin, XIVᵉ–XVᵉ siècle* (Paris: Taillandier, 2014); F. Cosandey, *La Reine de France, Symbole et pouvoir, XVᵉ–XVIIIᵉ siècle* (Paris: Gallimard, 2000), part III, focuses on a slightly later period, but many of its points hold for earlier times. "Gilles l'Augustin" is Giles of Rome and we might

Yolande certainly held a major influence over the young king in the 1420s: she was widely believed to be a key patron of Jeanne d'Arc.[60] Allied with constable Richemont, she helped remove Georges de la Trémoïlle as Charles VII's favorite and paved the way for the reconciliation with Philip of Burgundy. Christine de Pizan had a keen political mind, and we might think of her famous *Livre de la Cité des Dames* not simply as a classic presentation of the women's side of the *querelle des femmes*, but also as a clear statement about the nature of her contemporary political community, in which women like Isabeau and Yolande played major roles. The work is often misleadingly translated as the *Book of the City of Ladies*, yet the French word *cité* [Latin *civitas*] meant more precisely the political community of the citizens, not just a large town. Christine de Pizan wrote extensively on politics, and she knew the difference: the *Cité des Dames* shows a political community of female **citizens**, led by the three metaphorical Ladies – Reason, Rightness, and Justice – who founded any legitimate political community.[61] Moreover, de Pizan's other writings, like the *Book of Peace* or *The Book of Polity [Livre du corps de policie]*, offered trenchant analysis of contemporary politics.

Her influence on the political thought of her time, and of the later fifteenth century, has been grossly underestimated. Historians have been quick to trace the body politic image back to John of Salisbury, and to note that both John and Christine de Pizan attributed the metaphor to Plutarch. Christine's description, however, differed radically from John's: his description gave a major role to the clergy. "All desire for [*envie*] religion and for God" held the place of the "soul in the *corps du bien et du fait commun*." [body of the common fact and good] He assigned to "presidents" in the service of religion – i.e., the high clergy – the place of the "soul in this body." Who doubted that the ministers of holiness were not the vicars of God? Within the body, the "soul holds the seigneurie and principality." The prince held the seigneurie of all the "*corps du bien commun*."[62] The prince was the head [*chief*] of the "bien commun." The judges and presidents of the prince were his eyes, ears, and

---

wonder if Blanche owned both the Latin original and a French translation, the latter of which she left to Cresserel.

[60] See Rohr, *Yolande of Aragon*. Jeanne d'Arc came from the frontier village of Domrémy; her house was in the French part of the duchy of Bar, a region ruled in 1429 by Yolande's son, René, acting in part for his great uncle Louis, duke of Bar.

[61] Forhan, *The Political Theory of Christine de Pizan*; Adams, *Christine de Pizan*, which has a full bibliography on the extensive recent literature about Christine's political thought. A. Kennedy, *Le livre du corps de policie* (Paris: Champion, 1998), offers a modern critical edition, with a glossary, based on a manuscript held at Chantilly (Musée Condé 294). It can be compared with the edition of R. Lucas, *Le livre du corps de policie* (Geneva and Paris: Droz, Minard, 1967), based on BNF, M Fr 12439 [available on Gallica]. Gallica also has several other manuscripts, including one the catalog identifies as in the hand of one of Christine's known scribes (Arsenal, Ms 2681).

[62] Here using Denis Foulechat's translation of 1372, found in BNF, M Fr 24287, f. 117r.

tongue; the knights and officers were the hands; the financial officers and guards were the guts [*ventre*] and entrails, from whom might come great illness. The *laboureurs* were the feet, attached to the earth.

The visual image used in the *Avis au roys* of c. 1350 shifted John of Salisbury's description; the artist makes the seneschals, *baillis*, and other judges the sense organs (eyes, ears, mouth) of the head, the "councilors and wise men" the heart, the knights the right arm, the merchants the legs, and the peasants [*laboureurs de terre*] the feet. The text tells us that "li Roys est li chies par dessus le pueple subget" [the Kings are the heads above the subject people].[63] (See Illustration 3.1.) This description is basically identical to the one in Jean Golein's 1379 "translation" of *De l'informacione principum*, a text written by an unknown author in the 1290s:[64]

> One must know that the Royal majesty is in the chose publique as a body is composed of diverse members in which the king or the prince holds the place of the head and the seneschals and the provosts and the judges have the offices of the ears and the eyes and the wise councilors the office of the heart and the knights defenders the office of the hands and the merchants running about the world are in a manner the legs and the laboureurs cultivating the fields and other poor peoples are joined in the manner of feet, and thus it appears that the princes are in the body politic as the head

In France, Christine de Pizan popularized the secular body politic, providing the clearest exposition of the "chose publique" of any fifteenth-century French author. Given her connections with Trémaugon and Gerson, the influence of Marsiglio of Padua's body politic – also secular – seems assured, yet Christine – unlike Marsiglio – maintained the king as the head of the body, and she did not assign to *baillis* and seneschals the high status of the *Avis au roy* illustration. Fifteenth-century French lay speakers invariably used her secular body politic. She combined a trenchant description of the actual political system of her time with a detailed, respectful presentation of each of the members of the body politic. In her eyes, as in the eyes of her contemporaries who held political power – either nationally, in their region, or in their town – the common

---

[63] Sheman, *Imaging Aristotle*, 94, connects this work to Giles of Rome's *De regimine*, as a text designed for the education of royal children, but textually the image has closer ties to the *De l'informacione principum*. "Chies" or, later, "chefs," was a common term for head in this metaphor.

[64] BNF-Arsenal, M 5199, 3r "L'on doit savoir que le Royal mageste est en la chose publique ainsi comme ung corps compose de divers membres ou que le roy ou le prince tient lieu du chef et les senescaulx et les prevos les juges ont les offices des oreilles des yeulx et les saiges conseilliers l'office de cuer // et les chevaliers deffendeurs l'office des mains et les marchans courans par le monde sont a maniere des jambes les laboureurs cultiveurs des champs et les autres pavres peuples sont adioints a maniere des pies // et ainsi il appert que les princes sont du corps de la chose publique comme le chef //. Equipe Golein, "Remarques sur la traduction de Jean Golein."

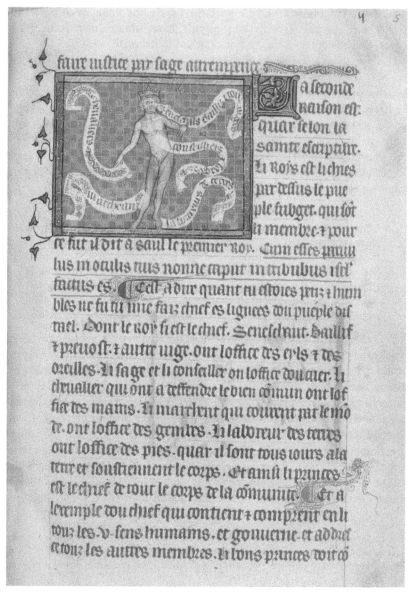

Illustration 3.1   Body politic: *Avis aus roys*: Morgan Library, Manuscript M 456, fol. 5r. Permission Morgan Library

people (artisans and peasants) had no business being involved in politics. The merchants and the bourgeoisie were to govern the cities, "because the common people do not generally have great prudence in word or, especially, in deed, in what touches governance [*policie*]." It followed that they should not interfere with the prince's laws, and that they should be led by the "merchants and the *gros*," who were to admonish the "simple and ignorant."

In her "chose publique", the prince was the head, "in that they [princes] are and must be sovereigns and from them must come the specific establishments, as well as the understanding of man." The knights and nobles were the hands and arms, defending the right [*droit*] of the prince and the *chose publique*. The people were the guts and the feet and the legs: just as legs and feet support the body, so, too, the *laboureurs* supported all the other estates. Her body politic has no special role for the clergy: they are no longer the soul of the body politic, and there is no discussion of the soul holding seigneurie over the body. The clergy were the highest of the three estates within the *cités*: clergy; merchants and bourgeois; and the "most common, like artisans and *laboureurs*."[65] The clergy was "high, noble, worthy of honor," but Christine de Pizan singled out their role in education, not spiritual guidance. She praised the students of the University of Paris, "disciples in the study of sapience," who sought the shining star of science, which was, along with the "height of knowledge" [*haultece de savoir*], the most worthy [*digne*] thing to which man could aspire. In an earlier passage, she made clear that by "man" she meant human: in a passage urging writers (*clers*) to praise the great deeds of worthy nobles for the edification of future generations, she argued they should also preserve the memory of those – any philosopher or man or woman – who surpassed others in wisdom or sapience. She cited "the wise Sybil" as her example. In the discussion of students, she cited the Stoics Cleanthes and Seneca, and praised Plato and Socrates, "who by the nobility of his engine was reputed the wisest of all mortals." Even her points of reference thus came from secular literature, not from the Bible or Patristic writing.[66]

Her description of the political life of towns accurately reflected actual practice in her time. She praises merchants and bourgeois, "of an ancient nation in lineages in cités": books, she tells us, call these men "citizens." They govern the *cités*, looking to the "fait du commun." The bourgeois and

---

[65] Her connection of the clergy to the urban body politic may reflect the tendency of the first and third orders to meet, with the nobles sometimes holding a separate session, at the bailiwick level. Such was certainly the case in many bailiwicks in both 1468 and 1484, for the "Estates General."

[66] On her sources, see Rigby, "The Body Politic," which has a clear summary. Evrard de Trémaugon, in his *Songe du Vergier* (1378), laid out clearly the importance of the "chose publique" to the legitimate prince, but he does not make specific use of – or describe – the body politic, although he does make reference to Marsiglio of Padua. Christine de Pizan clearly had connections to the Collège de Navarre intellectuals, among whom Jean de Montreuil deserves special mention in this regard, because of his interactions with Salutati. Montreuil's defense of Jean de Meung's *Roman de la Rose* touched off Christine's famous response and led to a literary quarrel with Montreuil on one side and Christine de Pizan and Gerson on the other.

the *gros* needed to restrain the *menu peuple*, to make sure no conspiracy came up against the prince. Calling to mind the riots of the early 1380s, she cautioned that in case of unduly heavy taxation, the "wisest and most discreet" should "humbly" go to the prince, to request redress. Far from the Aristotelian contempt of the world of commerce, she praised merchants as necessary to prince and society: without them, "the state of kings and princes and even the polity of *cités* and of *pays* could never survive."[67]

Christine de Pizan's body politic thus differed from that of John of Salisbury in fundamental ways. First, she rejected John's claim that the prelates were the soul of the body, with lordship over it. Second, she sided with the philosophers – those, like Oresme or Gerson, trained in the study of "sapience" at the Collège de Navarre – against the lawyers: again, she rejected the special place for "judges and presidents" as the eyes, ears, and tongue of the prince, thus moving beyond the *Avis aus roys'* image, too. Third, she provided an elaborated vision of the many roles of the common people, from the pursuit of knowledge by students to the many useful products created by artisans, and those circulated and sold by merchants. Fourth, with respect to Marsiglio, she differed in keeping the king as the head of the body politic. Fifth, as Tracy Adams has clearly demonstrated, she based her presentation on the actual political life of early fifteenth-century France, which she unmistakably viewed as a monarchical commonwealth, a "chose publique" or body politic in which the members, by carrying out properly their assigned roles, allowed society to function.[68] In her polity, the prince held supreme authority, but citizens governed the towns. She also applied this model in other works, like the *Book of Peace*.

In the fifteenth and sixteenth centuries, French orators returned again and again to the metaphor of the body politic. Members of the clergy might sometimes revive elements of John of Salisbury's body, with its special role for the clergy, but after Christine de Pizan's *Livre de policie*, the standard French body politic was **hers**, not John's. Christine wrote in French, making her ideas accessible to practical politicians; her secular political order, based on a monarchical commonwealth, with the king as the head of the body, made sense to the thoroughly profane citizens of late medieval and Renaissance France. In a world in which Isabeau of Bavaria and Yolande d'Aragon played such important roles in practical politics, we should not be surprised that a woman laid out the parameters of the key political metaphor.[69] Her *Livre du corps de policie*, *Livre de la paix*, and *Livre des fais* joined the canon of

---

[67] BNF, Arsenal, Ms 2681, f. 87v. : "l'estat des roys et des princes et mesmement la policie des citez et des pays ne se po[u]voit nullement passez."

[68] Adams, *Christine de Pizan*.

[69] Adams, *Isabeau of Bavaria*, reaffirms Isabeau's central role in the politics of 1400–1420 and puts to rest the many ridiculous slanders that have plagued her name since the 1420s.

fundamental vernacular texts created between 1370 and 1410 – Oresme's glossary to Aristotle, the *Songe du Vergier*, the *Songe du Vieil Pelerin*, and *Vivat rex* – that defined the French monarchical commonwealth for its citizenry. They were, in a sense, the counterparts to texts like Terrevermeille's royalist treatise, yet seeing contradiction in them pushes the contrasts too far. All agreed on the role of a strong king, on a unified monarchical commonwealth, and on the need for those charged with governance to look after the *bien de la chose publique*. Terrevermeille, after all, gave the estates the key role in establishing the law of succession: in December 1560, at the Estate General of Orléans, chancellor Michel de l'Hospital would make precisely the same argument.

3.2 *Vivat Rex*: Jean Gerson, Hero of the Commonwealth

> Those invited to council must fear [*Doutent*] God and conscience and put *le bien commun* before their own profit [*propre proufit*].
>
> Jean Gerson, *Vivat Rex*, 1405 [27v].

One of Christine de Pizan's intellectual companions was Jean Gerson, chancellor of the University of Paris.[70] Gerson today is best known for his role as the main driving force behind the Council of Constance (1414–1418); in an age with two (and, briefly, three) Popes, the supremacy of a council had considerable allure. Gerson remained for centuries one of the founding fathers of Gallicanism.[71] His political prominence, as one of the intellectual mainstays of French commonwealth ideology, is less appreciated. He gave his sermon, *Vivat rex*, to the Court in 1405; its staying power remained remarkable. The version of Gerson cited here was published by the *imprimeur du roi*, Vincent Sertinas, in 1561, at the height of the commonwealth revival, surely not a coincidence.[72] The

---

[70] That Gerson and Christine de Pizan interacted and shared ideas is certain; see C. Nederman, "Christine de Pizan and Jean Gerson on the Body Politic: Inclusion, Hierarchy, and the Limits of Intellectual Influence," *Del Storia Pensaro Politico* (2013): 465–480, for a summary of recent literature on this point. Christine also knew well Philippe de Mézières, author of the *Songe du Vieil Pelerin*. The standard modern biography of Gerson is B. McGuire, *Jean Gerson and the Last Medieval Reformation* (University Park: Penn State University Press, 2005).

[71] See Randall, *The Gargantuan Polity*, and J. Parsons, *The Church in the Republic: Gallicanism and Political Ideology in Renaissance France* (Washington: Catholic University of America Press) for details on this aspect of Gerson's life and work.

[72] Michel Simonin, "Peut-on parler de politique éditoriale au XVIe siècle: le cas de Vincent Sertenas libraire parisien" in *Le livre dans l'Europe de la Renaissance*, ed. H-J Martin and P Aquilon (Paris, 1988), cogently argues that Sertenas did, in fact, have a "politique éditoriale," and his status as the monopoly printer of royal edicts and ordinances suggests close ties to the chancellor, Michel de l'Hospital. One of the last books Sertenas published was a Latin *éloge* by the University of Angers, in honor of de l'Hospital. Simonon, p. 280, no. 122, makes no mention of *Vivat rex*, but does cite "plusieurs harangues" among the works issued in 1561.

same year, Sertinas also published two pamphlets about the Estates General of Orléans (which met in December 1560) and, remarkably enough, a copy of the Pragmatic Sanction [in French translation], another of the foundational texts of the monarchical commonwealth. Gerson's dual role as champion of conciliarism and hero of the political commonwealth made the connection between debates about papal and conciliar power in the Church especially relevant to concomitant French controversies over the powers of the king.[73] The rules governing succession to bishoprics and abbeys in France brought these two currents together, much as coinage brought together the economic and political dimensions of *la chose publique*. In these early decades of the fifteenth century, Charles VI issued ordinances about cathedral chapters electing new bishops, but actual practice did not catch up until 1438, when Charles VII issued the Pragmatic Sanction of Bourges, in which he made specific references to the precedents established by his father.

Gerson's sermon began with the thrice repeated "Vive le roi," once each for the corporal, spiritual, and civil bodies of the king. Speaking on behalf of the University of Paris, which desired "the good government of all la chose publique," he first denounced the "detestable schism" destroying the Church, and ended with a long diatribe about the loose morals and outrageous luxury of French elites.[74] The University, he told his listeners, had the medical faculty for corporal life; faculty teaching moral philosophy, ethics, economics, and politics, for civil life; and the theology faculty for spiritual life. The university took in students from all over France, indeed all over the Christian world, who came to acquire doctrine and sapience, a virtuous science that nourished "all the body of *la chose publique* in the guts [*ventre*] of the University, to give birth to men of all perfection." The king's corporal life, after all, required him to be accompanied by "preudes gens d'estat", of good morals, devoted to God and very loyal to the *bien public*.[75] Gerson and Christine de Pizan did much to popularize this latter term, *bien public*, which henceforth would appear in parallel with the earlier *bien de la chose publique*.

---

[73] Lange, *First French Reformation*, has renewed our understanding of this connection.

[74] The moral decline/wretched excess theme has existed since time immemorial, but Gerson had a point. The BNF's exhibit on *Paris 1400: les arts sous Charles VI*, presented some of the extraordinary artworks, in a wide range of media, produced in years around 1400. http://mini-site.louvre.fr/paris1400/paris1400/01parcours-expo/09.html, offers a sampling of works of extraordinary beauty, but whose cost surely rankled contemporaries. Gerson also provided a litany of the sufferings of ordinary French people: heavy taxes; goods seized by unpaid soldiers; women raped; churches violated. Juvénal des Ursins closely followed Gerson's lead in his description of the difficulties of the 1430s.

[75] Reading their texts, I get the sense of a fruitful dialogue rather than a straightforward influence of Gerson on de Pizan. Their texts differ in one important aspect: Gerson, unlike de Pizan, frequently cites the Christian Bible and Patristic writers, hardly surprising in a theologian at the center of conciliarism.

The king's second life, his "civil and political" life, which is called "estat ou dignité Royale," because of its link to the *bien commun*, was worth more than the individual life: the proof was that the king often risked his corporal life for the sake of the civil one. The civil king had to protect order, defined as the combination of four cardinal virtues: prudence, moderation, force, and justice, the last of which had inextricable ties to the love of God. These pillagers – flattery and lying; voluptuous living; rapacious barratry; and "estat oultrageux" – could destroy "the civil life [*vie civile*] of all the *chose publique* in the head and in the member" because they dissipated not only the "state of the Royal seigneury" but each of the three estates – clergy, nobles, bourgeoisie – of "this sovereign state."[76]

"Rex qui sedet in solio iudicii intuit suo dissipate omne malum.[77] Le Roy qui est assis au trosne de justice, dissipe par son regard tout mal ou toute malice." [The king sitting in the throne of justice dissipates by his gaze all evil or malice.] Later, Gerson repeated the theme, this time saying the king's gaze destroyed all malice. President Charles Guillart, in a speech to which Francis I took such strong exception in July 1527, perhaps had Gerson in mind when he repeated this phrase; *avocat général* of the Parlement of Toulouse, Pierre de Belloy, in his *De l'Authorite du roy et crimes de leze Majesté, qui se commettent par ligues* (1587) reproduced the quotation.[78]

Gerson focused particularly on tyranny: "like venom or poison kills the human body, so tyranny is the venom, the poison, the sickness that kills all political and Royal life." Why? Because tyranny wants to take everything for its own profit: where royal government wants strong subjects who develop their sapience, tyranny wants ignorance and weakness. "It prevents studies so that none can acquire science; it forbids all honest assemblies and nourishes division by false reports and envy." The only thing worse than tyranny, is sedition, "popular rebellion without rhyme or reason": here we see Gerson's consonance with Christine de Pizan, who similarly feared popular rebellion. Gerson's King "does not submit to his subjects, but to reason, to which according to divine and natural law, every seigneur and others owe obedience and subjection."[79] Gerson recommends that the king call both nobles and clerics from the principal parts of the kingdom to tell him of the miserable state

---

[76] Gerson, *Vivat rex*, 14v.

[77] In the wording of the Clementine Vulgate, *Proverbs* 20, 8: "Rex qui sedet in solio iudicii dissipat omne malum intuitu suo." Lefevre d'Etaples put it this way in his translation: "Le Roy qui sied au siege de iugement, dissipe tout mal par son regard."

[78] S. Daubresse, *Le Parlement de Paris ou la Voix de la Raison (1559–1589)* (Geneva: Droz, 2005), traces du Belloy's use back to Guillart.

[79] Gerson mentions Seneca, without specific reference, to support this point. He is also glossing Giles of Rome, *De regimine*. Alain Chartier, when giving a speech to the Emperor Sigismund, as ambassador on behalf of Charles VII, borrowed from *Vivat rex* in his discussion of princes.

of the people: "because they know it better by seeing and by experience than those who are only at their ease in their *hôtels* in Paris, where is all the fat of the kingdom." The king needs good counsel: "A King without prudent counsel is like the head of a body without eyes, without ears, and without a nose."[80] The king was not a "singular person," but a "public power established for the health/salvation [*salut*] of all the communality." This word "salut" carried two meanings, first, health (the "conservation of something in a happy and amenable state"), and second, eternal salvation. Centuries later, in a perfect example of the long-term linguistic shifts in terms for the polity, the first *Dictionnaire de l'Académie Française* (1694) chose as its initial example of usage, "Le salut de l'Estat, de la Republique. le salut public."[81]

The king was the head of a body, whose members consisted of the various estates of the kingdom, each doing their appointed task. The king's life was not simply corporal, but "civil and mystical." For Gerson, the most horrible sight imaginable was this mystical body tearing itself to pieces; throughout, Gerson emphasizes the responsibilities of the prince to his subjects and reminds Charles VI that just as poison kills the body, so the poison of tyranny kills "all Royal and political life."

What did the tyrant do? He oppressed the people by foreign men-at-arms, by heavy taxes, by preventing the study of sciences, by forbidding "honest assemblies," and by nourishing divisions based on false reports and rumors. Gerson here borrowed closely from the list provided by Évrard de Trémaugon, in chapter 131 of his *Songe du Vergier*, in lines spoken by the cleric.[82] Sedition – violent rebellion by the populace – was sometimes even worse than tyranny: Gerson here harkens back to the events of 1380–1382, and clearly worries that France, and Paris, would soon be consumed by similar violence.[83] How right he was.

Gerson's oration offers us an unparalleled explication of the term "Estat," as he and his contemporaries understood it: he has an entire section on "*estat outrageux*, which is against the fourth virtue, moderation [*attrempance*]." "Estat outrageux," like a famished werewolf [*loup garou*] is never satisfied,

---

[80] Here we can see Gerson [27v–28] glossing John of Salisbury and the *Avis aus roys*, and implicitly differing from Christine de Pizan in his body politic. She would not issue her version until two years later, perhaps in an effort to move beyond Gerson's less precise image.

[81] http://artflsrv02.uchicago.edu/cgi-bin/dicos/pubdico1look.pl?strippedhw=salut In Nicot's 1606 *Thresor de la langue francoyse*, he provided the coupling: "Pourchasser le salut public, Ad salutem reip. incumbere." His use of the term *res publica* (reip.), and the absence of any mention of "estat" make clear the primary sense of *salut* as referring to the body politic, that is, the commonwealth.

[82] The knight regularly refutes the cleric's positions when he disagrees with them; he did not do so in this case.

[83] Gerson was attending the Council of Constance in 1418, at the time of the massacres in Paris; he never returned to the city, fearing Burgundian retribution.

"it's an abyss without bottom or border." Bloodsuckers [a favored term for tax officials from the fourteenth to the seventeenth centuries] "eat all, day and night," letting no one rest. He cites famous historical examples of cruelty (Nero, et al.), but "*Estat outrageux* does it not carry out the same or worse cruelties? Does it not live from the blood and flesh of the poor?" It squanders the substance not of one or two or even 100, but 1,000 on excess in meat, horses, dogs, presumptuous buildings, pomp, and even on "vanities covered under the shade of alms or religion." No kingdom is so stable, strong, and honorable that it will not be lost "when this monstrous beast *Estat outrageux* rules and lives there." Gerson points to Greek and Roman examples, and to the Popes of the previous forty years. Taxes were to be levied in equity and equality "on all of the corps mystiq." Failing to do so introduced "a pernicious thing in the *chose publique*," that is, "Sedition." [40v][84]

Speaking of France, he asked, how it was possible all the taxes levied, together with demesne revenue, could not pay for "l'estat commun"? "*Estat* must properly be separated from *Outrage*, first among prelates, among great seigneurs: why? First for good example: because by the seigneurs are the people seduced." He soon launched into a long tirade about luxury at Court, by seigneurs and councilors, including the high clergy: he compared *la chose publique* to the king's mother, who seeks to feed him sustenance, only to have it stolen by those sitting at his table. "*Estat* in clergy, as in the knights [*chevalerie*] and the bourgeoisie must separate itself from *outrage* by instituting good ordinances and keeping them: moderation in food, dress, dishware, jewels, precious stones, and in those things that nourish *outrage*." One's consumption should not be to the prejudice of "the other members of *la chose publique*."[85] *Estat*, a term then sometimes used to describe the government, clearly here has its more usual sense, of Estate [as in Three Estates, or forms of status, or the Royal Estate, referring to the king]. The outrage, or perhaps one might say violence, attached to "estate" is the excess of its members, yet Gerson's connection of the prelates and the seigneurs to "Estat outrageux" carries clear overtones of the rulers, the leaders of *la chose publique*. He denounces excessive gifts, which "anger three or four for one made happy" and which impoverish 2,000 to gratify one: gifts to men of low descent, in particular, cause resentment among the "preux and valliant," who cannot afford to dress like the parvenu.[86] Gerson's text provided a clear statement of

---

[84] E. Kantorowicz, *King's Two Bodies: A Study in Medieval Political Theology* (Princeton, NJ: Princeton UP, 1957), 218–220 on Gerson and the "corpus reipublicæ mysticum." In his discussion of the French case, Kantorowicz ignores Christine de Pizan.

[85] Gerson, *Vivat rex*, 37v–39. A. Chartier, *De Vita curiali*, ed. F. Heuckenkamp (Halle, 1899) took up these same themes.

[86] This advice antedates by more than a century Machiavelli's comments about excessive princely gifts – the Florentine's comments about generosity have far more medieval resonance than is often believed.

the civil life of the French kingdom: it rested on justice, on Aristotle's giving to each his own, and on each order accepting its place, both its rights and its responsibilities.[87] Gerson's kingdom was a commonwealth, in which the tax revenues were to serve the needs of "la chose publique," the *res publica*.

3.3   The Assassination of the Duke of Orléans, 1407

Las ou sont ores les preux & les vaillans champions de la chose publique, qui pour le bien commun contre les tyrans exposoient iadis leurs corps & chevance, comme Iudas Machabeus, Mutius, Themistocles, Trasibulus, Mathatias & autres : ou sont tels personnages pour delivrer ce Royaume de miserable oppression ? A eulx doibt estre la voye de faire ce que dit Seneque ; qu'il n'est sacrifice tant plaisant à Dieu que la mort d'un tyran.

Gerson, *Vivat rex*, 1405.

The crime of human lèse-majesté divides in four degrees. The first is, when the injury is done directly against the person of the Prince. The second is, when the injury or offense is directly done against the person of his spouse. The third degree is, when it is done directly against the person of his children. The fourth is, when it is directly done against "le bien de la chose publicque."

Jean Petit, justifying the murder of the duke of Orléans, 1408.

Two years after his famous sermon, Gerson was involved in another controversy that would have a long life. On November 23, 1407, a group of eighteen armed men intercepted Louis, duke of Orléans, younger brother of Charles VI, as he walked down the rue Vieille du Temple, returning from a visit to Queen Isabeau. Jean sans Peur, duke of Burgundy had sent the assassins, a fact that he quickly admitted. Burgundy initially fled Paris, but he returned, with a large armed retinue, in March 1408. In an extraordinary session of an enlarged royal council, Duke Jean had the theologian Jean Petit justify his act, in a famous discourse defending this specific act of tyrannicide. Petit accused the deceased duke of Orléans of all manner of perfidy, including an attempt to use a poisoned apple to kill the king. Most of his contemporaries, most famously Gerson, denounced Petit's reasoning, but we need to get beyond the tyrannicide issue to look at the vocabulary used by Petit and by Orléans' later defender, the abbé of Cerisy (Thomas du Bourg), who shortly after Burgundy left Paris presented [September 11, 1408] the case of the dowager duchess of Orléans against Jean sans Peur, to virtually the same audience addressed by Petit in March.[88] Gerson himself, as we see above, had cited Seneca in praise of killing tyrants.

---

[87] Oresme's *De moneta* specifically said that sound currency is necessary in order to give to each his own fair share. Christine de Pizan shared these views.

[88] E. Emerton, *Humanism and Tyranny: Studies in the Italian Trecento* (Gloucester: Peter Smith, 1964, reprint of 1925 edition Harvard UP), reproduces four important contemporaneous Italian treatises on tyranny, including works by Salutati and Bartolus.

Petit accused Louis d'Orléans of all four types of human lèse-majesté – against the king, his spouse, his children, and "la chose publique." In his discussion of civil laws, Petit accused Orléans of being a traitor [Petit uses the word "trahaison"] on several grounds, not least of them making an alliance with the "mortal enemies" of the king and the kingdom: in so doing, Petit argued, Orléans had committed treason against the king, his sovereign lord, and against "la chose publique."[89] Later, in fleshing out his charge of lèse-majesté in the fourth degree, he noted that Orléans had made alliances with "enemies of the Kingdom," who were "expressly enemies of *le bien de la chose publique*"; he had also raised troops for fourteen or fifteen years, said troops having "eaten and forced into exile" the poor people of the kingdom, and he had falsely raised *tailles*, ostensibly for the king's needs, but really for his own. Speaking to the king and his council a few weeks later, the abbé de St-Fiacre, responding on behalf of the dowager duchess of Orléans, stated the duke of Burgundy had acted "hardly out of good cause, nor for the *bien commun*, but from ambition, covetousness, and desire to dominate."[90] Under Gerson's leadership, the University of Paris denounced Petit's doctrine as heretical (1408).

Gerson spent the next decade leading the charge against Jean Petit. The two men and Pierre d'Ailly had been part of the French delegation to Benedict XIII[91] in 1407, seeking to get him to agree to resolve the Schism. This mixed delegation well illustrated the relationship of the Schism to the Orléans-Burgundy conflict. The duke of Orléans supported the Avignon Pope: the duke of Burgundy stood strongly against him, and the army that laid siege to Benedict's palace in Avignon from 1398 to 1403 was led by Geoffroy de Boucicaut, brother of the marshal (Jean) and a close ally of the ducal family.[92] D'Ailly and Gerson allied with Orléans; Petit was a Burgundian. Petit had led the University of Paris' 1398 protest against Benedict XIII levying a tax on them; in 1406, at a large council of the French Church, speaking for the University, Petit called Benedict an inveterate schismatic and virtual heretic. That assembly insisted on clerical election to benefices – eliminating papal nomination – and continued the ban on papal taxation, but it did not claim Benedict had no jurisdiction over the faithful.[93] At the council, Pierre d'Ailly had been one of those

---

[89] Both Orléans and Burgundy had negotiated with the English at various times.

[90] Monstrelet, *Chroniques*, ch. XXXVI on the murder; ch. XXXIX for Petit's speech.

[91] The Catholic Church considers this "Benedict XIII" an anti-Pope and does not recognize his papal name. The official Benedict XIII was Pope in the 1720s.

[92] Marshal Boucicaut had accompanied Jean sans Peur on the Nicopolis expedition; Boucicaut was one of the few nobles not executed, supposedly because of his prior kindness to Muslim prisoners.

[93] Charles VI issued letters, in February 1407, declaring that benefices would be filled by election: bishops would be elected by the cathedral chapter. *Ordonnances*, IX, 180ff. These letters – in Latin – followed up July 1406 letters (IX, 110) – in French – in which Charles VI spelled out that benefices such as bishoprics would be filled by election, during the

supporting Benedict. The split between d'Ailly and Gerson on one side and Petit on the other thus had roots in church politics, and the connection between royal power and papal power – as in this case – did not always flow in the direction of the king allying with the Pope against the theoretical powers of a church council. On the contrary, Charles VI and Charles VII both sided with the conciliarists, and claimed the support of church councils for one of the most important intersections of Church and monarchy: nomination to benefices.[94] In royal ordinances, Charles VI and Charles VII would refer to these positions – archbishop, bishop, abbot, prior, dean of chapters and colleges – as *elective* benefices.

After the murder of Orléans, Jean sans Peur had sought advice from his councilors in a meeting at Lille: Monstrelet says the justification of the deed given then by Simon de Saulx, abbé of Moutiers-Saint-Jean, provided most of Petit's arguments.[95] Jean sans Peur ordered copies made – both richly illuminated and basic text – of Petit's four-hour speech of March 8, 1408; Petit personally supervised their production. After the abbé of Cerisy's September riposte, Petit wrote a *Second Justification of the duke of Burgundy*, which took a harder line.

This confrontation formed part of a war of words between the Armagnacs and Burgundians. Local officials must have spent most of the next decade or more scratching their heads, trying to make sense of the incessant flood of royal letters accusing first Jean sans Peur and then his opponents of traitorous deeds. The seneschal of Carcassonne received letters in September 1417 telling him not to recognize Jean sans Peur's title as duke of Burgundy, because of his "traitorous and damnable murder" of Louis d'Orléans, and then five months later, in letters sent by Isabeau, in conjunction with Jean sans Peur, heard that the count of Armagnac had attacked the "bien commun" with tyranny and violence.

Charles VI's September 1417 letters spoke of the great prosperity of "our kingdom, and its chose publique" at the time Jean received his duchy: Burgundy had raised up men of "small estate" who carried out several "commotions" in Paris (a reference to the Cabochiens of 1413),

---

Schism. Charles VII made specific reference to these letters – and to the fact that the civil war had made it impossible to enforce them – in the Pragmatic Sanction.

[94] The Council of Constance (1418) had recognized the right to election, except in three cases: death of the benefice holder while in Rome; benefices held by cardinals; benefices removed from the incumbent for cause. In France, by far the most important exception was the second one, because the archbishops were often cardinals. N. de Valois, *Histoire de la Pragmatique sanction de Bourges sous Charles VII* (Paris, 1906). Kings, Popes, and powerful aristocrats, it need hardly be said, regularly interfered in these elections.

[95] A. Coville, *Jean Petit* (Paris, 1935), provides the running narrative. Coville cites (119) Pierre de Marigny, who participated in the peace conference at Vernon in July 1413, and Pierre Aux-Bœufs, along with de Saulx and two others, as the team behind Petit.

issued letters "bad, scandalous and offensive to our Royal Majesty," and acted against the *bien public* of our kingdom. The February 1418 letters attacking Armagnac claimed, on behalf of Isabeau of Bavaria, "having for occupation the government and administration of this Kingdom," that she wanted to repair the "*chose publique* of his Kingdom." Armagnac and his accomplices had acted in "dishonor" of and "prejudice" against the "bien public of this Kingdom." Charles VI's 1416 letters to the seneschal, in Latin, make clear the meaning of "chose publique": "nobis & rei publice regni nostri" [in the French texts, *Nous et la chose publique de nostre royaume*].[96] What the poor seneschal made of the constant stream of contradictory messages – which went back to the time of the 1407 murder – one can only guess.

Gerson returned to the attack after the collapse of the Cabochiens and the Burgundian ascendency in Paris in the summer of 1413: he spear-headed an effort to have sixty theologians condemn Petit's arguments as heretical. The University duly ordered the text burnt in front of Notre-Dame: Jean Le Févre claims that the king had Petit's bones dug up at Hesdin, where he had been buried, to have them burned on the same spot; Monstrelet says Petit's enemies did indeed propose such a course of action, but nothing was done.[97]

Gerson was still not satisfied: he wanted the Council of Constance to condemn Petit's propositions, which it did on July 6, 1415, but, to Gerson's great regret, only on one point, and without mentioning Petit by name. Jean sans Peur, who heavily pressured the Council, did not disagree that the propositions condemned deserved to be so; he claimed, with some justifica-tion, that Petit had not made them in his speech, and so should not be cited by name. Gerson had cleverly modified Petit's wording: Petit had justified the killing of "this tyrant," meaning Louis d'Orléans, precisely on the grounds that Louis was a traitor both to Charles VI, his king, and to the *chose publique*. Gerson had the University and the Council condemn the proposition that it was licit to kill "all tyrants," in particular condemning those seeking the death of their prince. At Constance, Gerson went one step further: he added a condemnation of the proposition – rejected as not established in Petit's writing by the University of Paris – that "Every tyrant must and can be killed with praise and merit by any of his vassals or subjects and by any manner [. . .]

---

[96] Bessé, *Recueil des documents*, letters from September 5, 1417 begin on 119, those of February 1418 on 161. Virtually every document reproduced in this collection refers to the "chose publique" and/or the "bien publique." The double usage, as in the 1418 letters, appears multiple times: see, for example, the letters confirming powers granted to Louis de Guyenne, at that time Dauphin, in December 1409, for the "needs and affairs of our Kingdom and its chose publique" ("besognes et affaires de nostre Royaume & la chose publique d'iceluy," 51ff).

[97] Le Févre, *Chronique*, 155.

no matter what oaths or confederation has been made with him [. . .]." Petit's text makes no such statement, so rejection of this principle again could not be tied directly to him.

Gerson could point to other passages in Petit's speech and his *Second Justification*. In the speech, Petit had cited multiple other authors approving of tyrannicide: Thomas Aquinas, Cicero, and Boccaccio, among others. He may not have specifically justified the murder of any tyrant, but he did paraphrase Boccaccio that "There is no more agreeable sacrifice than the blood of a tyrant." Boccaccio, of course, was paraphrasing the same passage from Seneca that Gerson had cited in *Vivat rex*. Gerson won the public relations battle: Petit's *Justification* for the murder came down to posterity as a text justifying tyrannicide.[98]

In his final writings, a meandering text known as the *Treatise against builders of burials*, Petit continued to justify Burgundy's action. If it was reasonable to act in self-defense, Petit claimed, how much more so to "save several bodies [. . .], the *cité* or province and the *bien publique*." To the duke of Burgundy, above all others, belonged the obligation to defend the public interest: "First that Monseigneur of Burgundy in the degree of his estate was a loyal defender. The second that of the *chose et bien publique* he was a loyal defender."[99] From beginning to end, Petit and Gerson essentially agreed on the key point at issue here: the primacy of the *chose publique*.

This quarrel ended up transcending the Burgundy-Orléans divide. In the first decades of the seventeenth century, when Popes again asserted their supremacy in secular matters – above all through the writings of Cardinal Bellarmine – their opponents reached back to Gerson for support. Edmond Richer proposed to issue the collected works of Gerson but was unable to do so in France; Paolo Sarpi, in Venice, instead published two short works by Gerson and an abridged edition of Richer's defense of Gerson: Richer renounced it. Richer, unable to publish Gerson, instead published other Gallican texts, including writings of Gerson's old ally, Pierre d'Ailly. In the immediate aftermath of Henry IV's assassination, the Sorbonne faculty met to discuss tyrannicide. Led by Richer, they denounced any such doctrine, and on June 4, 1610 reissued their 1408 decree against Jean Petit![100]

3.4   From *Vivat Rex* to the Treaty of Troyes: The "chose publique," the "bien public," and the Civil War

Verbales sumus et voces, non res recipimus [We are verbal; we take more from words than things.] . . . Est virorum conventus, qui se ad invicem

---

[98] Coville, *Jean Petit*, 520–523, on the textual changes.
[99] Coville, *Jean Petit*, 295–296.
[100] The Parlement of Paris condemned and burned Bellarmine's attack on Barclay, much to the chagrin of Marie de Medici and the papal nuncio, Roberto Ubaldini.

decipiendum, boni communis simulatione, communicant [(The Court is) a convent of men, who, under the simulation of the public good, assemble in order to trick each other] ... Ecce nos curiales fortune servi [We at the Court are serfs to fortune.]

Alain Chartier, De vita curiali, ca. 1427.[101]

Alain Chartier's lament, which borrowed heavily from Gerson's *Vivat rex*, reflected the sorry state of affairs at Charles VII's court in the late 1420s. His portrayal of a vicious cycle of self-serving princes and counselors alike owed much to Seneca, whom he cited at the end, but it should not mislead us about their continued service to king and "patrie." The "corrupt Court" motif lasted until the end of the Ancien Régime, but relative few of the elite chose the life of *otium* for any extended period of time. Chartier belonged to a milieu – one that included other prominent figures like Miles de Dormans, Pierre d'Ailly, Jean Gerson, Nicholas de Clamanges, Jean de Montreuil, and Alain Chartier – that had absorbed the vocabulary of the republic, of "la chose publique," in the last quarter of the fourteenth century.[102] The concomitant development of this vocabulary by Italian Humanists, such as Salutati, affected the younger French generation, like Montreuil, whose 1384 meeting with the Florentine chancellor provided an impetus to French developments already well underway. Salutati provided writers like Gerson, de Pizan, Montreuil, and Chartier with a broader range of Classical citations with which to support the public good.[103]

In some ways, the Treaty of Troyes grew out of the legalities created by the Treaty of Calais. Charles V's insistence that all the fiefs regained in the 1370s were inalienable parts of the royal demesne, and that the king of France could not legally renounce his superior jurisdiction over any fief held of the Crown, meant that the logical step for Henry V was to take the Crown, not a collection of fiefs. The 1406 memoir attached to the *Grandes Chroniques de France*

---

[101] Chartier, ed., *De Vita Curiali*, 18–22.

[102] Dormans and Jouvenal des Ursins trained in law, at Orléans; the others in this group studied at the Collège de Navarre, so we see the same split evident from the 1350s onward. Montreuil served as Dormans' secretary.

[103] Literary scholars, concerned with the distinction between those whom many of them qualify as theologians, like Gerson, and those they call Humanists, like Montreuil, have noted the greater use of Classical references in Montreuil's work, but *Vivat rex* contains constant references to Classical authors and examples. On d'Ailly, F. Oakley, *The Political Thought of Pierre d'Ailly* (New Haven and London: Yale UP, 1964) and L. Pascoe, *Church and Reform: Bishops, Theologians, And Canon Lawyers In The Thought Of Pierre D'ailly (1351–1420)*, Studies in Medieval and Reformation Traditions, n. 105 (Leiden: Brill, 2005). Alain Chartier's *De Vita curiali* (1427?) shows the obvious influence of Italian Renaissance thought. P. Bourgain-Hémeryck, *Les œuvres latines d'Alain Chartier* (Paris: CNRS, 1977), has the text and offers valuable insights in her introduction. See also the helpful review by P. Santoni in *Journal des Savants* v. 3, 3 (1980): 217–224. This historiography sadly ignores Christine de Pizan and her original contributions.

reiterated the point that the king of France could not renounce "sovereignty and *ressort*" over lands belonging to the kingdom of France. Henry V solved that problem by getting Charles VI to name him as heir. Jean de Terrevermeille, in his *Tractatus de iure futuri successoris legitimi in regiis hereditatibus* (1419), anticipated that action: he insisted that the king of France had no right to name an heir – the law determined succession. Jean Juvénal des Ursins, later archbishop of Reims and brother of the chancellor Guillaume Juvénal des Ursins, made precisely the same argument in defending the rights of Charles VII on various occasions, such as his 1435 "Audite celi" and his 1439 speech at the Estates General.

The Treaty of Troyes is festooned with commonwealth vocabulary. Article 6 named Henry as Charles VI's heir,[104] while article 7 made Henry regent,[105] because of Charles' incapacity to rule: Henry was to rule "for the honor of God, of Us and our companion [the queen], and also for the *bien public* of the said kingdom." In article 8, Henry promised to maintain Parlement in its "sovereignty," while in article 9 he swore to preserve the "rights, customs, privileges, pre-eminences, liberties and franchises" of the peers, nobles, "*cités*," towns, and other groups. Like his grandfather, Henry insisted that the commonwealth's citizens swear to the treaty: he demanded that "the great seigneurs, barons and nobles and the estates of the said kingdom, both spiritual and temporal, and also the *cités* and notable communities, the citizens and bourgeois of the towns of the said kingdom" swear an oath to keep the treaty and recognize Henry as heir and regent.

The Treaty did maintain certain principles of French law: once Henry became king, lands, like the duchy of Normandy, that he had conquered, were to return to the Crown of France. Henry promised (article 23) to levy taxes only "for the *bien public* of the said kingdom of France" [*quam pro Bono publico ipsius Regni Francia*]. Here we see a remarkable direct influence of Trémaugon and of Philippe de Mézières: the former had stated that the king may tax free subjects only "for the defense of *la chose publique* and with their permission when the ordinary revenues do not suffice for defense of the *pays*"; the latter changed the wording just a bit, the king must tax his subjects only for "*le bien public*."[106]

---

[104] Article 24 stipulated that Henry's heirs would inherit both kingdoms, which had to remain united.

[105] The later Charles VII had already proclaimed himself regent for his incapacitated father. Article 7, in the official Latin, read in the key sections: "ad totam vitam nostram Facultas & Exercitium Regendi & Guberna Rempublicam praedicti Regni Franciae ... Quibus quidem Facultate & Exercitio Regendi, sic penes dictum Filium nostrum Regem Henricum existentibus, efficaciter, & diligenter, & fideliter laborabit & intendet ad id quod esse possit, & debeat ad honorem Dei, & Nostri, & dictae Consortis nostrae, necnon ad Bonum publicum dicti Regni." From Rymer, *Fœdera*, IX, 895–904, consulted online: www.british-history.ac.uk/report.aspx?compid=115256.

[106] Trémaugon, *Songe du Vergier*, I, 140; Mézières, *Songe du vieil pelerin*, 346. "Ordinary" revenues, prior to 1523, had the specific meaning of revenues from the royal demesne.

Parlement registered the treaty eleven days after it was signed: its new First President, Philippe de Morvillier, provided an explanation in French of the Latin text and each person present then swore an oath, in Morvillier's hands, to observe the treaty.[107] Ordinances issued in the name of Henry VI as "King of France" made reference to the "bien public": his renewal of the privileges of the University of Paris cited their services with respect to the "support of the Christian Faith, to the multiplication and growth of diverse sciences, and to the conservation of the *bien public* of our said Kingdom." In the next clause, he broadened his scope, the University now provided for the "exaltation of our said Faith and of the *bien public* of Christianity."[108]

The unity of the commonwealth had implications for matters such as the principle of the inalienability of the royal demesne, which undergirded the Troyes negotiations. This principle did not restrict grants of apanages to princes of the royal blood, but it did mean that the king always retained his "souveraineté et ressort" in the lands of an apanagiste, or in those granted as a *douaire* to his queen. One interesting dimension of the civil war was that the faction in control of Charles VI invariably used his authority to manipulate past grants of apanages. When Jean sans Peur had control of Charles VI in April 1412, for example, the king issued letters rescinding grants to various royal princes – his uncle, the duke of Berry; his cousins, the Orléans brothers; their allies. The king then stripped the officers of these areas of their posts, claiming to restore the order kept by his predecessors, "for the good of our Seigneury and of the public good."[109] In letters given under the influence of the duke of Burgundy, the king cited his legitimate possession of the lands in question at the times of the sales, alienations, or leases, but the letters issued on August 22, after the reconciliation of the princes at Auxerre, specifically rescinded all such sales and grants, and restored both lands and offices.[110] Three months later, in a session at which only the duke of Burgundy, among the princes, was present, the king shifted course, again recognizing the rights of those who had purchased or leased the confiscated properties.

---

[107] French text in Cosneau, *Les grandes traités de la Guerre de Cent ans*, 102–115; Latin official text in Rymer, *Fœdera*, IX, 895–904; I mention Morvillier here because we will see that his son would be Louis XI's controversial choice as new chancellor in 1461. D. Kern, "The Political Kingdom: Parliamentary Institutions and Laguages of Political Legitimacy in England and Castile, 1450–1520," Ph.D. thesis, 2012, Georgetown University, explains the expanded use of this term in England in the middle of the fifteenth century.

[108] *Ordonnances*, XIII, 168ff.

[109] *Ordonnances*, X, 3ff. The remarkable chronology of this incessant changing of key personnel has been carefully reconstructed by A. Demurger, "Guerre civile et change-ments du personnel administrative dans le royaume de France de 1400 à 1418: l'exemple des baillis et sénéchaux," *Francia* 6 (1978),available online: http://francia.digitale-sammlungen.de/Blatt_bsb00016281,00167.html

[110] *Ordonnances*, X, 20–21.

The Treaty of Troyes involved not alienation but royal succession: Henry V would get the kingdom, not parts of it as "lord," as his great-grandfather thought he obtained at Brétigny. By the 1370s, Charles V's lawyers had insisted that ancient laws banned women from the succession, or from the ability to transmit such a right; eight years after his death, a royal lawyer "discovered" the key clause in the Law of the Salian Franks, a sixth-century compilation; French lawyers would soon trumpet the Salic Law as a fundamental constitutional principle in France.[111] Charles VI voided his son's right to inherit by declaring him guilty of "horrible and enormous crimes" (article 29).[112] Little wonder that the lawyers defending the rights of the later Charles VII emphasized the inviolability of the Salic Law, but lost in that simple equation is the obvious fact that had his crimes made the young Charles ineligible to inherit, Salic Law would have passed the throne to the king's nephew, Charles of Orléans, then a prisoner in England.[113] If the chronicler Monstrelet is to be believed, Henry V's last words, to his brother the duke of Bedford, were that Orléans, the count d'Eu, and the lord of Gaucourt, then held in England, should not be released, under any circumstances, until the infant Henry VI reached adulthood.[114] Henry knew full well that excluding Charles, the Dauphin, alone did not, under French law, make Henry V or his son legitimate heir to the French throne.

Henry's words suggest that Barbey is certainly correct that the principles set forth in Terrevermeille's *Tractatus* had become widely known in elite circles, yet we must be wary about overemphasizing the importance of Salic Law.[115] Terrevermeille, born into a family of jurists at Nîmes, was a *docteur ès lois*, having studied at Montpellier with Jacobus Rebuffus. He served as a consul at Nîmes (1399) and was later an *avocat du roi* at the seneschalsy of Beaucaire.

---

[111] E. Viennot, *La France, les femmes et le pouvoir, Volume 1, L'invention de la loi salique (V^e–XVIe siècle)* (Paris: Perrin, 2006). A memorandum of 1406, added to the text of the *Grandes Chroniques de France*, uses the term "loi salicque" to justify inheritance "from male to male of male descent." See also C. Taylor, "Salic Law and the Valois Succession to the French Crown," *French History* 15, n.4 (2001) for a discussion of the sudden emphasis on Salic Law in the 1410s.

[112] Charles V's letters for his plenipotentiary at the Bruges negotiations in the 1370s had specifically stated that the king, holder of the *dignitas* of the Crown, would forfeit his right to rule, if he violated his coronation oath, so the principle of forfeiture for heinous, infamous crimes had been set by the Crown itself.

[113] In 1453, the Parlement of Paris officially ruled that Henry VI could not inherit France through his mother's rights, on the grounds of Salic Law, so that his "coronation" had been null and void.

[114] E. McLeod, *Charles of Orléans Prince and Poet* (NY: Viking Press, 1970), 158. Charles, count d'Eu, son of a constable of France and a direct male line descendant of Robert of Artois, brother of Saint Louis, was also legally in line for the throne.

[115] Barbey, *La fonction royale*.

Unsurprisingly, given his training in Roman law at Montpellier, Terrevermeille, in addition to bringing "Salic Law" front and center in royalist ideology, also further developed the ideas of a kingdom of France, distinct from other entities, and of the independence of the king's power. Rather than seeing Terrevermeille as a jumping off point for those traditions, however, in both cases the events of the 1360s to 1419 show that he merely systematized ideas already widely accepted by the political elite.

No manuscript of Terrevermeille's work survives, but it was published in Lyon in 1526. That published version brings us full circle, back to the political vocabulary of Terrevermeille's own day: the letters of permission from Louise of Savoy (then regent for her son, held in captivity in Madrid) allowed Constantin Fradin, "citizen of Lyon," to print Terrevermeille, whose work was "very useful and profitable to 'la chose publicque.'"[116]

In a time of royal incapacity, the coherent idea of a French Commonwealth strengthened. The fundamental laws theoretically limited the king's freedom of action, in the name of protection of the rights of the Crown: the Parlement of Paris long believed itself the guardian of this principle. The rules of royal succession had a short tradition in Charles V's lifetime; his lawyers, and those of his son, sought to solidify it. The Salic Law took succession rights out of the hands of the king: the son-less king could not, for example, claim his daughter would succeed – the Treaty of Troyes does **not** suggest, in any clause, that Catherine of France was bringing a right to the French throne through her marriage to Henry. In fact, several clauses deal with her new rights as queen of England and with rights she might have as a widow, with respect to her dowry and *douaire*. The Treaty specifies that **Henry's** heirs will get both kingdoms: it says nothing about Catherine's heirs.[117] Pierre Fevin, doubtless speaking for many of his contemporaries, wrote: "And this point seemed strange to many in the kingdom of France, but they could not do otherwise for the present."[118]

The commonwealth, however, specifically meant France. Decades later, when Charles VII's armies drove the English from France, in the negotiations between the count of Dunois and the seigneur de Montferrant, who had sided with the English, Montferrant promised to take an oath to the king to be a "good and loyal Frenchman." [*bon et loyaux François*] The inhabitants of the town of Acqs made the same promise: the count of Foix, acting for the king, gave them six months to decide to declare themselves "French" or to emigrate. The estates of the Bordelais, and the town government of Bordeaux, used

---

[116] On Gallica, image 4 contains the permission.

[117] In 1428, Parliament passed an act forbidding Catherine of Valois from re-marrying without Henry VI's adult permission [Henry VI was then seven years old], yet Henry V's male line died with Henry VI, while Catherine's grandson, descended from her liaison with Owen Tudor, became Henry VII.

[118] Émilie Dupont, ed., *Mémoires de Pierre de Fenin* (Paris, 1837), 137. Fenin [Févin] was royal provost at Arras, a town under Burgundian control.

a different formula: they promised to be "good, true, loyal, and obedient subjects of the King of France."[119]

These documents take us down to the local level, where the commonwealth vocabulary gradually came to be the basic framework for political discussions. Let us turn now to Louis XI's assault on the commonwealth, and to the reaction of three groups of citizens: clergy, nobles, and sovereign court judges. In Chapter 5, we will shift to the town and local records to see how the *cité* and the *pays* lent themselves so easily to the vocabulary of the *bien de la chose publique*.

---

[119] *Ordonnances*, XIV, 137 (Montferrant), 138ff (Bordeaux), 158 (Acqs). The fifteenth-century sources are unambiguous: the "chose publique" in question was France. The many works of Nicole Grévy-Pons, focused on the writings of Jean de Montreuil, provide abundant bibliography and clear presentation of the French "identity" issue in the primary sources.

4

The Commonwealth under Siege

Louis XI

4.1 The Tyrant

> There was demanded the duchy of Normandy, the Somme towns, and various other demands for each one [... and thus] the *bien public* was converted into *bien particulier*.
>
> Philippe de Commynes.[1]

> Louis XI, this tyrant who respected nothing.
>
> Jules Michelet.[2]

Louis XI was a tyrant. Blinded by Commynes' brilliant summation of the end of the War of the Public Good, many historians have not taken seriously the Ligue du Bien Public.[3] We are easily misled by the obvious particular interest [*bien particulier*] of each prince, and by their cynical and selfish deals with the king in the fall of 1465. Several of them paid with their lives for their stupidity. The chroniclers all agree that the princes made little effort to restore the *bien public* in September 1465, yet the evidence of those same chroniclers shows that Louis XI did restore the commonwealth, to some degree, and that pressure from the princes played a key role in his decision to do so. Thomas Basin, bishop of Lisieux, admits that some of the princes turned against "right and just" actions and sought personal gain. He minces no words about the

---

[1] Commynes, *Mémoires*, I, ch. 12.

[2] Michelet, *Histoire de France*, VI, 78. In many respects, Michelet began the process by which Republican historians in France turned Louis XI into the father of the centralized State – a tyrant, but also a ruler who overcame the feudal elite to help transform France. That dualism remains in modern biographies, like those of P. M. Kendall, *The Universal Spider, Louis XI* (NY, 1970), P.-R. Gaussin, *Louis XI, un roi entre deux mondes* (Paris, 1976), and Jean Favier, *Louis XI* (Paris: Fayard, 2001), who downplays the "tyrant" charge. A. Bakos claims the "tyrant" charge came after his death – the evidence suggests otherwise, in my view – and offers a fascinating book on *Images of Kingship in Early Modern France: Louis XI in Political Thought 1560–1789* (London: Routledge, 1997).

[3] Malcolm Vale, in his review [*Medium Ævum* 57, n. 1 (1988): 138] of Peter Lewis' collection of essays on fifteenth-century France, refers to the "smokescreen of the bien public."

"perfidy" of these [unnamed] princes, who prevented any benefit [*fructum*] from coming to the "*reipublice*."[4] Even so, he defends the princes against the charge of selfish intentions. Full restoration had to wait until after Louis' death, but we should not underestimate the immediate aftermath of 1465, nor should we underestimate the extent to which most of French society violently rejected the changes he made.

From his first days as king, returning from exile in Burgundian lands, to brave "the only army one risked encountering at the frontier or on the road, that of haranguers, flatterers, and solicitors who rushed ahead, who barred the passage," Louis XI's driving principle was to attack anything related to his father.[5] Quite apart from firing officials, he moved the primary royal residence in Paris out of the hôtel de Saint-Pol and into the Tournelles, and then the forbidding fortress of Vincennes, in the woods east of town. He also removed the keeping of the royal chronicle from the abbey of St-Denis. Virtually alone among French kings, he chose not to be buried at the royal necropolis of St-Denis, but at Notre-Dame de Cléry at Orléans.[6]

Philippe Contamine rightly sees the bigger picture: Louis was trying out a new method of governance of his kingdom.[7] The king's supposed remark that "We have as great a power [*puissance*] to remove them [offices] from you as to give them or re-give them to you, as seems good to us [*se bon nous semble*]" sums up his perspective. Breaking with the traditions of his father meant a wholesale attack on the commonwealth, which staggered under the blows. The commonwealth fought back in 1465, and Louis XI settled for a compromise that neutralized the group he thought most dangerous, the princes. When he died in 1483, the outpouring of opprobrium for his actions was unprecedented in monarchical history.

Louis XI rejected the commonwealth; in addition to abrogating the Pragmatic Sanction of Bourges from 1438, he carried out an unprecedented purge of royal officers. Fearing this rumored outcome, Philip the Good of Burgundy, at a royal banquet shortly after the coronation, had knelt and asked the king to confirm all the officers of his father, and to forgive those the king considered enemies. Louis specifically exempted seven [unnamed] people, but publicly promised to grant Burgundy's request. Replacing key members of the royal council at the start of a new reign was hardly innovative, and the practice

---

[4] C. Samaran, trans. and ed., *Thomas Basin, Histoire de Louis XI*, 3 vols (Paris: Société d'édition "Les Belles Lettres," 1963-1972), vols. 2-3 co-edited by M.-C. Garand, I, 176-177. In this bilingual edition, Samaran translates "reipublice" by "État" in all cases.

[5] Michelet, *Histoire de France*, t. VI, 7. As Dauphin, Louis attacked royal prerogatives: in 1453, he renamed the "conseil delphinal" a sovereign Parlement, implying it had final *ressort* in Dauphiné.

[6] Huguenots desecrated his tomb during the Wars of Religion.

[7] P. Contamine, *Guerre, état et société à la fin du Moyen Âge. Études sur les armées des rois de France (1337-1494)*, (Paris: EHESS, 1976), 404-407.

continued long after Louis XI, but his wholesale institutional slaughter of appointed officers had, and would have, no other parallel in French monarchical history, aside from the chaotic interlude between the death of Louis d'Orléans (1407) and the 1418 massacres in Paris.

Louis XI replaced the chancellor, the First President of the Parlement, the *procureur général* and both avocats at the Parlement, dragged his feet on renewing the Parlement and the Chamber of Accounts, and moved quickly to remove the officers of the Cour des aides, the generals of finance, the royal treasury [Chambre du Trésor], even local officials like *baillis* and *sénéchaux*, the provosts, the royal notaries, receivers, and the *grenetiers* of the salt monopoly. Philippe Contamine checked the accusations of the chronicles: he found that Louis XI removed seventy-five percent of the captains in charge of a *compagnie d'ordonnance*, seventy-five percent of the governors of provinces and major fortresses, and a similar percentage of the *baillis* and seneschals, as well as firing the generals of finance, and the receivers and controllers general.[8]

Louis later regretted this "folly and error," as he reputedly admitted to Philippe de Commynes. In the mid-1460s, he would rehabilitate many of those, like Antoine de Chabannes, whom he disgraced at the outset of the reign.[9] Louis XI himself believed his attack on the commonwealth led to the War of the Public Good. The most important outcome of that episode had nothing to do with the greedy princes; Louis restored many of the displaced officers and issued (1467) an edict that firmly established legal life tenure for royal officials. In the ordinance, he began by speaking of the "great mutation" in offices at the start of his reign; he blamed it on the machinations of unnamed individuals.[10] Because of the doubts engendered by this "mutation and destitution," many officers "do not have the zeal and fervor for our service that they would otherwise have without the said doubt." The king stated that – "considering that in our officers consists, under our authority, the direction of actions by which *la chose publique* of our kingdom is policed and maintained, and that they are the essential ministers of the kingdom, as members of the body of which we are the head" – henceforth they could lose their office only by death or legitimate resignation, or by seizure through judicial trial.

The judicial and financial officers, the key "members" of the commonwealth's "political body", thus obtained from the War of the Public Good a powerful reaffirmation of the principles of the commonwealth, and of their place in it. They wasted no time in making their power manifest: as soon as

---

[8] P. Contamine, "Louis XI, la prise de pouvoir, la foire aux places (juillet-septembre 1461)," in the collection of Contamine's articles, *Des Pouvoirs en France, 1300–1500* (Paris: Presse de l'ENS, 1992).

[9] Guillaume Cousinot, *bailli* of Rouen, offers a classic example: imprisoned in 1461, two years later he became a royal chamberlain, with an annual pension of 3,000 *l*. He became ambassador to Milan in 1466 and attended the Estates General of 1484.

[10] *Ordonnances*, XVII, 25ff, October 21, 1467.

Anne de Beaujeu had Charles VIII renew the entire Parlement (September 12, 1483), in an edict that recognized their sole jurisdiction over internal affairs – including disputes over offices – the Parlement began to settle disputes, and even to restore the exiled councilor, Martin de Bellefaye. Bellefaye was one of those aggrieved by Louis' unpopular henchman Olivier Le Daim; in a fitting symbol of the new order, the Parlement named him as one of its envoys to the Estates General of 1484. The Parlement tried and hanged Le Daim.

The treaty of Saint-Maur, October 29, 1465, which ended the War of the Public Good, began with the statement that the princes of the Ligue du Bien Public had taken up arms because they had tried to reach the king with "some remonstrances and requests touching the fact and order of justice and the bien public of the Kingdom," but that having been prevented from doing so, and fearing for their lives, they had taken up arms. The treaty marked an agreement with Louis XI to do "the necessary things for the good and utility of the chose publique of the Kingdom." Articles I–VI largely dealt with the conflict, and with matters such as amnesties and return of seized property, but article VII demonstrated an obvious concern for a key element of the "bien public": "that the towns and communities that adhered to one party or the other will not be mistreated for doing so, and there will not be done or given any trouble, disturbing, or preventing of their rights, privileges, estates, octroys, franchises, and liberties, which thus will remain as they were before the said divisions."[11]

Louis XI followed up the Treaty with letters for François II, duke of Brittany, recognizing the duke's right to the *régale* of Breton churches, and his rights of justice, *ressort*, safeguard, and sovereignty over them.[12] François II had done homage/obedience to Louis XI, in 1461, in the same manner as previous dukes had done to previous kings: in Breton eyes, that meant the duke of Brittany got recognition for his "sovereign" rights, which included the right to mint both gold and silver coins, to ennoble, and to pardon, and both *ressort* and "sovereignty."[13] Anne of Brittany shared her rights with Charles VIII, but when the king's death made her a widow, by the terms of their marriage agreement, she regained sovereign authority in Brittany. She immediately returned to the duchy, minted money showing her seated in majesty; identified as Anne, queen of France and duchess of Brittany; ennobled some of her subjects; issued pardons; and carried out "other marks of sovereignty," in the

---

[11] Dom Morice, *Preuves*, III, column 104–109. The letters for François II, duke of Brittany, begin on column 110.

[12] The *régale* gave the duke the right to the revenues of all Breton bishoprics between the death of the sitting bishop and the inauguration of the new one. The king generally had this right in the north of France, the pope in the south.

[13] *Journal de Jean Le Fèvre, évèque de Chartres*, ed. H. Moranville (Paris, 1887), t. I, shows a similar usage of "sovereignty" for the count/countess of Provence in the 1380s, when Marie de Blois convinced the various towns in Provence to recognize her son, Louis II, as Count.

words of the sixteenth-century Breton historian Bertrand d'Argentré.[14] A few months later, she had to marry Louis XII, and the duchy again reverted to at least partial royal control, although by all accounts Anne still maintained considerable authority. Louis XII immediately issued royal letters guaranteeing Breton rights, liberties, and privileges.

François II and Anne certainly protected their own rights and interests, but they could also rightly claim to protect the "bien public" of Brittany. They sought to preserve the principles that: Bretons would be adjudicated by Breton law in Breton courts, and that Breton bishops would come from Brittany. Anne sought to preserve the principle of the Estates voting all taxation. At the time of their marriage, Louis XII explicitly promised all three. She even included a clause in the marriage contract about the second son (or daughter, absent a son) inheriting Brittany, so that it would not fall to the heir to the throne of France.[15] The end result was mixed: the Estates did vote (and collect) the taxes, and Bretons remained subject to Breton law and courts; some bishops came from Brittany in future years, but others did not.[16] After Anne's death, Louis XII despoiled their second daughter, Renée, giving the duchy instead to their first daughter, Claude, who married Francis I, thus tying the duchy to the king of France. Renée would prove to have a profound influence on France in the 1560s and 1570s: she provided key leadership for the Protestant cause, while her daughter, Anne d'Este, duchess of Guise, would be a formidable figure among Catholics. Both women had superior educations, and we know from the inventory of Renée's library her access to leading works of political philosophy.[17]

Claude's son François was the last person to take the oath as duke [1532]. He did so in classic fashion: stopping outside the Sainte-Melaine gate of the city,

---

[14] D'Argentré, Histoire, 705. M. Walsby, The Counts of Laval: Culture, Patronage and Religion in Fifteenth- and Sixteenth-Century France (Aldershot: Ashgate, 2007), on the role of the Laval family, particularly Françoise de Dinan, countess of Laval, and governess of Anne in 1491, at the time of the marriage.

[15] Morice, Preuves, III, column 711ff, contract between Anne and Charles VIII; column 729, separate letters from Charles VIII in response to Estates of Brittany, in which he promises not to levy taxes except in following the procedures used by the dukes. D. Le Page, "Noblesse et pouvoir royal en Bretagne (1480–1540)," in J. Kerhervé, ed., Noblesses de Bretagne (Rennes: PUR, 1999): 129–149, emphasizes the considerably better terms granted by Louis XII, and Anne's expanded power in the duchy during their marriage, as against her union with Charles VIII.

[16] The cahiers of the Estates of Brittany invariably included an article about reserving Breton benefices for Bretons.

[17] E. Rodocanachi, Une protectrice de la réforme en Italie et en France: Reneé de France, duchesse de Ferrare (Paris, 1896), ch. 8. She turned her daughters over to the Italian prodigy Olympia Morata, who knew both Latin and Greek; the three girls – Anne, Lucrezia, and Eleonora – read the Classical sources, in both languages. See 182–184 for a list of books bought for the girls in the 1530s – Aristotle, Cicero, Euclid, Ovid, Erasmus, et al.

he received an endless parade of town militia units, officers, and clergy. **Outside** the city, after the bishop of Rennes had commanded the captain of the city to open its gates, François swore – on local relics and the Gospels – to protect the Church and its ministers in their "rights, privileges, and ancient liberties," and to do the same for the nobility, for the towns, and the "people." Only after having done so did young François ride around to the traditional Porte aux Foullons and enter the city.[18] The ceremony – similar to those used in other towns for the counts of Flanders or dukes of Burgundy, as well as kings – emphasized reciprocity: the prince receives submission, freely grants and recognizes privileges and liberties, returns the keys to the city, and only then enters. The exchange takes place outside, prior to actual, physical entry into the city, which was predicated on the reciprocal ritual at the gate. Free men, after all, accepted submission only on reciprocal terms

Basin compared the rebels of 1465 to slaves or mercenaries on a ship: could not even slaves or mercenaries revolt against a leader struck with a "sort of madness?" Surely a free people [*liberorum populorum*] could revolt legitimately against a leader who did not govern the republic according to the advice of good and wise men.

> He devastates and ruins everything, strips citizens of their patrimony and goods [*cives patrimoniis et bonis*], solely by his own will [*pro sola voluntate*] and not by any law [*iuris*], exiles men who deserve reward from the republic [*republica*], attacks the liberty of the Church, disdains all divine and human law, does everything according to his whim [*libito*], without reason, forces women to marry against their will and that of their families ... and in a general manner reduces all his subjects to misery and servitude [*servitutem*]

Why should not the leading men of the republic – "in such a devastated and desolated republic" – revolt against such a master, "for the common salvation" [*pro communi salute*] so that the republic could be governed by justice? Basin concludes by asking why any citizen who loves justice would not act against "I do not say so insolent a king, but more the most iniquitous tyrant and the cruelest beast."[19] [*non regis, sed iniquissimi potius tyranni et cruentissimæ bestiæ*]

Georges Chastellain, the Burgundian chronicler, condemned Louis in even harsher terms, in a famous dream sequence in which a regally dressed

---

[18] Morice, *Preuves*, III, col. 1001–1008. On Anne's legacies, see C. Brown, ed., *The Cultural and Political Legacy of Anne de Bretagne. Negotiating Convention in Books and Documents* (Cambridge: D. S. Brewer, 2010). Henry [II] succeeded his brother François as duke of Brittany, but never went through the ceremony. He was the last person to bear the title.

[19] Basin, *Louis XI*, I, 178–181. The litany of charges against Louis, such as the claim that he forced young women to marry against the will of their families, remains constant in all the sources, such as the manifestoes of 1465.

noblewoman seeks entry into the king's chambers. She asks: "How is it that the time has come now when the French royal dignity has descended on a bestial man, and the worthiest and the holiest crown of the earth sits on the hair of a non-human man [*homme non homme*]?" She warns the king that human voices murmured against him, and mouths ground their teeth at his deeds, "because in you [*toi*] appears nothing but ingratitude, but giving bad for good, and plain and evident intention to want to destroy your relatives and friends, on whom you turn your back, hateful and ill-counseled."[20]

Basin gets easily dismissed: after all, he personally suffered disfavor, disgrace, and exile, he participated in the Ligue du Bien Public, and was one of the thirty-six *commissaires* named in the agreement between the king and the princes.[21] Chastellain, another admittedly biased witness, cites the same errors by the king and denounces Louis XI. Yet Jean Maupoint's chronicle, which strongly favors the king, tells us, with respect to the massive dismissal of officers in 1461, there were many complaints about "such a sudden change and in such great number,"[22] and he relates as well, the great joy of "gens de bien" when the old officers were restored in the fall of 1465. Jean de Roye's chronicle baldly states that "most of these new men were not worthy [*dignes*]" of the positions.[23] He reminds readers that Charles VII left a peaceful, united, prosperous kingdom, a sentiment universally expressed by writers of the time and by French historians of the next three centuries. Louis XIV's official royal historian, François Eudes de Mézeray, castigated Louis XI for removing the "best officers" of the Crown, of Parlement and the Chamber, of lower courts, as well as seneschals and governors of places.[24] He "created new taxes, banned nobles from hunting on pain of death, abolished the privileges of towns and provinces, diminished the authority of offices, and every day introduced novelties."

---

20 J. Kervyn de Lettenhove, ed., *Œuvres de Georges Chastellain: Chronique*, t. V (Brussels, 1865), 141–142 (ch. CXXII). The use of "dignité," high office, to describe the Crown follows precisely the vocabulary used by men like Juvénal des Ursins.

21 Basin, distrusting Louis, skipped the commission and accepted the invitation of Philip of Burgundy to return to Louvain. Bakos, *Images of Kingship*, 15–16.

22 Contamine, "Louis XI, la prise de pouvoir, la foire aux places (juillet–septembre 1461)," in *Des pouvoirs en France*, 135. Francis I's creation of the Central Treasurer in 1523 marked the first clear separation between the revenue of the government and that of the king. Francis I also created the first quasi-public debt, the *rentes sur l'Hôtel de Ville de Paris*, perpetual annuities guaranteed by the city government of Paris, based on the proceeds of specified royal taxes, often duties on goods entering Paris itself.

23 A. Coulon, ed., "Chronique scandaleuse," in *Melanges d'archeologie et d'histoire* 15 (1895): 137–139, "Digne" here plays on "dignitas."

24 F. de Mézeray, *Histoire de France depuis Faramond jusqu'au règne de Louis le juste: enrichie de plusieurs belles & rares antiquitez & de la vie des reynes* (Paris, 1685), t. II, 681. Bakos *Images of Kingship*, ch. 2, does not discuss Mézeray. I. Durand-Le Guern, "Louis XI entre mythe et histoire," *Cahiers de Recherches Médiévales et Humanistes* (2004): 31–45, on his complex legacy.

Louis XI's dramatic increase in the taille, which produced about seventy percent of his revenue, was particularly unpopular. In 1484, the deputy Jean Cordier, a judge in Forez, proposed that the taille not be only cut to the level of Charles VII [1.2 million l.], but that the Estates approve it solely for two years, at which time a new meeting of the Estates General would have to vote any future taxes.[25] The government accepted this figure, along with a special grant of 300,000 l. in honor of Charles VIII's accession: combined, they still represented a massive reduction from the 4.4 million l. levied by Louis XI in 1483.[26] Despite some governmental noises implying acceptance of the two-year rule, Charles VIII and his successors all simply ignored it.

If we look at histories of France produced between the late fifteenth and eighteenth centuries, we can see that Louis XI comes in for a level of criticism simply not acceptable in reference to any other Capetian-line king, even if the monarchy applied censorship to books like the original printing of Bertrand d'Argentré's *Histoire de Bretagne* (1583), that carried such criticisms too far. Introducing Louis XI, d'Argentré painted a dark portrait indeed:[27]

> The king [Charles VII] dead ... entered the most suspicious and suspect king the earth ever bore: a man without faith, without alliance, vindictive and misshapen in all his actions, he doubted everyone and everyone doubted him ... no service, no good offices ever obliged him ... his principal rule of life, which he wished to teach to his children, was to dissimulate, never to speak of what he thought to contest

D'Argentré portrayed Anne de Beaujeu in a similar light, an "ambitious woman" who was the "image of her father, teaching from the first her brother [Charles VIII] not to hold either faith or loyalty." Unsurprisingly, the approved text published in 1588 eliminated such comments, even if it remained suspicious of Louis XI.[28] D'Argentré naturally took the Breton position with respect to the conflicts of the 1460s through 1490s, and other sixteenth-century

---

[25] The chancellor added the proviso that the sum be 1.5 million *l.*, to reflect the monetary devaluations that took place between 1460 and 1484: the silver mark, worth 8.5 *l.* in 1460, was worth 11 *l.* in the 1480s.

[26] J. J. Clamageran, *Histoire de l'impôt en France* (Paris 1868), II, 81.

[27] B. D'Argentré, *Histoire de Bretaigne* (1583), book XII, 970: "Le Roy mort ce fut une courte nouvelle: & entra un Roy le plus defiant, & deffié, que la terre portast, homme sans foy, sans alliance, vindicatif, & contrefait en toutes ses actions, il se doutoit de tous, & tous se doutoient de luy [...] nul service, nul office ne l'obligea oncq [...] sa principale reigle de vie, qu'il vouloit enseigner à ses enfans fut de dissimuler, ny iamais parler de ce qu'il pensoit debatre." Online on Google Books, the date appears as "1600" but as Kerhervé [next note] points out, many of the later editions were, in fact, the first edition with a false date: this version, from the princely library at Monaco, carries a handwritten note "Edition première," which is accurate.

[28] J. Kerhervé, "Écriture et récriture de l'histoire dans *l'Histoire de Bretaigne* de Bertrand d'Argentré. L'exemple du Livre XII," in N.-Y. Tonnerre, ed., *Chroniqueurs et historiens de la Bretagne* (Rennes: PUR, 2001), 77–109.

provincial historians, like the Burgundian Pierre Saint-Julien de Balleure, were just as negative about Louis XI.[29] The two authors most read with respect to Louis XI – Commynes and Seyssel – offered very different assessments, yet Commynes did not shy away from some of Louis' less edifying traits, and Seyssel gave him credit for strengthening the monarchy's rights.

Interested party or no, Basin had it right: Louis XI abandoned the commonwealth principles of his father and often sought to rule by arbitrary, personal fiat. Chastelain's dream woman makes that precise charge: the king ruled "comme tyran par volonté," like a tyrant, by will. According to Jean-Jacques Garnier, named "historiographe de France" in 1771, Guillaume de Chartier, bishop of Paris, told the city council, in his account of the 1465 meeting, that the nobles claimed the king had[30]

> left them no authority. They reproached him that everything was done by his will, that he himself was the law, the judge, and the parlement [...] in a manner that no one could be assured of his property [biens], or of his life, and that the most frivolous suspicions were followed by the loss or the exile of citizens: that wild animals were in greater surety and were freer than men.

Before going overboard in the comparison, however, we must remember that Charles VII created the permanent taille, and then claimed to have the right to levy it forever after, since the purpose – paying the *compagnies d'ordonnance* – had not ceased. Moreover, the staunchly Parlementaire Manuscrit Français 203 [see below] specifically endorses the principle that the king's will **does** make law, with the proviso that the law in question be subject to reason. These sorts of apparent contradictions merely reflected the importance of political reality both

[29] François II of Brittany, like Jean II d'Alençon, descended in direct male line from a king of France [Louis VI], and so remained in the line of succession. In very short order, the male lines of Dreux (Brittany), Alençon, Burgundy [including Montagu], Anjou, Valois, and Orléans died out, leaving only Angoulême, Bourbon, and Courtenay in 1515.

[30] J -J. Garnier, *Histoire de France* (Paris, 1770), IX, 61. Il "ne leur laisseroit aucune autorité. Ils lui reprochoient que tout se faisoit à sa volonté, que lui-même étoit la loi, le juge et le parlement ... de manière que personne ne pouvoit estre assuré de ses biens, ni de sa vie, que les plus frivoles soupçons étoient suivis de la perte ou de l'exil des citoyens: que les animaux sauvages étoient en plus grande sûreté et plus libres que les hommes." Garnier attributes this version to an author contemporary to the events, reproducing the speech given by bishop Chartier at the Paris city hall to report to the Parisians about the event. Other sources identify Jean, count of Dunois, companion-in-arms of Joan of Arc, first cousin of Charles VII, as the speaker. Bishop Chartier fell afoul of Louis XI during the War of the Public Good, for failing to offer sufficient support. After the bishop died (1472), Louis had a calumnious epitaph placed on his tomb; unknown hands replaced it in 1483–1484 with a more laudatory epitaph. Garnier contributed two final volumes of the *Histoire de France* begun by Paul-François Velly [vols. I–VII], continued by Claude Villaret [VIII]. Molinet, *Chronique*, 51, paraphrases this story in his continuation of Chastelain's chronicle.

in decision-making and in the use of political vocabulary by all royal parties. As with the sixteenth-century Parlement of Paris, where Marie Houllemare found a focus on the immediate political problem, rather than a coherent long-term strategy, so too, the monarchy itself invariably focused on the problem at hand, and then sought out philosophical and legal justifications for decisions taken on pragmatic political grounds.[31]

What interests us here is not the family quarrels of Louis XI and his relatives, but their vocabulary: constant references to the "bien public" or "la chose publique"; frequent accusations of tyranny. We must be particularly careful not to project backward onto the events of the 1460s and 1470s a logic derived from later events. At the time of the War of the Public Good, the nominal leader of the coalition, Charles of France, Louis XI's younger brother, was the heir to the throne. In the 1470s, when Louis XI actively prosecuted and executed many of the leaders of the Ligue du Bien Public, Charles was dead.[32] Louis had a toddler son as heir but given that his first three sons had died in infancy, a single male child could not have been all that reassuring. Louis' modern defenders, above all Jean Favier, point to a conscious policy of strengthening the monarchy against the great feudatories (most of them his relatives), but how are we to consider Louis XI's actions as focused entirely on strengthening the monarchy when he went to such great lengths to make sure one of his most likely heirs (Louis d'Orléans, who indeed became king in 1498) could have no children? He fought wars against the male heads of two other royal lines – Burgundy and Brittany (Dreux) – and tried for treason the head of a third, Jean II d'Alençon, who was also his godfather.[33] Moreover, as Dauphin, Louis had flouted the authority of the king of France and sought to create an independent, sovereign principality.

Even in purely dynastic terms, Louis XI focused on his petty, personal, vindictive goals, that is, on his particular interest, and ignored both the *bien public* and, in many ways, the interests of the wide "maison" of the Valois.[34] The assertion that Louis consciously set out to create a unified French state built around what would later be called "absolutism" seems an anachronistic misreading of events.[35] As Le

[31] Houllemare, *Politiques de la parole*.

[32] Louis' opponents, above all the duke of Brittany, tried to spread the rumor that he had poisoned his brother. We have little evidence to support the charge, but it is indicative of contemporaries' view of Louis that many believed it.

[33] Between 1515 and 1518, Jean d'Alençon's grandson Charles was heir to the throne.

[34] Mézeray argues that Louis deliberately gave his son Charles a poor education and a tiny household so that he would not have to worry that his son would be as unfaithful an offspring as he himself had been. A century earlier, d'Argentré, in his *Histoire de Bretaigne*, 1583 version, similarly claimed that Louis XI had done so. Mézeray recounts the story that the dying Charles VII worried aloud that Louis would be as bad a king as he had been a son.

[35] Favier, *Louis XI*. Contamine's introduction, "Le Moyen Âge Occidental a-t-il connu des 'serviteurs de l'État'?" in *Les serviteurs de l'État au Moyen Âge* (Actes des congrès de la Société des historiens médiévistes de l'enseignement supérieur public v. 29) (1998), 9–20, examines the tricky question of "functionaries of State" in the Middle Ages.

Roy Ladurie, who does see Louis XI as the founder of the French state, admits, "the common good [*bien commun*] in the sense of Aristotle and Aquinas remained present in his thought."[36] Peter Lewis, in his many fine articles, emphasizes the "state" building of the period, yet he recognized the "polity" element in French politics. John Watts' term, institutional thickening, offers a more precise description than "state" building.[37] Lewis is certainly correct, however, about the progressive rise of a professional class of royal officials, trained in the law. The expansion of Parlements, in particular, greatly improved the cohesion of the monarchy, even as it encouraged regional identity.

Contemporaries had a skewed sense of the numbers of royal officials – one chronicle says 60,000 – but the 4,000 or so actual officers in the judicial and financial systems still represented the largest such apparatus in Western Europe. To this number, we might add the annual tax collectors, chosen by each parish: they numbered in the tens of thousands, but were not actual royal officers. Royal sergeants, too, outnumbered the judges and financial officers.[38] The procès-verbal for the reformation of the customs of the bailiwick of Amiens in 1507 lists dozens of procureurs, representing the various justiciars: if Amiens, one of roughly eighty bailiwicks in the kingdom at that time, was at all typical, then France had thousands of procureurs, avocats, and *praticiens* scattered across its landscape, plying their trade in royal, seigneurial, ecclesiastical, and urban courts.[39] This situation would get infinitely worse in the sixteenth century: the cahiers of 1560, 1576, and 1614 all fulminated against the "plague" of lawsuits, and lawyers.

The statutes for Louis' Order of Saint-Michel, for example, specifically stated that the knights would aid the king in cases involving the "defense of the Christian faith," for the "liberty of the Church of God, upkeep of the crown of France, and of the chose publique of our Kingdom, and against our ancient enemies, or other just quarrels."[40] When a knight of the order died, his

---

[36] E. Le Roy Ladurie, *L'état royal, 1460–1610* (Paris: Hachette, 1987), 97.

[37] See Watts, *The Making of Polities*. My special thanks to Prof. Watts for several illuminating conversations about "polities" as against "states." P. S. Lewis, *Essays in Later Medieval French History* (London, 1985), see especially ch. 2, "France in the Fifteenth Century: Society and Sovereignty" and *Later Mediaeval France: The Polity* (London: Macmillan, 1968).

[38] *Ordonnances*, I, 752–753, contains a nominative list of the 234 sergeants of the Chatelet of Paris in 1321, a number the royal letters claim was a reduction from a previously abusive total. The *avocat* Laurière, editing the volume in 1721, noted (751, note a) that the Chatelet had far more sergeants by that time.

[39] In addition to Dupont-Ferrier's works on the local administration, see, for example, J. Dewald, *Pont-St.-Pierre, 1398–1789* (Berkeley and LA: University of California Press, 1987), I. Paresys, *Aux Marges du Royaume. Violence, société et justice en Picardie sous François Ier* (Paris: Publications de la Sorbonne, 1998). Bourdot de Richebourg, *Nouveau coutumier général*, I, 200ff.

[40] The statutes are in *Les Remontrances faictes au roy Loys*, 31, article 6. Throughout, Louis refers to himself as the "sovereign and head of the order," a good example of standard usage of the word "sovereign" at the time.

family had to return his collar of the Order, and the members, in classic commonwealth fashion, had to elect a replacement [art. 45–50]. The person obtaining the most votes, having been elected, took an oath in a more royalist vein: "you will aid to guard, sustain, and defend the highnesses [*hautesses*] and rights of the crown and Royal majesty and the authority of the sovereign of the order." [art. 50] The king and eight of the members would elect the chief clerk (*greffier*), the treasurer, and the herald. Article 64 even allowed the members to elect a temporary head of the Order, if the king were a minor.

The various articles of the statutes sought to circumscribe the actions of the great aristocrats invited to join. The statutes mentioned the initial members, who were essentially the military leadership of the kingdom. Louis honored them with special nomination, and the famous golden collar, but he simultaneously bound them with the articles.[41] These fifteen "brothers," and the king, were to elect the next twenty-one, to bring the Order to full strength. Louis XI was not about to allow an actual free election, but even he respected the principle.

They all promised not to leave to fight in wars outside the kingdom, without the king's permission, and not to fight each other: they even promised to report to other brothers any overheard insults or threats against them and further promised mutual defense if any brother were attacked. They would not "undertake any wars" without consulting with most of the brothers, to get their advice. Those brothers who knew of the sovereign's "enterprises" promised to keep them secret. The grounds for expulsion [art. 15] included heresy, treason, flight during battle, or "any other villainous, enormous and reprehensible case." In effect, the Order enabled Louis XI to create an institution that forced its members to swear loyalty to him, in the guise of doing so to the institution. Virtually everyone on the list was either discharged by Louis in 1461, subsequently disgraced, or tried for treason in the 1470s. The original group of those disgraced – du Bueil, d'Estouteville, Chabannes – returned to favor in the late 1460s, as did Jean II de Bourbon, one of the leaders of the Ligue du Bien Public. The Order of Saint-Michel, both in its statutes and its language, shows the extent to which Louis XI utilized a mix of techniques to enhance his power and reduce that of the great aristocrats, particularly military commanders.

Louis XI's creation was not "the royal State" of Le Roy Ladurie, however, but a temporary aberration in the history of the monarchical commonwealth.[42]

---

[41] The original fifteen were Louis' brother, Charles, the constable; two marshals of France; three men who held or had held the position of admiral of France; the master of the crossbowmen; five provincial governors; two seneschals (Poitou and Guyenne); and the grand master of the king's household, Antoine de Chabannes.

[42] The steady increase in royal presence, in terms of the size of royal officialdom and the jurisdiction creep of the royal writ, are incontestable. The massive increase, the quantitative jump so great as to be qualitative, however, took place in the late sixteenth century, not the fifteenth. One example will suffice: in 1620, Normandy alone had twice as many *élus* (local financial supervisors) as the **entire kingdom** had had in 1500.

What Louis XI did do – and what his later apologists, especially in the seventeenth century, would insist upon – was to demonstrate how the combination of royal prerogative unencumbered by respect for common-wealth principles and greater royal resources could enable a king to disman-tle the polity constructed by Charles V and Charles VII. Louis XI's suspension of the Pragmatic Sanction in particular, pointed the way to the fundamental change fully effected by Francis I in 1516. Just as the image of the "evil" Louis XI owes much to Basin and, in some parts, to Claude de Seyssel (praising his own master, Louis XII), so, too, the image of the king as conscious architect of "absolute monarchy" owes much to writers subsidized by Louis XIV.[43] They could find much in Commynes, above all, to justify the argument that Louis XI consciously sought to break the power of the *grands* in order to create a strong monarchy.[44] The "black legend" to which Favier refers overstates some of Louis' misdeeds, but the king really did carry out or countenance evil deeds; Masselin's account of the Estates General of 1484 makes clear that Louis XI's contemporaries found him morally repugnant.[45] As the eighteenth-century historian Garnier argued, "it is morally impossible that a prince find himself subject to the general hatred, without having contributed to it."[46] His sentiments revived a proverb cited by the *Songe du Vergier*: "He is not lord of his *pays*, who is hated by his subjects."[47] Let us look more closely at three key groups of citizens: clergy, through the abrogation of the Pragmatic Sanction; judges, through Louis XI's relationship with the Parlementaires; and the nobility, through the War of the Public Good.[48]

From the Parlement on down to the town governments, Charles VII had, in theory, created a broad system of election – of bishops, judges, and some other officials – by the 1450s. His contemporaries, and the next generation of French elites, looked to that system as the model of proper governance, as the Estates General of 1484 amply demonstrated. Never before or after did deputies so

[43] On which, see Bakos, *Images of Kingship*.
[44] Although Bakos is surely right about the *raison d'État* writers of the early seventeenth century, I am far less convinced about mainstream opinion. Seyssel, *Les louenges du roy Louis XII*, ed. P. Eichel-Loikine and L. Vissière (Geneva: Droz, 2009), written in 1508, offers much praise for Louis XI's clever defeat of the princes; he imputes entirely selfish motives to the League of the Bien Public. He famously drew the parallel, Louis XI:Louis XII = Domitian:Trajan. On Louis XII's management of his image, see N. Hochner, *Louis XII. Les dérèglements de l'image royal (1498–1515)* (Paris: Champ Vallon, 2006).
[45] Mézeray, *Abrégé*, II, 606, claims Louis XI executed more than 4,000 people, by diverse means, and that he sometimes watched their suffering for his enjoyment.
[46] M. Garnier, *Histoire de France*, v. X (Paris, 1770), 35.
[47] "Il n'est pas sire de son pais, Qui de ses subgetz est hays." The *Songe* attributed this comment to John, king of Bohemia, who died at Crécy (1346). He was the maternal grandfather of King Charles V.
[48] The towns are covered in Chapter 5.

relentlessly disparage any French king, or reject so completely his rulership, as they did with respect to Louis XI in 1484. In debate after debate, in article after article of the remonstrances, they urged the young king to reject the practices of Louis' reign and return to the ways of the good king of blessed memory, Charles VII.[49] One of their principal demands was the full restoration of the Pragmatic Sanction.

4.2   Elections: Louis XI and the Pragmatic Sanction of Bourges (1438)

> Against the sentiment and remonstrances of all his subjects, he revoked the Pragmatic Sanction.
>
> François de Mézeray.[50]

The commonwealth built on election had its clearest expression in the Pragmatic Sanction of 1438, in which Charles VII, acting on his own authority, but after consultation with a large assembly of bishops, abbots, and lay aristocrats, ordered that all vacant sees within the kingdom of France be filled by election (Illustration 4.1).[51] The "notable doctor" of Paris who wrote *M. Français 203* (c. 1500) tells us that a "pragmatic sanction is properly that which a prince orders and statutes with the counsel of nobles and barons for the affairs [*choses*] of the commune and university," that is, the community as a whole.[52] The Pragmatic began with a clear statement of royal right to govern, speaking of "the inscrutable providence of the divine highness by which kings rule and possess the governance of the *chose publique*." This divine highness "has ordered on earth the royal power."[53]

The Pragmatic and the French translation of c. 1500 differed on one key issue. The Pragmatic recognized the legitimacy of the "king or the princes" intervening in the election "by means of sweet prayers and benevolent recommendations, in favor of deserving subjects, zealous for the good of

---

[49]   This positive image of Charles VII conveniently overlooked the generally negative view of his early years and the princely discontent made manifest by the Praguerie of 1440. On Alençon's trial, see F. Collard, "Chronique judiciaire? Le procès du duc d'Alençon et la littérature historiographique du temps," *Cahiers de Recherches Médiévales* (2013): 129–143, online at: https://crm.revues.org/13082

[50]   Mézeray, *Histoire de France*, II, 689.

[51]   Charles VII was able to cite ample precedent for episcopal election in the canons of various Church Councils, especially that of Constance, where Gerson played a leading role, and Basel. The papacy fought this measure tooth and nail, even threatening Charles VII with an interdict on the whole kingdom. Valois, *Histoire de la Pragmatique*, vii–viii, suggests that English chapters at this time would not think of voting against the king's candidate.

[52]   BNF, M fr 203, f. 61v. "University" at this time often referred to a town government, as it does here.

[53]   *Ordonnances* XIII, 270ff; BNF, M Fr 203, fol. 4r, "L'inscrutable providence de la divine hautesse par laquelle les roys regnent et possedent le gouvernement des choses publicques a ordonné en terre la puissance royalle."

the republic"[54]; these "recommendations," of course, were not to degenerate into menace or violence.[55] The French translation and gloss, however, directly contradicted this point: the text says that "popes, princes, communities, and others of whatever degree or dignity" should "not write letters to the electors" or solicit them either in person or through procureurs. [f. 17v] Doing so would prevent a free election. The glossator mentioned that it was "well reasonable and profitable to the chose publique that the pope not attempt anything against the holy decrees," but he recognized that if an election led to an outcome that would disturb "the church of the *pais* or the bien public," then the cardinals in Rome could nullify it.

The controversy began in November 1461, when Louis XI abrogated the Pragmatic Sanction in Dauphiné; he re-established it in June 1464 and restored the abrogation in 1469.[56] Louis XI had promised Pope Pius II that he would also abolish the Pragmatic in France.[57] The Parlement refused to register the edict, and issued a remonstrance, probably written by Jean de Rély, to explain its position. The Parlement began by reminding Louis XI that the king was the "guardian" of the "liberties" of the French Church. French laws, such as the Pragmatic, had been made by kings in consultation with those of their blood, men of the Church, and other prominent subjects of the king. The Pragmatic assembly had listened to ambassadors both from the Council of Basel and from the Pope. The judges began their defense of the right of election with a call to Aristotelian justice: that each should "guard and observe what was his: that is to say, to Chapters the right to elect, to patrons the right to present, to ordinaries the right to confer." The king, as the guardian and defender of the Churches of his kingdom, naturally would wish to "work with all his power to maintain the said constitutions and decrees." [Art. XXII and XXIII] The people would naturally hold in higher esteem a bishop elected in the traditional way, and his doctrine and life could serve as an example.[58]

---

[54] *Ordonnances*, XIII, 274: "pro personis benemeritis & zelantibus bonum Reipublice," both of the kingdom and of Dauphiné.

[55] Valois, *Pragmatique*, lxxxiv, uses the word "kingdom," not republic.

[56] Here again, his successors went back to the commonwealth tradition, and restored the Pragmatic Sanction. In July 1492, Charles VIII issued special letters reiterating the point that no foreigners could hold bishoprics in Dauphiné (or in France). Chevalier, *Ordonnances*, piece 588. Needless to say, foreigners with the right connections did hold bishoprics. On the Pragmatic Sanction, J. Salvini, "L'application de la Pragmatique Sanction sous Charles VII et Louis XI au chapitre cathédral de Paris," *Revue d'histoire de l'Église de France* (1912); J. Combet, *Louis XI et le Saint-Siège* (Paris, 1903), on the gory details of Louis' relationships with the Popes of his day.

[57] Valois, *Pragmatique Sanction*.

[58] P. Pithou and P. Dupuy, ed., *Traitez des droits et libertez de l'Eglise gallicane* (Paris, 1731; original edition 1594); the Remonstrances are the first work in this selection of texts: "car si les elections n'ont lieu, le Roy pert ceste belle prerogative qu'il a, de donner puissance d'élire."

Illustration 4.1   Charles VII receives the Pragmatic Sanction; BNF, M Français 203, fol. 2r. Permission BNF

There followed the usual list of past French kings who had issued ordinances on election: Saint Louis took pride of place. In the discussion of Art. XXXI, the judges claimed that "those of Rome" had long sought to overturn elections, to weaken the power of the king of France: "because if elections do not take place, the King loses this beautiful prerogative which he has, to give the power to elect." We might extend this thinking to the entire commonwealth edifice: yes, elites supported election, but the king gave the power to elect in the monarchical commonwealth; we see in this article an argument that elections, far from detracting from royal power, in fact, expressed its centrality to the commonwealth. In art. XXXIX, they denounced the Pope's tendency to name foreigners [estrangiers], who were not from the pays of the benefice, and thus did not know its "mores and conditions." Later attacks on the Concordat of 1516 would pick up this theme and add that "foreign" bishops did not know the local language, and therefore the flock could not understand the wisdom of the shepherd. Article XLI suggested that it would be easier for the king to have his "serviteurs" gain such positions, because the electors "would gladly (as one might believe) please the King our Lord [Sire]." As Tyler Lange points out, the Pragmatic also marked an important step in royal power over the clergy, in the clause suggesting princes should make suggestions for appointments. The Parlement of Paris similarly expanded its writ, over first the secular and then the spiritual elements of ecclesiastical courts.[59]

French benefices existed in a kind of legal no-man's land for most of Louis XI's reign. The king's own procureur at the Parlement, Jean de Saint-Romain, spoke against the 1461 edict, as an assault on the rights of the Crown.[60] Louis XI himself essentially agreed; when he changed his mind, he tried to recall his emissary to Rome, Cardinal Richard-Olivier Longueil, who had enough sense to stay in Italy. Longueil was soon the subject of a royal arrêt denouncing those who sought to undermine the "sovereign authority" of the king and Parlement, whether "under the shade or color of Apostolic bulls or otherwise."[61]

When Cardinal Jean Balue, as papal legate, sought letters in 1469 abrogating the Pragmatic Sanction, Saint-Romain again spoke up, claiming that between 1461 and 1464, when the Pragmatic Sanction had not been enforced, more than 340,000 écus had been shipped from France to Rome for bishoprics,

---

[59] Lange, First French Reformation, 81–111.

[60] Michelet, Histoire de France (1844), VI, 86, citing the king's letter to the Pope in late September 1465, claims Louis XI thereby sought to eliminate the influence of the great nobility over the selection of bishops. Combet, Louis XI et le Saint-Siège, concludes that the Pragmatic was an effort by the clergy to get out from under both Pope and king. For the richest prizes, see Dauphant, Royaume des quatre rivières, map 22.

[61] R. Toustain de Billy, Histoire ecclésiastique du diocèse de Coutances. T. II (Rouen: C. Métérie, 1880), 293–294, reproduces the arrêt, from May 24, 1463.

abbeys, and priories, and another two million *écus* for "grâces expectatives" for other benefices.[62] When Louis reconsidered his rash step, the death of Pius II (1464) gave him the chance to restore some elements of the Pragmatic Sanction, relying on a memoir written by Thomas Basin, who argued that an agreement made with Pius II lapsed on the individual Pope's death.[63] From 1464 to his death, Louis changed the situation with respect to Church benefices so often that it was literally impossible to be certain at any moment who actually had the right of choosing the new holder. At the end of his reign, Louis XI again sought to abrogate the Pragmatic Sanction, and again Saint-Romain opposed him: Louis stripped the obstreperous *procureur* of his office, but the Parlement refused to seat his replacement, Michel de Pons, except as an auxiliary to Saint-Romain. The Parlement dragged out the process so long that Louis XI died before Pons got his office: Anne de Beaujeu then allowed the Parlement to decide who between Saint-Romain and Pons would be the *procureur du roi*. Jean de Saint-Romain became a hero to generations of French jurists for his courageous opposition to this attack against "French liberty."[64]

In 1484, no sooner had Parlement opted for Saint-Romain than he joined the First President, Jean de la Vacquerie, in a delegation to the regent to discuss the Pragmatic Sanction. The bishops had split on the issue of the Pragmatic Sanction: many of them joined with other delegates from the clergy to support its full restoration, but the archbishop-cardinals of Lyon and Tours denounced the Pragmatic Sanction as heretical.[65] Later, when de la Vacquerie went to the

---

[62] L. Morery, *Grande Dictionnaire Historique*, t. IV (Paris, 1707), 322, entry on Pragmatic Sanction. The deputies to the Estates General of 1484 repeated verbatim Saint-Romain's statement. The remonstrance of 1461 waxed long and eloquently about the disastrous financial effects of all that French money going to Rome for annates and "graces expectatives," that is, anticipated nominations, granted during the life of the current holder of the benefice. The 100,000 (*sic*) parishes of the kingdom would lose 25 *écus* each for such "graces," thus 2.5 million *écus* in all. The "bullionist" argument was especially strong in the fifteenth century, due to a perceived lack of silver and gold coins, on which H. Miskimin, *Money and Power in 15th-century France* (New Haven and London: Yale UP, 1984).

[63] T. Basin, *Advis de Monseigneur de Lysieux au roi*, 509.

[64] Mézaray, *Histoire*, II, 682. Garnier, *Histoire de France*, v. X, 25, speaks of Saint-Romain's tireless and courageous defense of the rights of the "State and of the Crown," a wonderful example of how eighteenth-century writers pushed the replacement of *res publica* by State.

[65] Charles of Bourbon, Cardinal-archbishop of Lyon, was one of the few holdovers from Charles VII's reign; he had obtained (1447) his archbishopric under the rules of the Pragmatic Sanction. The archbishop of Tours, Hélie de Bourdeilles, had obtained his first see, Périgueux, in 1447, with support from Charles VII; Louis XI made him archbishop of Tours in 1468. As cardinals, they could hardly oppose the Pope's position; de Bourdeilles even wrote a Latin treatise against the Pragmatic Sanction, published posthumously in 1486.

Estates General to give the Parlement's view, Saint-Romain joined him; they gave legal weight to the opinion of the lower clergy and the Third Estate that the Pragmatic Sanction should be restored. De la Vaquerie, like Saint-Romain, long remained a hero to Parlementaire partisans of the commonwealth political system. He offers a fine example of the ambiguity of their commonwealth ideology. De la Vaquerie stood up for the defense of the Pragmatic Sanction, a classic goal of almost all members of the commonwealth, but he also served as Louis XI's avocat in the king's seizure of Mary of Burgundy's duchy in 1477. Burgundians would hardly consider such a man a hero of the commonwealth, but Parisian Parlementaires would applaud this defense of the unity of the kingdom.

No matter what the legal situation of the moment, Louis XI regularly tried to interfere in these elections: the last letter in the ten volumes of his correspondence (#1914) was to the chapter of Uzès, to get them to rescind their election of Nicolas Maugras as the new bishop, and to elect in his stead Jacques de Saint-Gelays, who at that moment obtained a papal bull. After Louis XI's death, Charles VIII confirmed the chapter's choice, although the patient Saint-Gelays succeeded Maugras in 1503. Unsurprisingly, Louis had more influence over the choice of archbishop of Rouen [#1863, February 18, 1483]. Louis informed the chapter that he had written to the Pope that he would like to replace the late Cardinal Guillaume d'Estouteville as archbishop of Rouen with Robert de Croismare; the letters forbade the chapter to hold an election, despite a papal bull that gave the chapter the right to do so, even though d'Estouteville was a cardinal [by canon law, subject to replacement by papal nomination]. Louis got his way, as he often did with episcopal nominations – his letters show him interfering constantly not only in episcopal nominations, but also in chapter prebends and abbeys, yet he almost always chose someone who had ties to the local community.

Aside from the interlude under Louis XI, the *principle* of election remained in place until Francis I signed the Concordat of Bologna with Pope Leo X in 1516. The practice was more complicated, as Anne Massoni has demonstrated for the elections to the deanship, chantry, and cure of the Parisian parish of Saint-Germain l'Auxerrois, which sat right across the street from the Louvre palace. The nominal restoration of election in 1484, even if it did preserve the right for the head of the chantry, seemed to have little impact on the deanship, still named by the king.[66] Véronique Julerot's monograph on episcopal election under Charles VIII shows that chapters did regain their rights, but that the king often recommended successful candidates.[67]

---

[66] A. Massoni, "Élection et collégialité. La pratique elective au sein du chapitre de Saint-Germain l'Auxerrois à Paris au XVe siècle," *Cahiers de Recherches Médiévales et Humanistes* (2010): 161–179.

[67] V. Julerot, *"y a ung grant desordre; élections épiscopales et schismes diocésains en France sous Charles VIII"* (Paris: PU Sorbonne, 2006), whose title sums up the situation.

Chastellain and Maupoint both say the bishops and aristocrats reacted badly to Louis's abrogation of the Pragmatic Sanction in France, which deprived them of power and allowed the Pope to collect annates from many bishoprics. The Pope, the king, the aristocrats, and the chapters all sought a system that would maximize their influence, in part because bishoprics and abbeys often provided great wealth. A look at lists of bishops consecrated under Louis XI reveals the same line-up of aristocratic names as had dominated the episcopacy of his father: the Bourbons, for example, held the archbishoprics of both Lyon and Narbonne, and the powerful bishopric of Le Puy: their ecclesiastical writ thus ran from the Swiss border to the Pyrenees. The princes insisted on the restoration of the Pragmatic Sanction, which Louis granted in the Treaties of Conflans and St-Maur-des-Fossés (October 5 and 29, 1465).

Louis's persistent efforts to challenge the Pragmatic created a backlash after his death. At the Estates General of 1484, a dispute broke out, with a minority of prelates insisting that the Pragmatic was heretical, but a majority of the clergy and the lay orders demanding the full restoration of elections. The deputies [falsely] claimed that all but three of France's 101 bishoprics had changed hands between 1461 and 1483: many changed hands two or three times. At 6,000 ducats per episcopal exchange, and 500 ducats for each new abbot or prior, they claimed the total specie sent to Rome was denuding the kingdom of precious metals.[68]

The anti-Pragmatic bishops had protested to the king and the Estates that the Estates General had no right to rule on ecclesiastical issues, because bishops had not been summoned by individual letter to the Estates General. The deputies replied that all had been summoned to the bailiwick assemblies, that some bishops had attended such assemblies, that several of them had been elected as deputies, and that the deputy-bishops had often been chosen by unanimity. The Cardinal-Archbishop of Lyon then held a meeting at his residence of all the bishops, of a deputation from the Estates, and of a delegation from the king, headed by none other than Jean de Saint-Romain.

Refuting the Cardinal-bishops' position that the Pragmatic Sanction was heretical, Saint-Romain, claiming he was the "*procureur* of the *res publica* of the kingdom" whose job it was to secure the utility of the "kingdom," insisted the Pragmatic Sanction be restored, a position the non-Cardinal bishops supported. Saint-Romain argued that "the kingdom" got many benefits, both spiritual and temporal, from this "constitution" of the Church, such as the retention of money within the kingdom, and the election of capable clerics.

---

[68] They estimated that France had 3,000 abbeys and priories. Masselin, *Journal*. More than three of the bishops of 1484 had been in their sees since 1461. B. Guénée, *Between Church and State: The Lives of Four French Bishops in Late Middle Ages*, trans. A. Goldhammer (Chicago: UCP, 1991), gives a nice picture of how complicated the process really was. See his discussion of the elaborate negotiations between Thomas Basin and the Raguier family.

This second reason should be emphasized: every sixteenth-century *cahier* demanding the restoration of the Pragmatic Sanction picked up this argument. Saint-Romain threatened to take the case to the Parlement if the commissioners did not agree. The *cahier* of the Estates supported this position, and Anne de Beaujeu, surely seeking to solidify the Parlement's support for her regency, had Charles VIII re-instate the Pragmatic Sanction.

Saint-Romain died soon after this episode, and the method of his replacement reveals the regency returning to the mechanisms of Charles VII on another issue. In March 1484, the Parlement de facto regained the right to elect its members, choosing a president and a clerical councilor. After Saint-Romain's death in June 1484, the king nominated Pierre Pelet, but Parlement held its own election: Jean de Nanterre got fifty-seven of the eighty-six votes cast, and the king duly confirmed him, ignoring the complaints of Pelet. The Parlement filled the next sixteen vacancies on the court by election: they sent the names of the top three vote getters to the king, and he picked one of them, usually the top vote getter.[69] On the two most fundamental issues of election – bishops and officers in the Parlement, Charles VIII nominally restored the old commonwealth.

4.3 Citizens: The Parlement

> He admonished the court diligently to do justice, because this court is the sole refuge of justice that one can today have in this kingdom.
>
> Report of Chancellor Arnaud de Corbie's speech opening the Parlement's session in November 1408.[70]

The Parlement of Paris had multiple opportunities to assert its central role in the monarchical commonwealth, beginning with the mental incapacity of Charles VI. Quite apart from the crisis created by that incapacity and the Treaty of Troyes, the resolution of the Great Schism made necessary a clear statement of the relationship of the unitary Pope in Rome, and the Gallican Church.[71] In a sense, the Parlement of Paris' attitude toward that relationship, and not toward the succession, established its power to affect the making of law, in the 1420s, and provided its greatest opportunity to defend the king's unique right to make law in France, in 1713, with the quarrel over the bull *Unigenitus*.

---

[69] Elections applied to vacant offices, not to those transmitted by succession, with royal permission [for example, from father to son].

[70] Douët d'Arcq, *Choix de pièces inédites* I, document CXXXVI (p. 315).

[71] The Schism reached a particular intensity in France during 1398–1399, when Charles VI formally withdrew French submission to Pope Benedict XIII; Charles relented in 1403, but the University of Paris again withdrew French submission to Benedict in 1407, during Gallican Church Council at Paris.

The king, and Parlement, and the Church frequently quarreled over juris-diction, both over "moral" cases (like adultery) and over adjudication of clergymen for secular issues. The king's spokesmen had a clear view of the matter: on July 23, 1425, Guillaume Le Breton, archdeacon of Provins, stated the Parlementaire-Gallican perspective with no ambiguity: "to the King and to his sovereign court belongs the knowledge of his ordinances," that is, of all cases in which a royal ordinance came into play.[72] In practice that meant, for example, that a clergyman claiming exemption from a royal tax had to be adjudicated in a royal court, not an ecclesiastical one.[73] The Pope rejected this viewpoint. Every lay body in France, from the Parlement of Paris to represen-tative assemblies to town governments, supported the principle of secular jurisdiction over offenses against lay civil and criminal laws. Support for the king's position on this point went hand-in-hand with demands for **their** jurisdiction over clerics in their *ressort*.[74]

Right from the start, the three constitutional pillars – the Salic Law, the inalienable royal demesne, and the king of France's lawmaking independence – remained contested elements of the French monarchy, both in rhetoric and in practice. When the Dauphin Charles tried to declare himself regent in 1419, the Parlement objected, because doing so prejudiced the "authority of the king": Charles had no royal letters, nor had the Peers of France been called to name a regent.[75] The king, Charles VI, was literally a madman, so Parlement here really refers to the king of France, the royal office, which could have issued letters registered in the court. Parlement acted to protect its right to be the "sole interpreter" of French legal tradition and practice. The most important area in which it defended this right was in matters ecclesiastical, precisely where its jurisdiction faced the greatest outside threat, from the Pope.

Throughout the fifteenth and sixteenth centuries, French elites considered religious life to lie at the heart of the "bien public."[76] Innumerable documents, royal and otherwise, make the connection, both with respect to the Church

---

[72] Valois, *Pragmatique Sanction*, II, 16. Charles VII specifically ordered his Parlements to refuse to register papal bulls that contradicted the Pragmatic Sanction.

[73] In the 1370s, Saint-Flour had a seemingly interminable dispute with its bishop about this issue: did the clergy have to contribute to the upkeep of the walls? *Registres consulaires de Saint-Flour (1376–1405)*, 17ff. The king ordered the seizure of the Church's temporal property; the Pope excommunicated the town council. Every walled town had this same quarrel.

[74] Lange, *First French Reformation*, 89–111, for a detailed examination of this fifteenth-century process. The royal judges won in the third quarter of the sixteenth century.

[75] N. Pons, "Intellectual Patterns and Affective Reactions in Defense of the Dauphin Charles, 1419–1422," in *War, Government and Power in Late Medieval France*, ed. C. T. Allman (Oxford: University of Liverpool Press, 2000), 54–69.

[76] Douët d'Arcq, *Choix de pièces inédites* I, piece LXXIV, opinions given by dukes of Bourbon, Orléans, Burgundy, and Berry on the issue of whether to withdraw France from adherence to Pope Benedict XIII in 1398.

itself and with respect to universities. The king stood up for the rights of the University of Paris and of the Parlement on the grounds that those studying at the University "sustained very great labors" for "la chose publique" and "for the good of our Kingdom and Our salvation." Standing up for the rectors against an order of their expulsion from Rome's Apostolic Court, he noted the scholars could hardly work for "the good of our Kingdom and Our salvation" if they lost their positions. He thought the expulsion "against the tenor of their privileges [...] and the public good [*bien public*] of our Kingdom and the universal world where they flourish, and by which our Kingdom is decorated."[77] This early (1413) use of the term "bien public" in a royal ordinance unsurprisingly involved a matter that brought together the realms temporal, civil, and spiritual. Why? Gerson put it this way, in 1405: "Because there is nothing that holds as much men subject to the *chose publique* in obedience and unity under the King and the princes as religious faith."[78]

The Parlement of Paris' right to verify, not simply to register, royal edicts became explicit because of a conflict over Gallican liberties. A long, drawn-out process related to the 1407 French Church council's proposed rules for benefices ended with an edict sent to the Parlement in the name of the child "king," Henry VI of England, by the duke of Bedford.[79] The Parlement initially (November 1426) refused to register the edict; in the end, it relented, even though it found "the said letters greatly prejudicial to the liberties of the church and the public good."[80] Scarcely a decade later, Charles VII issued the Pragmatic Sanction, which overturned Bedford's edict and established the supremacy of church councils in France, as well as elections for benefices: the pillars of the Parlement's Gallican edifice.

Established practice after the 1420s made the necessity of Parlementaire registration of royal laws to make them operative an unquestioned assumption of everyone in France, the king included. Why? In letters about royal officers and the re-establishment of proper administration, in November 1446, Charles VII spelled it out. He insisted "that they be read, published, and registered at the Parlement." He sent an "expressed order" [*mandement exprès*] because he understood that the Parlement had been unwilling to do so without one: their failure to do so, he stated, "might be the cause of violation [*infraction*] of our Edict."[81]

---

[77] *Ordonnances*, X, 66–67 (1413).

[78] "Pource qu'il n'est rien qui tiene tant les gens subiects à la chose publique en obedience et unité dessoubs le Roy et les princes comme foy religieuse." [*Vivat rex*]

[79] Henry VI went through the French coronation ceremony, at Notre Dame in Paris, in 1431. English monarchs used the title king (queen) of France through the reign of George III. The Council encouraged Charles VI to support elections, which he did in an edict cited by his son in 1438.

[80] Maugis, *Histoire du Parlement de Paris*, I, 524ff.

[81] *Ordonnances*, XIII, 482.

In his 1408 speech, First President Arnaud de Corbie, devoted royalist, laid out the Parlement's view of its supreme place in the kingdom. He made his observation during the madness of Charles VI, but the judges certainly believed that they provided the institutional stability of the monarchy. Generations later, in 1574, when Charles IX died, First President Christophe du Thou insisted that the Parlement wear its traditional red robes, not mourning, for the lit de justice that would proclaim Catherine de Medici as regent for the absent Henry III. The "King" never died, de Thou told her, and his Parlement, as part of the royal body, needed to demonstrate the immutability of what Gerson had called the king's spiritual body.[82] Catherine and de Thou came up with a remarkable innovation that both expanded her power and theirs: the Parlement officially declared Catherine to be regent on behalf of her son, Henry III, then in Poland. Prior to 1574, French precedent held that only an Estates General could declare a regent; from that point forward, the Parlement would do so – in 1610, 1643, and 1715.

The Parlement of Paris, which had final jurisdiction and *ressort* over all other citizens, considered itself the apex of the hierarchy of citizens, but, at the same time, an integral part of the royal body.[83] The Parlement had its own reasons to insist on its superiority, summed up in the court's regular self-description as the "Senate" of the kingdom, and of the judges as "Senators." Jacques Krynen finds the first usage in a speech by First President Henry de Marle in 1412; he suggests that pleadings regularly used the term throughout the fifteenth century. A royal ordinance in April 1485 made the explicit comparison, which became commonplace in the sixteenth century. In the Ciceronian rhetorical world of these judges, within the commonwealth, the Senate – in Cicero's words – held authority (*auctoritas*), that is, the ultimate sanction of legitimacy. Cicero had situated power [*potestas*] in the people, but in late medieval France, there could be no question that "pleine puissance" rested with the king: royal legislation invariably said so.

Antoine du Prat chancellor of Francis I, did not take kindly to the term "Senate" and specifically repudiated the Parlement's use of it; in 1518, Francis

---

[82] S. Daubresse, "Christophe de Thou et Charles IX: recherches sur les rapports entre le parlement et le prince (1560–1574)," *Histoire, économie et société* 17, n. 3 (1997): 389–422. Further details in P. Dupuy, *Traité de la majorité de nos rois* (Paris, 1655), 28; Daubresse, *Voix de la Raison*, 50–51.

[83] The Grand'Chambre of the Parlement joined with the peers to form the Court of Peers, which had jurisdiction over the peers of France, such as Jean II d'Alençon. See Y. Lallemand, "Le procès pour trahison du connétable de Saint-Pol" [145–155] and O. Mattéoni, "'Couronne en forme sphérique ne se peut diviser sans perdre sa figure'. Une leçon de la souveraineté monarchique: le procès des officiers du duc de Bourbon devant le Parlement de Paris en 1480," [157–181] in Y.-M. Bercé, ed., *Les procès politiques* (Rome: École Française de Rome, 2007). On the use of this metaphor within the Church, Lange, *First French Reformation*, 54–55.

himself spoke against it, to a delegation protesting the Concordat.[84]
Manuscrit français 203, created in Parlementaire circles around 1500,
makes it obvious why the king and du Prat had such a reaction. The gloss
claimed that "Louis XI" had made a law [in 1489!] recognizing that "the
masters of Parlement can make a law, as could the Senate." To the glossator,
this point followed from the idea that the Parlement "was reputed to be part
of the body of the prince," a principle he traced to the commentaries of
"Jean Fabri" on the *Institutes of Justinian*, a text published in Venice in 1488
but composed in the 1330s by the French jurisconsult Jean Le Fèvre.[85] The
glossator here surely made reference not to Louis XI, but to the 1489
remonstrances made to Charles VIII, asserting that the king was the head
[*chef*] of the Parlement, just as the Emperor had been the head of the body
of the Roman Senate, and that the Parlement acted "all in authority of
senators representing the person of the king, because it is the final ressort
and sovereign justice of the kingdom of France."[86]

The glossator follows this point with the observation that "the will of the
prince is reputed for law [*loy*] when it is regulated [*reigle*] by reason."[87] Kings
of France were not about to recognize this first principle, nor was a Francis
I likely to accept the implication of the second one – that the Parlement judge
the connection between a law he promulgated and "reason." The Parlement, in
contrast, always claimed it had the right to check the consonance of any new
royal law and principles of reason and justice. Sophie Daubresse, in her study
of the Parlement of Paris from 1559–1589, sums up their view in her title: *La
voix de la raison*, the voice of reason.[88] As Arlette Jouanna has made clear, this
connection remained strong throughout the sixteenth century, but began to
unravel in the seventeenth, when kings insisted that no outside authority – like
a sovereign court – needed to assess the rationality of their actions.[89]

Charles VI had instituted a fundamental change in its workings in 1388,
following up in 1401, when he built on his father's practice of electing the

---

[84] J. Krynen, *L'idéologie de la magistrature ancienne* (Paris: Gallimard, 2009), part II, ch. 8,
for a full discussion of this important comparison.

[85] BNF, M Fr 203, f. 62v. Louis XI died in 1483. His reference likely has the date correct,
because of the well-known session of Parlement in 1489 that did make such an assertion.
King Charles VIII certainly did not issue an ordinance claiming the Parlement could
make law on its own. This text was printed in 1509 [released on April 12, 1508, o.s.] by
Gaspard Philippe, at Paris, as *La pragmatique sanction en Francoys*.

[86] Krynen, *L'idéologie*, 75, picking up on the discussion in Maugis, *Parlement*, I, 374–375:
tous en autorité de sénateurs représentant la personne du roi, car c'est le dernier ressort et
la souveraine justice du royaume de France.

[87] BNF, M Fr 203, f. 17v.

[88] Daubresse, *Voix de la Raison*, asserts [45] that the term "Senate" was extensively used for
the Parlement already in the fourteenth century.

[89] Jouanna, *Le pouvoir absolu*, 322, refers to an "autonomization" of "governmental action"
as the result.

chancellor; he mandated election by the sitting judges of all future judges.[90] In 1402, the contested choice of Henry de Marle and Pierre de Boschet for First President led to an election in which each judge (53) or bishop (20) whispered his choice to the chancellor; the chancellor reportedly claimed Marle had the majority of votes, in part because even though the voters recognized the great services rendered by the aged Boschet, they felt him too infirm to serve as First President: in fact, Marle had been the choice of the duke of Orléans, then dominant on the royal council.[91]

However dubious some of the "elections" might have been, the principle that the citizens in the "Senate" chose the new "Senators" fit perfectly with their ideals of a Classical commonwealth. In October 1446, Charles VII issued an ordinance reforming justice, in which the first article supposedly restored the "ancient" system of election by the judges, in the presence of the chancellor: the court was to offer one to three names to the king, of possible electees, making clear their opinion on the best candidate. Eight years later, Charles VII extended a related principle to the next level of the judiciary, the bailiwick courts: local judges, and any members of the king's Council who lived in the given jurisdiction, were to send the Council the names of proper candidates to fill vacancies in judgeships, offices of *avocat*, and *procureur*.[92] As late as the reign of Charles VIII, the king referred to this standard practice of electing judges at the Parlement, even if relatively few of Charles VIII's judges were, in fact, elected: the most common form of transmission was already resignation within a family, but absent such transmission, Charles VIII did respect the results of elections.[93]

Let me emphasize here the **theoretical** situation in 1454: the Pragmatic Sanction had codified the principle of election of bishops by cathedral chapters and of abbots and priors by their communities; the ordinance of 1446 had established the principle of election, by the sitting judges, of new judges at the

---

[90] To give some sense of the resonance of these rules, 400 years later, in his short summaries of important events of each year, Hénault, *Abrégé*, mentions both of these ordinances, even quoting from the second one. In the second case, it is the only event from "1400" [January 1401, n.s.] in his chronology for that year.

[91] Du Chesne, *Chancelliers*, 420–421 and Ducoudray, *Parlement*, 147. A typical version of the "Senate" description appears in a gloss from BNF, M Fr 203, f. 62r: 100 counselors: "12 pers de France 8 maistres des requestes de l'ostel du roy & 80 aultres consilleirs c'est assavoir 40 laiz et 40 clercs entre lesquelez sont 4 presidens laiz et ce a la semblance du Senat de Rome institute par Romulus du quel y avoit cent senateurs."

[92] *Ordonnances*, XIII, 471ff (1446 ordinance); XIV, 284ff (1454 ordinance).

[93] P. Pélicier, ed., *Lettres de C VIII, roi de France*, t. 3, 1490–1493 (Paris: Renouard, 1902), May 3, 1490, on the death of Guillaume de Montboissier, councilor, the chambers assembled chose three candidates, of whom the king picked Christofle de Brilhac [Brillac]. His letters stated he had followed the advice and deliberation of "princes and seigneurs of our blood and other notable *gens de conseil*." Maugis, *Parlement de Paris*, I, 107ff. Brilhac was one of the few judges elected in "traditional" fashion.

Parlement of Paris; and the ordinance of April 1454 had called for local officials to recommend "proper, learned, and sufficient *prud'hommes*" to fill vacancies in royal offices. The king created the ordinance of 1454, according to its preamble, based on the advice of "several lords of our blood and lineage, several prelates, archbishops, bishops, barons and seigneurs of our kingdom, the men of our Great Council, and some presidents and other men of our said Court of Parlement, and other judges and *prud'hommes* of this our kingdom." Toward the end of that ordinance (art. 118), the king asked officers in his courts, especial Parlement, to remember their obligation to "God, to Us and to our *chose publique*" to judge loyally, to make sure justice was not perverted, and to abstain from receiving gifts.

This 1454 ordinance laid down the key principles of the French common-wealth; in the sixteenth century, local elites regularly sought the implementa-tion of its principles, be it in the restoration of the Pragmatic Sanction or in the principle of lay elections to important offices, such as *bailli*. If we add in the April 1460 ordinance on the *tailles*, in which the king explicitly stated that he levied them for the "good [*bien*] and defense of the *chose publique*," we get a clear sense of the extent to which a commonwealth ethos had triumphed, from the royal administration down to town governments, by the end of Charles VII's life.[94] Yet this ordinance also illustrated the central government's efforts to get detailed information: *élus* had to sign and return to the generals of finance copies of every parish's tax roll, so that the generals could know the precise number of hearths in each *élection* [art. 5]. They even had to send names of all non-nobles who claimed to be exempt from the *tailles* [art. 11].

Years later, Francis I reiterated many of Charles VII's ordinances on tax-ation; in his major ordinance of 1517, article 11 reminded the *élus* that parishes had to elect their collectors; any *élu* who named parish collectors was to forfeit his office. Pierre Briçonnet, one of the generals of finance supervising the system, c. 1500, reminded the officers that the parish had twelve days to elect its assessors and collectors, or face a fine.[95] The election principle was never restored to the financial officers themselves, after Charles V converted them all into royal appointees (in 1372, 1373, and 1379). We might here distinguish between the financial structure and the judiciary: monarchs might issue legislation calling for a return to elected judges, but they did not issue similar

---

[94] *Ordonnances*, XIV, 484, ordinance on the apportionment and collection of the tailles, April 3, 1460. G. Jacqueton, *Documents relatifs à l'administration financière en France de Charles VII à François Ier* (Paris, 1891), conveniently brings together key legislation in this area. One of the final documents in this collection, from 1517, once again references the "*chose publique* of our said kingdom." [171] See Chapter 6, below.

[95] Jacqueton, *Documents*, 102ff on Briçonnet; 177 for the 1517 article. In 1599, Henry IV changed this system, on the grounds that assessors would be fairer if they also had to collect, and therefore be personally responsible for shortfall. From that point forward, the assessors and collectors legally had to be the same people.

legislation about tax officials, even though representative assemblies regularly called for a return to the original system of elections, from which the districts and officers [*élus*] took their names.

Within the Parlementaire world, what Krynen has rightly termed an "ideology" developed in conjunction with the royal version. This judicial ideology privileged justice as the first obligation of kings but recognized that "the prince is rarely a jurist." In December 1556, the Parlement spelled out clearly the implications of this separation:[96]

> God has established the king as monarch in his kingdom in unity of power and of jurisdiction and sovereignty is so closely conjoined with justice that separated it loses its name and would be a body without a soul. The king for the multitude of people and the grandeur of his state, not being able personally to exercise justice, had to commit it to worthy men [*hommes de confiance*] then to sovereign courts in various *pays*, who, for the relief of his subjects, judge in sovereignty and for this [reason] do not in their *arrêts* speak themselves but make the king speak.

The judges' defense of the rights of the king of France [as they defined them] against the actions of an actual, physical king was not some sort of existential conflict between the Parlement and the king. Louis XI certainly used political trials to try to expand royal prerogatives, but the Parlement of Paris cooperated as part of its own efforts to establish firmly its real jurisdiction and *ressort* in a kingdom in which large regions had largely ignored both.

Royal documents regularly referred to the need to preserve the Parlement's *ressort* over a given territory, whether an apanage or a province regained from the English.[97] Like his grandfather, Charles VII, both in the southwest and in Normandy, issued letters permanently tying regained towns and provinces to the Crown, and invariably stating their subjection to the *ressort* of the Parlement. By the time of his death, Charles VII had recognized the existence of two additional Parlements, in Toulouse and Bordeaux. The independent or semi-independent principalities – Dauphiné, Provence, Normandy, Brittany, and Burgundy – all had similar courts, which would be coopted into the royal judiciary, Brittany being the last, in 1554.[98]

---

[96] Krynen, *L'idéologie*, 53–61 on the king as non-jurist, citation from p. 60: the key passage reads: "le roi comme monarque en son royaume en unité de pouvoir et de juridction et de souveraineté est si étroitement conjointe avec la justice que séparée elle perdrait son nom et serait un corps sans âme."

[97] Dauphant, *Le royaume*, maps 13 a-d and 14a show the massive increase in appeals from the Loire area – the *généralité* of Languedoïl – after 1450 or so. See his discussion on pp. 130–133.

[98] Duke François II, in 1485, officially designated his Parlement as a sovereign court; Charles VIII, in 1493, changed the name to "Grands Jours," implying a temporary court under the jurisdiction of Paris. Louis XII, in 1499, as part of the "rights and privileges" recognized for Brittany in the aftermath of his marriage to Anne, restored

Parlement incessantly reminded the king of the need to maintain its jurisdictional supremacy: in January 1412, Parlement complained to the king about the need to preserve its jurisdictional rights over certain cases, because it needed to defend "the honor of the Crown and the good [bien] of the subjects."[99] Parlement unequivocally separated itself from other institutions, above all meetings of the "gens des trois Estats." It refused to go along with the Estates that met in 1413, during the Cabochien Revolt: the court argued that because it was "souveraine et capital, et représentans le roy sans moyen" [the highest and chief court, directly representing the king] it could not be part of a body, such as the "Estates General," that defined itself as distinct from the king.[100] Gerson had called the sentences and arrêts of the Parlement "the principal guardian of the civil life of the King"; he noted that even the king sometimes submitted to the justice of the Parlement.[101]

The language of the 1446 and 1454 ordinances on justice illustrated the connection between the commonwealth and the Parlement. In the first of the two, the king said he had gone back over the old ordinances on justice "for the good [bien] of Us and of the chose publique of our said Kingdom." Picking up the Parlement's language of 1413, he called it the "capital and sovereign" court of our kingdom and Seigneurie.[102] He wanted to preserve good order in the Parlement, "which is and must be the true light and exemplar of good equity and rightness [droiture] to all others." The 1454 ordinance mentioned that the king had regained Champagne, Vermandois, the Ile-de-France, Picardy, and Paris, restoring them to their "liberty and freedom," and had now done the same for Normandy, la Perche, Maine, Bordeaux, and Guyenne, where he had delivered his subjects from their "servitude." Having reunited the kingdom, and re-confirmed the rights and liberties of its inhabitants, the king now sought to restore justice to its proper form and order, "considering that without good order of justice, kingdoms cannot have any duration or firmness." Article 106 noted that he wanted to restore the Parlement to its

---

the "sovereign court" appellation, but it was not until 1554 that Henry II – the last person to hold the ducal title – officially created a royal Parlement of Brittany.

[99] Douët d'Arcq, Choix de pièces inédites, #CLI, 347.

[100] Maugis, Parlement, I, 657. This "Estates General" covered only Languedoïl. "Sans moyen" literally means without intermediary.

[101] Gerson, Vivat rex, 37. Such was also true of the Chamber of Accounts: when Louis XII issued letters saying that Suzanne de Bourbon could inherit various properties of her parents, the procureur du roi at the Chamber opposed them, on the grounds that the king could not thus harm the rights of the Crown [in this case, the reversion of an apanage to the Crown, absent a legitimate male heir].

[102] This dual wording offers a fine illustration of B. Guénée's point that contemporaneous French elites thought of themselves both as subjects and as vassals. "Y a-t-il un État aux XIVᵉ et XVᵉ siècles?" Annales E.S.C. (1971), 400.

old number of judges and "its former order, representation, and authority, to the honor of Us and our kingdom, and to the good of *la chose publique* and of our subjects, in uprightness [*honnesteté*], science, authority, and good renown."[103] Dauphant's figures on appeals show that Charles VII largely succeeded: Parlement did become a far more national court.[104]

The king's own men shared with other members of the French elite this ethos of the *res publica*. Perhaps the most telling statement of the principle came from the pen of Jean Jouvenal des Ursins, sometime *prévôt des marchands* of Paris, loyal royal servant, and father of an archbishop of Reims (Jean) and a chancellor (Guillaume). In the private journal [*livret*] he kept, Jean Jouvenal des Ursins wrote advice to his sons:[105]

> And to put and apply oneself to a good and honorable life, using good mores and avoiding sins and bad company, and following the virtuous, in order always to amend one's ways and acquire science, sapience and *office d'honneur*, to live from one's labor, fleeing idleness, which is the mother of all vices and sudden perdition of young people, and to tend loyally and honorably and reasonably to honor and power [*puissance*] to full faithfully serve God and one's prince and the republic

Louis XI's first act as king seems to have been to issue letters declaring vacant all royal offices (July 1461, while still outside France). We can contrast this action with the one taken by Charles V in 1364, when his first act had been to confirm temporarily all royal officers and then to issue specific letters about maintaining judges in the Parlement. Louis dispossessed chancellor Juvénal des Ursins and brought in Pierre de Morvillier, whose father, Philippe, had been the very man in whose hands the Parlement of Paris and the great men of the kingdom had had to swear to uphold the Treaty of Troyes. The king imprisoned the provost of Paris, Robert d'Estouteville, and removed d'Estouteville's brother, who was master of the crossbowmen, the powerful Masters of Requests, and the

---

[103] The ordinance made extensive mention of good practices to avoid "bad suspicions," such as bribery: bad practices had led to evils [*maux*] and inconveniences for "Us, our subjects, and the *chose publique* of our kingdom." Chancellor Guillaume Juvénal des Ursins, used the term "Senate" to refer to the Parlement in his writings. *Ordonnances*, XIV, 284ff. "à l'honneur de Nous & de nostre royaume, & au bien de la chose publique & de noz subjectz, tan ten honnesteté, science, auctorité et bonne renommée."

[104] The creation of a Parlement at Toulouse shifted southern appeals in its direction.

[105] "Livret de la famille Jouvenal," in *Écrits politiques de Jean Juvénal des Ursins*, v. III, ed. P. S. Lewis (Paris: Société de l'Histoire de France, 1992), 249, following BNF, M Fr 4752, fols. 111–117. "et soy mettre et applicquer a bonne et honnorable vie en usant de bonnes mœurs et evitant pechez et mauvaise compagnie et suivre les vertueux pour tousjours amender et acquerir science, sapience, et office d'honneur pour vivre de son labeur, fuyant l'oisiveté qui est mere de tous vices et soudaine perdition de jeunes genes, et tendre loyaulmant et raisonnablement a honneur et puissance pour bien fidellement Dieu et son prince et la republicque servir."

First President and king's men at the Parlement of Paris.[106] The new *prévot* of
Paris, Jacques de Villiers, was the son of Jean, seigneur de l'Isle-Adam, whom the
Armagnac faction held responsible for the Paris massacre of June 1418, in which
constable Bernard d'Armagnac and chancellor Henri de Marle died. For the
Armagnac/Orléans faction, Morvillier and Villiers were the most offensive
appointments imaginable.

Louis XI's attack on the commonwealth followed somewhat different tactics
with the military and judicial hierarchies: the former lost their jobs in 1461, but
the latter often just *changed* jobs. First President Yves de Scépeaux merely
dropped to Second President, a post he retained until his death in 1463. Louis
knew Scépeaux well, because the judge had been Louis' chancellor for six years,
leaving that job only in August 1457 – that is, at the point of Louis' exile – to take
the post as First President. His wife, Charlotte de Beauvau, was the niece of
Pierre de Beauvau, one of the two knights who had saved the Dauphin Charles'
life in Paris in 1418; the second knight was Tanguy du Chastel, who murdered
Jean sans Peur on the bridge at Montereau in 1419.[107] Mathieu de Nanterre,
who replaced Scépeaux as First President, later exchanged jobs with Jean
Dauvet, becoming First President at Toulouse (1465), then returning to Paris
as Second President. Louis XI charged him with running the Grands Jours in
Auvergne in 1479, as part of the king's effort to humiliate Jean, duke of Bourbon.

The wholesale removal of the Armagnacs did not mean their permanent
disgrace.[108] Louis removed chancellor Guillaume Juvénal des Ursins, but
Juvénal remained an important royal councilor, and represented the king on
several delicate diplomatic missions. Henri II de Marle may have lost his
position as Master of Requests, but Louis named him Fifth President of the
Parlement, and then First President of the Parlement of Toulouse, where he
took office in May 1465, at the height of the War of the Public Good: Louis
must surely have had great confidence in his loyalty to take such a step at that
time. Jean Dauvet may have lost his post as *procureur général* in 1461, but Louis
named him First President of the Chamber of Accounts, then First President of

---

[106] Jean de Bueil's father, master of the crossbowmen, died at Agincourt, along with as many
as fifteen family members. De Bueil wrote a famous fictionalized account of his life, and
of these events, *Le Jouvencel*. Masters of Requests prepared all preliminary documents
for the royal council, so the entirety of its business passed through their hands. In the
fourteenth and fifteenth centuries, their number varied between six and eight. They had
the right to sit in the Parlement, Chamber of Accounts, and all other royal courts; they
also had their own small court, reserved in Louis XI's time for cases involving members
of his households and cases involving the right of *committimus*.

[107] His nephew, Tanneguy du Chastel, served Charles VII, and paid for his master's funeral
out of his own pocket. Disgraced by Louis XI in 1461, he served the Breton dukes, but
later joined up with Louis XI.

[108] Chastellain, *Chronique*, IV, 99–101, says Louis discussed with Philip of Burgundy
"renewing" the Parlement, but that he made the many changes without taking counsel:
"tout de sa teste, sans avis de conseil."

the Parlements of Toulouse (1463) and Paris (1465). He negotiated Louis' agreements with François II of Brittany. Dauvet's replacement at the Chamber of Accounts was Bertrand de Beauvau, a relative of Scépeaux's wife. Rather than view Louis' actions as an effort to remove these men from public positions, his rearranging of their chairs might better be understood as an effort to emphasize their dependence on him: they now held positions to which Louis, not Charles, had named them.

In addition to replacing the king's men – the *avocats du roi* and the *procureur du roi* – Louis demoted the First President of the Parlement of Paris, Yves de Scépeaux, to Second President. The new First President, Hélie de Tourettes, died shortly after taking office. The chronicles claim the king had initially intended to remove all the judges, but Tourettes convinced him to keep the existing ones: "he demonstrated to him what a loss it would be for the kingdom to be deprived of these 'marvelous and scientific *clercs*, great and sovereign doctors in canon and civil law, both from the Church and laics'."[109] Tourettes argued it would be impossible to find "other judges having their prudence, nor as practiced and proven for *la chose publique*." The king relented, but made an exception for the Masters of Requests, whom he replaced.[110] The chronicler insists that Louis named men not worthy [n'en estoient dignes], "for which great murmuring was everywhere." Although he confirmed the existing seventy-four councilors and presidents, Louis quickly named replacements for the existing twelve vacancies **without** consulting the Parlement, mainly adding men with Burgundian connections. In the end, Louis also confirmed twenty-three officers at the Chamber of Accounts, testimony of his "singular desire for the *bien de la chose publique d'icelluy nostre royaume*." They had shown great assiduity in conserving the king's rights, superiorities, and demesne, "by which the said *chose publique* is maintained and defended."

The story of the Parlement of Paris in 1461–1465 offers an example of how the commonwealth's political elites had their own need for reconciliation, quite aside from conflicts between their princely masters.[111] Louis XI had

---

[109] Chastellain claims Louis tried to introduce twenty-five new judges into the Parlement, but only one could pass muster; the Court refused to seat the other twenty-four. Tourettes was already a president at the Parlement and had been one of the judges at the duke of Alençon's 1458 treason trial.

[110] Contamine, "la foire aux places," in *Des pouvoirs en France*, 136ff. "lui montra quelle perte ce serait pour le royaume que d'estre privé de ces merveilleux et scientifiques clercs, grans et souverains docteurs [. . .] d'autres juges ayant leur competence, leur prudence, leur souci de la chose publique." The chronicle in question says Tourettes warned Louis about the "destruction and annihiliation of his kingdom" if he did not restore the Parlement. A. Coulon, "Fragment d'un chronique du règne de Louis XI," *Mélanges d'histoire et d'archéologie* (1895); 103–140. This chronicler claims that all officers of the kingdom were dispossessed [*despointés*] by the death of Charles VII [137–138].

[111] F. Autrand, *Naissance d'un grand corps de l'État, les gens du Parlement, 1346–1454* (Paris, 1981).

initially favored the Burgundians, but Philip of Burgundy's suspicions that the changes were more cosmetic than real proved accurate. The old Burgundian faction, led by chancellor Morvillier, initially took over the Parlement, just as it gained control of the military. By 1465, however, Louis XI had three presidents in the Parlement from each faction: Dauvet, Marle, and Corbie from the old Armagnac faction; Nanterre, Thiboust, and Longueil from the Burgundian side.[112] The Longueil family, in particular, created marriage alliances that tied together the two factions, and enabled a more united Parlementaire elite to pass down to dominant sixteenth-century families like Harlay and de Thou.

The intricate web of marriages that connected the princes had a direct parallel among the judicial elite. The leadership of Louis XI's time invariably had marriage ties to the great families – d'Orgemont, Corbie, Dormans – of his grandfather's day. The great families of the fifteenth century later intermarried with the rising stars of the sixteenth century, like the Brulart, Le Maistre, Hennequin, and Harlay.[113] First President Christophe de Thou's mother, Claude de Marle, descended from the Armagnac Marle family and, through her mother, from the Burgundian du Drac family. Just as the princes tried carefully to regulate access to the military aristocracy, so, too, the judicial elite carefully regulated access to what would become the nobility of the State. Through these positions, this elite could dominate the commonwealth and, in time, the State. The continuity of a Parlementaire "ideology" owed much to these direct family ties, connecting the leadership of the Parlement in the seventeenth century with the legal elite of the fourteenth century. In town governments, like Amiens, local elites practiced the same technique, as we shall see in Chapter 5.

4.4   Noble Citizens: The War of the Public Good

His reign was very strange for the appetite of some people.

Jean Molinet, speaking of Louis XI.[114]

The disgraced military officers came from Western France – Estouteville, de Bueil, Laval, Dunois – and had long careers with a clear anti-Burgundian past. They had been the primary councilors of the final years of Charles VII; Louis partly blamed his father's break with him on them. In July through September 1461, prior to

---

[112] Robert Thiboust, kept in office in 1461, had joined the Parlement in 1436, which implies Armagnac connections, but his daughter Adenette married Jean du Drac, twice *prévôt des marchands* of Paris (1486, 1488), nephew of Jeanne du Drac, wife of Philippe de Morvillier.

[113] First President Achille de Harlay was a direct descendant of chancellor Morvillier, of First President Corbie, and a linear descendant of the Dormans brothers, chancellors of Charles V.

[114] *Chroniques de Jean Molinet*, I, 392. "Son règne fut assez étrange à l'appétit d'aulcuns gens."

Philip the Good's return to his own lands, Louis XI bent over backwards to defer to the duke. All the chronicles talk about Louis' obsequious behavior, even in public: the two men made a great show of mutual respect in the streets of Paris, and Philip lavishly entertained his royal master at banquets.

After first favoring the Burgundians, however, Louis turned his back on his former patron, first by breaking his promise to make Jean de Bourgogne, count d'Étampes [first cousin of duke Philip], the constable of France. Louis XI carefully navigated through the various branches of the royal family and the great aristocrats.[115] Louis XI, however paranoid and bizarre he might have been, was no fool. Catherine de Medici, in 1574, advising Henry III about how to deal with the grands of his time – Bourbon, Guise, and Montmorency – suggested that the young king read Commynes' passages on the War of the Public Good, and carefully contemplate Louis XI's actions. Historians have often treated this incident as an amusing anecdote, but Henry largely followed his mother's advice: like Louis XI, he called an Estates General (1576) and created a chivalric order, the Order of the Holy Spirit (December 1578).[116] Both kings issued laws about royal offices – Louis legalizing lifelong tenure (1467), Henry recognizing life tenure in the so-called Crown offices which were legally non-venal (1582).[117] Louis XI's reign marked a particularly difficult moment for royal relations with the upper nobility; the lesser nobility more often sided with Louis than against him. The chroniclers emphasize Louis XI's constant efforts to undermine the loyalty of the clients of the princes: as Commynes put it, "the king our master understood better the art of separating men than any other prince that I knew, and he spared neither money nor goods nor effort to gain not only the masters but also the *serviteurs*."[118]

Nobles lamented Louis' assault on their privileges, liberties, and franchises: one of the main demands of the League of the Public Good in September 1465 was the restoration of the rights and privileges of all nobles.[119] His contemporaries also objected to the king's avarice, hardly surprising given that he increased tax revenues by 135 percent.[120] Basin took practical offense at an

---

[115] On Louis' careful undermining of the Luxembourg family in Picardy, see D. Potter, *War and Government in the French Provinces. Picardy, 1470–1560* (Cambridge: CUP, 1993).

[116] Louis XI called an Estates General (1467) and created the Order of St. Michael (1469).

[117] The Chancellor, Constable, Grand Master of the Household, Grand Squire (in charge of the stables), Grand Chamberlain, and the Admiral of France.

[118] P. de Commynes, *Mémoires de Philippe de Commynes*, ed. É. Dupont (Paris, 1840), t. I, 116 [Book II, ch. 1].

[119] Hunting rights offer a classic example. Chastellain's dream woman mentions the infamous case of cutting off parts of the ears of two nobles caught with a rabbit; she made her "tyrant" comment referring to that incident. Louis restored hunting rights in 1465, but the *cahier* of the Estates General of 1484 demanded full restoration. Mézeray and other later historians insist Louis did abolish noble hunting rights, but no such ordinance survives.

[120] Contamine, "Guerre, fiscalité royale et économie en France (deuxieme moitié du XVe siècle)," in *Des Pouvoirs en France*, 123–130, 127. In his manifestos of the spring of 1465,

edict requiring all ecclesiastics to provide a detailed list of their worldly goods [i.e., real property], a step he assumed to be a preliminary to royal taxation of the Church's property. Basin, in his assessment of Charles VII, for whom he had been an important counselor in the 1450s, stressed the fact that Charles' word was his bond, "sa parole est parole de Roi" – his word was a king's word. Basin and many contemporaries condemned the dishonesty of Louis XI, who regularly broke his promises. Louis thus violated *droiture* and justice, the hallmark of the tyrant. The speakers of 1484 constantly came back to this point about the royal word.

Chastellain claims to have witnessed a remarkable exchange between Louis and the duke of Bourbon, whom Louis had stripped of the governorship of Guyenne. Bourbon had been one of the two main leaders who drove the English out of the Southwest in the early 1450s. Bourbon complained of the good service he had done for benefit of king and Crown, "If you wish to hold us in such rude terms and to be so hard to us, you will give us little occasion to love you and even less to serve you. Monseigneur, think about what I have said to you and tell if I have spoken truly." In this public quarrel, the barons sided with Bourbon, saying the king had made a mistake to disappoint such a lord in order to put in his place "un mendre et moins digne" [a lower and less worthy person].[121]

Maupoint says many seigneurs were angry at losing their pensions and offices. Louis promoted a tiny number of new men, entirely dependent on him: noble contemporaries, like Chastelain or Commynes, took particular objection to people like Olivier le Daim, the king's barber, and Daniel Bart. After Louis's death, the high nobility and the Parlement of Paris took quick revenge: Le Daim and Bart were tried and hanged within nine months.[122] The towns, it must be said, largely supported the king in 1465: urban governments were clever enough to side with the king, in the hopes (often fulfilled, as at Issoudun) of obtaining concessions from him – Paris, in particular, received considerable benefit for its royalism in the summer of 1465. In October, the king issued letters exempting the serving *prévôt des marchands*, *échevins*, town clerk [*greffier*], *procureur du roi*, and receiver of the city government from all taxes, because they were occupied in the "conservation and maintenance of the police and chose publique" of Paris.[123] We might also speculate that town elites had little faith in the princes' commitment to genuine reform. The Somme towns, in particular, show urban elites to be both cagey and cautious in the

the king took great pains to say that he had not raised taxes above what his father had levied, as proof that he had not harmed the *bien public*.

[121] Chastellain, *Mémoires*, IV, 117 (ch. XXIX).

[122] Basin, *Louis XI*, t. III, 383; the duke of Orléans got Le Daim's confiscated property.

[123] *Ordonnances*, XVI, 376. Louis made one exception: officials involved in "merchandise" of goods other than those produced by their own lands, had to pay *aides*. Commynes comments multiple times on Louis' ability to get along well with those of "medium estate."

constant transmission of power from royal to Burgundian authority and back
again: individuals lost power in the shifts, but families did not.[124]

Olivier Le Daim's case remained a staple of French history for centuries to
come.[125] Le Daim [aka, de Neckere, Flemish for the Evil One], had been
renamed and ennobled by Louis XI, who made him count of Meulan and,
later, royal chamberlain.[126] Basin condemns Louis for bringing into his inner
circle men with no learning and "no sentiment of justice." The Franciscan
preacher Antoine Fradin, in Paris in 1478, spoke of "justice and of the
government of the king"; Fradin preached that the king was "ill served and
had around him *serviteurs* who were traitors, and that he if did not kick them
out, they would destroy him and the kingdom both."[127] Louis sent Le Daim to
Paris to ban Fradin from preaching (May 26, 1478): many of Fradin's listeners
cried that it was folly and that the king knew nothing of the matter.

Everyone in Paris was "in danger of body and goods" at the hands of Le
Daim; 110 witnesses testified against him, from towns as far away as
Tournai.[128] The Parlement of Paris ordered him hanged, not beheaded,
a symbolic gesture of unmistakable power: it was privilege of nobility not to
be hanged. Jean de Roye extends the climate of fear of the king to the whole
kingdom: "there was no one in his kingdom so great, even those of his own
blood, who slept soundly in his house."[129] Two centuries later, Mézeray would
say that Le Daim might not have been the guiltiest of Louis' collaborators, but
he was certainly the most "odious," an obvious reference to his commoner
origins.

In the seventeenth century, the Dupuy brothers (royal librarians) put
together a collection of letters from the War of the Public Good. An initial
letter (March 26, 1465) of Charles, duke of Berry (the king's brother),
explained why he was levying troops:

> Having been alerted and informed by those of the blood of France and by
> other noble men and councilors of our late very beloved lord and father,
> whom God absolve, we have been remonstrated about the great calamity

---

[124] Towns are discussed in detail in Chapter 5.

[125] J.-P. Boudet, "Genèse et efficacité du mythe d'Olivier le Daim," *Médiévales*, n. 10 (1986): 5–16.

[126] Jean de Roye's chronicle always refers to him as "Olivier le Diable, dit Dain." Boudet, "Genèse," 7.

[127] Jean de Roye, *Chronique*, II, 70–73. Jean Molinet, in his continuation of Chastelain, composted a poem about Le Daim: "Jay veu oyseau ramage,/ Nommé maîstre Olivier, / Voilant par son plumage / Hault comme un esprevier,/
Fort bien savoit complaire Au Roy. Mais je vis qu'on / Le fit pour son salaire /Perchier à Monfaucquon" (48). Montfaucon was the site of the royal gibbet.

[128] The town council of Tournai sent an official delegate, with a detailed list of the damages done by Le Daim.

[129] Jean de Roye, *Chronique*, II, 138.

in which is *la chose publique* of this kingdom by the means of several of its
enemies being around my lord the king

Charles claimed these "enemies" of the public good had cases judged in
Parlement according to their will, levied heavy taxes that the people of the
kingdom could barely support, forced children into marriages, without the
consent of their parents and relatives, "the which things are against all order of
right, and are to the dishonor and vituperation of the kingdom, and confusion
of the *chose publique*": he demanded the expulsion of these "enemies of the
bien public" and the return of good order and form.[130] Louis naturally
responded that Charles' action would bring harm to "*la chose publique.*"

Louis wrote to the other princes, such as Jean, duke of Bourbon, to seek their
aid and justify his conduct. Bourbon had been stripped of his position as
governor of Guyenne as part of the general house cleaning of Louis XI's
accession, so he, like so many others, had a specific grievance against the king.

> for a long time it has been considered and weighed generally by the
> seigneurs and princes of your blood and lineage who have seigneuries,
> lands, and *pays* in your said kingdom and under you, and who after you
> have interest in the good, prosperity and maintenance of your said
> kingdom of which after you they have good part, each in his own place,
> the means which have been held in the fact of justice, police and
> government

Bourbon accused the king of "grand and excessive charges on the poor
people"; the princes have "heard, seen and know" of complaints, sadness,
suffering, heavy taxes "beyond all order, due and accustomed manner."
Princes and others have complained to those the king named to run the
kingdom: such complaints deserved action for the "*bien*, utility and conservation of the *chose publique*" of your said kingdom "and also for the estate
of the said seigneurs and princes." The kingdom had been "long prospering
in good justice, tranquility and ordinary police all of which things are well
known [*notoires*]." The duke suggested that all of those involved in the
revolt "could not have blame or reproach before God, your Crown or
justice."[131] [March 1465]

---

[130] BNF, M Dupuy 539, fol. 19ff. "gens du sang de france et autres nobles hommes et
conseillers [...] la grande calamité en quoy est la chose publicque de ce royaulme par le
moyen d'aucuns ennemis d'icelle estans environ monseigneur le roy." Virtually all the
documents of this period, and on up to those from the Estates General of 1484, mention
this charge of daughters being married, often to men of inappropriate status, against the
wishes of their parents: "font faire mariages outre le gré volonté et consentement des
peres et meres et autres parens lesquels choses sont contre tout ordre de droit deshon-
neur et vitupere du royaulme confusion de la chose publicque."

[131] The Estates General of 1484 and all early modern historians treating the fifteenth century
return to this theme that the kingdom was at peace and enjoying prosperity in the late
1450s. BNF, M Dupuy 539, ff. 25v–27: "qui ont interest apres vous au bien prosperité et

René d'Anjou, "king" of Sicily, great-great-grandson of King John II, tried to mediate between Louis and the princes. He told Charles of Berry that the king "was well content" with his remonstrances, "which everyone could know to be true and reasonable."[132] Berry then told René that he feared for his life, because the king did not love him: the "good king René," as his Provençal subjects called him, relayed Louis XI's reply that Charles had nothing to fear. Louis castigated those, like the duke of Bourbon, who had spoken against his "authority and royal majesty," and who had attacked his councilors, such as the chancellor and the seneschal of Poitou (who had become marshal of France). The duke of Berry claimed that the "seigneurs of the blood, the clergy, the nobility, the poor people, and even 'justice'" knew of the disorders. He later insisted the king call an Estates General to look to "the good of the king, of the crown and of the *chose publique*."[133] [fol. 61] Louis XI's public response emphasized Berry's youth and inexperience, and insisted that "the king is his head (*chief*), his king and sovereign seigneur," so that Berry owed him "homage, obedience, fidelity and service."

Berry wrote (July 4) to the count of Vendôme[134] that the greatest and most powerful princes and "seigneurs du sang" together sought a remedy for the "disorder which is in all the estates and facts of the kingdom, for the good and honor of the kingdom and good and honor of the crown and to the profit of all *la chose publique*." Vendôme begged off: he held his castles for the king, but in his reply, he said nothing in support of the king, nor did he deny the justness of Berry's complaints. He just wanted to spare his county from war and taxes.

In April, the conspiracy hardened. Philip of Burgundy told (fol. 71) his Estates they had always been loyal to him as "their seigneur and head [*chef*] of the *chose publique*": he reminded them that he had several times exposed his goods and life for them, that "by justice he has maintained them in good union, and by his clemency, *bonté* and pity has been as benign and gracious to them as ever prince has been to subjects." Speaking of the "great mutations" in France and their cause, he ended by asking them to swear loyalty to Charles, his heir, who would, in fact, soon inherit his father's dominions. In describing those mutations, Philip referred to letters sent by the duke of Berry, similar to those he had sent to the duke of Calabria.[135] Berry claimed the new royal councilors

---

entretennement de vostredit royaume auquel apres vous ilz ont bonne part chacun en son endroit, les facons qui ont esté tenues tant ou faict de la justice police et gouvernement d'iceluy"

[132] Brother-in-law of Charles VII, René also held the counties of Maine, Provence, and Guise, and the duchies of Bar and Lorraine. Kekewich, *René of Anjou*.

[133] BNF, M Dupuy 539, fol. 38. Folio numbers in the text in this section refer to Dupuy 539.

[134] Jean VIII de Bourbon-Vendôme, descended from Robert de Clermont, youngest son of Saint Louis; King Henry IV was Jean's great-great-grandson.

[135] Jean II of Anjou, duke of Lorraine and titular duke of Calabria; he was the son of "king" René. Seeking to make good on the offer of the crown of Aragon, made by the Catalans in

sought their own good, not that of king, kingdom, and *chose publique*. The princes, he claimed, want to "make justice reign, maintain and guard the authority of the church and liberty of the nobles, cease and make cease all acts of force and violence," and eliminate all taxes on the poor people, other than the *taille* levied for men at arms.

Philip's son, Charles, count of Charolais, wrote to the town government of Amiens [fol. 89] claiming that Louis XI's councilors had created enmity with longtime allies, like the kings of Castile and Scotland. Charolais, like the duke of Berry, lamented that "the authority of the church is no longer guarded, justice is neither done nor administered, the nobles are not maintained in their rights and usages of nobility, and the poor people are not supported or protected from oppression." The town of Amiens arrested the herald who brought Charolais' letters: he graciously forgave the town government, claiming that the chancellor (Morvillier, whose eponymous cousin was Amiens' mayor) had taken this unworthy act. Charolais' letters about the arrest of the herald duly noted that bad councilors would have their profits confiscated and would be punished for their faults and "evil counsel." [fol. 100]

The soldiers of the two sides ravaged various parts of the French countryside, fought an indecisive battle (Montlhéry) outside Paris in July, and finally laid down their arms in September. Chastellain ridicules the forces of the two sides, especially the Burgundians; indeed, the descriptions of the battle make it sound like two completely undisciplined, ill-trained noble mobs more interested in loot than in fighting. Both sides squandered chances at victory by stopping to pillage baggage trains; both commanders, Charles of Burgundy and Louis XI, came within a hair's breadth of death, through undisciplined bungling.[136]

The treaties of Conflans (October 5) and St-Maur-des-Fossés (October 27) did address the "bien public." In the preamble to the Treaty of Conflans, Louis XI stated that Charles of Burgundy and the other princes had assembled with him to discuss various matters related to the "bien public et universel de nostre royaume."[137] The king said he met with many leading seigneurs, trying to restore peace, and together they had taken "several good and notable overtures done as much for the *bien public* of our kingdom, police and government of the same, as to have peace and union with our said brother and cousin the count of Charolais." The Treaty of St-Maur suggested that a commission was to seek remedies for "the good of the King, the said lords, of his subjects, and the chose publique of the kingdom." It singled out the conservation of the "rights,

---

1466, Jean went to Barcelona, where he died of poisoning. His sons, Jean (1471) and Nicolas (1473) died soon after: contemporaries suspected Louis XI of poisoning Nicolas.

[136] After the battle, having heard of the duke's wound, Louis sent letters to supporters, and to many towns, claiming Charles had been so badly wounded that he was either near death or dead.

[137] *Ordonnances*, XVI, 355–356.

liberties, and franchises of the Church, the nobles, and of other vassals and subject" : here we see a fine example of the deliberate omission of the word "privileges."[138]

The commission of thirty-six men – twelve each from the nobility, clergy, and men of "council and justice" – to advise Louis was supposed to come up with recommendation for the good of the "chose publique." Louis promised to act on their recommendations within a fortnight, by sending letters patent to the sovereign courts. The commission's power was to lapse on December 15, 1465. Louis naturally just ignored them. Even so, Louis's behavior changed for good; as Jean Favier puts it, "after 1465, the impulsive Louis XI became a wise man."[139]

In theory, the big winner was Charles of Berry, who now received Normandy as an apanage. Charles of Burgundy, now become duke, got the Somme towns: Louis agreed to this transfer acting "as much for the *le bien public* of our kingdom, the administration and government of it," as for any other reason. The duke of Bourbon (and his wife, Louis' sister Jeanne), got extensive authority in their vast territories in the Midi.[140] In return, the leaders – the Captal de Buch, the count of Armagnac, the duke of Nemours et al. – took an oath of loyalty, renouncing previous oaths given "to any person or seigneur or seigneurs whether it be under the pretext of the *bien public* or otherwise."[141]

Louis' various actions – the temporizing, the creation of obligations within the Order of St. Michael, the use of an Estates General (1468) – helped him defeat the princes, one by one. His brother Charles quickly lost Normandy – Louis had the ring of the duke of Normandy smashed at Rouen, in front of the local elite – and died childless in 1472.[142] Jean V d'Armagnac would be condemned for treason and was later murdered by one of the soldiers of Antoine de Chabannes sent to arrest him. Jacques d'Armagnac, duke of Nemours, likewise was condemned for treason, as was Jean, duke of Alençon, who had supported Louis during the 1465 crisis. In both cases, as had been true of Alençon's 1458 trial, they stood charged with lèse-majesté against *la chose publique*, as well as against king and Crown.

Jean d'Alençon's son, René, also faced charges of lèse-majesté in 1481. His trial documents indicate a new direction, an important shift in vocabulary.

---

[138] *Ordonnances*, XVI, 378ff.

[139] Favier, *Louis XI*, 922.

[140] BNF, M Dupuy 539, folios 166 and 206. Bourbon did not get new territories, but he and Jeanne got much greater authority in their existing ones and the prized governorship of Languedoc, to go with restoration of that of Berry.

[141] M Dupuy 539, 368ff. In a note on fol. 375ff, Nemours took an oath to be faithful to king, even against previous allies, who had united "soubz couleur du bien public."

[142] Commynes, *Mémoires*, I, 109, says Charles of Burgundy wanted Louis to have to give up Normandy to his brother, because it would reduce the king's strength by one-third.

Louis' letters patent ordering René's arrest in August 1481 begin with the usual vocabulary: they accuse him of acting "to the prejudice of Us and *la chose publique* of our said kingdom."[143] The letters later refer to the loyalty a "good subject" owes to his sovereign, a novel usage of that term for the time. Placing the disloyalty purely in the realm of subject-sovereign changes the political system: we do not see reference to disloyalty by a vassal to his "souverain seigneur." Given Louis XI's long history of seeking personal revenge, to avoid anachronism, we should probably see this particular usage as Louis focusing on the personal disloyalty to him, but the early use of the term "sovereign" in something like the sense that would become normative in the last third of the sixteenth century does presage those later developments. Louis XI died in 1483 and this usage died with him, at least insofar as concerns Charles VIII and Louis XII. As for René, his letters and other writings, such as his complaint to or demands upon the king, demonstrate precisely the sort of "particular" interest cited by Commynes, and no interest at all for the *bien public*.

These princes made a dubious defense team for the "*bien public*": they plotted incessantly against the king and made alliances with France's enemies (above all, England). Princes like Jean d'Alençon felt genuine grievance about inadequate compensation for great sacrifices made for the Crown, but their grievances were, above all, "particulier" not public. We should not therefore conclude, however, that the War of the Public Good had nothing to do with the *bien public*. Louis XI's subjects strenuously objected to his repudiation of the commonwealth: the Estates General of 1484 tried to reestablish the full Commonwealth, even to push beyond anything Charles VII had practiced.

In fact, Louis XI himself recognized his initial act as a catastrophic mistake. In his testament, Louis specifically warned his successors against repeating his foolish error: "We remonstrated to him the great evils and irreparable damages that arrived to us shortly after coming to the throne, for not have maintained the lords and officers of our kingdom in their estates, charges, and offices," leading to destruction in "many of our lands." Anne de Beaujeu, as regent, followed her father's advice: the first act of the child Charles VIII was to confirm all the judges of the Parlement of Paris.[144] Louis himself, in the *Rosier des guerres* he had composed on rulership, as a guide for his son, told young Charles: "I send you this present *Rosier* touching upon the guardianship and defense of *la chose publique*." Harkening back to Giles of Rome, he told his son to

---

[143] F. Bouviers des Noes, *Procédures politiques du règne de Louis XI*, v. II, document 15.
[144] *Ordonnances*, XIX, 125. Maugis, *Parlement de Paris*, I, 80, rightly points out that in recommending this course of action, Louis XI preserved intact the administrative personnel **he** had named.

make sure he "did nothing" without consulting his conscience to see that he acted "according to God and reason."[145] The monarchical commonwealth, deeply wounded, nonetheless survived for another century.

---

[145] Cited in Y. Labande-Mailfert, *Charles VIII* (Paris: Fayard, 1986), 21. Favier, *Louis XI*, 883, attributes the *Rosier* to Louis' doctor, Pierre Choisnet.

5

The *chose publique* and Urban Government

When did the transitions in vocabulary take place at the urban and regional levels, and what relationship did those changes have to broader events? The first vocabulary shift gives us a strong indicator about the political integration of a given region into the functioning kingdom of France and into its political community, its *chose publique* [*res publica*]. The term *chose publique* carried multiple meanings in urban vocabularies: in a political sense, it could mean the kingdom, the province or *pays*, or the town itself.[1] Documents regularly used the term "chose publique" to refer to the larger economic community, which shared common interests in matters such as fair exchange and transportation. The smaller town council, almost always run by merchant and legal oligarchies, invariably consulted a larger assembly when deciding matters of great concern to the "chose publique," such as the creation of a new tax or military decisions likely to affect the town and its surroundings. These larger assemblies seem to have been less comprehensive in the south than in the north, but still included far more members than the smaller council.[2] The use of "chose publique" instead of "respublique" for "res publica" surely resonated with townsmen from the world of commerce.

As we have seen in Chapters 1 and 2, in 1358–1360, commonwealth vocabulary became normative in the areas participating in the Estates General of Languedoïl: the Paris basin, Normandy, the Loire Valley, Champagne, and Picardy, as well as Brittany and Burgundy. It arrived much later in the south and Flanders. In the southwest, the constantly shifting territories of the kings of France and England made towns like Bergerac or

---

[1] At the local level, the word *pays* could refer to an entire province, like Brittany, to a bailiwick, or to a city and its immediate surroundings. All contemporary scholars working on this topic build on the pioneering work of B. Chevalier, *Les bonnes villes de France du XIVe au XVIe siècle* (Paris: Aubier, 1982).

[2] C. Fargeix, *Les élites lyonnaises*, 429. I have used her doctoral thesis, which is available online:

http://theses.univ-lyon2.fr/documents/lyon2/2005/fargeix_c#p=0&a=title

Dozens of guild masters participated in the Lyon assemblies: see the table on 426. In 1427, she cites [427] an assembly, precisely about a new tax, with 600 participants.

Saint-Jean d'Angély reticent to use the French royal vocabulary, and Bordeaux remained, until 1453, in English hands.

Neither Dauphiné nor Provence was part of the traditional kingdom of France and royal edicts long referred to the "kingdom and Dauphiné." Francis I kept separate his title as count of Provence and distinguished, in his 1515 alliance with Jean d'Albret, king of Navarre, between the kingdom and the duchy of Brittany, and other [unnamed] duchies and counties he possessed.[3] For these outlying areas, particularly those not part of the medieval kingdom of France, inclusion in the French "chose publique" was far from clear. Towns in the south remained closely tied to Italian political vocabulary of the urban "republic" [*civitas*]; moreover, cities from Arles to Toulouse or Bordeaux did not keep their registers in French.[4]

The commonwealth vocabulary had many variants, and these various regions displayed distinctive urban usages.[5] The walled towns, the "bonnes villes," provided a specific and powerful interest group in French politics. Such towns had many critical roles, but we might single out five of them, with respect to kingdom-wide politics. First, the walled towns provided essential bastions against enemy armies. These towns, in their negotiations with the central government over tax payments could thus make the argument that the upkeep of their walls served the "bien de la chose publique" of the entire kingdom. Charles V accepted this line of argument and invariably shared the proceeds of the new royal taxes with walled towns. In later centuries, towns on or near the frontier – like Amiens, Dijon, Lyon, or Narbonne – effectively used the same argument. In his 1547 ordinance banning royal judges from holding municipal office, Henry II cited the need to have merchants, who had knowledge of administering money, run the towns, so that the finances of the town would be capable of paying, above all, for the upkeep of the walls.[6]

---

[3] In 1515, naming René, bastard of Savoy the royal lieutenant general for Provence, Francis I referred to himself as "Francis by the grace of God king of France, count of Provence, Forcalquier and the adjacent lands." *Ordonnances des rois de France: règne de François Ier*, v. I (Paris, 1902), #28, 109. Louis XIII's edicts sent to the Parlement of Aix still listed "comte de Provence" as one of his titles. Francis's 1515 alliance with Jean d'Albret. D'Albret, #38, 144.

[4] AC Arles, BB 1, first image, Arles is a "civita[ti]s." The first entry is for the election of the consuls of the "civitatis" of Arles. [image 5r online]. BB 5, image 267v, the "civitate" pledges loyalty in 1480 to the new count of Provence, Charles IV, in return for his promise to respect the "conventions, statutes, and liberties" of Arles. In voting 8,000 florins to Charles IV, the consuls [image 265r] had cited the "bonis dicte civitatis" – the good of the said *civitas*. On Dauphiné, see G. Lurie, "Citizenship in Later Medieval France, c. 1370 – c. 1480," Ph.D. thesis, 2012, Georgetown University, ch. 7, available online through Georgetown's library.

[5] On the process of meetings, Fargeix, *Les élites lyonnaises*, part III, ch. 2.

[6] Isambert, *Recueil*, XIII, 34.

Second, the walled towns provided a substantial share of the revenue from the new indirect taxes on sales of wine and other goods. The disturbances of the 1350s and 1380s made clear urban opposition to these taxes; the royal triumph of 1382–1383 put an end to serious resistance and marked the transition to permanent indirect royal taxation. At the Estates General of 1484, the Normans sparked outrage from the royal council when they spoke against the legitimacy of taxation: no one should be surprised that having sworn to defend the "interests of the people [*rem populi*]" that they carried out their oath. First, the *tailles* having been established because of a war, should have ceased when the war ended. They claimed they would not be fulfilling their mandates if they voted a tax [the *taille*] that brought "servitude" and "damage" [*perniciem*] at a time when the "republic was not in great danger [*reipubicœ majori periculo*]." By "grave corruption," the *gabelle* and the tax on wine, voted to deal with a danger, instead, like the royal demesne, had become eternal [*jam velut domanium, œterna perseverant*]. The members of the royal council reacted sharply, accusing the Normans of criminal intentions, and asking if they believed the subjects could be permitted to resist payment for the necessities of the republic [*reipublicœ necessitatibus satis*], against the laws of all kingdoms? Did they wish "to write the laws of an imaginary monarchy?"[7] [*imaginatœ monarchiœ leges velle prescribere*]. Towns also collected such taxes, for their own needs, but they could justly point out that large assemblies had invariably approved the taxes in question, often after acrid debate about the form the tax would take.

Third, as the proceeds from the indirect taxes made obvious, towns were where the money was: commerce took place there and cash settled in urban coffers. Fourth, many towns housed royal administrators: bailiwick courts; *élections* of the financial system (which were also law courts); demesne officers; monopoly salt warehouses. Royal administration of the countryside emanated out from the towns. Fifth, the combination of commercial and governmental roles made the towns the critical hubs for the dissemination of information. Caroline Fargeix's work on Lyon shows that the council established in 1460 a "*porte-parole*," or rapporteur, to present the agenda at the start of the meeting: she lists the *porte-parole* for the years ending in "7" from 1467 to 1517: each one was a Doctor of Laws, giving us a clear indication of why legal vocabulary played so important a role in municipal affairs.[8]

---

[7] Masselin, *Journal*, 418–421, has the Latin text and French facing translation. Masselin translated the French proceedings into Latin for his journal, so the French version is a double translation. Isambert, *Recueil*, XI, as part of its presentation of Masselin reproduces Garnier's eighteenth-century "translation" of this passage (78–79), which provides fascinating insights into the political discourse of the 1770s.

[8] Fargeix, *Les élites lyonnaises*, table on 467.

Within the group of walled towns, an important dividing line separated cities like Paris and Lyon, whose inhabitants were exempt from the *tailles*, and the taxpayers of most smaller walled towns, who had to pay.[9] The small-town bourgeoisie and the *laboureurs* (ploughmen) of the villages paid the lion's share of direct taxes: these two groups thus had a special interest in the central government's demands for direct taxation – which skyrocketed under Louis XI. The survival of the cahiers for both the city of Lyon and the governorship of the Lyonnais in 1576 neatly illustrates the difference: Lyon's *cahier* calls upon Henry III to maintain this privilege; the *cahier* of the Lyonnais insists that all should have to pay taxes for rural properties.[10]

Over the course of the period 1356–1560 the balance of forces shifted in many towns, and the local political discourse shifted with it. In towns with a sovereign court, or even a bailiwick, the power shifted toward the legal elite. This process accelerated dramatically in the sixteenth century because kings starting with Francis I sold so many new offices, in both financial and judicial administrations. Whereas fourteenth-century urban political conflict often pitted merchants against guild artisans, in the sixteenth century, the merchants squared off against the men of the law, led by the most powerful local judges. Whether it was Agen in the southwest or Amiens in the extreme north, sixteenth-century town councils debated royal legislation about banning royal judges from sitting as mayors or *échevins* or consuls.[11]

Amiens offers a fine example of this lengthy struggle among the artisans, merchants, and royal officers. Many northern towns had chosen violent resistance to the taxes in 1382; Amiens' merchant elite blamed the artisans and sought royal approval to strip the guilds of their share of political power. The merchants petitioned the king to overturn the election of 1382, when the "maieurs des bannières," or guild representatives had elected Henri de Roye as the city's treasurer [*grand compteur*]: the royal government removed Roye and

---

[9] Some small towns also won exemption: when Francis I became king, he granted his birthplace, Cognac, exemption from the *tailles*.

[10] AM de Lyon, BB 94, fols. 170v and ff. [Online: image 165] In their section "de l'estat et pollice du royaulme" [f. 179; online: image 173], the first article noted that past kings had gratified towns by "recognizing" their "privileges, liberties, franchises, and immunities," which new taxes introduced by "evil spirits" [*malins espritz*], most of them "Italians and foreigners" had undermined. The second article [179–179v] asserted that all *"villes franches"* had paid "onerous" sums in the fourteenth and fifteenth centuries for this exemption. The governorship *cahier* is in the journal of the noble deputy Pierre Blanchefort, BNF, M Fr 16,250, starting on fol. 95. Lyon had the complicated situation that its bourgeois often owned land in the Empire or Savoy.

[11] Agen, which had a bailiwick court, protested Henry II's 1547 ban on royal officers serving on town governments. J.-B. Bosvieux, *Inventaire Sommaire des archives communales antérieures à 1790. Ville d'Agen* (Paris, 1884), entry for BB 27. The *avocats* typically sided with the merchants.

substituted Jean de Beauval. Parlement's *arrêt* said Roye had little wealth and "did not know how to read or write."[12] The king thereupon eliminated the guild masters from the electorate choosing the mayor. They would not get their rights back until 1484, when Anne de Beaujeu, acting for the young Charles VIII, solidified popular support for the king in a vitally important town on a hostile border.

Royal letters of 1385 mentioned that in 1382 the *maieurs* and several other men of "small status," without the consent of the better part of the bourgeois and inhabitants of the town, had committed "rebellions, disobedience, abuse, assemblies, monopolies, conspiracy, seditions, and other excesses and delicts against our royal majesty and the bien de la chose publique." The royal commissaires had beheaded some of the *maieurs*, banished others, and enforced the political ban.[13] This episode marked a typical royal intervention in town politics: the central authority intervened – at the invitation of the locals – not so much to expand its own authority, but to support a given faction or social group within the town.

The relationship between the "good towns" and the Crown encompassed such a wide range of elements that simplistic views of royal encroachment onto municipal liberties disguise more complex developments. The simplest illustration is the endlessly contradictory royal attitude toward officers holding municipal office. Louis XII, in an edict of September 1503, banned royal officers from municipal government in Amiens. Citing the need for the mayor and council to allow the inhabitants to live in "good peace, love and union, to the good, profit and utility of us and of all the chose publique of this town and the surrounding *pays*," he excluded royal officers, whose royal duties "could prevent them from seeing to and understanding the affairs and police of the said town."[14]

Henry II emitted directly contradictory laws: in October 1547, he banned all officers of sovereign courts, bailiwick and seneschalsy courts, *élus*, and royal lawyers from serving as mayors, *échevins*, or other urban officers. He mentioned the fiscal knowledge of merchants and their ability to devote time to the "utility and bien public" of the towns. Judges, in contrast, were busy rendering justice, "and do not have such knowledge and experience in the handling and administration of money," as did the bourgeois and merchants. The ordinance further stipulated that the bourgeois should vote to elect mayors and such; anyone voting for a royal officer was to be fined 200 *écus*, half each to the king and the town coffers. If an officer were elected, the town would forfeit its right to elect, and the king would name the mayor or *échevins*. The royal officer would forfeit his office.[15]

---

[12] Thierry, *Recueil des monuments inédits de [...] Amiens*, I, 708. Twenty-four different guilds had been represented by two "*maieurs*" each up through 1382.

[13] Thierry, *Recueil [...] Amiens*, I, 736.

[14] Thierry, *Recueil [...] Amiens*, II, 496.

[15] Isambert, *Recueil*, XIII, 34ff.

In May 1552, Henry II called into question his father's 1542 edict on Amiens, and directly contradicting his own reasoning of 1547, claiming that merchants and men of the short robe "could not well satisfy the needs of these positions, not having the knowledge of letters, or laws and customs, which is very necessary for the administration of justice." Furthermore, they were not experienced in the "conduct of the great affairs concerning the republic [*respublique*] of a town like this one." The inhabitants of Amiens had thus petitioned the king to let them choose a mayor and *échevins* from any honorable estate, whether "royal officers, men of law, gentlemen, merchants, or others."[16] Two years later, when the lieutenant general of the bailiwick filed a suit against the mayor and *échevins* for having chosen men of the long robe, the city council arrested him; the king's council, in direct contradiction of the 1552 edict, dismissed the 1552 election result – the king's procureur, Me Jean de Thérouane had been elected mayor – and again forbade any judge of the long robe from serving as mayor. Henry II's April 1554 letters mentioned the names of all the *échevins*, five of whom were royal officers, including the receiver general of Picardy.

In 1557, Henry II asked the council to continue Jérôme Dainval as mayor, but the royal procureur pointed out that Dainval had just bought the new office of *garde du sceau royal* at the bailiwick of Amiens; the electors chose Antoine Louvet. The king's council sided with Louvet, but Henry added a clause stating that Amiens would be exempt from his 1547 blanket ban on judicial officers. Nineteen years later, Charles IX sent letters permitting one or two men of the long robe to serve.[17] The *cahier* of the bailiwick of Amiens in 1576 asked Henry III to legalize the right of judges of the long robe to hold municipal office, but the city of Amiens, in its *cahier*, specifically asked the king to ban them. Fortunately for them, Jean de Morvillier, descended from a family with almost two centuries of service on Amiens' town council, was one of the secretaries of state, and they made sure to send their delegation straight to him.[18] In so doing, they followed a typical technique: in 1576, just as delegates from Amiens went to Morvillier, who, even though from Blois, had family connections to Amiens, so, too, delegates from Lyon would go to Pomponne de Bellièvre, whose father had been on their town council.[19]

---

[16] Thierry, *Recueil [. . .] Amiens*, II, 631ff.

[17] Thierry, *Recueil [. . .] Amiens*, II, 765; 817. Charles IX had prepared letters allowing open eligibility, including for nobles, but died before he could issue it, so they went out under Henry III's signature.

[18] Morvillier, bishop of Orléans, was one of Catherine de Medici's chief counselors; he was the great-grandson of the Philippe de Morvillier who was chancellor of France under Louis XI.

[19] Towns also made use of powerful aristocrats. Louis de la Trémoïlle, governor of Burgundy, wrote extensively to the mayor of Dijon about a 1521 royal visit. In a letter

The bailiwick *cahier*, in contrast to Amiens' town articles, noted that in order to "avoid abuses and connivances of merchants who hold the government and police of towns, the which merchants and bourgeois have in their hands and administration all of the said police, whether for wines, grains, wood or other sorts of merchandises," that the king allow men of the long robe and other notable and capable persons to hold such offices, as had been long practiced in Amiens. In an assembly dominated by royal judges, they unsurprisingly demanded the consular (merchant) courts be suppressed. The merchants of Amiens struck back, asking to maintain the consular court, to keep the traditional method of choosing *échevins*, and to ban officers of the long robe from sitting in Amiens' government. The royal government compromised: the merchants kept their consular court – in Amiens and elsewhere – but the judges remained eligible for municipal offices.[20]

This quarrel repeated itself at the bailiwick estate meetings. Normandy long had a rule banning royal officers from sitting as deputies in its provincial estates or for the Estates General, but they made an exception for royal officers who were also municipal officials: in practice, that meant royal officers from Rouen often participated. In Champagne and in Burgundy, in 1588, non-officers protested against the presence of royal officers on the delegations: in Champagne, merchants led the charge; in Burgundy, it was the *avocats*.[21] These cases held multiple motives: in Champagne, the merchants sided with the Catholic League, and they sought to exclude royal officials – felt to be too supportive of Henry III – from both the town council of Troyes and the delegation to the Estates General.[22] The *cahier* of the city of Troyes, and that of its bailiwick, had specifically called for the maintenance of the consular

of May 6, he mentioned that the duchess of Alençon (Marguerite, the king's sister) had received a gift from the city of Troyes during the entry there: he urged them to do the same, "because she can give you a great deal of pleasure [*plaisir*] in your affairs." Garnier, ed., *Correspondance de la mairie de Dijon*, I, 298. At Limoges, the city pulled out all the stops – including a special viewing of the preserved skulls of three local saints – for Charles, duke of Bourbon, who was so pleased he promised that "he will gladly employ himself both with the king and elsewhere as for his own [*propres*] affairs." *Registres consulaires de la ville de Limoges*, I, 57–59.

[20] Thierry, *Recueil [. . .] Amiens, II*, 861ff. Deputies from all the major towns joined together to lobby the king's council about the consular courts.

[21] A compromise allowed deputies already chosen in 1588 to serve but ruled that henceforth royal officers would be banned from representing the bailiwicks. In 1614, neither province respected this rule. The Guise faction naturally wanted to remove royal officers, assumed to be loyal to Henry III, from the group of deputies, but both of the first two orders, and the non-royal officers of the Third, brought up the contradiction at every meeting; in 1614, they believed the stranglehold of officers on the Third's deputation led to the failure to abolish venal offices.

[22] M. Bailly de Barbery and R. de Saint-Maruis, eds., "Mémoires et livre de famille de Nicolas Dare" in *Collection des documents inédits relatifs à la ville de Troyes*, t. III (Troyes, 1886). Dare was a prominent and wealthy cloth merchant.

(merchants) court, but the royal judges serving as deputies from the seven bailiwicks in the governorship of Champagne, in their *cahier*, had inserted the demand that these courts be abolished.[23]

The conflict between merchants' consular **elected** judges and royal judges evident at Troyes appears in every city with a royal court. At Blois, in 1566, the town council recommended a royal officer and a merchant as the incoming *échevins*: the assembly, which included a large group of royal officers, chose instead two royal officers, one of whom, Florimond III de Robertet, was a *secrétaire d'État*.[24] One problem with reform of the judicial system – particularly with the demand, made from 1484 to 1576, to restore election of judges – was that from 1484 to 1614, a remarkably high percentage of the Third Estates' deputies were the lieutenant general (chief judge) of the bailiwick.[25] The merchants and *avocats* put up a fight at the bailiwick assemblies, whose *cahiers* regularly included an article calling for the election of local judges and highly detailed recommendations about improving legal and administrative practice, but must have known the elected deputy would ignore this suggestion.[26] The bailiwick assembly of Blois in 1576, dominated by judges and lawyers, chose *noble homme* Me Simon Riolle, lieutenant general of the bailiwick of Blois, as their deputy, but then voted an article to insist on triennial elections of royal judges, despite the argument from another royal official that the king had recently appointed only highly qualified men.[27] Autun's 1576 deputy, a local ecclesiastical judge, Georges Venot, who had several times been *vierg* (mayor), objected to articles about abolishing ecclesiastical courts, on the grounds that he could hardly be expected to petition the Estates General to abolish his own job. He initially refused to serve as deputy, but he finally relented, and the article stayed in.[28]

Municipal authorities trod a fine line, as we can see in the remarkable fifteenth-century oath of office taken by the mayor of Dijon. He swore by all

---

[23] Dare, "Mémoires," 35–36. For the election to be valid, at least fifty merchants had to participate. The deputies from each of the thirteen governorships met together once at the Estates General; the Champagne *cahier* is in Lalourcé and Duval, *Recueil*, IX, 191ff.

[24] Jacques Viart, *bailli* and governor of Blois, chaired the meeting. L. Bergevin and A. Dupré, *Histoire de Blois*, v. II (Blois, 1847), 189–190. AM Blois, BB 5, fols. 120ff for the meeting and *cahier*. Viart's wife, Françoise de Phélypeaux, was the aunt of Paul Phélypeaux, founder of the dynasty of secretaries of state.

[25] On the failure of these reforms, Greengrass, *Governing Passions*.

[26] Blois's *cahiers* in both 1576 and 1614 contained mind-numbing detail on proposed reforms in legal and administrative practice, right down to who should be allowed to witness notarial documents. AM Blois, BB 17 for the lengthy documents of 1614, BB 5, fols. 150ff for the *cahier* of 1576.

[27] AM Blois, BB 5, 138v–141 on election of judges. Three of Blois' town officers spoke in favor of the article. Jacques Viart spoke in defense of royal judges.

[28] H. Abord, *Histoire de la Réforme et de la Ligue dans la ville d'Autun: précédée d'une introduction et suivie de pièces justificatives* (Paris, 1855), v. II, 470–471.

his power [*pouvoir*] to guard the "honor, estate, right, prerogatives and nobilities of the King our Lord [*Seigneur*]." In a second clause, however, he had a contradictory responsibility:

> That he will guard the good, honor, estates, rights, privileges, franchises and liberties of the said town in the way in which they are written and thus that one will enjoy and use them without suffering them to be restrained [*enfraindre*] in any way by the King our Lord's sergeants, officers, and others

The oath required the mayor to make sure all the town council's deliberations got written down, with nothing taken out or added in.[29] A royal officer, taking an oath to protect the city's rights against infringement by royal officers, faced an obvious conflict of interest.

Town governments thought as well about the "bien public" of the *cité*: the *échevins* of Reims cited that phrase in agreeing to help pay for a lawsuit of a local citizen, who claimed he was defending the *cité's* rights.[30] These early uses of the term *"bien public"* were unusual, but in the sixteenth century the terms "bien public" and, by mid-century, "respublique" became more common. At Chalon-sur-Saône, at the 1539 election of the new officers, they pledged to look after the "urgent affairs of the said town and its bien public."[31] Twenty-one years later, electing deputies to the Estates General of Orléans, the inhabitants were to "speak and discuss the written articles both on the fact of religion and of the republic [*respublique*]." The assembly, with more than sixty-five men present, picked a three-man commission to draft articles on the "complaints and grievance to make to the Majesty of the King and his estates general both on religion and on the republic."[32]

5.1 La chose publique of the economy

The vocabulary of "la chose publique" suited townsmen particularly well because the phrase invariably turned up in royal edicts related to commerce

---

[29] AM Dijon, GG 3, on parchment. "qu'il gardera le bien honneur estat drois privileges franchises et libertez de lad ville en la maniere qu'ilz sont escriptz et ainsi que l'on en a joy et usé sans les souffrir enfraindre en aucune maniere par le Roy nre dit Seigneur sergens officiers et autres." Dijon's mayors in this period tended to be lawyers like Pierre Sayve, who served from 1514–1517, 1528–1529, and 1534–1537. Bernard Des Barres (1573–1575), councilor and later president at the Parlement, marked a significant break in this tradition.

[30] Varin, *Archives administratives*, III, document DCCCXXXIX, 1378.

[31] AM Chalon, BB 2, July 4, 1539.

[32] AM Chalon, BB 3, general assembly of November 29, 1560. The follow-up meeting on December 1 named a twelve-member commission – four each of men of letters, merchants, and clergy – for "the fact of religion and of the Republic." See Chapter 6 for more on the use of "republic."

and manufacturing, such as those about markets and guild privileges, or the abolition of all rights and tolls created since Philip IV (December 1380).[33] Town governments regularly brought up the "bien de la chose publique" or the "bien public" when funding public works, such as street or bridge repairs. Given the link between coinage and "la chose publique," the marketplace was, by definition, a place of rhetorical intersection. The confirmation of the privileges of the wine measurers of Auxerre, in 1383, like most such letters, spoke of the "good, profit and utility of 'la chose publique', and of the merchants who from various lands [*pays*] and countries [*contrées*]" shipped and sold wine on the Seine, Marne, Yonne, and Loire rivers: they needed to be protected from fraud and malfeasance, so the king renewed the privileges of the official measurers, so that all could have confidence in transactions.[34] A few days later, in letters for the Prior of La Charité-sur-Loire, the king allowed him to change the local wine measure to conform to those nearby, to help prevent fraud against merchants, wishing in this way to act for "*le bien public* of the said town and its countryside."[35] In 1393, the town government of Abbeville set up rules for selling herring in the city, "for the good of the *chose publique* and of the government of the said town."[36]

More than a century later, in letters granting the continuation of a tax on salt to help pay for repairs of the Pont Notre-Dame in Paris (1506), Louis XII cited the "bien, profit and commodity of the *chose publique*, as they say."[37] In Paris, deliberations regularly made use of the commonwealth vocabulary. In 1512, when they decided to clean up the Bièvre sewer, they spoke of the "bien et utilité publique"; later that year, in deciding to repair the city's walls, in case of invasion, they praised the military supervisor as one always known for his "zeal for the *bien public* of this town of Paris."[38] The Paris town government continued to use this vocabulary for public works, such as the Pont Neuf, in the early seventeenth century. The "chose publique" was thus not only the translation for *res publica*, but also the term for places of public interaction, like markets: context in each document usually makes clear the sense, but it should be emphasized that the term was by no means used **only** to refer to the *res publica*, in the sense of commonwealth. The nearly universal pattern of initiating usage of the term "bien de la chose publique" in princely ordinances related to coinage neatly captures the intimate bond between public commerce and the commonwealth: coinage cemented that bond.

---

[33] Isambert, *Recueil*, VI, 551, December 7, 1380; the letters speak of the "great prejudice to *la chose publique* and damage to the said merchants."
[34] *Ordonnances*, VII, 17–18, May 1383, also cites the public utility.
[35] *Ordonnances*, VII, 19–20, June 5, 1383.
[36] Thierry, *Recueil* [. . .] Abbeville, IV, 193.
[37] *RDBHV Paris*, I, 121.
[38] *RDBHV Paris*, I, February and April 1512.

Town documents demonstrate that the urban elites of Languedoïl quickly adopted the "bien public" and "chose publique" vocabulary, particularly with respect to commercial matters. In November 1358, when the Dauphin and his council created a toll on the Seine, for goods coming to Paris, to pay for the siege of Melun, they noted that the locals had supplicated them, on behalf of the "common profit and *bien public*" of the said *pays* and the whole kingdom, to allow merchants to ship goods. Their inability to do so "greatly damaged the merchants and other men of these *pays* and of all the kingdom, and the *bien public*."[39] In May 1360, Constable Robert Moreau de Fiennes mediated a dispute between the officers of Troyes and the master drapers. It seems the drapers, without royal permission, had been holding "assemblies, unions, monopolies, and conspiracies against my said Lords (John II and the Dauphin) and the *bien public*."[40] John II later confirmed their privileges, citing the "great damage to the common people and *la chose publique*" done by the dispute.[41] Antoine de Marronie, mayor of Rouen, in April 1361, issued letters about the need for the guild to affix a seal to all draperies produced in the city, because "it would be a very profitable and honorable thing for *le bien public* and the community of the *métier* of drapery" to have certification of quality.[42] In Amiens, the local government, granted remission to a bourgeois for participating in the revolt "against the Royal Majesty of our said Lord [John II] and us [Charles], to the grave prejudice of the *rei publice* of the said *civitas* of Amiens."[43]

Guild statutes everywhere in northern France regularly mentioned the "bien de la chose publique" from the reign of Charles V onward. The town archives of Dijon have a remarkably complete collection, so we can follow them over time. Burgundian guild statutes invariably drew their wording from Parisian examples. Why Paris? Philip the Good, in his July 1443 letters for the goldsmiths of Dijon, who borrowed the Parisian statutes, mentioned that some of them sold at a lower alloy than was done in Paris, "which is the most notable and capital town of the Kingdom of France and in which, as one says and commonly holds, all things are and were accustomed to be better." Parisian guilds thus had "the great rule" [*reigle*] and ordinances for goldsmiths. Philip began his letters saying he sought the "good, honor, and utility of the said commune," and ended by expressing that he "desires with all his heart that his towns and *pays* be well conducted and governed for the good and profit of the *chose publique*."[44]

The first letters in the Dijon collection come from King John II, who wrote of the "comoditae publique" and reformed the statutes of Parisian goldsmiths

---

[39] *Ordonnances*, III, 298.
[40] *Ordonnances*, III, 410.
[41] *Ordonnances*, III, 510.
[42] *Ordonnances*, III, 494. John II and Charles approved this decision, on behalf of the "bien public."
[43] Secousse, *Charles de Navarre*, 169–170.
[44] AM Dijon, GG 3, fols. 11–12.

for "the profit of the King of the common people of the said town [Paris] and of all the Kingdom."[45] The remaining initial letters in the collection date from the reign of Charles V, and they immediately use the "bien de la chose publique" vocabulary.[46] This practice greatly assisted in the spread of the new political vocabulary, which focused on a specifically vernacular French translation – *chose publique* – of *res publica*.

Charles V's 1378 letters about the goldsmiths claimed that the old statutes were not being followed, "to the damage and lesion of the *chose publique*," so he sought advice, in his desire to provide "good government" to the people of the kingdom and, especially of Paris. Four years later, in letters about the pewterer's guild, the provost of Paris cited the "good and utility of the *chose publique*," while the statutes for the linen weavers cited the need to prevent "frauds and inconveniences and malicious acts" which were to the "lesion and prejudice of the common people and also to reform this *métier* to be better and better for the utility of the *chose publique*." The provost then merely reproduced Charles V's letters for the weavers, of 1373.[47] These statutes gave exceptionally strong rights to widows: a widow who knew the trade could keep her husband's shop open; if she did not know how to "work" (weave), then she could hire workers. Upon remarriage, she could remain open if she knew the trade, but if not, she had to close.[48] The ubiquity of this economic usage of the term "chose publique" surely helped make it a staple of political discourse, too, particularly given the efforts of guilds to increase their political role.[49]

Over the course of the late fourteenth and fifteenth centuries, the various statutes and regulations issued by the Dijon town council used several variations on the theme. The 1384 letters for the shearers cited the obligation of the *jurés* to look after the "profit of the King and of the chose publique" and those of 1415 referred to the "good and utility of the said *métier* and of the *chose publique*." The fullers' statutes of May 1443 noted that "because of our office and royal privileges appertains the government and the police and decoration of this good town" [Paris] the king makes the rules for all *métiers*, for the "profit and utility of the said *métier* and merchandise and of the *chose publique*." The town council of Dijon, issuing rules (1425) about barbers, did so for

---

[45] AM Dijon, GG 1, f. 1v.

[46] These dossiers contain guild statute letters up through the eighteenth century.

[47] AM Dijon GG 1, folios 1v, 6, 11v, and 17. The letters for the shearers (1384) added the "profit of the king."

[48] AM Dijon, GG 1, f. 27. In contrast, the dyers guild statutes of 1375 banned widows from taking on new apprentices and forced them to sell if they remarried someone other than a dyer. [f. 56] The barbers (1425) and the fullers (1443) followed the dyers' model. [f. 47]

[49] Flemish towns already had their own guild statutes, in Flemish, well before the events of the 1350s, and they did not copy Parisian examples, so that the "bien de la chose publique" vocabulary is absent.

the "good, honor, profit and utility of the police and of the *bien public* of the said town." The barbers' letters are the first ones to use the term "bien public," which became a standard formula only in the sixteenth century.[50]

In the fifteenth century, the "bien de la chose publique" remained the point of reference. The shearers guild (1437) cited the "good, honor, profit and utility of all the common of this town and of the *chose publique*,"[51] while the hosiers in 1490 just kept to the "good and profit of the *chose publique*." They chose to copy the Parisian statutes because Paris is "the mirror and example of all the others in police." The linen weavers perhaps best summarized the general reasons in 1468: "good, utility and profit both of the bourgeois *manans et habitans* of the said town of Dijon and of others coming and frequenting it and also of the *chose publique* which above all other things must be preferred."[52] Later renewals of guild statutes, up through the early seventeenth century, largely preserved this vocabulary of the "bien de la chose publique" but sometimes shifted to the "bien public." Because guild statutes largely reproduced an earlier text, simply reissued by a new monarch, they remained consistent in vocabulary until the seventeenth century. Statutes from that period often had a precise linguistic shift, from "bien public" to "bien du public" [good of the public], a phrase more suited to a political culture in which the "bien de l'Estat" had replaced the "bien public."[53]

At Amiens, as in Dijon, whenever the town government issued regulations for a guild, it referred to the "bien de la chose publique," whether for the statutes of the weavers in 1502, for regulations about apothecaries in 1529, or in the royal letters of 1545 confirming the town's right to regulate the *métiers*.[54] Those letters contained a fascinating point about local governments: the king argued that the town council, because it contained no craft master, could focus on the "bien public." The masters themselves, in contrast, would be concerned only with their particular good. Ruling themselves, the "artisans, men of the crafts, and mechanics" would have abandoned their customary obedience, and

---

[50] AM Dijon GG 2: fol. 39 [fullers, 1415], 45v [fullers, 1443], barbers [43–43v and 47], 45 [dressmakers]. From the 1576 statutes of the metalworkers (*taillandiers*) into the early seventeenth century, the phrase became "public good and utility" [*bien et utilité publique*]. [GG 3, f. 242v.]

[51] AM Dijon GG 3, f. 1.

[52] AM Dijon GG 2, fol. 46v (hosiers) and fol. 50 (linen weavers). All the letters of guilds mention good (bien) and profit, some, like the bonnet makers in 1490, add "honor" and some, like the apothecaries and grocers (*épiciers*) in 1490, add "utility." A few, like the carpenters in 1525, cite only the "bien de la chose publique." [GG 3, f. 231.] On the linen weavers, GG 3, f. 50: "aussi de la chose publique qui avant toutes autres choses doit estre preferez."

[53] Henry IV pushed this change in the late 1590s, as is clear from communications with Abbeville and Amiens; the town council of Lyon shifted to the phrase shortly after 1600.

[54] Thierry, *Recueil [. . .] Amiens*, I, 488, 582.

would, in an important town like Amiens, set a bad example for those in other towns.[55]

Commercial activity often provided early examples of the vocabulary shift in outlying regions, like Flanders, where the "bien de la chose publique" had not taken over public political discourse prior to 1400. The extensive series of renewals of town charters at the start of Jean sans Peur's reign (1406) made no mention of "le bien de la chose publique"; in some cases, they cited the common or public utility, hearkening back to an earlier discourse. Letters written to Ghent in 1411 by Charles VI (two), Marguerite of Burgundy (daughter of Jean sans Peur), and by the town government of Paris refer only to saving the king, his lineage, and his kingdom from the evil Orléans faction: none of the letters refers to "la chose publique."

Yet Jean sans Peur slowly began to use the "chose publique" in his ordinances, particularly those dealing with commerce. In 1406, extending the privileges of Venetian merchants in Flanders, he initially referred to the "bien commun" of the *pays* of Flanders, but later in the ordinance spoke of the importance of trade (*marchandise*) to "*le bien de la chose publique* of our said *pays* of Flanders."[56] His political treaty with Guillaume, count of Hainaut and Holland, and with Jean's brother Antoine does not use the term, focusing instead on the honor and good [*bien*] of the three princes. Jean's contemporaneous treaty with England, however, had been signed "for the common profit of the *chose publique* and the advancement of commerce in our said county and *pays*."[57] In the letters Jean sent to various towns, such as Lille, to inform them of the treaty with England, he invariably cited "le bien de la chose publique" as the reason for the treaty. Similarly, following the royal pattern again, Jean regularly referred to the same in his multiple ordinances on coinage.

The town archives of Ypres show how the vocabulary of the commonwealth took over at the peripheries of the kingdom. In 1411, Jean sans Peur modified the way in which Ypres chose its city government: his letters mentioned the need to eliminate potential ill will between rival families as a reason to move to princely nomination of aldermen. He cited the bad effects of poor government. In 1430, Philip the Good, again changing the election rules, claimed that some of the town officials were paying more attention to their own commercial affairs than to town business. They lacked experience for the "good of justice and of the *chose publique*" of the town. He mandated that the *avoué* [mayor] and the first alderman be men knowledgeable of the law. "Men of law" [*gens de*

---

[55] Thierry, *Documents [...] Amiens*, II, 622ff. In 1540, creating a new marketplace for tanned hides, the letters again referred to the "bien public." The 1570 letters establishing the new *métier* of *sayeterie drapante* also spoke of the benefit for the *bien public*.

[56] *Ordonnances de Jean sans Peur*, 40–41.

[57] *Ordonnances de Jean sans Peur*, 31 and 54–55 (England). Some of Jean's other ordinances, whose topic would have used this vocabulary in Languedoïl, did not always do so.

justice] should run the city so that it "will be kept in good administration [*pollice*] for the *bien public*" of the city. He returned to this theme in summing up, saying he had acted for the "bien public" of Ypres in making the change.[58]

For the next forty years, Philip the Good and his son Charles consistently used the vocabulary of the "bien public" in their correspondence and negotiations with representative assemblies, such as the general estates of Burgundy.[59] Unsurprisingly, when Charles the Bold died in 1477, after severely restricting the rights and privileges of the Flemish towns, the patriciates of Bruges, Ghent, and Ypres took advantage of the weak bargaining position of young Mary of Burgundy to insist, in the name of the "common good," on the restoration of the old order.[60] They simultaneously had to restrain efforts of the guilds to restore some of the power they felt they had lost in the century after the disaster of Roosebeke (1383).

Brittany belonged to the commonwealth rhetorical area from the start, and Bretons like Evrard de Trémaugon helped diffuse the terminology. When Philip the Bold of Burgundy became the "tutor" of Jean V of Brittany, in 1404, he promised to act for the "good government, to the honor, profit, and for the *bien public*" of the duke and his duchy.[61] [#2] Jean V issued a "constitution on the fact of justice" in September 1405, which dealt with "Justice, lawyers, pleadings in Brittany and other things touching the public good and utility." [#96] When the duke granted Rohan the right to have his own officers collect and keep the ducal *fouage* levied on his "men and tenants," he noted the *fouage* was levied for the "good and utility of our *pays*." [#573] Granting the parishes in the marches on the border with Poitou an exemption from the *fouage* (which they kept to 1789), the duke said he wished to act "to the good and public and common utility of the *pays*." [*bien et utilité publique et commun du pais*] [#1052]

As in France proper, commercial activity regularly gave rise to the use of the term "chose publique": on an inquest into roads in 1409 [#1056]; in a lawsuit

---

[58] I, Diegerick, *Inventaire analytique et chronologique des chartes et documents des archives d'Ypres*, III, 309–316. Count Louis de Mâle had taken away Ypres' right to elect the council in 1380.

[59] Examples in: *Recueil des édits, déclarations, lettres-patentes [...] concernant l'Administration des Etats de Bourgogne* (Dijon, 1784). In 1447, for example, Philip the Good reformed the town government of St-Omer, to look to "the police and bien public" of the said town. When Philip of Habsburg did the same in 1506, he simply cited the 1447 ordinance: Pagart d'Hermansart, *Histoire du bailliage de St-Omer, 1193–1790* (St- Omer, 1898), t. II.

[60] J. Haemers, *For the Common Good: State Power and Urban Revolts in the Reign of Mary of Burgundy, 1477–1482* (Turnhout: Brepols, 2009). Charles the Bold's brutal treatment of Dinant (1466) and Liège (1468) meant that Flemish towns had an extremely negative view of ducal power in 1477.

[61] R. Blanchard, *Lettres et mandements de Jean V*, 5 vols (Nantes, 1889–1895). Blanchard numbers all the entries; the parenthetical numbers in the text refer to his numbering.

about illegal selling of wine, "against the *bien public*," at Nantes in 1414 [#1166 and 1175]; about market stalls in Vannes [#1224]; or again about damage done to roads near Buzay, owned by monks [#1197]. The unknown perpetrators had acted "in prejudice of the *bien de la chose publique*" so the duke, "wishing that we, of our royal rights, sovereignties and nobilities, as guard and protector of churches and their ministers in our duchy and of the *bien de la chose publique*," will see that "punishment and correction will be made."

5.2   Southern France: *civitas* and *chose publique*

Town council deliberations in Bergerac, Bordeaux, Poitiers, and Saint-Jean d'Angély confirm that the southwest generally avoided the "bien de la chose publique," even in the fifteenth century.[62] The southwestern regions around Bordeaux, under the control of the king of England, used far less of this vocabulary when communicating with Henry V. They might use the phrase "utilitat publica" or "good and public and common utility [*ben et utilitat publica et comunia*] of all his land beyond the river" but the vocabulary of commonwealth rarely appeared either in the correspondence between Henry V and either Bordeaux or the Estates of the Bordelais. The oath of the *jurats* of Bordeaux makes no mention of *bien public* or *chose publique*; they swore only to do right (*dreit*) reason and justice to poor as well as rich, to show no favoritism, to keep the ordinances, and not to give away town's property (*bens de la comunia*). Unsurprisingly, the first usage I have been able to find came in letters complaining about currency in 1414: the Third Estate of the Bordelais spoke of the "ben et utilitat de la causa publica."[63]

In contrast to this relative lack of such terminology in communication with Henry V, the local towns like La Réole, Bazas, and Bordeaux, among themselves, did speak of the "ben comun." The *jurats* of Bordeaux claimed in November 1415, on hearing of the king's victory at Agincourt, that it would send a delegation to congratulate him, for the "ben comun de la ciutat," here using the local vernacular term for *civitas*.[64] Bordeaux and the other southwestern towns usually used the phrase "lo Rey, nostre senhor" for Henry V. At this time, French towns invariably referred to the king as "nostre souverain seigneur" and the absence of the word "souverain" was clearly not accidental in the southwest, where towns regularly changed hands.

The town records of Bergerac show the careful diction of the town's consuls. In 1379, just after shifting from English to French control, they told a local

---

[62] The inventories of archives in Agen and Narbonne imply a similar absence of the vocabulary.

[63] "Causa" was the local equivalent of "chose" in French-speaking regions.

[64] Examples from the *Registres de la Jurade, Délibérations de 1414 à 1416 et de 1420 à 1422* (Bordeaux: G. Gounouilhou, 1883), letters to the jurats of La Réole, Bazas, and Saint-Macaire in 1415.

noble that they had taken "an oath of loyalty to the king of France, our lord" and would keep it to the best of their power [*poder*]; they made sure to mention that when they had been "subjects" of the king of England, they had been loyal to him, too.[65] In 1424, they spoke of the "profit and utility of the commune" and took an oath to "well and loyally rule and govern [*regit e governat*]" the said town and to be "good and faithful to our said very sovereign [*tressobiran*] lord [*senhor*] the king of England and France."

In 1450, safely in French hands, the town council of Bergerac asked Charles VII, for the sake of "le bien de la chose publique," to reduce the number of consuls from eight to five, with his *baile* to choose who among the five chosen consuls should be mayor.[66] The consuls were to have charge of the "government and administration of the town and its *chose publique*." In 1456, their "very sovereign lord" was the king of France, and in 1463 their oath now bound them to "sustain the town, both the small and the grand" and to do justice to all. By 1482, the consuls, who had long just spoken about the "profit and utility" of the king and the town, now added the "bien public" to their vocabulary, initially, as in so many cases, on a commercial matter: the rules governing opening a city gate for commercial entries.[67]

Throughout the south, towns had a long tradition of Roman vocabulary. Arles had especially close commercial and intellectual ties to Italian city republics, and to the vocabulary of the *civitas*. In the register of deliberations for Arles, the clerk always referred to the assembly as the council of the "*civitas*" of Arles.[68] Arles had two "constitutions," of 1251 and 1385: in these charters, the count of Provence promised "to protect the persons, goods, and rights of the citizens of Arles."[69]

Like Arles, the towns across Languedoc continued to refer to themselves as a *civitas* and preferred for most of the fourteenth century the language of rights, liberties, customs, and privileges. In time, however, they ardently adopted the new *langue* (French) and *langage*. In 1479, in Marseille, the meeting to choose a new town council decided to continue for four years the existing group "for the good government of the Town and of the *chose publique*."[70] The municipal government of Toulouse, in March 1525, on

---

[65] G. Charrier, *Les Jurades de la ville de Bergerac* (Bergerac, 1892), v. I, 54.

[66] *Ordonnances*, XIV, 111.

[67] Charrier, *Jurades de Bergerac*, I, 313.

[68] Arles had been part of the Empire and had held the status of a free imperial city. Besançon, in Franche-Comté, offers parallel example of such status. Arles briefly had a *podestà* in the early thirteenth century, a further example of its filiations with Italian political practice.

[69] Article 15. See the eighteenth-century collection edited by N. Anibert, *Mémoires historiques et critiques, sur l'ancienne république d'Arles*, III (Avignon, 1781), 230: "personnes, biens & droits des Citoyens d'Arles."

[70] P. Mabilly, *Ville de Marseille. Inventaire Sommaire des archives communales antérieurs à 1790*, series BB (Marseille, 1910), I, 225, deliberation of April 28, 1479.

hearing the news of the capture of Francis I at Pavia, during the meeting of the general assembly referred to the *capitouls* as the "head and having the guard of the town and *chose publicq[ue]*".[71] The deputies from the Parlement and the seneschal promised to "live and die with the said town and make one single body together."[72] When the archbishop's vicar general gave his "advice," he told the assembly that he was "of the advice that the *bien public* be preferred to the *bien particulier*," so that, if the military commanders so ordered, the houses within twenty feet of the walls should be torn down.[73]

The Estates of Languedoc, in 1539, referred to themselves as the "men of the three Estates of the *pays* of Languedoc, the Church, nobles, and common estate, representing the mystical body of its *chose publique*," when seeking confirmation from Francis I of their jurisdictional privileges. They insisted on being judged by the written law [*droict escript*] customary in the south, "according to which the judges and ordinary jurisdictions had been made and instituted for the good and relief of the republic [*république*]."[74] Arles' consuls, meeting in October 1560, said they would discuss "the affairs and negotiations of the said town hall and *cause publique*." This vocabulary had become normative there.[75]

In the east, the county of Burgundy (Franche-Comté), which had close ties to France, but legally lay in the Empire, long stuck to the old vocabulary. Besançon, in its 1290 charter, spoke of "franchises and customs" that they had used since a time beyond memory.[76] Just as in the kingdom of France, however, sound coinage came high on the list of their rights: the first article insisted that the money of Besançon could not be changed by "force de

---

[71] AM Toulouse, BB 9, f. 5v–6 [online, image 13]. "lesd capitoulz comme chief et ayans la garde de la ville & chose publicq[ue]." They promised to do their duty as "good, true, and loyal subjects" of the king.

[72] "vivre et mourir avecq lad ville & faire ung mesmes corps ensemble."

[73] "est dadvis que le bien public soit p[re]fere au bien p[ar]ticulier." Lautrec, the king's lieutenant for Languedoc, insisted that the houses be torn down, but the *capitouls* – rightly as it turned out – feared they would have to pay for the damage.

[74] "les gens des troys Estatz du pays de Languedoc, l'Esglize, nobles et comun estat, représentans le corps mistique de la chose publique d'icelluy [...]suyvant lequel les juges et jurisdictions ordinaires ont esté faictes et instituées pour le bien et soulagement de la république." *Inventaire Sommaire des Archives Communales . . . de Narbonne, série AA* (Narbonne, 1877), 364 [entry for AA 182]. This clause appeared in the document making the official grant of money – about 300,000 *l.* – to the king.

[75] AC Arles, BB 14, image 247 online [f. 225r]

[76] Request for confirmation of privileges made to their "very high prince and sovereign King," Rudolph of Habsburg, King of the Romans, in 1290. A. Castan, *Origines de la commune de Besançon* (Besançon, 1858), Pièce justificative XXI, 180. During the reign of Charles V, when the key vocabulary changes took place in the kingdom, the countess of Burgundy was Margaret, great-granddaughter of Philip V. She married Charles V's brother, Philip, duke of Burgundy, uniting once again the two Burgundies after the death of her father, Louis de Mâle.

seignor" but had always to be maintained in good alloy. The "citizens" of Besançon were to have a "community or university" with its own seal.[77] The general goals in a Besançon or an Arles were no different from those in Paris or Dijon, but they delayed taking on the French political vocabulary from the 1350s.

5.3 Communications: The Key Role of the Towns

Marcial de Verit, a "poor shepherd, mad and without sense," overheard a bourgeois of Limoges, recently returned from Paris, tell someone that the kings of France and England had just made peace. Out in his field, tending the sheep, poor Verit, who had supposedly lost his senses in an English prison, later told his companions, in so many words, that he did not believe it, "because the king had gone to destroy and pillage the *pays* of Flanders and did the same to Paris." Young Charles VI would have done even worse, "if it were not for the seigneur of Coucy who brought him a hoe and a spade, saying to him, 'when he would have destroyed his *pays*, he would have to accommodate himself to using this'."[78]

This 1388 pardon recounts a famous anecdote of 1383, when the royal army, returned from its triumph in Flanders, treated Paris like a conquered city. Unlike most of the pardon documents in the collection, this one carries no date, but the surrounding pardons date from events in 1383, and one might surmise that Verit, off in his isolated mountain hamlet, was repeating the latest news from Paris. If shepherds high in the Limousin hills heard these sorts of stories from Paris, we must surely consider that political news traveled farther afield than we have imagined. The bloody events at Paris in 1383 would have made an impression – kings rarely attacked their own capital cities, executing the leading citizens – and a bourgeois of Limoges certainly would have taken notice. The restoration of the *aides* affected everyone, especially merchants: townspeople, and their governments, had to engage with the central government's discourse in order to resist in a non-violent manner. A century before printing transformed human communication, the king, the princes, town governments, and bishops had regular recourse to a public sphere of action, in word as well as deed.[79]

---

[77] "Université" here meaning the political community.

[78] Douët d'Arcq, *Choix de pièces inédites*, I, piece XLVII (90–91).

[79] Guenée, *L'opinion publique*, looks at the perspective of the author of the Chronicle, Michel Pintoin, with respect to the existence of, and the means of affecting the "public opinion" of his day. In Pintoin's view, ordinary people – the *vilissimus populus* – did not have a real role in establishing public opinion, but they did intervene, in a sense, by means of their periodic outbursts (as in 1413 or 1418 in Paris). Cazelles, *Société politique sous Jean II*, on public opinion in the fourteenth century.

Opposition to the new taxes sparked considerable public discussion, quite apart from open rebellion. A group of merchants from Macon, drinking in Paris in 1382, started grousing about taxes on commerce. One of the group was heard to say that Charles V "when he was alive, had been very avaricious and a gatherer of money, and that he much coveted gold and silver." At which point, Raoulet Mathei had drunkenly exclaimed that they were better off with the king [Charles V] dead than if he had lived another ten years.[80]

Guillaume a skirt maker from Orléans, had gone even further in his 1382 tirade against the royal family, denouncing the duke of Anjou, whom he claimed had "pillaged, robbed, and taken the money to Italy": Anjou was now "dead and damned, and the king Saint Louis, too, like the others." Guillaume complained about going from "king to king, when their only real king was God." These supposed kings taxed and re-taxed him [*ilz me taillent et retaillent*]: "what are they doing to take away from me what I gain from my needle? I would rather that the King and all Kings were dead than my son be sick in his little back." Originally sentenced to have the fleur-de-lis tattooed on his head, Guillaume fortunately had his sentence reduced to a 50 *l*. fine.[81] All of these men objected to permanent taxation. Poor Moreau du Bourc, "Jewish usurer" living at Montargis, faced charges of lèse-majesté for saying "the king is a bigger usurer than he."[82] The intersection of commerce, taxation, and coinage necessitated a vocabulary that brought in all three: the *bien de la chose publique* admirably filled the bill.

These pardon letters remind us that news traveled informally, by means of merchants, wandering laborers, vagabonds, and soldiers, to say nothing of official messengers. Jean Verdon highlights the tavern, the fair, the market, the mill – any place people gathered – as inevitable sites of information and disinformation.[83] In the markets, women, who did much of the buying and selling, played a particularly important role in spreading both. The town registers of Limoges show another way women would have known about, and indirectly played a role in, politics: in October 1511, after an interminable and remarkably complex lawsuit about who should be the town civil judge, Limoges' city government sent out Leonard Veruhaud, their trumpeter, to

[80] Douët d'Arcq, *Choix de pièces inédites*, 100–101.

[81] Douët d'Arcq, *Choix de pièces inédites*, 58–59. Chevalier, ed., *La Loire Moyenne* [# 1048], Etienne Thorel, butcher's apprentice, one of the ten people who did not come back to Orléans after the king's letters of amnesty for the tax revolt at Orléans [#1054], Regnault Lermede, "compromised in the revolt of Orléans," who had fled received remission (January 1384), as did Pierre Caqus, soldier, who "participated in the revolt against the tax at Orléans" [#1094; June 1384], and Guillaume Lermede, prisoner at Orléans, who had participated in the revolt against the aides [#1114]. This revolt, in December 1382, led to the city losing its government and to the destruction of the city gates. Charles VI restored the government in 1384.

[82] Chevalier, ed., *La Loire Moyenne*, [#1090] [May 1384], letters of remission.

[83] J. Verdon, *L'information et désinformation au Moyen Âge* (Paris: Perrin, 2014).

summon the electors to make their pick. Me Pierre Bermondet, – lieutenant general of the seneschalsy, who had been a party to the lawsuit – was somehow in Poitiers for fifteen days: his mother spoke to Veruhaud and promised to let Bermondet know when he got back. In house after house, poor Veruhaud spoke to wives, mothers-in-law, daughters, servants: the men did not wish to participate in the election, and so had a woman answer the door and take the message.[84] The electoral assembly took place the next day, with the voters instructed to choose the "most sufficient and professionally qualified [*ydoine*], most profitable and suitable to the *chouse publique* for civil judge."[85] We may reasonably assume these women knew what was happening and surely discussed it.

Royal, princely, and municipal governments had well-worn methods of publicizing their acts, which used the same general language. In 1385, when Philip, duke of Burgundy, sent word to Bruges that he and the king had reached a peace agreement with Ghent, he suggested they post it around the town "so that all of the common people [*le menu*] would better know of the said peace, and that it be common knowledge to all."[86] In the conflict between the houses of Orléans and Burgundy, the dueling princes regularly issued manifestos designed to influence public opinion. As Lethenet has shown for Macon, the city had a well-developed system of spreading news already in the late fourteenth century.[87] In 1484–1485, when openly seeking control of the young Charles VIII, Louis, duke of Orléans, sent letters to towns all over the kingdom claiming the regent, Anne de Beaujeu, was not acting to protect the "bien public."

Town governments had important roles to play in the dissemination, or non-dissemination, of information of all kinds. The town council of Troyes, a city that 'miraculously' returned to Charles VII's camp in July 1429 – reputedly when the local royalists insisted agreements made for the "bien public" had to be honored – carried on an extraordinary series of exchanges with the king, first about changing sides (July 8–10, 1429) and then about coinage. The royal army arrived at Troyes short of food, money, and artillery; according to the *Chronique de la Pucelle*, and the testimony of Dunois at Joan of Arc's rehabilitation trial, the entire royal council opposed continuing the

---

[84] *Registres consulaires de la ville de Limoges*, t. I, report starts on 49. In a few cases, a male child answered.

[85] *Registres consulaires de la ville de Limoges*, t. I, 55. They avoided men involved in the lawsuit and elected Me Aymery Essenaud, who was later chosen to give the welcoming speech to Charles, duke of Bourbon.

[86] "afin que tout le menu sache mieulx la dicte paix et qu'il soit notoire a touz." On similar developments in England, see J. Coleman, *Medieval Readers and Writers, 1300–1450* (New York: Columbia University Press, 1981).

[87] Lethenet, "Comment on doit se gouverner," ch. 9.3.

siege. Summoned to the council, Joan implausibly insisted the city would be theirs, by love or force, within two days.

Just as Joan predicted, the bishop, Jean Léguisé, and a delegation of bourgeois came to the king, to seek pardon and favorable terms of submission, which Charles granted in letters patent. He then made a "treaty" [*traité*] with the city. In the letters, he pardoned all crimes, delicts, and offenses against his authority and confirmed Troyes' franchises, liberties, and privileges. The "treaty" placed the city under royal safeguard, promising the death penalty to any soldier caught looting. He allowed the Burgundians to leave and gave them two weeks to collect their possessions.[88] Troyes' citizens would collect royal taxes, and the city received royal permission to continue for ten years its own taxation, which would be used for the walls and other purposes: Charles required only that they get duly registered royal letters for this tax. This last clause established the clear precedent that even the patrimonial taxes levied for the city required the king's authorization.

The illuminated manuscript of the *Vigiles de Charles VII*, from the late 1450s, has illustrations of Joan convincing the king to stay the course and of the city council rendering the keys to the city to Charles (Illustration 5.1). Leaving aside the considerable impact of Joan's presence, the three most important members of Troyes' clergy – Bishop Léguisé, dean of the cathedral chapter Jean Pougeoise,[89] and dean of the collegial of St-Etienne, Guillaume Jouvenel – were all confirmed royalists.[90] All three men regularly participated in the general assemblies of 1429–1432, as did Me Oudart Hennequin, *avocat du roi*. Whatever Joan's role might have been, Troyes' submission to Charles VII was surely a royalist coup spearheaded by these four men.

The surviving register of municipal deliberations from this period shows the complex calculus a town government had to consider, and the vocabulary invariably used in exchanges with the king.[91] Troyes' town government referred to themselves as the "council of the *chose publique*" of Troyes, a usage showing "chose publique" to be their term for the political community

---

[88] Joan of Arc intervened to prevent removal of their prisoners; Charles guaranteed their ransoms.

[89] Charles later ennobled the Léguisé and Pourgeoise families for this service. Pougeoise had been the chapter's envoy to Pope Martin V, to overcome the duke of Bedford's objection to Léguisé's 1426 election.

[90] The Jouvenal family's sixteenth-century house in Troyes survives. The Hennequin family would provide important members of the Paris robe, as well as leaders of later city governments in Troyes.

[91] A. Roserot, *Le plus ancien registre des délibérations du conseil de la Ville de Troyes (1429–1433)* (Troyes, 1886), counts over 200 meetings in this period, for which six months are missing. The council called thirteen general assemblies, to deal with matters like taxation, coinage, and military affairs. The largest assembly had over 300 men present, from a wide range of trades in the city.

Illustration 5.1   Jeanne d'Arc and Charles VII: *Les Vigiles de Charles VII*, Martial de Paris, dit d'Auvergne, BNF, M Français 5054, fol. 61v. Permission BNF

of the *cité/civitas*.[92] When Troyes submitted to Charles, he promised, in addition to a full pardon and exemption from most taxes, that he would maintain the currency. Six months later, however, he sent letters – to be read aloud in the usual places – devaluing the small coins by twenty percent.[93] The public reading of the letters created such a crisis that a general assembly, involving about 150 men, including Bishop Léguisé and the two deans, convened to discuss the matter.[94] They refused to implement the change, and sent letters to the king, to the count of Vendôme, and to the chancellor that in order

---

[92] Roserot, *Délibérations du conseil de la Ville de Troyes*, 247.

[93] Roserot, *Délibérations du conseil de la Ville de Troyes*, 53.

[94] Léguisé, like so many of the political leaders we have encountered, attended the Collège de Navarre. The king's confessor, Gérard Machet, was a fellow student there. J. M. Hayden and M. Greenshields, *Six Hundred Years of Reform: Bishops and the French Church, 1190–1790* (Montréal: McGill-Queen's UP, 2005), 522, single out Léguisé as one of their seven outstanding episcopal reformers of the period 1410–1469. Jouvenel belonged to the prominent Jouvenel/Juvénal des Ursins family.

to "succor the poor people and the *bien public*" the coinage had to be kept at its current value. They pointed out that Troyes drew its food supply from Burgundian regions and expressed alarm at the damage to "the king, his bourgeois and subjects, and all of the *chose publique*." Vendôme sided with them, and forwarded temporary letters restoring the old value, subject to later action by Charles VII.[95]

The flurry of royal ordinances on coinage in March 1431 used a similar vocabulary. Acting first to reform the coinage in Dauphiné, Charles VII acted for the "bien de la chose publique" of our said *pays* of Dauphiné, "in order that the fact of commerce does not cease in the said *pays*."[96] A week later, the king issued major legislation about coins, reducing the number of authorized mints, of which Troyes was one. He acted because "to Us by our right, authority, sovereignty, and royal majesty belongs to order and institute coins in our Kingdom." Those disobeying these letters would be guilty of lèse-majesté, because they committed "irreparable damages or prejudice to Us and the *chose publique* of our said Kingdom." The king "desired and wished with our heart the *bien public* of our said Kingdom and seigneurie."[97] The follow-up letters of April 5 laid out specifications for the coins, and again the king cited the "chose publique" and the "bien public" of both the kingdom and of Dauphiné.[98]

Troyes' town council took a different view; they thought changing the alloy would be to the "very great prejudice and damage to the King our lord [*sire*] and *la chose publique*."[99] Two days later there was murmuring in the town against the decrying of the coins, and the council heard remonstrances about how it harmed the king and the *chose publique*. The next day, another massive assembly heard there was "great noise [*bruit*] and rumor in the city among men of moderate estate [*estat moyen*] and others." One of the deans asked the bishop to preach to the people the great perils of "treason," and to warn them that "evil traitors loving the contrary party" would be excommunicated.[100]

In October, the council received the king's edict of July 31, 1431 about the reminting of all small coins, "for the *bien de la chose publique* of our kingdom"

---

[95] Louis I de Bourbon, count of Vendôme, was one of the witnesses to Charles VII's "traités" with the city on July 9, 1429. Charles put Vendôme in charge of their relief, should they be attacked.

[96] *Ordonnances*, XIII, 151.

[97] *Ordonnances*, XIII, 164ff. "Comme à Nous de nostre droit, auctorité, souveraineté & Majesté royal, et non à autre, appartiegne de ordonner & instituer monnoies en nostre Royaume {. . .} "dommages irreparables ou prejudice de Nous & de la chose publique de nostredit Royaume [. . .} Desirans & voulans de notre cuer le bien publique de notredit Royaume & Seigneurie."

[98] *Ordonnances*, XIII, 168, 5 April 1431 [n.s.].

[99] Roserot, *Délibérations*, 93.

[100] Jouvenel was one of two chapter deans who were regularly present at the council meetings at this time.

and other considerations. The council took an extraordinary step: they chose NOT to allow these letters to be read aloud in the city, because doing so would damage "the king, his subjects and the *chose publique*." They again reminded Charles VII that they got their food from enemy territory, where people did not take the king's money "because it was not as good as that of the English or the Burgundians."[101] The master of Troyes' royal mint and the city's money changers told the council they together had only 20 *l.* of the said money, so that changing the coinage was literally impossible.[102] In the end, the king did mint the new silver coinage and it remained stable for some years afterwards. Peace with the duke of Burgundy made it a lot easier to collect taxes, which in turn lessened the incentive to re-mint the coinage to produce revenue.

These exchanges remind us of the key role played by town governments and bishops in dissemination of the royal government's messages. The king's letters would go to the town council, with orders to have them read, at the sound of a trumpet, in the "usual places." Letters to bishops might encourage them to have a royal circular read from the pulpit of all the parishes in their diocese: in 1709, when Louis XIV explained to his subjects why he had refused the peace terms offered by the Dutch and the English, he used precisely this method, for which we also have ample fourteenth-century examples. Town governments might turn to the bishop, or a preacher, to reach the people. In July 1431, after news of the death of the highly regarded governor of Champagne, M. de Barbazan, the town government asked Bishop Léguisé to tell the people that Barbarzan had died fighting in a "quarrel of Monseigneur the duke of Bar" not for Charles VII. They convoked all the town militia and 2,000 "very content" people listened to the bishop acquit himself well for "the good of the King and the town of Troyes."[103]

Communicating with towns meant writing – and speaking – in a language that made sense to the audience. Town governments in France usually contained a mixture of merchants, lawyers, and, in many cases, judges; some governments included guild representatives, but they typically formed part of a larger, general assembly. As in the case of Bishop Léguisé's speech about Barbazon, the town government took pains to mobilize and manipulate public opinion. As Lethenet has pointed out, town governments and royal officials had to control "rumor," often referred to as the "bruit commun," the common

---

[101] Roserot, *Délibérations*, 148. From 1424–1429 local coins bore the name of Henry "Rex" and a lion next to the fleur-de-lis, so Charles VII naturally wanted to re-mint the coinage with his own name and a double fleur-de-lis.

[102] On the vagaries of royal minting policy, see Miskimin, *Money and Power*. The Troyes mint was a minor producer. He claims (59–60) that silver coins lost thirty-eight percent of their value in 1428–1429, but recovered full strength by 1430, when they stabilized.

[103] Roserot, *Délibérations de Troyes*, 115–118. Barbazon died on July 2; the bishop spoke on the 8th.

noise, which spread by word of mouth.[104] The term "chose publique" fit far better into this oral world of communication than a Latinized "respublique." Jean Jouvenal des Ursins' letter to his sons, and various documents related to the Parlement of Paris, suggest that some in the legal elite already used "respublique" for the forms of *res publica* in the first third of the fifteenth century, but in everyday politics, where the audience was far larger and did not have a Latin-based education, "chose publique" remained the term of choice well into the sixteenth century – an obvious indication of the need for politicians to reach a broad public.

Kings wrote to towns about a wide range of matters. Both Henry VI and Charles VII gave clear examples of learned discourse in their university charters, always issued in Latin. Henry VI, as "king of France," confirmed (1431) the privileges of the University of Paris, an institution necessary for the "defense and sustenance of the Christian faith" and the "conservation of the *bien public* of our said kingdom." Creating a law school at Caen, he cited the prejudice caused to the "republic" by the lack of legal education. Charles VII, for his part, told Angers he renewed and expanded the privileges of **their** university for the "promulgation of science" and the "growth of the Republic." In granting permission to the city of Nîmes to have a bell tower to ring the alarm, Charles cited the "common good" [*bien commun*] of the town.[105]

Just as town governments played a key role in disseminating information for the royal government, so, too, they had jurisdiction over injurious speech. In the case of insults directed at the king or blasphemy, their judgment could be appealed to a royal court, or to the king, for a pardon: after 1350, for other verbal abuses, they had final say. Burgundian records contain regular prosecutions for "mauvaises paroles" spoken against the king or duke. In 1355, several inhabitants of Villaines had to pay fines for disrespecting the "coins of the king." One Perrinot, of Verrey, paid 1 florin for having said "that it would be better to be the devil's man than the duke's, and he said it because of the overly great *taille* placed on him." When Yolande, wife of Jean Humbert of Châteauneuf, recently moved to Burgundy, complained that "no one was bold enough – not any lord, lady, duke or duchess – to speak up against the nobles," she pleaded innocent because she was "simple by her nature, and spoke openly without thinking what she said": her fine had been the enormous sum of 100 *moutons d'or*, suggesting her words struck close to home.[106]

---

[104] Lethenet, "'Comme l'on se doit gouverner," ch. 2.1.

[105] *Ordonnances*, XIII, 169 (Paris), 176 (Caen), 186 (Angers), 196 (Nîmes). University charters used the relevant forms of *res publica*, here translated as republic.

[106] These places cannot be fully identified but are likely to be Villaines-en-Duesmois, Verrey-sous-Salmaise and Châteauneuf-en-Auxois, all royal properties.

Various other cases involved assaults on royal sergeants and Burgundians speaking ill of Jeanne d'Auvergne, dowager duchess of Burgundy, who was then effectively ruling the territory for her son, Philippe de Rouvres.[107] Shortly after the fiasco at Poitiers, Jean Bisot of Fontaine,[108] was branded on the lips and cheeks for having spoken ill (*mauldit*) of the king and his company at the battle. Burgundian discontent peaked on April 23, 1359, when a serious uprising took place at Dijon. A crowd burned down the Jacobin church and broke into the houses of rich bourgeois like Jean Gauthéron, where they found and carried off their main target, Jean Rosier, councilor of Jeanne d'Auvergne. He had overseen levying the new taxes. Poor Rosier died at their hands. In response, the authorities burned Adeline, the hatmaker and executed Laurent the painter.[109]

Other French towns took similar actions. Amiens banished the "large woman Marion" in 1427, for having spoken "insults and villainies against the town government and the honor of the town." Thirty-two years later, Hué Demay insulted Jacques de Coquerel and the good people of the town, going so far as to call them "English, which is a great insult."[110] Both Amiens and Abbeville had posted lists of the punishments for each specific insult. Nor were such insults restricted to the common people: in a 1412 lawsuit pitting Jean Bourquetot, viscount of Le Bec-Crépin against Jean sans Peur, the latter's lawyer claimed Bourquetot had said several times "in the presence of notable men that Monseigneur of Burgundy was a false traitor, murderer, and executioner."[111]

Town records all over France show the municipal court fining people for verbal insults or, far less often, for blasphemy. Quotidian matters took up the vast majority of their time: sanitation, upkeep of streets, policing of markets (especially the all-important grain market) and, in some towns, of trades, collecting rents, paying for some schools, and, above all, military expenses such as maintaining the city's most essential possession, its walls and moat.[112] In periods of internal warfare, and, prior to the late fifteenth century, even in

---

[107] Petit, *Histoire des ducs de Bourgogne*, t. IX, 36, n. 2. Jeanne was by then the second wife of King John II.

[108] Petit, *Histoire des ducs de Bourgogne*, t. IX, 74, n. 2. "Fontaine" could mean Fontaines-en-Duesmois, which would place this case near the others, or Fontaine-lès-Dijon, right outside the city.

[109] Villani, *Cronica*, II, 210, calls it an uprising against the richest citizens. Petit, *Ducs de Bourgogne*, IX, 148–149.

[110] Gauvard, *"De grace especial,"* 744.

[111] Gauvard, *"De grace especial,"* 729. Bourquetot's lawyer was Jean Jouvenal des Ursins, giving some idea of the resonance of this case.

[112] The first dictionary of the Académie Française, in its definition of "ville" began this way: "Assemblage de plusieurs maisons disposées par rues & fermées d'une closture commun qui est ordinairement de murs & de fossez" [An assemblage of several houses arranged by streets and closed by a common closure ordinarily made of walls and moats].

intervals of peace, due to wandering bands of furloughed mercenaries, the walls kept the town's citizens and their goods protected. All these services required volunteer officials – the men who would have considered themselves to be citizens – and, of course, money. That's where the king or a territorial prince came in: towns had the bulk of the actual cash in circulation, and so kings always had to turn to them to get specie.

These towns also provided the skeletal structure for every level of government; courts sitting in towns invariably dominated the countryside. Bishops in their "*cités*" drained grain, wine, and other resources from the countryside: in times of famine, thousands of starving peasants might descend on a town like Troyes, believing that their tithes entitled them to some of the grain in the hands of the bishop and the cathedral chapter.[113] The relief efforts spearheaded by Bishop Léguisé in fall 1432 did not alleviate the crisis, and an exceptionally large city assembly on December 9, 1432 complained that so many had come into the city that grain was running out, which "required" expelling "a great number of people, which is a thing pitiable to support," but which had to be done to prevent even greater problems.[114] The four constables, and their sixteen sergeants, were to draw up lists of all "foreign persons recently come to this town, of their estate, government, and how well they are supplied with food." If they found any "coquins, maquerelles et gens de mauvaise vie," they were to expel them immediately.[115]

At Limoges, in 1528, the "sterility of food" in the Limousin area meant "a greater number of poor than had ever been seen" came to the city. The council created a written list of all the poor and assigned each inhabitant of the city, according to his or her means, a daily obligation of six pence, or a bread loaf of that value, to the poor. In this way, "the said poor were nourished from the first of March until the first of July."[116] Food insecurity remained an issue in the region for several years; in 1532, the registers noted that people were living from oatmeal porridge, a "strange" circumstance never before seen. The consuls augmented the city watch and often personally participated, "for the conservation of the *bien public* and correction of the bad."[117] In April 1533, the city organized a massive procession of the poor, 1,600 or 1,700 strong, stopping

---

[113] Troyes' city council passed a series of ordinances expelling recent immigrants, due to a grain shortage in 1432. [Roserot, *Délibérations*, 191; 198] The bishop and other clergy led the way in providing grain to the city's markets, to be sold at a price well below the going rate. In the 1640s, St-Malo followed the typical pattern: first an ordinance emphasizing poor relief; then, an ordinance combining relief for the local poor and funding for a "chasse gueux" to drive vagabonds out of the city.

[114] Roserot, *Délibérations*, 232.

[115] A *maquerelle* was a woman running a brothel; the other two terms apply as well to people leading "immoral" lives.

[116] *Registres consulaires de la ville de Limoges*, I, 177.

[117] *Registres consulaires de la ville de Limoges*, I, 210, comment added at the end of the year/s minutes.

at each intersection in the city, joining hands and crying out for the mercy of God. Three days later it was the turn of 1,000–1,200 torch-carrying good citizens, led by the canons, all the city's clergy, and the consuls. A few days later, the cold intensified, and the entire population of the city turned out, some just in nightshirts, some barefoot and without hats – "religious, priests and other people, young and old, women and children, small and tall, it was something terrifying to behold and to hear."[118]

5.4   The *bien public* and the *chose publique*

Town archives all over royalist France show that by the 1430s at the latest, reference to the "*bien public*" or the "*bien de la chose publique*" had become standard practice in justifying municipal action.[119] In the sixteenth century, town governments regularly referred to the town as a "respublique"; the local priest Claude Haton, in his memoirs, for instance, regularly referred to the town government of Provins in this way.[120] This new usage – which had been extremely rare in the fifteenth century – came from legal circles, and, given the significant increase in the number of royal judges on town councils, the increasing popularity of the term was not surprising.

One key distinction between royal and other usage of the term *chose publique* stands out: Charles VI usually spoke of "le bien de la chose publique de nostre royaume"; others simply used the term "la chose publique" on its own. Royal edicts slowly began to shift to a more varied usage of the term "la chose publique." In April 1412, when Charles VI dismissed all the officers on the royal demesnes granted as apanages to Orléanist princes, he stated that his predecessors had created the demesne "for the good of our Seigneurie and of the '*chose publique*'." The next ordinance allowed Parisians to buy, and foreigners to import, arms and armor to help defend the city: the king claimed that the armorers guild of Paris, which had a monopoly on such sales, could not provide sufficient arms in time. He cited the "good, utility and surety of our Kingdom and of its chose publique"; later, he came back to the need to protect "the good of mercantile activity (*marchandise*) and of the '*chose publique*' [of Paris]." Charles VII exempted the members of the Parlement and the Grand Conseil from the *ban-et-arrière-ban* [feudal military aid] because of their

---

[118] *Registres consulaires de la ville de Limoges*, I, 212–215. In an aside at the end of this narrative, the clerk mentions that the city built a new brothel with six bedrooms and staffed it with "filhes de joye."

[119] In Agen, new residents had to take an oath to be "good inhabitants and good citizens" of the town. Urban records almost all refer constantly to the "citizens" of the town, and individuals, even in documents as private as a last will and testament, regularly called themselves "citizen of Autun" or of any other town.

[120] *Mémoires de Claude Haton*, 4 vols., dir. L. Bourquin (Paris: Collection des documents inédits sur l'histoire de la France, 2001–2007) vols. 28, 31, 33, 40.

continuous service "for the good of Us and of all the *chose publique* of our said Kingdom." The king noted that his "men" [i.e., his *avocat* and *procureur*] and "ministers" [judges], above all other men, needed to "live in freedom (*franchise*) and liberty, as is reasonable."[121] The "chose publique de nostre royaume" phrasing remained common even under Charles VIII (1483–1498).

Royal letters soon referred regularly to local administrations having charge of "la chose publique of the said town" (Langres, 1446) or even "le bien public" of their town, as was the case with the *épiciers* of Paris (1450) or the drapers of St-Lô.[122] Princes such as the dukes of Brittany and Burgundy had long used those formulæ. The "chose publique" in a political sense could thus mean the entire kingdom, a principality like Brittany, a *pays*, or just a town.

Charles VII kept to the old formula, "le bien la chose publique de nostre Royaume" in almost all his ordinances prior to 1440: his 1437 letters on privileges for apothecaries in Paris offer a rare exception. In the 1440s, in contrast, he shifted back and forth: his July 1443 edict on coinage simply used "la chose publique" but another edict on coinage in November added the familiar "de nostre royaume."[123] In December 1443, banning cloth importation from Normandy, he did not add the modifier; edicts in 1444 went back and forth, with about equal numbers having the "de nostre royaume" and not including it. In his April 1460 edict on levying the *tailles*, Charles VII said they were levied "for the good and defense of *la chose publique* and the payment of our soldiers."[124]

In the 1440s, the king also started to make more regular use of "bien public." The letters creating the Parlement of Toulouse, in October 1443, spoke of the

---

[121] *Ordonnances*, X, 3–4; 5–6; 9–12. "Franchise" carried, throughout this period and into the seventeenth century, the sense of being able to speak freely. The renewal of an *aide* from the Estates of Artois (p. 9) used the traditional phrase "Us and the *bien public* of our kingdom"; the letters establishing the rules of the vinegar makers' guild at Paris (pp. 16ff) refer to the "good and utility of the King [...] and of the *chose publique*."

[122] *Ordonnances*, XIII, 455, January 1446, allowing Langres to elect four *échevins* to look after the "fait commun" of the town, so that "*la chose publique* of this town" could be maintained and "governed in *bonne police*." The *échevins* were to have "charge of the fait commun de la police et de la chose publique de ladite ville." Épiciers of Paris (Ordonnances, XIV, 115), drapers of St-Lô (XIV, 493). *Ordonnances*, XIII, 551, similar usage in an edict about La Rochelle (1447); *Ordonnances*, XIV, 360–361, on the tailors of Caen (1455), or 409, on the bakers of Dun-le-Roi (1456), where the letters also speak of "the common affairs of *la chose publique*" of the town; *Ordonnances*, XIV, 55, on the privileges of Bourgneuf, where a local prior speaks of the taxes necessary for the "republic," doubtless a translation of an original Latin.

[123] *Ordonnances*, XIII, 244–245 (apothecaries) and 369ff. The many cases of the traditional usage include the ordinances on coinage (1436, XIII, 221–222), on mounted sergeants in Poitou (XIII, 316), on benefices granted by the Pope before the Pragmatic Sanction (XIII, 332), on abolishing transit taxes on certain rivers (405), on re-establishing the fairs of Champagne or creating news ones at Lyon (399).

[124] *Ordonnances*, XIV, 395 and 484.

"bonum Reipublice Patrie nostre Occitane et Ducatus nostri Acquitanie."[125] In letters affirming or re-establish guild privileges – for bakers at Bourges (Dec. 1443), weavers at Issoudun (Dec 1447), or *tondeurs* at Tours (Feb 1448) – the king now referred to the "bien public": the Tours letters spoke of the statutes of the *tondeurs* as being "good and profitable for the *bien*, utility and common profit of the said town and the said inhabitants"; the lack of such statutes had been to the "great prejudice and damage of the *bien public* of our said town, and of the *manans*, inhabitants, merchants and other people frequenting the said town." The letters for Issoudun cited "le fait et bien publique."[126]

Town records used the language of citizenship and public good: the registers of Lyon invariably refer to the "citizen consuls" and regularly make note of someone being a citizen of Lyon or of some other city, like Vienne.[127] When the large council, which included masters from twenty-five guilds, discussed safety measures in the spring of 1465, they referred to the "bien, honneur et profit du Roy, desd. ville et pays et de la chose publique dud. Royaume."[128]

That town governments used such language is hardly surprising: as David Rivaud has pointed out, many municipal officials came from the middling ranks of royal officers.[129] The same was true of deputies from the towns to the Estates General of 1468, forty percent of whom held a royal or seigneurial office, and even more true of those of 1484, nearly two-thirds of whom were royal officers.[130] These Aristotelian citizens ruled their local commonwealths, and were ruled in turn, within the larger commonwealth of the kingdom, by the king and his councilors. They shared in royal power because they had to execute it and in the use of royal vocabulary, the *langage* of their métier.

We thus have two shifts: 1) the near universal acceptance of the need to refer to the "la chose publique" or the "bien public," often as distinct from the king

---

[125] *Ordonnances*, XIII, 384.

[126] *Ordonnances*, XIII, 531 (Issoudun), 534 (Tours).

[127] AM Lyon, BB 4, f. 122 (June 28, 1450) is one example among many. Fargeix, *Les élites lyonnaises*, cites many examples of the *chose publique* vocabulary. Online: fifth BB 4 link, image 11.

[128] AM de Lyon, BB 10, fol. 45–46. The phrase referred to the good offices of the clergy, who needed to participate in the defensive preparations (and costs); their representative was Barthélemy Bellièvre, procureur of the archbishop. Bellièvre was the great-grandfather of the later chancellor, Pomponne de Bellièvre. Online BB 10, 2nd link, images 15 and 16. The archbishop was Charles II de Bourbon; Lyon remained staunchly loyal to Louis XI, a fact the city council regularly brought up in later correspondence with French kings.

[129] D. Rivaud, *Les villes et le roi. Les municipalités de Bourges, Poitiers et Tours et l'émergence de l'État moderne (v. 1440 – v. 1560)* (Rennes: PUR, 2007), ch. X.

[130] Figures from the invaluable N. Bulst, *Die französischen Generalstände von 1468 under 1484. Prosopographische Untersuchungen zu den Delegierten* (Sigmaringen, 1992); see also J. R. Major, *Deputies to the Estates General of Renaissance France* (Madison: University of Wisconsin Press, 1960).

himself; and 2) the frequent substitution of "bien public" for "bien de la chose publique," a shift particularly noticeable from 1440 onward. Many speakers and writers used them interchangeably, but "bien public" had a sense beyond that of the simple vernacular translation of the Latin *res publica* (*chose publique*); it brought to mind the Aristotelian theme of the "good life," the end of any properly constituted polis. In the post-1300 Christian world, it also brought to mind the religious dimension of secular life.[131] During the Wars of Religion, this aspect of the "bien public" would abet the death of commonwealth ideology.

5.5   Louis XI and the Towns

Louis XI quickly assaulted the independence of the towns, interfering in municipal elections throughout the Loire Valley and in Amiens. His letters to the town council of Amiens contained a breathtaking interpretation of royal power:[132]

> Because of our sovereignty and royal majesty, to us alone adheres and belongs the general government and administration of our kingdom, either in offices, jurisdiction or otherwise, and also in all our walled towns and cités, the mayoralties, laws, and councils, the which mayoralties, laws, and councils we can renew, create, and order at our good will [*bon plaisir*], without anyone interfering.

The town council, which had always elected the mayor, took exception to this radical change. Louis's candidate, chancellor Morvillier's eponymous cousin, had, in fact, already served several terms as mayor. The council proposed to Morvillier that they could not name him mayor until he had been freely elected: they had no doubt of his success, as they told him he was "much loved by the people."[133] Morvillier, ever the king's man, said he could only take

---

[131]   We might think of the *Traité de la Police*, of Nicolas de la Mare, composed under the late Louis XIV, in which the author tells us that "religion is the first and principal object of the Police, and at all times the care of it has been given to the two powers, spiritual and secular."

[132]   Thierry, *Recueil [. . .] Amiens*, II, 271ff: "à cause de notre souveraineté et majesté royale, à nous seul complette et appartient le général gouvernement et administration de nostre royaume, soit en offices, juridicions ou autrement, et aussi en toutes nos bonnes villes et citez et mairies, oys et eschevinages, lesqueles mairies, loys et eschevinages nous pouvons renouveler, créer et ordonner à nostre bon plaisir et volonté, sans que nulz y ai que veoir." Rivaud, *Les villes et le roi*, documents the same process in the Loire Valley. *Archives Historiques de Poitou* for the letters interfering in Poitiers. The classic thesis of H. Sée, *Louis XI et les villes* (Paris, 1891), provides many details about Louis XI's attack on local liberties, but overstates the permanence of the king's success. Sée is certainly right, however, that Louis was unusually intrusive and did augment royal power in the towns.

[133]   Louis allowed the council to keep its right to elect the new aldermen and town fiscal officials.

office by virtue of the king's orders. The council then chose to hold an election, followed by the customary ratification of "the people." They unanimously chose Morvillier.

The matter did not end there. In November 1465, when Louis XI handed Amiens over to Charles of Burgundy, Morvillier resigned as mayor and a new election, using the traditional method, took place.[134] This royal interference was far less severe than it appears: Morvillier had been mayor of Amiens in 1455 and 1457, and an *échevin* in almost all other years since 1450. In 1467, the town elected Jean Le Normant as mayor; in 1469, the town picked Fremin Le Normant. The Morvillier and Le Normant families had a long history of intermarriage; both had been on the town council since at least the 1350s. Jacques Clabault, who displaced Morvillier as mayor in November 1465, and Jean Le Normant were both on the "royalist" town council of 1464–1465, on the council under Charles the Bold, and on the council again with Morvillier in 1470 and after. Clabault and Morvillier were, in fact, both cousins of the chancellor, so hardly an example of ham-handed outside interference in Amiens' affairs.[135]

Louis XI's "intervention" did not even cause a ripple in the local political pond. Fourteen years later, Louis urged the lieutenant of the *bailliage* to suggest to the town electoral assembly that they re-elect Jacques Clabault's first cousin, Antoine, who had done a fine job, "good and praiseworthy service" for the king "in the said town and government and good police of the *chose publique* of this town."[136] Antoine Clabault served sixteen terms as mayor and died in office in 1504; Amiens held a massive public funeral to mourn its loss. In October 1482, after Antoine had served three years as mayor, the electoral assembly named him again as one of its five top vote-getters; before they could go to the large assembly, a delegation from an assembly headed by the *bailli* of Amiens, consisting of a "large number" of *avocats*, merchants, and inhabitants came to the electoral group and demanded they renew Clabault. He asked to be excused, they insisted, and he relented; the assembly used precisely the same language Louis XI had used in 1479 to describe Clabault. In 1484, when he finally stepped down, his relative Jean Le Normant took his place, and he took Le Normant's spot as first *échevin*. Several other members of the Clabault family served as mayor in the sixteenth century.

---

[134] Favier, *Louis XI*, 461, sees the use of chancellor Morvillier as envoy to Amiens as a positive development, and ignores the entire episode of the coerced election. All the evidence suggests Amiens had royalist and Burgundian parties, roughly evenly divided; the king and the duke of Burgundy alternated control of the city for nearly twenty years.

[135] Janvier, *Livre d'or*. Clabault's mother, Isabelle de Morvillier, daughter of Jean, mayor of Amiens in 1421, was thus the niece of First President Philippe de Morvillier.

[136] Janvier, *Livre d'or*, 369. Jacques Clabault's father, Pierre, had been mayor of Amiens in 1422 and 1441. Antoine, like Jacques, was a cousin of Morvilliers. All these families had been on the council in the fourteenth century and some as early as 1241.

Louis XI interfered in municipal elections and government in town after town, but only the sort of detailed empirical work done by scholars like Rivaud, for the Loire towns, or Fargeix, on Lyon, can help us understand how much the process varied from one town to the next. A city like Bourges, which had a troubled history with the king, differed sharply from one like Troyes, where the town council, Louis XI's arbitrary interference in local affairs notwith-standing, remained staunchly loyal.[137] The same tightly knit oligarchies dom-inated all these towns, royal "interference" be damned. In the sixteenth century, however, descendants of these families often divided along profes-sional lines, with the mercantile branch lined up against the legal one.

Louis had given his brother Charles the duchy of Berry, and Charles' men held Bourges for him during the War of the Public Good: it was the only town in Berry not to be taken by Louis' army in the spring of 1465. Issoudun, Bourges' long-time rival, used its loyalty to the king to request, and get, expanded privileges. In 1471, Louis abolished the traditional farming of the royal provost at Bourges and made it into a permanent office.[138] In 1474, after a rebellion against new taxes, he sent troops to carry out a severe repression, including the hanging of more than a score of the guilty: Louis' henchmen strung up the corpses on the front of the artisans' houses. Louis then abolished the traditional municipal government, but his imposed system did not last long. Even his less manipulative revised system did not survive him: in one of her first acts as regent, Anne de Beaujeu restored Bourges' ancient system of "public" election of four *échevins*, from among the "degreed men, in both laws, and bourgeois and merchants, and not those who work with their hands."[139] Louis' vaunted imposition of royally chosen mayors was often more symbolic than substantive: Rivaud shows that the imposed mayors of Poitiers did not, in fact, participate in town government, and rarely lived in the town.[140] In March 1465, Jean Jenoillac, Poitiers' envoy to court, wrote to the town govern-ment to tell them Louis XI believed Lyon and Poitiers were the two most loyal towns in the kingdom, and said he planned to live in Poitiers and "finish out his days there." Both towns did remain loyal – and regularly reminded later kings

---

[137] Fargeix, *Les élites lyonnaises*; Rivaud, *Les villes et le roi*.

[138] This step had broad support; the Estates General of 1484 asked the king to eliminate the farming of royal provosties and to put them into the hands of trained judges.

[139] L. Raynal, *Histoire de Berry*, v. III (Paris, 1841), 138–139. Louis had similar problems with the Church: it took him several years – and severe punishments – to impose his choice for one of the cathedral canons, and he had trouble imposing his choice as archbishop, Pierre Cadouet, who had to make a private agreement with the chapter's choice.

[140] Favreau, ed., *Poitiers (. . .) registres des délibérations du corps de ville*, v. II–IV, provides extensive examples of Louis XI's interactions with the town government of Poitiers. In 1475, the town elected Maurice Claveurer, instead of Louis' choice [IV, 130–131], Perrochon; Jean Hébergé, bishop of Evreux, their protector on the king's council, got Louis to accept Claveurer.

of that loyalty. Poitiers hoped to translate its loyalty into the creation of a Parlement, and managed to get support of other nearby towns, like Tours, on the grounds that the great backlog of cases in Paris "wounded sovereign justice in this kingdom." They met Paris' main argument with the contention that "one does not [in creating a Parlement in Poitiers] divide the unity of the crown and sovereignty of France," because "in this kingdom there is only one king, one crown, and one sovereignty." Negotiations dragged on for years, but Poitiers never got its Parlement.[141] In Bourges, in Amiens, it was the same story: great families, like the Clabault of Amiens, retained control of local power. New families gradually insinuated themselves into these elites, usually by marriage.

5.6 Towns and the King: The Invasion of 1552

> to all soldiers and others who wish to do service for the King, the City, and its chose publique.
>
> Recruiting poster, Paris, 1552.[142]

Town governments continued to use commonwealth rhetoric, especially in times of crisis. The Lyon town government, faced with the devastating news of the capture of Francis I at Pavia (1525), called a series of meetings of the leading citizens. Louise of Savoy was in Lyon when she got the news, but the town records say she was in such a state of shock that she could not speak to their delegates. Their assembly reminded her that Lyon had always remained loyal, whether during the captivity of John II or during the "bien public" [War of the Public Good]; they promised to do something very useful and necessary "à la chose publique de ce royaume." That meant repairing their fortifications, in fear of an invasion: the ensuing town deliberations provide a less-than-edifying portrait of the local disputes to which raising the money for these repairs (and for an immediate loan of 10,000 *l.* to Louise) gave rise.[143]

---

[141] Favreau, *Poitiers (...) registres des délibérations du corps de ville,* II, 362, 365, 369.

[142] RDBHVP, t. 4, October 16, 1552.

[143] AM Lyon, BB 44, f. 16 [online: image 13], news reached Lyon on February 28, 1525 of the disaster at Pavia, where the king had been captured and "a great number of the men of the said lord dead." The next day they ordered a full military review of the security of the gates, of the state of the artillery and ammunition, and food supplies. They sent "*espyes*" to the frontiers of Burgundy "and other places where the enemies" might enter the kingdom. Claude Bellièvre, Pomponne's father, was one of the *échevins* at the time. The subsequent general assembly held a remarkably open debate, to judge from the records. The assembly that took the final decision included sixty-five bourgeois and two members each from the thirty-six represented trades. A steady parade of inhabitants of Lyon requested an exemption from the new tax: an eighty-year-old widow; a supposed household officer of the king; various officials whose positions supposedly exempted them.

The *chose publique* and the *bien public* remained key terms with respect to other topics, like commerce or secondary education: the 1529 discussion of Lyon's schools and *collèges* highlighted their importance and their "interest" to the *chose publicque*.[144] Taxes, too, elicited the usual rhetorical recourse to the "great damages" that might ensue to the town and its "chose publique" if the farm of its tax duties were not well managed.[145] When the duke of Montmorency suggested M^e· Jean Petit be chosen as the new *avocat* for the Amiens in 1558, the town council told him that the *avocat* had to be a native of Amiens and that he could only serve the "respublique": Petit, a non-native, worked for the bishop of Amiens, so that ruled him out on two grounds.[146] The town government used the same term in a different context in 1562: Protestants, the Catholic council members claimed, were "perturbateurs de la respublique," who should be punished.[147] Here we can see how "respublique" had taken over from "chose publique" in urban political discourse, at least among the elite – many of them legal men – on the town councils.

Ordinary citizens used the vocabulary of the "bien public," as we can see in the flier posted up in Lyon during the Grande Rebeyne uprising of the spring of 1529, in the name of "Le Povre" [The Poor Man]:

> First to all those who desire to uphold the bien public, to contradict the malice and fury of false usurers, it please you to take notice how the shortage of grain falls on us who have not deserved it, because of their barns full of grain, the which they desire to sell at their last word, which is not reasonable.
>
> [Premièrement à tous ceux qui ont désir de soustenir le bien public, pour répugner la malice et fureurs des faux usuriers, plaise vous à avoir regard comme le détriment du blé nous tombe sus sans l'avoir mérité, à cause de

---

[144] AM Lyon, BB 46, fol. 27ff [online: second link, image 5] on the schools, fol. 33v [image 12] and following on the need to provide grain for the city and "la chose publique."

[145] AM Lyon, BB 46, fol. 73v–74 (March 1529) [online: image 52] and fol. 96 (April 1529). This second meeting took place during the Grand Rebeyne, a grain riot and tax protest that lasted for ten days: those present complained about the small participation at the meeting – the authorities by and large hid out during the uprising. The seven men present stated they waited from 2 pm to 5 pm for their colleagues to show up. The authorities later hanged several of the so-called ringleaders. D. Potter, *A History of France, 1460–1560: The Emergence of a Nation State* (London: Macmillan, 1995), 16, on this revolt, and response, as symptomatic of the increased local restrictions on exports of grain from any given region.

[146] *Documents [. . .] Amiens*, 658. Montmorency gracefully backed down, saying he had meant no attaint to the city's privileges.

[147] *Documents [. . .] Amiens*, 718. The complaint sought to prevent Antoine de Bar from becoming the town's *procureur* at the bailiwick, but he obtained the office anyway. Bar was a suspected Protestant, but his father-in-law, Simon des Essars, longtime *procureur* of the city, was a pensioner of the bishop. After his first choice failed to win the nomination, the cardinal of Bourbon, lieutenant general of the king for Picardy, supported Bar, who won an election held by the *échevins*.

leurs greniers pleins de blé, lesquels ils veulent vendre à leur dernier mot,
ce que n'est de raison]

The poster addresses all those who wish to sustain the *bien public* and
denounces grain hoarders in a time of famine. This vocabulary of the public
good can be seen from the town records of Lyon in the south, to those of
Rennes in Brittany, to Paris, and even in the far north, in Tournai (lost to
France in 1521) where the former royal prosecutor, Pasquier de la Barre, in his
journal of the 1560s, regularly referred to the "chose publique," the "bien
public," and the "patrie."[148]

For a case study, let us look at the protracted correspondence among Paris,
nearby towns, royal military commanders, and Henry II in 1552, in response to
the Imperial invasion of Picardy. To set the mood, we can listen to the speech
given to the papal nuncio on behalf of the town government of Paris, in
August 1552: "the citizens, bourgeois, and inhabitants of Paris" greeted him,
said the *prévôt des marchands*, speaking on behalf of himself, the *échevins*, the
rest of the 'corps' of this City, capital city not only of this kingdom, but of the
whole inhabitable world." The *prévôt* told the nuncio that they knew how
important to "all the *chose publique chrestienne*" was the amity and enmity,
union and separation, of the king and the Pope. The nuncio graciously replied
that he was delighted to be greeted by such excellent personages, and to be in
the most Christian, renowned, and excellent city in the world.[149]

Henry desperately needed money to relieve Metz, to which Emperor Charles
V laid siege in the fall of 1552. To add to Henry's problems, an army of about
35,000 men, led by Adrian de Croÿ entered Picardy: Croÿ claimed to have
burned 5,000 farms, villages, *bourgs*, and towns, among them Noyon,
a cathedral city and home to one of the six ecclesiastical peers of France.
Given the commitment of the main royal army to the relief of Metz, this
invasion caused consternation in the area north and east of Paris. Towns
such as Senlis and Compiègne, only 20 km from Noyon, worried they would
share its fate. Thomas de Lorrain, an *échevin* of Paris sent out to gather
information, visited Noyon after the attack and reported that only the cathedral was left standing.[150] Compiègne wrote to the town government of Paris,
asking for aid in men and money, for the "service of the King and the
conservation of the *pays* in his obedience."[151] Christophe de Thou in Paris
convoked the twenty-four *conseillers* and the sixteen *quarteniers* to discuss the

---

[148] Pasquier de le Barre, *Mémoires*, v. II, 6. In February 1567, even Philip II used the term
good of the "*république*" in creating the commission to root out Protestantism. [II, 175].
[149] RDBVP, t. IV, 7ff.
[150] He blamed the city's disaster on the fact that its judges and leading men were heretics!
RDBVP, IV, 48. Noyon was the birthplace of France's most notorious "heretic," John
Calvin.
[151] *RDBVP*, IV, 18.

matter, but he could not raise a quorum, and so wrote to the king and the cardinal of Lorraine for permission to remove artillery pieces from Paris. Compiègne sent another letter, saying the king had already approved aid to them. The next day the Parisians replied that "in similar things of such importance, we have no desire or power, if not to do what we are commanded by the king." Senlis reported the "astonishing" and "terrifying" burning of Noyon, and asked for help, but again Paris hid behind the need for royal authorization.

A large council meeting in Paris, meeting under the aegis of the cardinal of Bourbon, lieutenant for the king in Paris, decided to raise 500 troops willing to serve the king, the city, and its *chose publique*. These troops were to help Compiègne. When they heard that the enemy had retreated (de Croÿ went back to home base for supplies and cash; Mary of Hungary, regent in the Low Countries, reportedly ordered him back), the Parisians told the soldiers to return home, with each one getting an *écu* for his trouble.[152]

Here we have an existential threat to important nearby walled towns, like Compiègne and Senlis, the last two fortresses between Croÿ's army and Paris. No large enemy army had ever got anywhere near the area of Compiègne-Senlis-Paris, so the panic of town governments regarding the inadequate state of their fortifications and artillery was surely not unreasonable. Paris had to think first of its own defense, thus denuding the city of artillery was not a popular option; but allowing the only two substantial fortress towns on its northern front to fall into enemy hands was not a decision to be taken lightly.

Royal officials and town governments displayed a mixture of the traditional commonwealth vocabulary and the new discourse. In late October, Constable Montmorency wrote to the Paris city government, asking them to be "diligent and vigilant to do service to the King, to the City and its *chose publique*." Henry II used a different vocabulary on October 24, when he praised the Parisians, who had been ready to do all for their "great affection and fidelity toward us and the good of our Kingdom."[153] His simultaneous letter to the cardinal of Bourbon, his lieutenant in Paris, shows an even more aggressive use of the new vocabulary: Henry thanked him for preparing men to go to the relief of Senlis, and for his "wise and prudent dexterity in manipulating the Parisians and

---

[152] The Parisians had agreed to pay these 500 men for a month. They raised the money through a forced "loan" on the wealthy.

[153] RDBVP, IV, 45–46. A letter sent from someone in Charles V's army at Metz to Philip of Spain in early November said that Croÿ had gotten to about 50 km from Paris, but returned to Habsburg territory, under orders from Mary of Hungary, to re-provision. Croÿ planned to return to do more damage. *Journal du siège de Metz en 1552: documents relatifs à l'organisation de l'armée de l'empereur Charles-Quint et à ses travaux devant cette place, et description des médailles frappées à l'occasion de la levée du siège*, ed. M. F.-M. Chabert (Metz, 1856), 125–126. The description of the siege is by Bertrand de Salignac, an eyewitness.

disposing of the things that are useful to my Kingdom and the good of my service." Here we see a precocious use of the phrase – "the good of my service" [or "king's service"] – that would soon replace the "bien public" in royalist discourse.

The Parisians carefully calibrated their responses to the audience: writing to the provost and officers of Pontoise, they spoke of the good of the king, the city, and *la chose publique*; writing to Montmorency, they referred to the king saving "all of *la chose publique chrestienne*." Writing to the king, they took a different approach: referring to the "small service" they had done, to which they were held by all "law natural, of men, and civil," they insisted that the "greatest reward that a subject might have in this world, is to find grace in the eyes of his King, of his sovereign."[154] Whatever else such rhetoric might have been, it was not the language of the commonwealth.

---

[154] RDBVP, IV, 49. In 1552, the new town council of Metz took an oath to the "bien commun" of Germany and the Holy Empire.

6

The Orléanist Offensive

Puissance absolue and Republicanism

> Oh how happy would be our poor patrie if our sovereign Monarchy had always around his majesty people like those mentioned above [good old captains, expert and sharp judges, Ecclesiastical doctors and prelates who were alienated from the avarice of simony, of adulation, and of envy]
>
> Yves Magistri, 1584.[1]

Yves Magistri, in his lament about the sorry state of French affairs in 1584, longed for the day when the king governed the Republic with the aid of worthy councilors. He wanted all those at court and in Paris to have roses before their noses, ears, and eyes, and in their hands, to banish "all stink and spiritual infection" from the Palais Royal (where Parlement sat). The goal of a good prelate "must be to have occasion better to save his soul, and to aid others of his Republic to save themselves."[2] Magistri here uses "republic" for the political community, an example of the shift away from "chose publique" in sixteenth-century French political discourse, but he maintains the focus on the needs of the collective political unit.

In the middle of the sixteenth century, the landscape of political discourse was remarkably confusing because of the monarchy's use of so many different terms, even in the same clause. The monarchy began to make limited use of the term "respublique" and greater use of the word "state," still lower case and closer in meaning to Machiavelli's sense of the "state" of Florence being a personal possession of the Medici [*lo stato di Medici*].[3] Moreover, the early royalist champions of *respublique* were invariably legists trained in Italy, above all at Padua. Chancellor François Olivier's father had been Louis XII's chancellor for the duchy of Milan; chancellor Michel de l'Hospital got his doctorate in both laws at Padua in 1533 while the great jurist Jean de Coras was studying

---

[1] Y. Magistri, *Bibliothèque vergier et jardin des ames desolees es esgarees* (Bourges: P Bouchier, 1584), 128.

[2] Magistri, *Bibliothèque vergier*, 128 and 151.

[3] C. Nederman, "Niccolò Machiavelli," *The Stanford Encyclopedia of Philosophy* (Summer 2019 Edition), Edward N. Zalta (ed.), URL: https://plato.stanford.edu/archives/sum2019/entries/machiavelli/. Consulted June 2019. Section 5, "The State and the Prince: Language and Concepts," has a clear presentation of Machiavelli's use of the term "stato."

there.[4] The Parlement of Paris particularly liked "republic" in this sense, because it fit their self-image as "Senators."[5]

In the *lit de justice* held December 1527, Francis I spoke of the duty he had to his subjects and to the "chose publique du royaume de France," an interesting shift from the older "de notre royaume."[6] He needed their counsel for "the good of himself, the kingdom and the chose publique." Harkening back to Gerson's distinctions about the king's various bodies, he noted that in prison he determined not to give up the duchy of Burgundy, because of the "danger there would be in leaving such a duchy" and in "dismembering the crown of France": he thought about how he was just "a man, who was only for dying" [*homme, qui estoit pour mourir*], and that it would be better for him to die than to dismember the duchy. The first use of "respublique" in royal legislation that I have tracked down came in documents related to lèse-majesté cases in 1539, when Francis I ruled that those convicted of having "conspired, machinated, against the person of the king our lord nor against the state of the republic of his kingdom" would forfeit their property to the Crown. This combination of "state" and "republic" popped up again in the letters of remission for admiral Chabot, who had been convicted of lèse-majesté, Francis avowed that Chabot had not committed such acts against "our person, nor the state of the republic of our kingdom" [*l'estat de la république de nostre royaume*].[7] In 1543, issuing a document about articles of faith approved by the theology faculty at Paris, the king noted that those who did not conform would be "held and reputed seditious, and disturbers of the repose and tranquility of our very Christian republic" and as "conspirators against the good and prosperity of our state."[8] The next year, confirming that nobles did not derogate – and hence lose tax exemption – by serving as judges (in Brittany), Francis praised "the authority and dignity of the said estate of justice, by which every republic is conserved" [*toute république est conservée*].[9] The jumbled vocabulary came up again in a lèse-majesté case, this time against marshal Oudart de Biez, accused of "infidelities, disloyalties, *practiques* and even intelligence of the said prisoner

---

[4] Jean de Coras studied at Padua from 1532–1535. N. Bingen, "Le chanoine Antoine du Ferrier et son ami Jean Daffis à Padoue," *Bibliothèque d'Humanisme et Renaissance* 74, n. 2 (2012): 353–368 and J. Dupèbe, "Un chancelier humaniste sous François Ier: François Olivier (1497–1560)," *Humanism and Letters in the Age of François Ier*, ed. P. Ford and G. Jondorf (Cambridge, 1996), 87–114.

[5] Houllemare, *Politiques de la parole*.

[6] Isambert, *Recueil*, XII, 287 (piece 150).

[7] Isambert, *Recueil*, XII, 590 (piece 285) and 773ff (piece 340). Volume XI, which covers the years 1483–1515, has no mention of the word "république," aside from a speech by the "men of the [royal] council" at the Estates General of 1484 referring to "an imaginary republic" but that is merely the modern translator's version of Masselin's Latin. The 1539 usage is the first one in volume XII.

[8] Isambert, *Recueil*, XII, piece 368 (827).

[9] Isambert, *Recueil*, XII, piece 381 (870).

with enemies of the kingdom, concerning the good of the king and the state of his republic."[10]

Local elites stuck longer with the old vocabulary about the "chose publique." The government needed to act, as the town council of Bourges, seeking two annual fairs, told the king in 1484 "for the interests of the kingdom and of the *chose publique.*" What was that interest? The town council, seeking to explain why the fairs should be at Bourges rather than Lyon or Troyes, argued that only a handful of "great and powerful merchants" would benefit in those two cities. Bourges was a better choice because it would benefit middling merchants. In Lyon or Troyes, the rich and powerful would take all the profit, "against the *bien de la chose publique*, for which it is better if each town has 30 or 40 rich merchants rather than 10 or 12." They told the king, switching to Latin, that "interest rei publice subditos habere locupletes," the interest of the "republic" is to have rich subjects.[11] Their use of the Latin *rei publice*, in a French text, reflected the extensive use being made of "respublique" in the Parlement of Paris.[12]

This exchange illustrates the *chose publique*'s common economic meaning. Bourges' town government, like Philippe de Commynes or Machiavelli, used the language of interest and practical benefit. Their argument had obvious roots in an Aristotelian view of society, in which a large middling group provides not simply the best economic outcome, but the best social and political one, too.[13] This middling group dominated local assemblies and, in terms of sheer numbers, meetings of the Estates General. They believed themselves to be the commonwealth, which they governed (locally) under the aegis of the king.

In the king's immediate entourage, the seemingly eternal conflict between jurists and philosophers for the soul of the French monarchy developed a new dimension in the sixteenth century for the simple reason that the number of royal officers grew so rapidly. The Ordonnance Cabochienne (1413) had complained that seven treasurers-general were far too many: what would that commission have said about the more than 20 treasurers and *généraux* of 1515, or the more than 100 of 1583, or the 650 of 1630?[14] Courts proliferated

---

[10] Isambert, *Recueil*, XIII, piece 154 (186). De Biez and his son-in-law, Jacques de Coucy, took the blame for the English capture (1545) of Boulogne. Henry III rehabilitated their memory in 1575.

[11] *Histoire de Berry*, III, 528. Charles VIII granted Bourges two fairs, because it was the best locale for the "bien and profit of la chose publique." [535] Bourges later lost the fairs back to Lyon.

[12] The copy of the rare 1484 procès-verbal of the Estates, printed by Jean du Pré, at the Bibliothèque Sainte-Geneviève [OExy 58], indicates Jean de Rély and the *cahier* of the Estates still used "chose publique" rather than "respublique."

[13] Aristotle was not making such remarks about merchants, whom he disparaged, but about landowners.

[14] The individual officers of 1413 were extremely powerful; those of 1630 included some effective local administrators and a larger number of place servers (and investors). The treasurer-general of 1630 was a minor official in comparison with a *général* of 1413.

and within tribunals the number of judges and lawyers grew exponentially. Quite apart from incessant complaints about the increasing numbers of royal officers, civil society objected to the alteration in the "natural" order of things. In their *cahier* for the Estates General of 1614, the bailiwick estates meeting at Bourges asked the king to eliminate all the law schools in France, except those of Toulouse, Poitiers, and Bourges, because "they give many young people occasion to study instead of employing themselves in commerce, one of the principal means for bettering [*bonnifier*] the towns."[15] This deluge of new officers helped create important divisions within the group. In the first half of the seventeenth century, deep fissures developed among the jurists: the sovereign courts, particularly the Parlements, grew more distant from the subordinate ones; and the judges split off from the lawyers.[16]

In the first half of the sixteenth century, the legal world remained far more united than it would be a century later, and the new vocabulary of "respublique" could thus spread out more easily from the Parlementaire milieu. The beliefs of the so-called constitutionalists, like Claude de Seyssel, and the so-called absolutists, like Charles de Grassaille, had far more in common than our teleological rendering of their positions allows. We have already seen the overlap at the start of the fifteenth century, in the positions of Jean de Terrevermeille and Jean Gerson: even a "constitutional" text like Gerson's *Vivat rex* recognized the unique authority of the king of France to make law. De Seyssel famously posited three checks on the king's power: religion; justice; and what he called "la police." The first two are precisely the traditional limits to the king's power, reason and justice, itself discovered through reason; the third "brake" on the king's power was entirely practical. The king had to carry out his laws, and those charged with "la police," that is, local governance, were the means by which he did so. Their action, or inaction, presented a fundamental "brake" on the king's will.

Seyssel's famous trio thus merely combined the traditional limits to the king's power, elaborated by Jean Gerson in the early fifteenth century but equally emphasized by Hardouin de Péréfixe in the middle of the seventeenth century, and the quotidian realities of governance well known to a man of Seyssel's extensive practical experience.[17] Grassaille would hardly have disagreed with any of Seyssel's points – although he had far less actual

---

[15] AM Bourges, AA 38, documents for the Estates General of 1614, article 1 of the chapter on "la police." This connection soon became a cliché.

[16] M. Breen, *Law, City, and King: Legal Culture, Municipal Politics, and State Formation in Early Modern Dijon* (Rochester: University of Rochester Press, 2007); J. Collins, "La formation et la reproduction des magistrats du Parlement de Bretagne: question sociale ou question politique?" in *Les Parlements de Province*, ed. J. Poumarède and J. Thomas. (Toulouse: Framespa, 1996), 601–620.

[17] P. Eichel-Lojkine, ed., *Claude de Seyssel. Écrire l'histoire, penser le politique en France, à l'aube des temps modernes* (Rennes: PUR, 2010), contains many fine essays.

governmental experience, so he little understood that practical dimension – and his "absolutism" consisted mainly in his assertions that the king could tax without consent, in cases of necessity, and that the king made the law. In a practical sense, war meant necessity, so Grassaille could (and did) argue that the king could raise taxes in wartime without consent. Such a position long had broad support: in the early fifteenth century, speakers like Gerson or Jean Courte-Cuisse had accepted taxes raised for urgent military expense as legitimate, but, glossing Évrard de Trémaugon, had protested that money raised for this purpose could not go to other purposes, such as the luxuries at court.[18]

With respect to law, however, in a fundament shift, Grassaille argued the king could override the objections of traditional guardians of Crown rights, like the Parlement. Later in the sixteenth century, the king of France used precisely this argument, his "puissance absolue," to override the objections of the Parlement or other sovereign courts to given royal actions, but he stuck with "pleine puissance" and "autorité royale" and "certaine science" to justify actually making a law.[19] The Parlement of Paris adapted to this change by insisting on its role as a "Senate" verifying the "reason" of each law, and therefore its consonance with God's law, natural law, and pre-existing French law. As Tyler Lange has demonstrated, this shift owed much to French monarchical attraction to the papal position in the pontiff's controversy with conciliarists. Gerson's heirs at Paris provided a particularly strong conciliarist presence in France, and, as Lange points out, the ebb and flow of Parlementaires with degrees from Paris' canonical law faculty matched precisely the views of given kings on royal authority: a quarter of Louis XII's appointments to the Parlement of Paris held a Parisian canon law degree, as opposed to fewer than four percent of Francis I's appointments.[20] This trend notwithstanding, the counter trend of Parlementaires studying in Italy – particularly at Padua, a stronghold of republican ideology – must be recognized, particularly since so many of the judges either inherited their office or got it through a family transaction.

6.1   The Estates General of 1484

Et touchant la justice, qui est dame et princesse des autres vertus, sans laquelle nulle monarchie ne chose publique peult estre entretenue en félicité et prospérité, ne parvenir au souverain bien, qui est le bien du pays; car c'est

---

[18] Their position differed little from that of the rebels of 1314, who protested that the scuttling of the invasion of Flanders meant the tax being levied to pay for it had to cease. In Trémaugon's *Songe du Vergier*, when the cleric claims royal taxes were tyranny, the knight replies that taxes collected for the defense of the *chose publique* were legitimate, if used for that purpose alone.

[19] Isambert, *Recueil des loys*, XIII – the laws issued by Henry II – has no use of "puissance absolue."

[20] Lange, *First French Reformation*, 71–74.

celle qui enseigne à vivre honnestement, prohibe et deffend offenser son prochain, et rent à chascun ce qui est sien.

Opening words of the articles on justice, cahier of the Three Estates, 1484.[21]

The section on justice in the cahier of the Estate General of 1484 was remarkably brutal. They began with the usual comment that justice was the "lady and princess of the other virtues," and that no monarchy or "chose publique" could be maintained in felicity and prosperity without it. Previous kings, they said, had the fear of God and love for their people: they mentioned Saint Louis, Philip the Fair, John, Charles V, and recently, Charles VII. These kings therefore chose officers of justice by seeking advice from "officers, men of counsel, and other good prud'hommes in sovereign courts, bailiwicks, seneschalsies, and lower courts." These courts held an election and sent the names of three men to the king; he chose one, "and in so doing was the conscience of the king discharged and acquitted toward God and the world, and the offices given to appropriate people."

> Nonetheless, since the death of the late king Charles, the said ordinance was not kept; offices were often filled with non-expert men, who bought the offices [. . .] blank letters of appointment were sometimes sold through factors [. . .] leading to several difficulties, oppressions, and injustices

Judges, viscounts, provosts, and other officers needed to be experts in judicial matters and finance, and the *élus* had to be "learned, experienced, prudent men of conscience and great circumspection, in order, without favor and in great equity, to do justice." Here, as throughout the cahiers and discussions, the deputies drew invidious comparison between the good king, Charles VII, and the bad one, Louis XI. If they did not simply say "Louis XI was a tyrant," they came closer than anyone familiar with the discourse of monarchical France can imagine.

The discussions at the Estates General of 1484 enable us to integrate the two key elements of the development of political discourse. Writers like Commynes and Machiavelli combined three major elements in their analysis of politics: Classical history; philosophy; and current history. Machiavelli's *Prince* lays out general principles of princely action, basing those general principles on an analysis of actions taken by contemporaneous political leaders, like Louis XII.[22] The Estates General rooted its critique of Louis XI both in general principles – above all, that the king's word must be his bond – and in the pernicious practical results of Louis XI's failure to honor such principles.[23]

---

[21] *États de Tours*, Bibliothèque Sainte-Geneviève, OEXV 558, image 68 of 132 (unpaginated). Online: https://archive.org/stream/OEXV558_P3#page/n0/mode/2up

[22] Machiavelli had two extended stays in France, as part of delegations from the Republic of Florence.

[23] Charles the Bold of Burgundy, writing to the mayor of Dijon to demand the city send him its artillery, promised, "en parole de prince," to return it as soon as the campaign was over. Garnier, *Correspondance de la mairie de Dijon*, I, 183, March 8, 1476.

They focused on the contrast between Charles VII – "his word was the word of a king" – and Louis XI; while Seyssel, writing a few years later, applied the same criteria to his invidious comparison of Louis XI and the "father of his people," Louis XII. Seyssel's *Monarchie de France* (1515) became a fundamental text defining French elites' understanding of their political system and its discourse, but we need to ground Seyssel's arguments in the debates of 1484 and the framework of comparison and analysis they laid down.

Several precise documents about the meeting of 1484 survive; the most famous is the journal kept by the deputy Jean Masselin, doctor in both laws, later dean of the cathedral chapter of Rouen. Masselin kept his journal in Latin, translating from the French used by the speakers. We can confirm parts of his version with the actual *procès-verbal* of the meeting, attested by Jean Robertet, royal secretary, on March 23, 1484 (n.s.). This document begins with the list of deputies, in procedural order, followed by: the speech of Jean de Rély, presenting their *cahier*; the *cahier*; and the royal council's response.[24] A chronicle of the time tells us Masselin spoke several times at the meeting, "in front of the king and princes, he gave speeches full of eloquence on behalf of the public good [*pro bono publico*]."[25] The chancellor, Guillaume de Rochefort, as was custom, spoke first, praising the French above all "foreign nations" for their loyalty to their king: he cited the dolorous example of England, where the murderer (Richard III) of two young princes had just become king by public acclamation. The deputies had come from great distances, all within the kingdom, not to see a foreign king, but their own king, in whose person the "salvation and the glory of the *chose publique* resides."[26] The king is the soul [*animo*] of the political community and he knows that justice is essential to it, that justice "is the nutrition, even the life of the body [politic]." He who offends justice, offends the king.

What was this political community? The chancellor turned to Cicero for an answer, paraphrasing a passage from *De re publica*.[27] Rochefort focused on the second segment of Cicero's definition, leaving out the first, negative

---

[24] https://archive.org/stream/OEXV558_P3#page/n0/mode/2up The note at the start of the volume, from an 1897 bookseller's catalog, provides an explanation of possible attribution to printer Jean du Pré. Hereinafter *États de Tours*.

[25] A. Bernier, ed., *Journal des Etats Généraux tenus à Tours en 1484 sous le règne de Charles VIII par Jehan Masselin* (Paris, 1835), iii, note 1, citing Rouen's episcopal chronicle.

[26] *Journal des Etats*, 42–43. Bernier's French translation renders Masselin's *res publica* as État, but in a few places, such as the quotation from Cicero, he uses "république." At Bourges, the royal letters of 1484 all refer to the "profit" or "bien" that "la chose publique of this Kingdom" might get from the meeting. AM Bourges, AA 13. Bourges and Lyon always both cited the "bien de la chose publique" in requests for the fairs.

[27] Given that only a small portion of *De re publica* was known to Europeans prior to 1819, Rochefort likely knew much of it second hand, from Augustine. Rochefort had worked for Charles the Bold but fell out with him after the Morat disaster; Louis XI made him chancellor just before the king's death in 1483.

part: a republic is not simply an assemblage (*coetus*) of men, rather, as Rochefort says, it is "a multitude in agreement on law and sharing a common utility" [*sed coetus multitudinis iuris consensus et utilitatis communion sociatus: De re publica*, I, xxv, 39].[28]

Historians have focused on the speech by Philippe Pot, former chancellor of the duke of Burgundy, setting forth supposed ideals of popular sovereignty [here popular means the citizens only]. As one might expect, Pot emphasized the public good and the special obligation of the deputies to preserve and protect it.[29] Yet the speech of Jean de Rély, a royal counselor, deserves closer attention. De Rély's speech remained well known throughout the sixteenth century; orators often took passages from it, and it long remained one of the foundations of the commonwealth heritage. The procès-verbal printed in 1484 had only de Rély's speech and the general *cahier*, with royal responses.

De Rély told the Estates that the kingdom was like a body (*corps*) "whose blood had been evacuated by various bleedings, so much that all its members are empty."[30] Reaching back to Oresme, he tied the public good to sound money: "just as blood is the sustenance of the corporal body, so are the finances of the Kingdom the sustenance of the *chose publique*."[31] The "chapter of the commons" continued with an interesting neologism: the members of this body were the clergy, the nobles, and the men of the Third Estate [*gens du tiers estat*] – here we see a break with the traditional third element, the good towns (*bonnes villes*). The *cahier* focused on mistreatment of ploughmen (*laboureurs*) by soldiers, and on the heavy *tailles*, which reduced the French to being less than serfs, "because a serf is fed." Parishes taxed at 20 *l.* or 40 *l.* under Charles VII, paid Louis XI 1000 *l.*

De Rély, presenting the *cahier*'s wording, emphasized the commonwealth's fundamental principal: election. Just as the Pragmatic Sanction, which he strongly supported, enshrined election of bishops, so, too, the *cahier* insisted on the need to elect royal officials: "procureurs, avocats, lieutenants general of bailiwicks, baillis, seneschals, *élus*, *vicomtes*, officers of the Chamber of

---

[28] D. Hollenbach, *The Common Good and Christian Ethics* (Cambridge: CUP, 2002), 65, gives "common good" as his translation for this passage in Cicero, obscuring the important distinction between "common good" and "common utility": Cicero here uses *utilitas*. Bernier's translation reads: "La république est le rassemblement d'un grand nombre d'hommes, associés par une même loi, par un même consentement, pour une même utilité."

[29] Randall, *The Gargantuan Polity*, 92–93, calls Pot's speech "perhaps the most overt claim for a completely consensual notion of power in the fifteenth century."

[30] *Etats de Tours*, 58, opening sections of the "Chapitre du commun." He complained about the gold and silver sent to Rome under Louis XI. "com[m]e ung corps qui a este evacuee de son sang par diverses seignees/ et tellem[n]t que tous ses membres sont vuydez."

[31] The *cahier* and de Rely's speech both contain this sentence. "Et comme ainsi soit que le sang est le sousteneme[n]t de la vie corporelle/ aussi sont les finances du royaume le soustenement de la chose publique."

Accounts, *généraux*, councilors in the courts of aides, of the treasury, councilors and examiners of the Châtelet, and members of sovereign courts of Parlement and other officers of justice." The electors were to be either the court in question, such as the Parlement, or local notables, often in conjunction with sitting officers (as in a bailiwick). Officers would serve for life, in keeping with Louis XI's 1467 edict. These "elections" were thus mechanisms for co-optation, much like the "elections" in many French towns, in which the previous mayors and *échevins* chose their successors.[32]

De Rély and the *cahier* demanded not simply the election of officers, but that candidates had to be "gens suffisans" in professional competencies in law and finance. This demand protected the legal men, especially royal officers, who made up sixty percent of the deputies of the Third Estate. The most common deputy for each bailiwick was its chief judge. One cannot imagine a clearer example of the connections between professional knowledge and the creation of a power elite, so well explained by Bourdieu for contemporary France. Nor did the connection disappear: Louis XIV had strict rules about the required professional background to be an intendant and he virtually never granted an exception.[33] From the Collège de Navarre in Louis XII's time to the Collège de Clermont (Lycée Louis-le-Grand) in Louis XIV's or Macron's time, the pattern has remained the same.[34]

Jean de Rély allows us to clearly see the long continuities in the commonwealth ideology in France: his speech, as we have seen, was part of the commonwealth group of texts published by Vincent Sertanas in 1560–1561. Sertanas published the *Relation* of the Estates General of 1484, with the speech of Jean de Rély and the cahier (i.e., the procès-verbal in the Bibliothèque Sainte-Geneviève's collection). The first remonstrance of that Estates General was the restoration of the Pragmatic Sanction, and reprinting Jean de Rély's speech enabled the deputies to the Estates Generals of 1560 and 1561 to have ready access to a fundamental text of commonwealth ideology.[35]

---

[32] This practice was nearly universal in northern France. *Élus* were the court of first instance for most tax cases. *Vicomtes* were local judges in Normandy. This list notably does not include any officer involved in collecting money but focuses entirely on judges and royal attorneys.

[33] A. Smedley-Weill, *Les intendants de Louis XIV* (Paris: Fayard, 1995).

[34] President Chirac attended Louis-le-Grand; President Macron attended the lycée Henri IV. All recent Presidents of France, except for Nicolas Sarkozy, have attended the École Nationale d'Administration [ENA]; all of them also attended Sciences Politiques, from which all but Sarkozy are graduates. President Macron announced plans in April 2021 to close the ENA, but the school's website, consulted on September 9, 2021, provides details on an incoming class for fall 2021.

[35] Simonin, "le cas de Vincent Sertenas." In 1576, local *cahiers* continued to insist on ecclesiastical elections: one example among many, AM de Troyes, BB 15.

6.2   Uncoupling the King and the *bien public*

Francis I and Henri II transformed the basic structures of government so that the French monarchy of 1559 scarcely resembled the one Francis inherited in 1515. Francis made fundamental changes, starting with the abrogation of one of the commonwealth's foundations, the Pragmatic Sanction. In 1516, he signed the Concordat of Bologna, with Pope Leo X [Giovanni di Lorenzo di Medici], giving the king of France the right to nominate to French bishoprics and restoring key financial rights to the Pope. The mastermind of this step was Francis I's chancellor, and former preceptor, Antoine du Prat: in the seventeenth century, Eudes de Mézeray blamed du Prat for the separation of the king and the *bien public*, and singled out the Concordat as one of his chief crimes:[36]

Mézeray recognized that the *bien public* lived on, but his point that a rupture had taken place was well taken. In addition to ending the Pragmatic Sanction, Francis created twenty new offices of councilor at the Parlement of Paris (1522), in the process institutionalizing the practice of venality in that court.[37] Francis' elimination of election of judges and of bishops and abbots marked a decisive alteration of the monarchical commonwealth: up through the Estates General of 1588, the *cahiers* consistently demanded the restoration of the Pragmatic Sanction's clause on election of archbishops, bishops, abbots, and priors, and the restoration of election of all judges, including those of the Parlements. The royal government moved away from the commonwealth model between 1516 and 1559; the social groups running the State – segments of the judicial elite and the aristocracy – did so during the War of the Catholic League (1588–1598); but the local elites had not fully given it up even in 1614.

As Michael Randall points out, the French polity moved away from a system run by a king but relying on consensus, to one with greater central, unified authority.[38] This process moved slowly, and for all his self-proclaimed independent power, Francis I regularly sought consensus for important actions. Within towns, royal officials steadily sought more local political power, although, as we saw in Chapter 5, several kings, including Henry II, sought to prevent royal officials from serving in town governments.

Because the political dialogue of Francis I's time took place in a fundamentally different polity from the one Charles VII had ruled, the same vocabulary thus took on a different meaning. Moreover, the gradual shift toward terms such as "bien public" and "respublique" accelerated rapidly in the 1540s and 1550s. By the time of the Estates Generals of 1560 and 1576, the usage of "bien public" had eclipsed the older "bien de la chose publique" among the legal elite, in the central government, in the Parlements, and in

---

[36] Mézeray, *Abrégé*, 144. See above, the introduction for his precise wording.

[37] The sale of new offices touched off conflicts with all the Parlements.

[38] Randall, *The Gargantuan Polity*, uses the term "absolute," which I would avoid, but the larger point is certainly true.

some local assemblies. Francis I was developing what Philippe Hamon has aptly called "state-lite," a rapidly evolving set of institutions and practices that would gradually coalesce into the early modern State.[39] In terms of royal finance, Francis I created the Central Treasury (*Épargne*, in 1523), that is, an institution separate from the king's personal finances: henceforth, even the king's private treasurer would get money from a public treasury. In a financial sense, the creation of the *Épargne* (and its treasurer) marked a first step in the creation of the State.

Having instituted legal venality of office, Francis I created the *parties casuelles*, a special office for receiving money from such offices, and instituted (1522) the *rentes sur l'Hôtel de Ville de Paris*, annuities guaranteed by the Paris town government, which received revenues from various royal taxes to assure the payments.[40] These *rentes* in time became the foundation of a State debt, but the necessity of an intermediate guarantor – the town government of Paris – makes obvious the absence of a genuine public debt. The financial arrangements created in 1522–1523 demonstrate the inadequacy of the term "State" for the polity of Francis I; Philippe Hamon justly called his book on Francis I's finances, *L'argent du roi* [*The king's money*], because in 1547 France was still a long way from a system of State finance. By the time of the death of Henry II (1559), the French monarchy had a Central Treasury, a set of officers to run and oversee it, and a nascent regional taxing and receiving system, but all these institutions lacked coherence, and the failure of the Grand Parti de Lyon (1557–1558) made manifest the absence of a genuine State or public debt.[41]

Late in his reign (1542), Francis I amplified the system of regional financial districts known as *généralités*, creating sixteen of them, each with a *recette générale*; Henry II added Brittany in 1552, and later kings added five more by 1600.[42] Francis I levied a wide range of new taxes, such as a special subvention on walled towns, a tax for 50,000 infantry (levied on walled towns), special "*crues*" (surtaxes) on clergy, and a tax on belfries, all without benefit of approval by estates, even in provinces where custom dictated he needed such approval.[43]

---

[39] P. Hamon, *Les Renaissances 1453–1559. Histoire de France*, sous la direction de J. Cornette (Paris: Éditions Belin, 2009), 275.

[40] Charles IX and Henry III issued such *rentes* backed by sale of Church properties.

[41] The Grand Parti de Lyon (1555–1558) was an amortization fund of a syndicate of Italian and German bankers, who secured their loans on revenues of indirect taxes: R. Doucet, "Le Grand Parti de Lyon au 16ème siècle," *Revue Historique* 171 (1933): 473–513 and 172 (1933): 1–41. On the central apparatus, M. Antoine, *Le Cœur de l'État* (Paris: Fayard, 2003).

[42] P. Hamon, *L'argent du roi* (Paris: CHEFF, 1994) and *Messieurs des finances* (Paris: CHEFF, 1999) are the classic studies of this financial system, which evolved in fits and starts from the 1520s to the 1580s.

[43] *Catalogue des Actes de François I*[er], IV, contains numerous examples from 1543 and other years. #12872 for the provosty and viscounty of Paris (180,000 *l.*), #12877 on the seneschalsy of Toulouse (108,000 *l.*), #12876 on Lyon [3,000 men for four months].

He consistently had his agents argue on behalf of "urgent necessity," and many of the letters about the tax for the 50,000 infantry specifically stated that both privileged and unprivileged were to pay the tax. The king issued special letters to groups like the cathedral chapter of Notre Dame of Paris and the University of Orléans to confirm their exemption from even this tax. Emperor Charles V's armies invaded France on several occasions, so the argument had real merit. In 1560, the deputies of the Third Estate of Touraine emphasized that Henry II had had to run up large debts, maintaining simultaneously six armies, in different provinces, but that with the return of peace, heavily taxed subjects had a **right** to expect taxes levied for the "urgent affairs" to be reduced or ended. It was "a pitiable thing to see" that two-thirds of the people lived on "bread and water," even "under such a great King, in time of full peace, with not even a whiff of war in the air."[44] The other deputies of 1560 agreed with them, but to no avail.

Francis I and Henry II had profoundly different relationships with their judiciary:[45] Francis emphasized his own authority, perhaps because he came to the throne via indirect inheritance. Henry II had advantages over his father. First, he inherited directly from his father. Second, from his mother, Claude, he inherited Brittany: Francis I, as Claude's husband, had the usufruct of the duchy, but was not its legal heir. One of Henry II's earliest acts as king was formally to create a Parlement of Brittany: he did so in part for financial gain, but his inherited right to the duchy gave him a legal standing in Armorica that his father had not had.[46] Yet both kings had authoritarian personalities; together, they consistently thickened the institutions essential to the development of the early modern state. They made the greatest changes, in my view, in the financial sphere, although France lacked a genuine state debt – which I would consider a sine qua non of an early modern state. In that sphere, Francis I's arguably greatest innovation was the infantry tax on the walled

---

#13079 shows Lyon getting permission for a new tax on hooved animals entering the city, with the proceeds to be split between upkeep of the city walls and contributed to this infantry tax. Town archives from Narbonne to Dijon or Nantes show the large cities seeking to gain control over the manner in which they met their assessment, or, as in the case of Lyon, to get at least partial exemption on the grounds that they had to pay for the upkeep of walls in a key frontier city. R. Knecht, *Francis I* (Cambridge: CUP, 1982), 383, on Lyon receiving back only 27,000 *l.* of the 60,000 *l.* it levied as a "loan" for those soldiers in 1543.

[44] C. Grandmaison, ed., *Plaintes et doléances de la province de Touraine aux États généraux du royaume* (Tours, 1890), 23. Francis I added permanent *"crues"* of 600,000 *l.* and 300,000 *l.* to the main *taille* (which had been 2.4 million *l.* in 1515). Nominal direct taxation doubled but remained stable in real terms.

[45] Houllemare, *Politiques de la parole*, provides a brilliant analysis of this difference.

[46] A. Croix, *L'Age d'Or de la Bretagne* (Rennes: Éditions Ouest-France, 1993). The offices officially generated 350,000 *l.* The edict does not mention the public good (Isambert, *Recueil des loys*, XIII, 361ff.), but highlights the union, repose, and tranquility of Breton subjects.

towns. This tax meant that wealthy urban patriciates in places like Lyon or Paris, who had avoided regular direct taxation, now had to pay. The tax soon came to include *bourgs*, and even in a few cases the countryside, but it remained largely the responsibility of the major cities. This tax disappeared during the Wars of Religion, a practical triumph of the great cities that has been virtually ignored in the historiographical image of their loss of independence, particularly under Henry IV.[47]

Francis I continued the project begun under Charles VIII and Louis XII to write down, print, and publish the customary laws of the various *pays* of France. The king had strong local support for codification, as the massive turnouts at the meetings made clear. Estates General – and provincial ones – regularly demanded the institution of a single system of weights and measures. Royal apologists in Francis I's reign ramped up the arguments for "puissance absolue," providing philosophical justification for the royalist arguments set forth – and then retracted – by the king's representatives at the Estates General of Tours in 1484. Yet we can see in documents such as the *cahier* of the governorship of Orléans of 1614 that the principle of the king and the Estates General jointly making binding law remained vigorous into the seventeenth century.[48]

Building on his father's initiatives, Henri II made profound changes in the structures of French government. He created intermediary appellate jurisdictions, the presidial courts; he instituted a new tax for the gendarmerie, the *taillon*, and a tax for the mounted constabulary (*crue des prévôts des maréchaussée*); he formalized (1558) the title, "secretary of state," and sent out temporary investigating commissioners called *intendants*.[49] The *taillon* and constabulary tax offer fine examples both of the legalism of the monarchy – because Brittany was part of the kingdom of France when these taxes came into being, it paid both of them, but it did not pay the *taille*, because it had not been

---

[47] Henry IV, acting on the advice of the Assembly of Notables of 1596, created a five percent sales tax, the *pancarte*, but soon backed away from this unpopular measure. Kings regularly assessed forced "loans" on major towns; town governments often raised much of this money through direct assessments.

[48] AM Bourges, AA 38, papers of the Estates General of 1614, which include both the *cahier* of the bailiwick of Bourges and the *cahier* of the governorship of Orléans, which covered a vast region of central France – five seneschalsies and thirteen bailiwicks. Both *cahiers* insisted on the inviolability of laws made by the king and the Estates. Bailiwick and provincial *cahiers* all over France repeated this demand in 1614 and in 1789.

[49] The *prévôt des maréchaussées*, the marshals' provost, initially provided oversight of royal soldiers within France; they were a sort of sixteenth-century military police. They evolved into a nationwide police force, with jurisdiction only outside walled towns, especially on royal roads. The *taillon*, de facto, came to replace the levy for the infantry, shifting the burden from the towns to the countryside. In many parts of France, like Champagne, the existing bailiwick judges bought the offices of the presidial, so the judges were the same people.

present at the 1439 meeting of the Estates General that supposedly voted the *taille* – and of the Crown's newfound willingness to create a tax, without consent, for "evident necessity."[50] Henry II created the new controller general, who audited all accounts and supervised the Central Treasurer; the intendants of finances carried out a wide range of activities, starting with the central division among the *généralités* of the direct tax burden.

The kings of France from Charles VII through Henry II also created key regional institutions; these institutions both de-centralized the monarchy and provided it with effective levers of royal power in what had been the great fiefs. Kings created Parlements for southern France (Toulouse, 1442) and for the reconquered Guyenne (Bordeaux) and transformed pre-existing local courts into Parlements in Dauphiné, Burgundy, Provence, Normandy, and Brittany. The main fiefs, like Brittany and Burgundy, also had financial courts: each had a Chamber of Accounts (in both cases, simply the co-optation of a ducal court). The vast territory of Languedoc seemed too big to administer from Toulouse alone, so Montpellier got a *Cour des aides,* a Chamber of Accounts, and, in the reshuffle of 1542, a *recette générale.* The *Catalog of Acts of Francis I* lists an astounding array of offices newly created, particularly in years like 1543 when military expenses ran amok.[51] All of these men invested money in their offices, creating what Robert Descimon has rightly called a sort of proto-public-debt: they all needed the state financial system to function effectively in order to get their *gages,* that is, the return on investment.[52] Henry II followed his father's example in selling offices to access urban capital.

The proliferation of offices legalized French society: nearly every little town now had royal officers, many of whom had had legal training, especially in the expanded judicial system.[53] The number of criminal appeals heard by the Parlement of Paris doubled between 1540 and 1600 and the number of civil

---

[50] Brittany did pay the tax on walled towns and the levy for the infantry created by Francis I, so Henry II, in creating the *taillon* without a vote by the Estates of Brittany, followed the precedent set by his father.

[51] *Catalogue des Actes de François Ier,* IV, has the entries for 1543; the king created new judgeships in places like the Parlements of Rouen (an entire new chamber) and Toulouse. He also levied in-kind contributions: the bailiwick of Dijon had to provide 250 *muids* of wine, 10 heads of cattle, and 500 sheep per week for the royal armies (May 1543; #13080). A *muid* held about 270 liters, so roughly 65,000 liters a week.

[52] R. Descimon, "La vénalité des offices comme dette publique sous l'ancien régime français. Le bien commun au pays des intérêts privés," in *La dette publique dans l'histoire,* ed. J.-Y. Grenier (Paris: CHEFF, 2006), 177–242. Descimon, 188ff, emphasizes the "imperfect modernization of the debt" through means of venal offices.

[53] In 1700, in the small Norman town of Coutances, twenty percent of the men worked in the royal court system. J. Collins, *State in Early Modern France* (Cambridge: CUP, 2009), 233. In the sixteenth century, leading towns of major fiefs – like the duchy of Nevers or royal apanages – still had their own, substantial princely administrations answering to the fief holder.

arrêts it issued jumped 800% between 1525 and 1550 and nearly doubled again by 1600: the 173 *arrêts* of 1525 thus became the 5,752 *arrêts* of 1600.[54] The king's attorney told Charles IX in 1572 that in the twelve years of his reign he had issued so many edicts and ordinances that it took seven volumes to register them; Louis XII, in seventeen years of rule, the attorney told him, had issued only enough royal acts for a single volume.[55]

Because royal officers combined the attributes of executive, legislative, and judicial power, it made perfect sense for elites to share power **within** the structure of government. Estates Generals gave local judicial officials and provincial nobles a powerful institutional base to share central power; central elites – the royal council, but also the sovereign courts and the High Court nobility – did not necessarily view with equanimity such a power-sharing arrangement. For them, sharing power within the emerging State made more sense. As we look at the evolution of republican discourse in the sixteenth century, we have to keep these realities in mind.

6.3   The Last Days of Charles VII's Commonwealth, 1485–1515

> It's commonly said that the king [Louis XI] frightened not only men, but even the trees.
>
> Testimony of Elisabeth Fricon, annulment proceedings of Louis XII and
> Jeanne de France, 1498

The French monarchy suffered from dynastic weakness between the death of Louis XI and the birth (and survival) of three sons to Francis I between 1516 and 1522. Charles VIII was only thirteen when he inherited the throne, and his legal successor, Louis, duke of Orléans, married to Charles' sister, Jeanne, had an uneasy relationship with the adolescent king. At his annulment hearing in 1498, Louis d'Orléans claimed that the dreaded Louis XI had forced him into the marriage, in violation of canon law. He had plenty of witnesses, like Elisabeth Fricon, to back up his claim. In 1484, Orléans had tried, unsuccessfully, to gain control of the king, relying on his right as first prince of the blood; Charles' half-sister, Anne de Beaujeu, and her husband, Pierre, kept the reins of government. Orléans sent letters to the main towns in late 1484, claiming Anne was subverting the monarchy, and that he wanted to protect the "bien public," through means of calling another Estates General. Anne, in Charles VIII's name, naturally countered with letters defending the government and implying Orléans had been led astray to make these "very strange" charges, about things she "had never thought."[56] Orléans plotted with other princes,

---

[54] Houllemare, *Politiques de la parole*, Table 5.

[55] Houllemare, *Politiques de la parole*, 148.

[56] AM Bourges, AA 13, has copies of this correspondence, which can be found in multiple town archives.

above all with François II, duke of Brittany. Their combined forces were routed at St-Aubin-du-Cormier (1488), ending the "Mad War": Orléans spent the next three years in prison, hardly a dynastically reassuring abode for the heir to the throne. Charles VIII's first-born son, Charles-Orland, a healthy child, succumbed to measles at age three; his two younger brothers died soon after birth. When Charles VIII died in 1498, Louis d'Orléans became king. He, too, failed to produce a male heir, and the throne passed to his cousin, François d'Angoulême (Francis I), in 1515.[57]

The thirty years of dynastic instability encouraged Anne of Beaujeu, as regent, Charles VIII, and Louis XII to reach out to the most powerful "members" of the French body politic. Both Charles VIII and Louis XII maintained most of the members of the royal council of their predecessor, although Charles VIII shifted its composition back in the direction of the nobility.[58] A study of the counselors of Charles VII reveals that among the forty-nine most prominent, a quarter were princes, just under a half other nobles, and twenty-nine percent commoners; Louis XI reversed those two final percentages for his overall group of councilors (forty-seven percent commoners), but his inner circle statistically resembled that of his father, with twenty-one percent princes and forty-seven percent nobles.[59] These raw numbers, however, give insufficient weight to Le Daim's network, which included men in key administrative posts, above all in finance. All these kings mixed princes of the blood, great aristocrats, nobles (often personal friends), and professionals, both financial and juridical, in their core group of counselors.

Documents from Charles VIII's reign show the government was deeply embedded in the rhetoric of commonwealth. Coins were, as one edict put it, "the interest of the king and of the *chose publique*," an interesting effort to combine the positions laid out in the fourteenth century by the royalists and by those who followed Oresme's argument: the deputies to the Estates General of 1484 had taken the Oresmian position that coinage was a public good, not a princely monopoly. In 1490, Charles VIII wrote to the Parlement of Burgundy to inform them about changes to the royal coinage, undertaken

---

[57] They descended from the sons of the Louis d'Orléans murdered in 1407.

[58] Charles VIII kept nineteen of the twenty-nine chief counselors of Louis XI; Louis XII kept fifty-nine percent of Charles VIII's counselors and removed only two of the major ones. In contrast, Henry II, in 1547, kept only one major counselor of his father, the chancellor François d'Olivier, a professional jurist. Lange, *First French Reformation*, points out that both Charles VIII and Louis XII were far more receptive than Louis XI or Francis I to conciliarist ideas, and judges.

[59] P. R. Gaussin, "Les conseillers de Louis XI," in *La France de la fin du XVe siècle. Renouveau et apogée*, ed. B. Chevalier and P. Contamine (Paris: CNRS, 1985), 105–134, and "Les conseillers de Charles VII," *Francia* (1983): 67–127; see also Claude Michon's fine summary in his edited volume *Les Conseillers de François Ier* (Rennes: PUR 2011). We see here how Louis XI could be laid open to the charge that he brought in too many "vile bourgeois," yet his inner circle remained heavily noble and aristocratic.

for the "good of us and of the *chose publique* of our kingdom." Charles had taken this step, he told them, with the advice of princes of the blood, of members of his great council, of the Chamber of Accounts, of the heads of the mints and of royal finances, and of "several great and notable personages of the *bonnes villes*," gathered in "great number" to see to the reform.[60]

This assembly, although not an "Estates General" or an "Assembly of Notables," in the later, legalistic sense, was a typical example of the consultative bodies regularly convened by French kings to consult the body politic. Although no official "Estates General" met between 1484 and 1560, French kings consulted large assemblies of key members of the political society on many occasions, from this one in 1490, about currency, to Henry II's informal assembly to raise money in 1558.[61] The bailiwick assemblies convened to swear to uphold the Treaty of Cambrai (1529) seem to have had particularly large attendance.

With respect to the currency, the 1490 change hardly solved the problem, so the king called another assembly in 1493: his letters of June 27, 1493, on the "disorder in the fact of the currency," sent to the town government of Lyon, asked them to send two experts. The king had already consulted "princes and seigneurs," but now he wanted the advice of "several great personages experienced and knowledgeable in the fact of minting"; he was inviting such experts from all the "countries and outlying regions of our kingdom, *pais*, and seigneuries," to have their opinion on the way to proceed "to the greatest profit and relief that can be had for the *bien de la chose publique*." The town government of Lyon decided to save the money of sending a delegation, and appointed Claude Thomassin, already in Paris on other business, as their delegate.[62] Town records, as at Lyon, or regional ones, as in Brittany, reveal

---

[60] P. Pélicier, ed., *Lettres de Charles VIII, roi de France*, III, 1490–1493 (Paris: Renouard, 1902), document DXIX. The king's edict of December 8, 1484, against using foreign coins, had similarly referred to the "prejudice" done to the king and to the "chose publique de nostre royaume."

[61] I am not suggesting here a "Renaissance Monarchy" in the style of J. Russell Major. The king came with a set agenda, particularly at meetings not officially called an Estates General, and expected the deputies to discuss the specific agenda. In these other meetings, deputies did not bring *cahiers de doléances*, although urban deputies could, and did, bring requests specific to their town. Major is certainly right, however, that French kings of this period regularly consulted their subjects, seeking advice – as in the case of the assemblies on coinage – or simply public support for a given royal policy, as in 1506.

[62] AM Lyon, BB 20, fol. 104ff. [Online: BB 20, 2nd link, images 66 and ff.] The letters refer to "especes d'or et monnaie." The small council of July 17 called a larger one, consisting of current and former counselors, and the "notables" – fifty men – which met on July 21 and 22 to elect the deputies. The meeting on the 21st heard several nominations and initially thought about sending two delegates, one focused on money and the second on the Lyon fairs. The king soon thereafter sent Thomassin to Lyon, to deal with another pressing matter: the failure of Charles' choice as archbishop of Lyon, Cardinal André d'Espinay, to

how expensive delegations sent to the king could be, and further reveal that both town governments and provincial estates regularly sought to use interlocutors already at court – often the *avocats* they had on retainer at the Parlement of Paris – to save money.

Local political leaders did **not** want to be involved in quotidian governmental decisions in Paris; they wanted control over implementation at the local level. The central government largely supported this arrangement. The "chose publique," the commonwealth, mainly became a sphere of conflict over issues related to money: commerce; coinage; and, above all, taxes. We might recall here the argument of the town government of Bourges in 1484–1485, that the interest of the republic was rich subjects. Charles VIII and Louis XII often paid for their Italian campaigns through loot or land grants (especially in the kingdom of Naples); for a century after his death, Louis XII's relatively low level of taxation became proverbial – representative bodies ritually demanded a return to the level of taxation of the "father of the people." Starting with Francis I, the level of taxation changed rapidly and permanently: Rivaud's figures on the nature of royal correspondence with the Loire towns illustrate the shift. Whereas Louis XI regularly sought to interfere in municipal affairs, Francis I rarely did so: more than half of the time a letter from Francis I to Tours or Bourges was simply asking for more money.[63]

Royal ordinances continued to use the commonwealth vocabulary, and so did Charles VIII in his letters. He wrote to Ludovico Sforza of Milan in 1490, seeking restoration of goods seized many years before from a merchant of Lyon, on the grounds that Jean du Perat, the aggrieved party, a "citizen of Lyon," was a "good merchant and man of good conversation," and that the king always wished to support those who traded for the "bien de la chose publique." He used similar terms in discussing the wine trade at Bayonne. Perhaps the clearest expression of the larger meaning came in Charles' letters to the sovereign courts of Dauphiné, in 1491, when he explained his marriage to Anne of Brittany: he wanted to combat rumors that the marriage had been contracted by illegitimate means [i.e., that Anne had been forced to marry him], and he wanted "the truth to be heard and known by everyone." The two courts were to inform everyone in Dauphiné that the king had married "for the good and utility of us, of subjects and of the *chose publique* of our kingdom and *pais*."[64] This letter shows us both the king's concern with public opinion, and

---

wrest the metropolitan see from the rival elected by the canons, Hugues de Talaru. It took six years before he bought out Talaru. The entries in BB 20 for August 1493 provide the details.

[63] Rivaud, *Les villes et le roi*, chart on 188. The published deliberations of Poitiers for the reigns of Charles VII and Louis XI shows those two kings regularly asking for money, too.

[64] Pélicier, *Lettres de Charles VIII*, letter of December 8, 1491. Writing to the courts of Dauphiné, the king took care to use the term *"pais"* [for Dauphiné] in addition to "kingdom."

the use of the argument that the royal marriage was legitimate, in part because the king had contracted it on behalf of the commonwealth. Francis I, in contrast, when speaking of the betrothal of his son François [then two] to Mary Tudor [four], referred to the "good of the kingdom," and made no mention of the *chose publique* or *bien public*. Yet Francis did not hesitate to accuse Charles, constable of Bourbon, of violating his faith and oath [*serment*] "to us and to the *chose publique* of our kingdom" in informing the city government of Dijon about Bourbon's treason in 1523.[65]

As soon as he became king, Louis XII called a large assembly to meet at Blois and issued (March 1499) a long ordinance on justice, often renewing legislation created by his predecessors. Louis began with a clear statement of the centrality of justice, the first and cardinal of the virtues, in all well-ordered monarchies, kingdoms, and principalities, "as it is ordered by God."[66] The king claimed that some officers had forgotten the laws, or failed to carry them out "due to the variety and change of time," so he needed to add to or adjust them. He wanted, above all things, that his subjects be well "ruled and governed by good and due justice and police." To that end, he had called together prelates, the presidents and some councilors of the Parlements of Paris, Toulouse, and Bordeaux, as well as some seneschals and *baillis*, the chancellor [Guy de Rochefort], the bishop of Albi [Louis d'Amboise, brother of Cardinal George d'Amboise], the royal chamberlains, and members of the Grand Conseil to give advice on these matters. After getting the recommendations of the Blois assembly, the king discussed their suggestions with the princes of the blood. Louis then issued the ordinances on the basis of "nostre plus ample puissance et auctorité roial." When he made several modifications, in June, based on suggestions from the Parlement, he spoke of acting for "the good of our said kingdom and its *chose publique*," but issued the changes using his "plaine puissance et auctorité roial."[67] Louis XII, in letters about the sale of clothing (March 1499) had already stated that "Be it known that we, to whom belongs *la cure totale, regime et gouvernement principal* of all our subjects, and also the protection, good treatment in our kingdom of all foreigners, merchants and others" – the term "cure" had a distinctly religious and spiritual overtone, reminding everyone of the "cure" of souls of a curé (parish priest).[68]

We could hardly ask for a clearer statement of the commonwealth's political praxis: the king consults with the "members" of the body politic – in this case,

---

[65] Garnier, ed., *Correspondance de la mairie de Dijon*, I, 307.

[66] *Les ordonnances Royaulx nouvellement publiées à Paris de par le Roy Loys douziesme de ce nom le 13 juin 1499* [unpaginated; downloaded from Gallica, image 4]. The ordinance also appears in *Ordonnances*, XXI, 177ff.

[67] Charles VIII attributed to the Grand Conseil in 1497 the right to hear judicial cases evoked to the royal council. The Parlement of Paris and the Grand Conseil traditionally had extremely bad relations, the former seeking always to have the latter abolished.

[68] *Ordonnances*, XXI, 167.

related to laws, he consults with the leading authorities on law, the ecclesiastical and secular judges, and, as always in this family monarchical corporation, with the members of the royal family. Having listened to their counsel, **he** then acts on the basis of royal power and authority; in so doing, he gives voice to the will of the body politic. We might consider as well Louis XII's entry into Paris, in which at the Châtelet the decoration presented him surrounded by Good Counsel and Justice, that is, precisely the two main secular limits placed on the king's power by Claude de Seyssel – justice and "la police." As Nicole Hochner has suggested, the scene was less a glorification of the king than of a perfectly balanced system of governance.[69] Louis XII worked hard on this image of the king within his commonwealth, not simply in using the commonwealth vocabulary in his ordinances but in his regular use of large assemblies, constituted from a mixture of hand-picked delegates (such as those from the Parlements and his council) and deputies chosen by "capital cities," such as Lyon, Paris, and Troyes.[70]

Given that the "first and principal part of justice is religion," Louis XII began his March 1499 collection of "constitutions, statutes, and ordinances" with a reaffirmation of the Pragmatic Sanction and the decrees of the Council of Basel.[71] He singled out residence in one's benefice, preaching, and proper divine services. Articles 35 and 36 dealt with the election of new councilors in the Parlements: they were to be vetted by presidents and councilors chosen by the court; if not "ydoine" [professionally capable], they were to be refused (art. 35). The king claimed (art. 36) that there had been abuses in past elections of presidents and councilors, so now all voters had to swear, on their honor and conscience, in hands of the First President or presiding officer, that they voted for the most lettered and experienced candidate, "useful and profitable for the said offices respectively to be exercised for the good of justice and the *chose publique* of our kingdom." To avoid fraud, the elections were to be held by public voice vote; only one of the three candidates sent to the king could be from Paris. Later articles (40, 48) dealt with the election system for local judges and forbade the sale of judicial office. The ordinance reiterated longstanding prohibitions for seneschals and *baillis* to be officers of, or take pensions or gifts from, any aristocrats or prelates, and for royal attorneys to work for private clients. Judges had to recuse themselves from any case in which a powerful lord or prelate was involved if any member of the judge's family had received benefits from that lord or prelate (art. 37).

This long ordinance contains a remarkable statement about the nature of the king's "souveraineté" because it spells out (art. 70) the abuses governors and their lieutenants had been committing on the "pretexte" of royal letters

---

[69] Hochner, *Louis XII*, 62.

[70] The town records of Tours, Bourges, and Poitiers show that Louis XI also convoked such meetings, such as one in 1470 in which he assembled merchants from the major towns to get their advice on where to establish fairs to handle the commerce formerly conducted in Flanders, with which he had forbidden trade. Rivaud, *Les villes et le roi*, 195.

[71] *Ordonnances*, XXI, 177ff.

granting them certain rights and privileges reserved to the king.[72] Louis stated that as king he had the right to issue pardons, remissions, and grace, "and with that right we have several singular rights and privileges that belong to us and to our successor kings of France reserved in sign of sovereignty." He then enumerated the exclusive royal rights: pardoning; creating fairs and markets; ennobling and legitimizing; and judgment of civil and criminal cases without right of appeal, that is, *ressort*.[73] If we add the rights to coin money, levy taxes, name magistrates, make public law, and to negotiate with foreign princes, we get a clear delineation of royal power in 1499. Louis XII carried the burden of the "bien public," as Jean Marre put it in his *Instructions au roi Louis XII*.[74]

The three largest principalities – Brittany, Burgundy, and Provence – had fallen into royal hands, either by marriage (Brittany) or inheritance.[75] Two of the four most important branches of the royal family – the houses of Anjou and Burgundy – died out in the male line within a four-year span (1477–1481), and with the death of Charles VIII, a third major branch, the Orléans, inherited the throne, so its possessions, too, were reunited with the royal demesne.[76] The fourth major branch, the Bourbons, continued to hold vast areas of southern France, although its stranglehold on the key bishoprics – Lyon, Le Puy, Clermont – largely disappeared between 1485 and 1488 due to the deaths of Charles, cardinal-archbishop of Lyon (1488) and nominal bishop of Clermont from 1475–1488, and of Jean III de Bourbon, bishop of Le Puy (1485). Charles de Bourbon was Anne de Beaujeu's brother-in-law, and a strong supporter of the Regency she shared with his brother. At the Estates General of 1484, he was among the government's chief spokesmen, and one historical tradition identifies him as the "senior lord" who made the sweeping claims for royal rights over the property of subjects, claims the chancellor later disavowed. From 1483 until 1522, when Francis I's first son (Francis) turned four, no king of France

---

[72] The sixteenth-century French word *pretexte* could mean reason and/or pretext; it did not carry the modern connotation of a false reason, but more the sense of the publicly stated reason, which need not be the true one.

[73] We notice the consistency of these rights with those enumerated in 1545 by Grassaille. The Parlement had established by this time the principle that it had to register a royal edict before that edict became law.

[74] Marre was vicar general of the archbishopric of Auch and a close friend of Jacques d'Amboise, bishop of Albi, singled out by name as one of those consulted for the March 1499 edict discussed above.

[75] In French royal eyes, Burgundy had returned to the royal demesne by law, as an apanage lacking a direct male heir; the Burgundian-Habsburg position was that Burgundy had not been granted as an apanage in 1361, but as a personal inheritance of John II, given to his son Philip. Provence passed to Louis XI by means of private inheritance; the county had never been part of the kingdom of France.

[76] The conflict between Francis I and Emperor Charles V simply maintained the old division between the Orléans and Burgundy branches: Francis was the great-grandson of the Louis d'Orléans murdered at Jean sans Peur's order in 1407; Charles was the great-great-great grandson of Jean sans Peur, who ordered the murder.

had a living son over the age of three: thirty-nine years was a long time for that sort of dynastic instability.

The Salic Law, of course, identified the legal heir, but we grossly overestimate its importance. In hindsight, we know that the Salic Law-designated heir actually did become king in each of the three lateral transmissions (1498, 1515, and 1589), but the political behavior surrounding each succession makes it obvious that no one took it for granted that Salic Law would literally determine the succession, although it did define the range of the most likely candidates.[77] Each new king made sure to have control of the woman most likely to pose a threat to his possession of the throne. Louis XII faced rumors that his rebellion against Charles VIII, in 1488, made him ineligible to succeed;[78] Francis I took care to marry his predecessor's daughter; Henry IV faced a civil war in which his opponents called an Estates General to select a new king.[79] Let us look closely at the background to the second transition (1515), to see how the commonwealth functioned at the beginning of the sixteenth century.

6.4   Royal Wedding

Ad coronam Franciæ non potest succedere fœmina, nec masculus ex ea descendens.

> C. de Grassaille, Regalia franciæ, 349.

It's a very perilous thing in a kingdom when it is subject to fall in succession to daughters as well as sons; because once a woman has authority to command in a republic, if she is not wise enough to take honest counsel from prudent and virtuous men, all will not go well; and even so, should the woman herself be very wise and furnished with good counsel, it is the case that the grands over whom she has the power of command do not take much account of her ordinances, if they are not accorded to their wishes, as they would those of a man, and they have little fear of offending [her].

> Claude Haton, 1558.[80]

---

[77] The Bourbons promulgated an interesting twist to the Salic Law: they claimed only those descended from Saint Louis (Louis IX), father of Robert de Clermont, founder of the Bourbon line, could claim rights through Salic Law. In the 1660s, Louis XIV ruled that the Courtenay family, incontestably descended in the male line from Louis VI, had no right to call themselves princes of the blood or to inherit the throne. The Courtenay had sought designation as princes of the blood since the 1580s.

[78] Machiavelli speaks of such rumors: Hochner, Louis XII, 37.

[79] The primary sources make it obvious that French elites had no intention of following the letter of Salic Law, should Henry IV die without legitimate male issue, but elites did focus on the Bourbon princes.

[80] Haton, Mémoires de Claude Haton, ed. Bourquin, I, 118–119, 1558, paragraph 29.

The king recognized the importance of the commonwealth's acceptance of succession, and nowhere is that clearer than in the events surrounding the engagement of Francis I and Claude de France in 1504–1507. Louis XII and Anne of Brittany had promised their daughter, born in 1499, to the young Charles, grandson of Emperor Maximilian I (to whom Anne herself had been briefly "married," by proxy, in 1490).[81] Louis XII had gotten himself into trouble pursuing his claim to the kingdom of Naples, so he promised Claude a dowry that included, among other territories, the duchies of Brittany and Burgundy, and Louis' personal lands, such as the county of Blois and duchy of Milan.[82] The king orchestrated the 1506 campaign by major towns and the nobility to break off this engagement; he convened a sort of "Estates General" (as contemporaries often called it, but really more like an Assembly of Notables) at Tours in May 1506 to demand that the young princess be affianced to a "French prince," that is, to Francis of Angoulême, Louis XII's cousin and presumed heir.[83] All of the documents carefully note that the "*bonnes villes*" proposed to the king that he approve the engagement of Claude and Francis, and that the princes, nobles, prelates, and high personages of the Council had heartily approved this humble request from the town deputies.

The town archives of Troyes, Paris, Amiens, and Lyon contain some extraordinary documents about this process. Troyes sent deputies to the meeting, with orders to join with other leading towns, such as Paris, Rouen, Bourges, and Amiens, and to demand the repudiation of the Blois treaty and the engagement of Francis and Claude. The king gravely received this request, which he granted after two days of supposed deliberation. Royal letters seem to have gone out even to small towns. In the bailiwick of Auxerre, mounted sergeants brought letters about the prospective marriage to "seven of the large *bourgs* or towns" of the bailiwick.[84]

---

[81] Anne had married Maximilian by proxy, in Rennes, in 1490, prompting a French invasion of Brittany. Charles VIII forced Anne to marry him in 1491 and Pope Innocent VIII recognized that marriage, not the proxy one, as legitimate in 1492. Anne pushed for the marriage of Claude and Charles, which Louis opposed.

[82] Louis XII's alliance with King Ferdinand of Aragon to split the kingdom of Naples led to a disastrous war, ending with Spanish control of Naples in January 1504. The agreements signed at Blois a few months later, in addition to placating Anne of Brittany, also bought Louis time to recover from the Naples fiasco.

[83] This meeting was not a formal Estates General, because no letters of convocation were issued. The king invited specific people, and representatives from "capital" cities. The term "Assembly of Notables" was not in use prior to 1583. Many sixteenth-century sources call this meeting an "estates general," but the royal government did not do so.

[84] M. Quantin, "Le comté d'Auxerre au XVIe siècle," *Bulletin de la Société des Sciences de l'Yonne* (1890), 263–287, online at Gallica, p. 267. Unfortunately, Quantin does not indicate whether the sergeants brought letters announcing the assembly or letters

If that procedure was followed throughout the kingdom, at least 600 small towns got copies of the letters in question.[85]

That Louis orchestrated the episode is hardly in doubt, particularly given that when ill in early 1506 he had prepared a will that mandated the marriage of Claude and Francis, but what interests us here is that Louis XII used the *langage* of a meeting of representatives of the commonwealth making a demand of him, to justify his action. Moreover, Louis XII carefully made sure that the deputies of the towns alone made the original request. In the letters he sent to Bourges about taking an oath to support the actions of the assembly, he emphasized that **their** deputies and others had not simply counseled him to engage Claude to Francis, but "prayed and supplicated" him to do so. He "prayed them nonetheless ordered them" to do so, because it "touches the *bien* of you and all the *chose publique* of our said Kingdom." They were to order prayers to God and solemn processions once the oaths had been taken.[86]

At Troyes, as in all the other major ("principal" and "capital") towns, citizens had to take an oath to support the marriage of the couple, "when they came of age to consummate it." The oath continued: "And if the King, which God not wish, dies without leaving a male child, we will hold and will repute the said Sr de Valoys for our King and sovereign seigneur and as such will obey him." The register lists 465 men who took this oath, with the formula "and many others in great number."[87] The register gives few occupations, but among those identified we find a shoemaker, two sergeants, and a draper, as well as lawyers, royal and town officials, and priests. The Salic Law may well have indicated that Francis was the next king, but Louis XII and Francis were taking no chances: they got the citizens of the kingdom to take an oath to support Francis' claim and made sure he would be married to the king's legal, personal heir.

The Parisian documents from 1506 spell out the same oath taken there. A meeting held at the Hôtel de Ville on April 23, 1506, to charge the deputies sent to Tours, included the First President of the Parlement, several masters of requests, and other leading royal officers, as well as the aldermen. They instructed their deputies to demand the marriage for the "bien, paix et union

---

announcing its results. By definition, a *bourg* had no town wall, but could have a population as large as one of the small towns (*villes*) that did have one.

[85] If each of the roughly ninety bailiwicks sent letters to seven towns, that would be 630 towns, and many of those bailiwicks had a much denser network of towns than the sparsely populated Auxerrois. M. Quantin, "Histoire des impôts aux comté et élection d'Auxerre au XVIe siècle," *Annuaire de l'Yonne* (1874): 11.

[86] AM Bourges, AA 13, letters of May 31, 1506.

[87] Boutiot and Babeau, eds. *Documents inédits tirés des archives de Troyes et relatifs aux États-Généraux* (Troyes, 1878), I, 7ff.

de la chose publicque du Royaulme."[88] We might particularly emphasize the final term, "union of the commonwealth of the Kingdom," as evidence of the strong sentiment on behalf of such unity, outside the king's person.[89] The king's letters of May 24 said the princes and seigneurs of royal blood, "whom the thing touched," had not simply counseled but "prié, supplié et requis" [prayed and supplicated] him and he had liberally condescended to go along with a request that was "very just and reasonable and for the good of our said Kingdom." The deputies in Tours had all sworn the same oath later administered at Troyes; in his letters to Paris, the king noted that "the which oath and promise, inasmuch as it touches you, there is need to ratify." He repeated that "it touched your good [bien] and that of all 'la chose publique' of the said Kingdom"; later, he used again the term "the universal good of our said kingdom."

The reply letters sent out by the Parisians began, "for the universal good of the *chose publicque* of the kingdom of France, and of its security and union," their deputies and those of the other principal "bonnes villes" of the kingdom had requested that the king agree to the marriage of Claude and Francis. In Paris, representatives of each "corps" and quarter took the oath on behalf of those whom they represented.

Lyon had a strong tradition of commonwealth ideology. In 1503, when Philip of Habsburg passed through the town, the two giant figures prepared for his entry were "Bien Publique" and "Bon Police."[90] In 1506, Lyon sent three deputies to Tours, for the "*bien*, profit, and utility . . . of the kingdom of France and its *chose publique*." The chief deputy, Claude Le Charron, doctor in law, chief judge of the bailiwick, reported back that the king had approved the towns' request that he arrange the marriage and that François d'Angoulême "had now been created Dauphin [*créé dauphin*] and declared successor to the crown of France."[91] Here we have a highly trained lawyer, the chief judge in the third largest city in the kingdom, telling his constituents that Francis had been "created" Dauphin and declared successor to the Crown, a phrase that suggests the Salic Law had precious little to do with the succession as a practical matter,

---

[88] RDBHVP, I, 117ff. The deputies included members of all three estates, beginning with two royal officers (one of them *prévôt des marchands* as well); two doctors of theology, regents of the University; a merchant; a lawyer (avocat); the town receiver, and two nobles (one of them also an officer, Master of *Eaux & Fôrets*).

[89] G. Oestreich, *Neostoicism and the Early Modern State* (Cambridge: CUP, 1981), pointed out the fundamental role of representative bodies in "national" unity.

[90] J.-B. Monfalcon, *Histoire de la Ville de Lyon* (Lyon, 1851), I, 564, says the second figure was "Ardent Desire for Peace," with a young woman between them: she made the harangue to the prince.

[91] AM Lyon, BB 25, fol. 18v, consulted online [BB 25, 1st link, image 19]. Lyon sent three men, among them the Claude Thomassin we have met above. The list of signatories at the general meeting begins on f. 22 (image 22).

even in a lawyers' eyes.[92] Charron added that Francis became Louis' heir only if the king failed to produce "a male heir and not otherwise."

The Lyonnais drove a hard bargain for their support: Louis XII confirmed their four fairs (ending the attempt of Bourges to retake two of them), authorized some new local taxes, and responded positively to other remonstrances.[93] A few days after the report, the town council gathered together 107 notables and 66 guild masters "in the accustomed manner" to "treat the affairs of the city and the *chose publique*." The three deputies from Lyon had promised the king they would get the "ratification and consent" of the "manans et habitans" of the "ville et cité" of Lyon. The town council records cite the "bien, seureté, utilité et tranquilité de lad ville" as well as the *chose publique*: the large assembly, which had "power [*puissance*] in this matter" to act "for us and all the community" readily gave its assent. Imagine the response of the *vigneron* Jean Romain or the ploughman Benoist Pellet, to say nothing of the mason Pierre Pellu or the grocer Pierre Faye: all of them took the oath at Lyon, giving their assent, on behalf of their guild or group, to the engagement of the king's daughter and to the "creation" of François d'Angoulême as the Dauphin and as heir to the throne of their commonwealth. At Amiens, Raoul Lecouvreur, *avocat*, one of their deputies to the assembly, spoke to the large assembly meeting to discuss matters related to the good of the kingdom and its *chose publique*. He reported that the town deputies had determined that "for the good of the said kingdom and the *chose publique*, it was necessary and very appropriate to ally Mme Claude de France to monseigneur the duke of Valois and Angoulême." The members of an even larger assembly – a great number of "citizens, bourgeois and inhabitants" – the next day took the oath to support the marriage and to recognize Valois (Francis I) as "our king and sovereign seigneur and to obey him as such," should Louis XII die without a son.[94]

A century later, the royal historiographer, Pierre Mathieu, claimed that Francis had made Antoine du Prat chancellor of France because du Prat had given him good counsel in his youth, "to break a design of youth and love that could have distanced [*esloigner*] him from the succession of the Crown."[95] Mathieu, who held a doctorate in Roman law, does not elaborate, but he clearly believed Francis **could** have forfeited his right of succession, an interesting

---

[92] According to the agreement attaching Dauphiné to the kingdom of France, the king's oldest son was to be Dauphin, so in the case of a collateral inheritance, the heir to the throne was not legally Dauphin.

[93] In 1484, Lyon lost its fairs, but it got back two (Quasimodo, the first Sunday after Easter, and All Saints Day) in, and in 1494 regained the two (Epiphany and August) lost to Bourges from 1487–1494.

[94] Thierry, *Recueil [...] Amiens*, II, 504ff.

[95] P. Mathieu, *Histoire de France*, (Paris, 1631), 9. Mathieu here refers to Francis' supposed infatuation with Mary Tudor, sister of Henry VIII, who came to France in 1514 to marry Louis XII.

legal commentary on the Salic Law. In the case of all three collateral successions – Louis XII, Francis I, and Henry IV – contemporaries raised the issue of whether the heir designated by Salic Law could be legitimately excluded from the succession; all three kings took seriously these attempts to deprive them of the throne. Given the precedent that the members of the Parlement of Paris sitting in Paris in 1422 had pronounced Charles VII "unfit" to be king and cast aside the Salic Law to recognize Henry VI of England as king of France, one can hardly blame them.

6.5   The Royal "Bride"

And a marriage is made between the said Seigneur and his said subjects; and by the law [*droit*] of this marriage the said Seigneur is bound to guard and uphold and conserve the rights of his Crown.

Jean de Selve, First President of the Parlement of Paris, speaking against the
Treaty of Madrid, December 20, 1527, at a *lit de justice* in Paris.

Henry II's coronation, in 1547, marked a decisive symbolic moment in the evolution of the French royal commonwealth: for the first time, in the coronation oath, the king "married" the Crown, whose dowry was the kingdom, France. In French law, the husband obtained the usufruct of his wife's immoveable possessions (like land), but not ownership: he could not sell, alienate, or exchange lands she brought.[96] Grassaille, often cited as the source of this metaphor, in fact, used a fundamentally different one: the king was said to be "husband of the commonwealth" [*reip.*], in a "moral and political marriage." He kept the metaphor of the body politic, but with a new twist: "And if the man is the head of the wife, so the wife is truly the body of the man [*vir*]."[97] Ernst Kantorowicz reminds us that Grassaille did not originate this marriage metaphor, but took it verbatim from the fourteenth-century Neapolitan legist Luca da Penne, who also used the specific formulation of "moral and political" marriage.[98] Luca da Penne, in turn, borrowed from Cino

---

[96] Jackson, *Vive le Roi!* and *Ordines Coronationis Franciae,* for the late medieval *ordines.* Leyte, *Domaine,* on the evolution of law related to the demesne. In the second half of the sixteenth century, writers like François Hotman made the inalienability of the royal demesne, precisely as the "dowry," a fundamental law of the monarchy. F. Hotman, *Francogallia* (Geneva, 1573). The date makes us think immediately of the work's relationship to the Saint Bartholomew's Day Massacre, but Ralph Giesey demonstrated the likelihood of a pre-August 1572 composition of the original version of *Francogallia*: "When and Why Hotman wrote the *Francogallia,*" *Bibliothèque d'Humanisme et Renaissance,* 29, n. 3 (1967): 581–611.

[97] Grassaille, *Regalium Franciae,* 218.

[98] In Luca da Penne's day, Robert of Anjou, scion of a branch of the French royal family, ruled the kingdom of Naples. Robert led opposition to the Emperor in Italy, and we may surely hypothesize that Luca's contractual theories of monarchy had a direct tie to the

da Pistoia. In his 1314 commentary on the Digest, Cino da Pistoia had written that "just as the husband is called the defender of his wife ... so is the emperor the defender of the *respublica*."[99] As for the king as the head of the body politic, Grassaille could reached back to Christine de Pizan, or, in a slightly different formulation (used by de Rély in 1484), all the way back to Seneca's comment to Nero: "You are the soul of the republic and the republic is your body."[100]

Yet even in France, Grassaille followed in the footsteps of others. The marriage metaphor had appeared in many places. The Normans used it in the ceremony crowning the duke, who married his duchy: when Louis XI had the ring in question smashed in a ceremony at Rouen in 1469, his envoy specifically mentioned the marriage. Michel de Pons, procureur général of the Parlement, arguing Louis XI's case to take the duchy of Burgundy after Charles the Bold's death, compared the king's "moral and political marriage with la chose publique" to a carnal marriage of husband and wife; the royal demesne, of which the duchy of Burgundy was a part, was, like a dowry, "inalienable." Alain Bouchart, in his 1514 *Grandes chroniques de Bretagne*, used the same image of the ring signifying the faith the king promised to keep to the "chose publique," just as a husband swore his troth to a wife. In yet another royal family lawsuit about an apanage, this time the Auvergne, Pierre Lezet, pleading for Louise of Savoy, referred to the demesne of the Crown as the dowry that the "chose publique" brought to the king, its spouse.[101]

6.6 The Treaties of Madrid and Cambrai

The said Capitouls named above, having charge and administration of the *cause publique*, committed to them by the King, our Sovereign Lord (*Sire*), in the cité of Toulouse ... acting for and representing the mystical body [*corps mystique*] of the said Town, and its inhabitants ... for themselves and all inhabitants, present and future, have protested and protest that they intend [...] nothing in prejudice of the King, our Sovereign Lord, his Kingdom, and the Inhabitants of

---

practical political agenda of King Robert. The 1509 Lyon edition, published by Jean Petit, contained a dedication to none other than Antoine du Prat.

[99] Kantorowicz, *King's Two Bodies*, 213. Quotation from Luca da Penne on 214: Kantorowicz translates Penna's *respublica* as "state." Cino da Pistoia spent time in Paris and later taught Bartoldus at Perugia, yet another example of the close personal ties among so many of these key legal and political theorists.

[100] Cited in R. Descimon, "Les fonctions de la métaphore du mariage politique du roi et de la république. France, XVe-XVIIIe siècles," *Annales. Histoire, Sciences Sociales*, 47, n. 6 (1992): 1127–1147, 1129.

[101] BNF, M Fr 5079, f. 30v. Descimon, "Les fonctions de la métaphore," 1134. A. du Crest, *Modèle familial et pouvoir monarchique (XVIe–XVIIIe siècles)* (Aix: PU d'Aix-Marseille, 2002), ch. 1 on the marriage metaphor.

> Toulouse, nor to contravene in any quality that might be, to the privileges given
> to the Inhabitants of France, either by the King or by our Holy Father the Pope.
>
> Protest of the town government of Toulouse against their forced acceptance
> of the Treaty of Cambrai, February 13, 1530 [n.s.].[102]

Jean de Selve, First President of the Parlement of Paris, used this marriage metaphor in the famous *lit de justice* of December 20, 1527, at which the leaders of French society – princes, prelates, judges, nobles, town government of Paris – had repudiated the Treaty of Madrid, which gave Burgundy to Charles V. Speaking for the judges, de Selve argued that the king could not do so: de Selve had been one of the negotiators of the Treaty, which added a special irony to his speech.[103]

Francis I had been taken prisoner at Pavia (1525) and languished in a Spanish prison; he became so ill that he was given up for dead. Desperate, by the Treaty of Madrid, in return for his freedom, he agreed to "return" the duchy of Burgundy to Charles V (grandson of Mary of Burgundy, who had lost the duchy to Louis XI in 1477), to give up his claims in Italy (Milan, Asti, Naples), and to renounce his "droit de ressort de Souveraineté" in the counties of Flanders and Artois.[104] Francis granted Burgundy and the attached lands "purely, freely, perpetually and forever, to the said lord Emperor" and his heirs, both female and male, in "all sovereignty, preeminence and exemption from the Crown of France, without reserving anything of any kind for the said Crown of France." [Art. 3] Francis's negotiators, however, managed to convince Charles' emissaries to include article 5, which stated that the hostages

[102] B. Durosoy, *Annales de la ville de Toulouse*, II (Paris, 1772) *Divers titres et actes, pour servir de preuves*, 14–15; AM Toulouse, BB 9, session begins on image 120. The original says "cause publique," Durosoy reads as "chose publique," the more usual term. "Cause" here reflects the Occitan influence: the phrase in Occitan was "causa publica." G. de La Faille, *Annales de la ville de Toulouse* (Paris, 1701), t. II, "Preuves," 8, also uses "chose." Jean de Bagis, doctor of laws, one of the consuls of 1528, led the opposition; he had been Toulouse's deputy to the Estates of Languedoc, which had formulated opposition to some clauses; he moved, and the general assembly of about fifty men agreed, to second the objections of "those of Paris" and of the three estates of Languedoc. [fols. 116–116r].

[103] Mary of Burgundy, grandmother of Charles V, believed that the family had received Burgundy as a private inheritance, not as an apanage [a point open to debate], and that the royal ordinance about inalienability of apanages postdated the grant of Burgundy to Philip the Bold [true]. She believed Louis XI had robbed her of her inheritance, an opinion passed down to her son Philip, and to his son, Charles. De Selve received his legal education in Toulouse and held a doctorate in Roman law. R. Kalas, "Jean de Selve (1475–1529)," in *Les conseillers de François Ier*, 189–198.

[104] Charles V was count of Flanders and count of Artois; he had done homage for both fiefs in 1515. In addition to Burgundy, Charles was to get the counties of Charolais and the Maconnais, as well as the towns and surrounding territories of Saint-Laurent (across from Macon) and Auxonne. Charles renounced any claims he might have to Ponthieu, the Boulonnais, Guines, Mondidier, and the Somme towns.

Charles would take (Francis' two oldest sons) would be returned after Estates General of the "kingdom and *pays*" had approved the treaty, and it had been registered in all the Parlements and in the Chamber of Accounts. The *pays* in question was Burgundy; Francis and his legal advisors immediately (in the form of a notarized statement taken in prison) made the argument that he could not alienate Burgundy, because it belonged to the Crown and because in his coronation oath he had sworn not to alienate any rights or lands belonging to the Crown. Shortly after Francis' return to France, he and his advisors insisted he could not act without the consent of the Burgundians, and that he could only carry out the parts of the Treaty subject to his "free will" (*libre arbitre*), not those subject to the will of another.

The government certainly orchestrated a campaign by which Francis would not give up Burgundy, but it naturally sought legal justifications. Initially, as we can see in his instructions to the royal commissioners sent to the Estates of Languedoc in August 1526, Francis sought to get out of **all** the clauses related to the Crown's rights. The document mentions that under duress he had been forced to give up not only Burgundy and the attached counties but to relinquish "the sovereignty of Flanders and Artois, which are the *fleurons* and royal and sovereign rights of our crown, which cannot and must not be alienated."[105]

Henri Hauser has documented the actions taken by Francis I and Louise of Savoy (his mother, acting as regent) to make sure that Charles did not get his hands on Burgundy. Although he establishes beyond reasonable doubt that Francis had no intention of giving up Burgundy, Hauser wrongly assumes that the legal arguments made in 1526–1527 had no basis in public law or legitimacy in the eyes of contemporaries.[106] The procès-verbal of the meeting of the Estates of Burgundy on June 3, 1526 says that the deputies all agreed that the

---

[105] *Ordonnances de François Ier*, IV, 88ff for the notarized document; 299ff for the instructions to the commissioners sent to Languedoc. In the notarized document, Francis stated that it was "illegitimate" to give up these rights. Hauser (n. 108) cites a letter from Henry VIII of England to his ambassador in France saying that Francis should not give Burgundy to Charles because he could not dismember the Crown's rights and property, which offers further evidence of the wide currency of this idea. "quitter la souveraineté de Flandres et Arthois qui sont les fleurons et droys royaulx et souverains de notre couronne."

[106] H. Hauser, "Le Traité de Madrid et la cession de la Bourgogne à Charles-Quint. Étude sur le sentiment national bourguignon en 1525–1526," *Revue Bourguignonne* t. XXII (1912). Joseph Declareuil, in an article published in 1913, rightly took Hauser to task for ignoring the legal history behind the documents. R. Descimon, "Declareuil (1913) contre Hauser (1912). Les rendez-vous manqués de l'histoire et de l'histoire du droit," *Annales. Histoire. Sciences Sociales* 57, n. 6 (2002): 1615–1636, provides a brilliant analysis of the wider meaning of the quarrel between the two historians. Two of Declareuil's objections to Hauser are surely right: 1) feudal law held that the suzerain could not transfer suzerainty over a vassal without his consent; and 2) ultimate jurisdiction or *ressort* could not be alienated. Those points were precisely the ones made by John of Legnano in the Guyenne case of 1369–1370. The existence of the papal bull on inalienability

content of the Treaty was "against all reason and equity." As Robert Knecht has argued, "[O]n the issue of Burgundy's inalienability, the king and his subjects were in perfect accord."[107] In their remonstrances, they were more explicit.

Picking up on royal discourse, they called Burgundy one of the "principal *fleurons* of the Crown of France, united and inseparably incorporated into it, and that reason and justice did not permit that Kings could or must alienate the titles of this crown or put them outside the accustomed obedience of France." They humbly begged the king to administer justice, "of which he was the holder, and had sworn to uphold at his coronation, and had also sworn not to alienate the titles united and incorporated into the said Crown." They asked him to think of the evils and scandals that would occur if the door of justice, always open to all in France, were closed to subjects from Burgundy. Here, the Burgundians made a point that all French elites agreed upon: the king could not unilaterally change their relationship to the kingdom of France, or to its *chose publique*.

They found it difficult to believe that Francis had given away Burgundy, "given that it would be an unjust and unreasonable thing, and in right [*droit*] and according to the law of France, impossible." The king's first oath, given to God, was to "guard the rights of the crown and not to alienate any land incorporated into it." The king had to keep faith with religion by upholding this oath taken to God. He was obliged to guard those in his kingdom "like a pastor is held to guard his sheep." They were not to be alienated or divided from "the union with the French people, of whom they were members, and it would be doing them as great a wrong and as great a violence as it would be to remove an arm from a human body."[108] After citing the precedent of the duchy of Guyenne in 1369, they argued that while the French ambassadors had sought the sought the best interests of the Crown, "nonetheless the inhabitants and the three estates, who have the principal interest in this affair, cannot and must not remain silent." In protesting and sustaining their rights, they assured the king that they meant no attack against him or the Crown. This document clearly demonstrates that the deputies believed in a body politic that existed outside of both king and Crown, and that as members of that body they had rights that even the king could not abrogate.

The Treaty of Cambrai spoke directly to most of these points. The Imperial negotiators added much more detailed language about what Francis I would give up in Flanders and Artois. Article 2 stated that all elements of the Treaty of Madrid would be enforced, except articles 3 and 4 [on Burgundy and the

suggests that contemporaries surely did look upon it as something like a fundamental law, but that precise terminology might be an anachronism in 1526.

[107] R. J. Knecht, "Francis I and the '*Lit de Justice*': a legend defended," *French History* 7, n. 1 (1993): 53–83, 69.

[108] Hauser, "Traité," reproduces the documents, 164–167.

attached counties], and those parts of articles 11 and 14 related to the Maconnais, Auxonne, and Bar-sur-Seine. In the interests of peace, the Emperor reverted to claiming his rights to Burgundy with the framework of a "friendly way and in Justice"; he expressly reserved all those rights. In article 6, Francis now renounced all "rights of Jurisdiction, Ressort, and Sovereignty" held by him and his predecessors in Flanders and Artois, and some rights in Arras, Tournai, and the feudal right of *rachat* in Lille, Douai, and Orchies.[109] Article 7 reiterated that Francis surrendered all fiefs, homages, peerages of France, oaths of fidelity and all Subjection, Jurisdiction, Superiority, Ressort, Sovereignty, and all other Rights held by the king and predecessors over counts and countesses of Flanders, prelates, nobles, vassals, towns, town governments, castellanies, "manans et habitans." Article 10 reiterated these clauses for Artois.[110]

Charles still wanted the Treaty confirmed, and Francis duly summoned the men of the three estates bailiwick by bailiwick and sent the treaty to the Parlements and the Paris Chamber. Dumont reproduces some of the relevant documents. Throngs of people attended some of these meetings – the procès-verbal of the Estates of the Bourbonnais, where Louise of Savoy was duchess, lists the names of hundreds of deputies – and they generally went along with the king's "pleasure and will." At Montargis, the greffier and notary who attested to the deputies' approval said that those present had acted as "public persons, to whom in such acts and most important matters [*greigneurs*] one adds faith."[111]

Some had their doubts: the nobility of Périgord carefully added to their approval that they "made the ratification without prejudice to their estate," a clause that strongly suggests concerns – precisely in the area at issue in 1369 – over the principle that the king could unilaterally transfer the homage of his vassals. Francis had to send *lettres de jussion* (mandating registration) to the Parlements of Toulouse and Bordeaux on October 4, 1529. He told them to register the Treaty, without revision, and not to make any difficulty "under the shade or color of Oaths, which you may have made not to consent to or suffer any alienations of the Domaine and Rights of our Crown, from which Oaths we have, to the extent there would be need, discharged and released, discharge and release you by these present letters signed by our hand."[112] The rights in question were sovereignty and *ressort* over Flanders and Artois.

---

[109] In 1537, during a later war with Charles, Francis I had Parlement issue a ruling reasserting his rights over Flanders and Artois.

[110] J. Dumont, *Corps universel diplomatique du droit des gens contenant un recueil des traitez d'alliance, de paix, de treve* . . . . [Amsterdam, The Hague, 1726), t. IV, part II, pp 7ff, Treaty of Cambrai; part I, 397ff, Treaty of Madrid.

[111] The greffier and notary claimed they had to do so because many deputies were illiterate. Jean Bodin used precisely the same idea about "public persons" in his *République*.

[112] Dumont, *Corps universel*, IV, part 2, 24–25.

Francis himself had similar scruples: he sought and obtained a papal bull absolving him from his violation of the coronation oath. The Pope asserted that although the king had taken an oath at his coronation not to alienate goods or rights of the Crown of the kingdom of France [*bonis aut Juribus Coronae Regni Franciae*], and had violated that oath at Cambrai, he did so for the peace of Christendom, and could therefore be absolved. Relying on his "certain science and *potestatis plenitudine*," Pope Clement VII absolved Francis from the violation, notwithstanding "Constitutions and Ordinances of the kingdom's laws and of its Parlements," this last turn of phrase surely related to the king's problems with the Parlements of Toulouse and Bordeaux.[113]

At Toulouse, Raymond Sabbaterii, the procureur général of the king had given an impassioned speech about the dismemberment of the Crown and insisted that an appeal be made to the Pope as soon as the young princes were back in France. He began by urging the Parlement to register the Treaty and claimed to make this request as the simple procureur of *Francis I*, declaring that for peace and the recovery of the "inestimable treasure" of the two boys, he requested, as a "simple and particular procureur," the registration of the Treaty. Having done so, he then gave a long speech as procureur général of the king, protesting the Treaty, and handed the clerk of the Parlement a written protest that the rights of the Crown were violated by the clauses related to Burgundy and Flanders.[114] Charles V got wind of this extraordinary event and insisted that the Parlement register the Treaty a second time, in the presence of his representatives and of the *avocat* and *procureur du roi*; the Parlement duly held such a session on February 3, 1530, about six weeks after the original session.[115] The capitouls of Toulouse, who, like other town governments, were also asked to approve the Treaty, did so only under the king's "expressed command." Their protest against the violation of the privileges granted to inhabitants of France by kings and Popes speaks to the same key point made by the Burgundians and the nobility of Périgord: no one wanted a precedent that allowed a king of France to violate basic feudal law (by giving away suzerainty without a vassal's consent) or to violate the coronation oath.[116]

---

[113] Dumont, *Corps universel*, 53, November 1529. Clement VII was born Giulio de Giuliano de Medici; uncle and guardian of Catherine de Medici, he married her off to Francis' son Henry in 1533. At the time of this bull, Clement VII was in the power of Charles V, whom he crowned at Bologna in 1530, the last such Imperial coronation ceremony.

[114] Devic and Vaissette, *Histoire générale de Languedoc*, V, 130. Document XLVII of the "Preuves" (88–89) provides the ratification of the Treaty of Cambrai by the Estates, making clear that they did so only to obey the king. They made sure to mention that their share of French taxes should not go up because of the loss of provinces.

[115] J. B. Dubétat, *Histoire du Parlement de Toulouse* (Paris: Rousseau, 1885), v. I, 160–161.

[116] AM Toulouse, BB 9, fols. 116 and ff.

In the 1527 assembly that rejected the Treaty of Madrid, four men had spoken on behalf of the assembly: the Cardinal of Bourbon, who offered 1.3 million *francs* from the clergy; the duke of Vendôme, for the nobility; de Selve, for the magistrates, and the *prévôt des marchands* of Paris, Germain de Marle, a royal secretary-notary.[117] After making his offer, the cardinal of Bourbon asked that the king do three things: 1) help the Pope escape from captivity; 2) drive heretics out of France; and 3) confirm the "franchises, liberties and rights [Droicts] that concern the Gallican Church." Francis I, in his later remarks, agreed to the first two requests, and slightly modified the third: he would preserve the "**privileges** and franchises" of the Gallican Church.[118]

Vendôme brings us into the realm of civic discourse. His remarks assumed the king would not return to Spain and promised that nobles present would give half their goods for the ransom of the two princes. His language about them came straight from the vocabulary of commonwealth: nobles would contribute so much because "the cause is the liberty and deliverance of Messeigneurs the children of the said Seigneur, who are not only his children but those of the *chose publique* of the kingdom." Vendôme suggested that governors or *baillis* call bailiwick assemblies of all nobles to vote their share of the ransom aid.[119] Godefroy has Vendôme formulate his remarks about those assemblies in classic commonwealth terms; he had no doubt that the king "in guarding and conserving their liberties and franchises of Nobility" would be able to get whatever he pleased from the nobility.[120] Francis I, after famously declaring that he was born a gentleman, not a king, replied that no one had greater desire to "augment, maintain, and observe" the **privileges** of the nobility.

[117] Three generations of this Marle family – Germain I (1502–1503), Germain II (1527–1528), and Guillaume (1560–1563) – served as *prévôt des marchands*. The family were royal secretary-notaries. See A. Lapeyre and R. Scheurer, *Les notaires et secrétaires du roi sous les règnes de Louis XI, Charles VIII et Louis XII (1461–1515): notices personnelles et généalogiques* (Paris: Bibliothèque Nationale, 1978), 2 vols. On this *lit de justice*, S. Hanley, *Lit de justice of the Kings of France. Constitutional Ideology in Legend, Ritual and Discourse* (Princeton, NJ: Princeton UP, 1983), 86, and E. A. R. Brown and R. Famiglietti, *Lit de Justice: semantics, ceremonial, and the Parlement of Paris 1300–1600* (Sigmaringen: Jan Thorbecke Verlag, 1994).

[118] The Treaty of Cambrai specifically states that Francis gives up his right of *régale* over bishoprics in Artois and Flanders, so the "Gallican" liberties of the French Church were directly involved.

[119] Nobles did contribute a considerable sum to the ransom; Francis here could rely on a basic right of a feudal lord, whose vassals were bound to contribute to his ransom.

[120] The summaries of the speeches can be found in Godefroy, *Le ceremonial françois*. II, 490ff. Cramoisy described himself as "the regular printer of the King and Queen Regent." De Selve also proposed local assemblies to apportion the levy. Vendôme on 493 "en leur gardant et conservant leurs libertez & franchises de Noblesse, ledit Seigneur ne fasse d'eux ce qu'il luy plaira." Francis' reply on 500.

Jean de Selve went much further than his colleagues. Like Vendôme, he insisted that the two royal boys were not simply the king's sons, but those of the "French people and the *chose publique* of the kingdom." Selve sought to reply to three questions: 1) should the king return to Spain; 2) should the king give Burgundy to Charles V; and 3) what should be done to seek the return of the young princes? For the first, de Selve emphatically said no, the king should not return to captivity because "nature abhors when the head is separated from the body, the which being removed, there is no more life; So too the French people, which is the mystical body, of which the said Seigneur is the head, would remain, without him [...] without life."[121]

De Selve insisted that not one person in the assembly believed the king should keep the Treaty that de Selve had helped negotiate. He started by showing historical and recent examples of how a promise forced from a prince in captivity was not binding. As for Burgundy, "it is the first Peerage of France, which is inalienable, and cannot be removed from the Crown. [...] Moreover the said Seigneur could not do it; because he is bound to uphold the rights of the Crown, which belongs to him, to his people, and to his subjects in common: to him as the head, and to his peoples and subjects as the members [of the body politic]." Many of de Selves' arguments came directly from Michel de Pons' 1479 pleading on behalf of Louis XI, therefore they were less innovative than has sometimes been believed.

Germain de Marle, as a royal secretary-notary perhaps the most in tune with royalist discourse, used a different metaphor: the king was the father of the *chose publique*. Later in the century, the king would shift precisely from the metaphor of himself as head of the body politic, to the metaphor of him as the father of his people.[122] The governor of Burgundy (Philippe Chabot), President Denys Poillot of the Parlement of Paris, who was from Burgundy, and the First President of the Parlement of Dijon, Claude Patarin, told the king, on behalf of Burgundy "that the said Seigneur cannot alienate the said Duchy without the consent of his subjects, who do not wish it, nor do they wish to be separated from the Crown."[123] Merle also told the king that should he decide to try to return to Spain, the Parisians would do everything in their power to prevent him from doing so, because he was "father of the *chose publique*, which by his absence would remain an orphan."

These speeches reveal some fundamental assumptions about elite conceptions of the political system. First, the king was the head of the body politic, a part of a larger whole. The statements by Vendôme and de Selve that the royal

---

[121] De Selve here glosses a point made by Gerson in *Vivat rex*.

[122] Cesare Cuttica has demonstrated precisely this same discursive shift in England. See, Cuttica, *Sir Robert Filmer*.

[123] Godefroy, *Cérémonial*, II, 499. "Que si sa sacrée personne, & Maiesté royale, avoit deliberé d'y retourner, ils mettroient toute la peine qui seroit possible pour l'empescher; d'autant qu'il est Pere de la chose publique, qui pour son absence demeuroit orpheline."

boys belonged as much to the "*chose publique*" as to the king, and, in de Selve's view, to the French people, clearly make the point that the *chose publique* had rights separate from the individual king.[124] Second, the French people were the "mystical body," that is, the body politic, of which the king was the head.[125] Third, the "goods" of the "chose publique" of the Crown, meaning both its real property and its rights, did not belong to the individual king: he could not give them away any more than he could break Salic Law by naming his second son as heir to the throne. Fourth, the Burgundians put forward the fascinating idea that the lord (seigneur) could not give away his subjects without their consent; Charles V had the Aquitanians use the same basic argument in 1369–1370, that the lord could not give away his vassals without their consent, so that the vassals of Aquitaine could not have been passed from the king of France to the king of England (as *Dominus* of Aquitaine), because they had not consented to it. Once again, vassals took up an argument that limited an individual king's royal power in defense of the territorial integrity of the Crown.

De Selve, following de Pons, explicitly drew together the marriage metaphor and arguments about the inalienability: the royal demesne was the property of the body politic, the dowry of the Crown. Ten years later, the king's *avocat*, Jacques Capel, speaking at a *lit de justice* that again involved Francis I's relationship with Emperor Charles V, slightly modified de Selve's formula. Arguing that Charles had forfeited his rights to his French fiefs (Flanders, Artois, Charolais), Capel stated: "the king is the husband and political spouse of the *chose publique* which brings to him at his *sacre* and Coronation the said domain as the dowry of his Crown."[126] The king, as the husband of the *chose publique*, thus logically became the father of his people, the same formula used by Germain de Marle in 1527.

---

[124] De Selve referred to the "French people and his subjects," referring to all the king's subjects, both in the kingdom of France and elsewhere. De Selve specifically mentioned that the king should raise the 2 million gold *écus* for the ransom from "the kingdom of France, Dauphiné, Provence, and his other lands and seigneuries." Local records, such as the town archives of Arles, continued to refer to the monarch as "King of France and Count of Provence and Forcalquier and the *pays adjaçents*" [attached lands, of which Arles was part]. http://archives.ville-arles.fr/

[125] As Descimon has pointed out, the mystical and political bodies were not one and the same in learned discourse, but most political actors of this time used them to mean much the same thing, as we see here.

[126] Godefroy, *Ceremonial*, II, 501ff on this ceremony. Capel mentions that Philip of Habsburg did liege homage for Flanders and Artois in 1499, at Arras. He pointed out the Charles, as count of Flanders and Artois, parts of the Crown of France, was legally bound to defend to the integrity of that entity. Parlement had confiscated Charles V's fiefs in 1523 for failing to appear when summoned, and therefore being guilty of felony. Capel argued that in case of notorious – that is, widely known – felony, no trial was needed for confiscation. He claimed that the Treaty of Cambrai was extorted from Francis, due to the captivity of his sons, and therefore null and void.

Thirty years after Capel (February 1566), Charles IX's chancellor, Michel de l'Hospital, issued the Edict of Moulins, which made explicit the promise embedded in the coronation oath after 1547: the Edict said that a king of France could not alienate or sell any part of the royal demesne (which included not just lands but a wide range of rights, such as the weights and measures of royal towns), except to provide an apanage for a younger royal son or, on a temporary basis (with right of permanent repurchase) to raise money for war. This principle had long existed, and had been clearly stated, with respect to royal minors, in an edict issued by Charles V (1374), but the Edict of Moulins, in its own words, restated the principles because "some of the ancient rules and maxims about the union and conservation of our demesne are badly known, and others little known." Many contemporaries took this Edict to be a fundamental law of the kingdom. For them, it formed one of the three Fundamental Laws of France: the Salic Law of succession; the inalienability of the royal demesne; and the *puissance absolue*, that is, exclusive right to make public law, of the king. The Edict offered a fine example of the new usage of the term "*estat*" in the mid-1560s: Charles IX called the demesne "one of the principal sinews (*nerfs*) of our state."[127]

Michel de Pons had made one remarkable argument in his 1479 pleading: he revived the arguments made by Charles V in disavowing the Peace of Brétigny-Calais: "Some doctors say that when Kings of France, using their *plaine puissance*, wish to do it [permanently alienate a fief in France], they cannot do it, because it would have no effect or vigor without the consent of the subjects of the said lands [*terres*], and by convocation of the Three Estates of the Kingdom, because of the interest in the matter to the Crown and to the chose publique of the Kingdom."[128] De Pons then specifically cited the case of Guyenne, referring back to the 1369–1370 confiscation of the duchy of Guyenne from Edward III and the Black Prince. Even the king's own procureur general, in the time of Louis XI no less, admitted that the citizens had an interest in the integrity of the Crown, the commonwealth, and the rights of both that lay outside the interest of the king himself. Charles V, Louis XI, Louis XII, and Francis I had all used this argument for their own purposes, and having made this point so often that it had become a core element of the French "constitution," the monarchy could not simply ignore it in later royal discourse.

---

[127] Isambert, *Recueil*, XIII, 185ff.
[128] BNF, M Fr 5079, f. 30.

~

Conclusion

The demons loosed in 1559–1561 transformed the French monarchy and hastened the arrival of a new rhetoric of politics, soon to be built around "the State" [*l'Estat*].[1] Practical political crises, such as the capture of John II, had often accelerated rapid changes in practice, theory, and justification, and I would argue did so precisely in that order. John's capture led to the most fundamental change in the history of the French monarchy – permanent taxation – and, under his son Charles V, to a new monarchical discourse seeking to legitimize it. Permanent taxation required both a theoretical foundation and a public justification: that Charles V's subjects rankled at this innovation is obvious from the events of 1380–1382. Charles V's new discourse emphasized the "chose publique" of the kingdom of France; the "bien de la chose publique" lasted for nearly two centuries as the monarchy's key justificatory phrase. After rampant rhetorical confusion between the 1560s and the 1590s, the neologism "bien de l'Estat" permanently took its place, as French (and other) monarchs sought to convince their subjects that the State was the new form of the *res publica*. Governments everywhere still do the same.

Where John had spoken of "my enemy, the King of England," his grandson Charles VI referred to "our ancient enemies, the English.[2] "Lèse-majesté," in Gerson's *Vivat rex* sermon to Charles VI, involved not simply attacks against the king and the immediate royal family, but against the "chose publique": Charles VI's grandson, Louis XI, would prosecute, and condemn to death, Jean II, duke of Alençon, for lèse majesté committed against both king and "chose publique."[3]

---

[1] In the late sixteenth century, the more typical modifier was "mon"/ "son." "The State" [l'Estat] gradually became normative in the reign of Henry IV, a transition I follow in *From Monarchical Commonwealth*. I take the critical moment to run from the mercuriale at the Parlement of Paris in June 1559, to the Colloquy of Poissy (9/1561).

[2] Beaune, *Naissance de la nation France*. The royal government used the concept "France" to appeal to the political body of citizens, who constituted its "chose publique."

[3] Jean's sentence was commuted, but he died in prison; Louis restored his confiscated lands to Jean's son, René. The Alençon line descended from Philip VI's brother, Charles. René's only son, Charles, was heir to the throne from 1515 to 1518. He died without issue.

The ongoing confusion between loyalty to God – and thus to his two lieutenants, the Pope and the "rex christianissimus" – and loyalty to the "bien de la chose publique" or "bien public" made manifest in a body politic of which the king was the head, lingered long into early modern times. The first formulation posed major problems: the nobles at Pontoise (1561) stated they had "after the honor of God nothing in greater recommendation than the good and *salut* of their prince and the conservation of his crown to all posterity, under the authority of the laws and customs of the Kingdom."[4] This phrase, the "honor of God," would soon have tragic consequences: both Jacques Clément, according to his defenders, and François Ravaillac, at his trial, justified their "parricides" of Henry III (1589) and Henry IV (1610) by reference to the "honor of God."[5] The greatest proponents of the secular version were always the Parlementaires, but their idea of the body politic and the conception of it prevalent among its noble and urban citizens differed fundamentally.[6] In the end, that division proved fatal to the commonwealth as a body politic.

Why? I would posit four major reasons: 1) the differing versions of the monarchical commonwealth held by the major power groups; 2) the democratization of politics during the sixteenth century, particularly from 1560 onward; 3) elite (and non-elite) exasperation with the inability of the commonwealth system to solve major problems, such as the corruption within the Catholic Church and the seemingly endless civil war; and 4) the Estates Generals from 1560 onward overwhelmingly focused on the main goal of each order's deputies: for the clergy, protection of their property; for the nobles, defense of their privileges; for the Third, defense of property in their offices. The innovation of 1560 – having each order debate separately – encouraged precisely this sort of emphasis.[7] The ferocious conflict about jurisdiction between the Ordinance of Orléans (1561) and that of Blois (1579) pitted the royal judges against the clergy, who wanted to maintain civil jurisdiction over their members, against rural nobles, who wanted exclusive control of their "subjects," and against merchants, who first got (1563),

---

[4] BNF, M Fr 3970, fol. 15ff.

[5] Jean Chastel, who tried to assassinate Henry IV in 1594, similarly claimed to act for the "honor of God."

[6] See the chronology on "Corps Politique, Corps Mystique" compiled by Nanine Charbonnel: www.editions-areopage.com/html/chronologie.pdf. Speakers, especially in assemblies involving all three orders, might conflate the "body politic" and the "mystical body" (*corps mystique*), which inevitably involved religion, and by extension, the Church, and thus the Pope. The judicial elite wanted to avoid seeing the two terms as co-equal, for this reason.

[7] In 1484, both the Estates General and the bailiwick assemblies met with the orders together, although in some local cases the Third and the clergy met together, and the nobles on their own. Greengrass, *Governing Passions*, provides a detailed and compelling analysis of this problem.

then lost (1566), then regained (definitively in 1577) royal sanction for merchants' courts to settle their disputes.[8]

Everyone had specific economic, social, and political interests to defend, and their *cahiers* contained articles related to such interests, as well as the "red meat" clauses for the home audience, **and** articles presenting a clear sense of how a legitimate polity should function. The monarchy regularly consulted elites, in assemblies of all shapes and sizes. The Third Republic's obsession with the Estates General – above all with its failure to become the equivalent of the English Parliament – has warped our understanding of the many other consultative bodies – most of them local – used by the monarchy.[9]

The distinct "commonwealth" visions of the Parlement and of the groups represented at the Estates General became obvious as soon as the government of Charles IX tried to implement the Ordinance of Orléans, drawn from the general cahiers of the Estates General of 1560–1561. Deputies at representative assemblies always insisted their actions should **not** be subject to review by the Parlements: just as the Estate General fought with the Parlement of Paris on this point, so, too, did provincial estates, such as those in Brittany, with their own Parlements.[10] The deputies clearly believed that acting for the commonwealth, the Estates General recommended laws, under the aegis of the king and **directly issued** by the king, and that the non-elected judges of the Parlement had no authority over such laws, aside from registering and enforcing them.

The narrative of state building has often ignored the monarchical commonwealth, seeing instead nothing more than the rise of the State, emerging from the political wreckage of the Wars of Religion.[11] In stark contrast to the historians who have ignored the Estates of Orléans and Pontoise, French local political elites long took the Ordinance of Orléans to be the legitimate legal foundation of their polity.[12] They insisted at every possible opportunity

---

[8] The clergy also sought to regain lost jurisdiction over things like morality and marriage, but that lost cause was far less serious than allowing clerics to face civil judges: in Burgundy, this matter came to a head in the 1560s, with the Parlement ultimately codifying civil control. In both 1576 and 1588, major towns like Amiens, Troyes, and Paris joined together to send merchant delegations to the king to protest against the judge-deputies' power grab.

[9] As far back as 1960, J. Russell Major emphasized this consultative process.

[10] In Burgundy, two of the seven members of the commission [*Élus*] that ran affairs for the Estates in between their triennial meetings were Masters in the Chamber of Accounts, and the king's *Élu* invariably came from the Parlementaire elite. First Presidents of the provincial Parlement were always one of the king's representatives to the provincial estates.

[11] Three examples among many: Le Roy Ladurie, *L'état royal* simply ignores the Estates General: in his chronology of events, he does not even mention the Estates of 1576 (475); A. Burgière and J. Revel, eds., *Histoire de la France. L'État et les pouvoirs* (Paris: Seuil, 1989); and O. Carpi, *Les Guerres de Religion (1559–1598)* (Paris: ellipses, 2012).

[12] On Orléans, Major, *The Deputies to the Estates General*; N. de Valois, "Les états de Pontoise (1561)," *Revue de l'histoire de l'Église de France* 29 (1943): 257–276.

that the king actually implement the articles, which, they reminded him in several of the 1576 regional cahiers, were **royal** legislation.[13] Henry III was the only adult French king between Louis XI and Louis XVI to call a meeting of the Estates General: he called **two** such meetings (1576; 1588), and an Assembly of Notables (1583), very nearly fulfilling a common demand of the *cahiers* of 1484, 1560, 1561, and 1576, that the king call regular meetings of the national body.[14]

Cahiers built their polity on a simple principle: election. The meeting of the Estates General at Orléans in December 1560–January 1561, and the confused follow-up assemblies that culminated in an "Estates General" at Pontoise in August 1561, brought forth an unprecedented volume of written expressions of the various versions of commonwealth ideology.[15] The lay *cahiers* set forth what local elites viewed as a historically viable system of governance: election of local leaders (bishops; *baillis*; royal judges);[16] local supervision of tax collection, by men selected in a bailiwick assembly; term limits; reform and clear publication of a new legal code; local representative bodies meeting once a year, and called together by law not royal fiat; unambiguous civil jurisdiction over clerics. Where the general *cahiers* demanded restoration of episcopal elections, local ones often extended this point to parish *curés*, who were to be elected by the parishioners. The lay orders insisted, both in local and general *cahiers*, that all ecclesiastics were to be subject to royal courts for civil and criminal cases. *Cahiers* demanded respect for customary laws and usages, directly contradicting articles on creating a uniform set of weights and measures or uniform laws, and redaction of all law in "the clearest language that there could be."[17]

The system they demanded was a genuine, if idealized historical construct having to do with a polity built on a restricted group of free citizens, not some sort of idyllic "feudal" paradise on earth. This system had allowed local elites and aristocrats to manipulate the process to their own advantage. Their model electorates would have empowered the cathedral canons to elect bishops, the noble fief holders to choose *baillis*, and the *avocats* and sitting judges to elect new judges to serve limited terms. Merchants naturally would play a role in

---

[13] Local *cahiers* in 1588 and 1614 often repeated such an article.

[14] Cahiers suggested two-, five-, and ten-year intervals.

[15] The Pontoise meeting involved only thirty-nine deputies: one per order per governorship. The clergy soon split off to the Colloquy of Poissy, leaving just the twenty-six lay deputies.

[16] The *bailli* had jurisdiction over the nobility; royal letters of convocation for the nobility to estates went to him. The nobles wanted only another noble to have jurisdiction over them, a demand made in the charters of 1314.

[17] Everyone insisted, like the nobles at Blois (BNF, M Fr 16,250, f. 187v) and Jean Bodin that kings respect custom, which should regulate individual's property. Philip V, in 1321, tried, and failed, to create uniform measures.

choosing one among their number to supervise local tax collections (and voted each year on the consular judge).

The Parlement of Paris insisted it had the right to assure that all laws, including those made with input from an Estates General, did not violate existing ones or reason and justice. After months of delay, the king accepted several of their emendations to the Ordinance of Orléans (1561), thereby establishing the precedent that the Parlement *did* have the right to evaluate even legislation created with an Estates General.[18] In Brittany, from the time of Henry IV, both the Parlement of Brittany and its Chamber of Accounts registered all contracts signed by the Estates and the king. Conversely, champions of the power of the Estates General, like François Hotman, naturally expressed harsh criticism of the "Kingdom of Lawsuits," which "put under its foot and supplanted all the authority of the Council of Estates."[19]

In this single dispute, we can see how the legal elite in and around the Parlement of Paris, in particular, sought to prevent the Estates General from becoming more powerful and to undercut any efforts to make it a regular body. Drawing the non-aristocratic personnel of the royal council exclusively from this group, as increasingly became the case, formed a central royal administration hostile to sharing power with the local elites represented in the Estates. With their self-image as the French equivalent of the Roman Senate, the Parlement of Paris provided the most anti-democratic political force in the kingdom.[20] Their version of commonwealth ideology, championed by men like the First Presidents Christophe de Thou (1562–1582) and his son-in-law Achille de Harlay (1583–1611), provided the theoretical foundations for the royal State, which we wrongly assume was their antithesis. Jurists from the late sixteenth century up to the Revolution praised de Thou and de Harlay as great champions of the commonwealth, yet de Thou masterminded the Parlement's theft of one of the Estates General's most prized powers: choosing a regent.[21]

In the early sixteenth century, the conflicting currents of royal centralism and of commonwealth made for a discursive balance, but the Wars of

---

[18] The Parlement, which had strenuously opposed the Concordat in 1516, objected to article 1, which restored the Pragmatic Sanction, on the grounds that the king of France could not unilaterally abrogate a bilateral agreement with the Pope. They also successful modified the Ordinance of Blois, finally issued in 1579.

[19] F. Hotman, *La Gaule françoise* (Cologne, 1574), ch. XX.

[20] On their "Senate" image in the mid-sixteenth century, see M. Houllemare, "L'imaginaire politique du Parlement de Paris sous Henri II, Sénat de la capitale," in *Cités Humanistes, Cités Politiques (1400–1600)*, ed. E. Crouzet-Pavan, D. Crouzet, P. Desan (Paris: Presses Sorbonne Université, 2014).

[21] In 1574, he and Catherine de Medici had the Parlement approve her regency for the absent Henry III. In 1560–1561, the Estates General at Orléans and the follow-up meeting at Pontoise had declined to name Catherine regent. The historiography almost universally calls her "regent" for Charles IX but, in fact, she did not get this official title (and its legal rights). Later regencies – 1610, 1643, and 1715 – were all approved by the Parlement.

Religion – whose chaotic conditions many elites attributed to a lack of a strong central authority – accelerated the transition from the monarchical commonwealth to the royal State. The vocabulary of the monarchical commonwealth, which had dominated French political life for two centuries, slowly disintegrated into a confusing mixture of discourses. The jurists' term *respublique* steadily replaced the *chose publique* in political language. At Troyes, the *éguillotiers* [pinmakers], in their 1576 *cahier*, called for abolition of the new import-export duty (*foraine*), because it was "a thing against the common republic." The hatmakers lamented: "As for the fact of the Republic, we say that it is so trampled upon that it can no longer sustain itself because all of the substance of its labor is employed in subsidies." The castellany of Méry complained about men becoming judges at twenty or twenty-two, "which is a very pernicious thing and carries great damage both to your majesty and to the republic of all the kingdom."[22] The unprofessional hand and the shaky printed signatures of guildsmen Pierre Gode and Jehan Thibault make it clear that the hatmakers wrote their own *cahier*. The "republic" vocabulary had penetrated even down to the artisan world by 1576.

The second factor in the demise of the monarchical commonwealth was the meteoric rise of popular participation, evident in the hatmakers' belief that they could make comments about tax policy in defense of the "republic." One of the tensions exacerbated by religious conflict was precisely the desire of elites to restrict real citizenship to their membership. The remarkable democratization of politics – in the massive meetings about redacting customary law, in the bailiwick and urban assemblies to approve the Peace of Cambrai, and in the meetings, and redaction of local *cahiers*, for the Estates General of 1560 – raised the issue of broad social participation in politics in ways unprecedented since the Cabochiens. The even broader local participation for the Estates at Blois in 1576, made this trend all the more disturbing to elites.[23] The Estates at Orléans laid down an elaborately developed practical and theoretical "respublique françoyse" – what the nobles thought of as an aristocratic monarchy, tempered with some elements of "popular" government. Nobles and legal elites, however, feared too broad a definition of "popular." Pierre de Saint-Julien de Balleure, in his history of Burgundy [1581], denounced the "seditious word" that "all are equal!" [*Tous esgal!*][24] In his discussion of the "antiquities" of his hometown of Chalon-sur-Saône, he lamented the intervention in urban politics of a "confused mass of persons, more often pushed by fury than by reason."[25]

---

[22] AM Troyes, BB 15, liasse 3: éguillotiers [#15]; hatmakers [18]; the castellany of Méry [67].

[23] Daussy, *Le parti Huguenot*, on the specifically Protestant element of "democracy."

[24] P. Saint-Julien de Balleure, *De l'Origine des Bourgongnons et antiquité des estats de Bourgogne* (Paris: N. Chesneau, 1581), 126, italics in the original.

[25] Saint-Julien, *De l'Origine*, 431. "confus amas de personnes . . . plus poussez de fureur que de raison."

The third element in the commonwealth's demise as a system was its utter failure either to reform the Catholic Church or to end the civil war. Complaints about clerical abuse were ubiquitous and the *cahiers* of the two lay orders, whether in 1560 or 1576, show a remarkably consistent program of Church reform, which the Ordinance of Orléans spelled out in great detail: restoration of the Pragmatic Sanction; mandatory residence for benefices having cure of souls; elimination of underaged, undereducated, and foreign prelates; moral and educational reform of the clergy; greater Church spending on primary and secondary education. Henry IV and Louis XIII certainly did not restore ecclesiastical elections, but they – in conjunction with a post-Tridentine generation of Church reformers – did, in fact, make substantial progress on rectifying the other abuses. Henry IV radically reduced the percentage of foreign (especially Italian) bishops, and appointed almost exclusively men of canonical age, who held advanced degrees either in canon law or theology.[26] In 1614, the Estates General barely made a peep about the Pragmatic. Henry also ended the civil war, sword in hand.[27]

The three elements of French monarchy – practical, philosophical, and discursive – evolved in a complex symbiotic relationship from the moment of John II's 1356 capture. Debating currency reform in 1356–1358, Charles V's future subjects directly tied the new term for their collective political identity – the *chose publique* – to that term's economic overtones. Both the *bien de la chose publique* and the *bien public* long remained prominent in economic discourse, such as the preambles to guild statutes. New statutes often just repeated earlier versions, but from 1600, many statutes – and town government records – shifted away from the "bien public," of which the "salut" of the body politic formed the essence, to the "bien du public" (good of the public), an anodyne phrase focused solely on material well-being.[28] The "bien de la chose publique" became increasing rare in statutes by the late sixteenth century.

Charles V also oversaw a radical transformation in the publicity of the monarchy – symbols like the scepter of Charlemagne, but also the justificatory introductions to royal legislation. His legacy, cemented by Christine de Pizan as that of "Charles the Wise," cast a long shadow over his successors.[29] Charles VI's thirty-year mental illness and the civil war led to two powerful traditions

---

[26] J. Bergin, *The Making of the French Episcopacy, 1589–1661* (New Haven: Yale UP, 1996), table 5.3 and 185–187; Hayden and Greenshields, *Bishops and the French Church, 1190–1789*, Annex 4 G.

[27] Henry IV also compromised with elites, both on religion and other matters, like the nature of taxation.

[28] The Catholic League – which contemporaries called "the party of the Church" – regularly cited the "bien public" in its justifications; unsurprisingly, Henry IV discouraged use of the phrase after he gained full control of France.

[29] Already in the 1420s, the "advice to Yolande d'Aragon" referred to "le saige roy Charles" as the model.

in political discourse. The historiography has long privileged the royalist group, focused on the figure of the king. Yet the second group, led by people such as Gerson, Christine de Pizan, and the Jouvenal des Ursins family, rather emphasized the commonwealth as the political unifier. Given the incapacity of the actual king, this tradition, with its emphasis on the *bien de la chose publique* and the *bien public*, attracted broad support. Two of its key principles – *quod omnes tangit* and *cessante causa* – long continued to be touchstones of political discourse, especially in town councils and bailiwick and provincial assemblies. *Quod omnes tangit* even lay behind actions such as Louis XII's special assembly of 1506 to approve the engagement of Francis and Claude, or of Francis I's process for dealing with Charles V in 1527–1529. The monarchy made effective use of *cessante causa* in its perennial argument that the continued existence of the royal army, the *compagnies d'ordonnance*, justified the perpetuity of the *taille* voted in 1439.

Francis I proved to be a transformational monarch, beginning with the 1506 assembly that "created" him Dauphin and "begged" Louis XII to engage Francis to his cousin Claude, for the sake of the good of the king and of *la chose publique*. Once king, Francis I operated a staggering shift of a key element of power: ending ecclesiastical elections and giving the king unprecedented new powers to distribute the *bienfaits* craved by every noble family.[30] The long tradition of aristocratic revolt against an adult king, due to dissatisfaction with reward for service – the Praguerie of 1440, the "treasons" of Alençon or Luxembourg in the 1470s, the Constable of Bourbon in the 1520s, the Guise family in the 1580s – came to an abrupt end with the trials and executions of the dukes of Biron (1601–1602) and Montmorency (1632).[31]

On *bienfaits* and many other issues, one Burgundian family, the Bauffremont, provides us with insight into the continuities and changes in noble political ideology between the late thirteenth and early seventeenth centuries. Nicolas de Bauffremont, soon to be *bailli* of Chalon-sur-Saône, gave the nobility's official speech at Pontoise in 1561. Nicolas' son, Claude, would do the honors at Blois, in 1577, and his grandson, Henri, did so at Paris, in 1615. Nicolas had a conscious connection to two of his "ancestors," Geoffroi de Charny and Jean de Joinville, famed biographer of Saint Louis.[32] Jacques de

---

[30] Francis also codified venality of office and created the Central Treasury and a proto-public debt.

[31] Louis XIV's memoirs for the Dauphin recognized the importance of *bienfaits* and his duty to provide them, but also rejected out of hand any "right" to dissatisfaction by nobles seeking greater rewards.

[32] Saint-Julien, in a book on prominent Burgundian noble families, and Claude de Rubys, in a passage about the battle of Poitiers, took pains to tie directly Bauffremont to Geoffroi de Charny: Saint-Julien de Balleure, *Meslanges Historiques* (Lyon, 1588); C. de Rubys, *Histoire véritable de la ville de Lyon* (Lyon, 1604), 311. Rubys was the nephew of Nicolas' mother-in-law. Saint-Julien, *De l'Origine*, 68, told a story about resistance to

Thou tells us that the nobility chose Nicolas to speak because of "his science, a quality rare among our warriors."[33] He picked up this learning from his upbringing (in his mother's extended family) and enhanced it through his marriage to Denise Patarin, daughter of Claude, the First President of the Parlement of Dijon who had argued to Francis I in 1527 that he could not detach the duchy of Burgundy from the kingdom. Two of Nicolas' closest noble friends – both also his vassals – were themselves Humanists of considerable reputation, the historian Saint-Julien de Balleure and the Pléaïde poet Pontus de Tyard, bishop of Chalon-sur-Saône.[34]

Nicolas de Bauffremont spoke twice to defend the commonwealth system.[35] He reminded the deputies they had been summoned to help the king pay off debts of 42 million francs, "in order that the king, head of our political or mystical body, can be relieved by its members and well-affectioned subjects." Bauffremont emphasized that in any assembly treating public matters, one had to proceed in a manner to protect, guard, and observe as well as one could the position of each, so that none would be reduced or diminished. The deputies needed to find what will be "necessary in the present constitution of our *republique fransoeze*" and to render "better and happier the condition of his republic." They had to seek, within the framework of their instructions, the honor, relief, and commodity of all, according to the grace of God, "of whom the honor and fear alone must be our motive." They needed to help the king regain his "civil liberty, which no one indebted to another can have."[36]

Bauffremont's final speech for the nobles at Pontoise repeated the standard themes, starting with a request that the king keep them in their centuries-old "liberties, franchises, privileges, pre-eminences, prerogatives, and authorities."[37] Nobles were naturally ready to give up their lives and persons

---

unreasonable taxation by Charles the Bold, in 1476, led by the "lords of Jonville, who was also lord of Charny [Antoine de Luxembourg, husband of Antoinette de Bauffremont] and of Mirabeau [her uncle, Jean de Bauffremont], and other true Burgundians." This story proved how vital great lords could be "when they have their affection well turned to the *chose publique*."

[33] Jacques de Thou, *Histoire universelle* (London, 1734), VI, 415. G. Chapuis, trans., *Le parfait Courtisan du comte Baltasar Castillonois* (Lyon, 1585, dedicated his translation to Bauffremont, whom he praised as the French personification of Castiglione's ideal courtier. http://gallica.bnf.fr/ark:/12148/bpt6k754790/f6.image.r=Courtisan%20casti glione.langFR

[34] Pierre's ancestor, Claude de Saint-Julien, a page of Louis, duke of Orléans, witnessed the duke's murder in 1407.

[35] Contemporaneous account of Jacques de Montaigne, BNF, M Fr 15,494. Bauffremont's speech on fol. 32–33v.

[36] Bauffremont blamed God's ire, due to the clergy, in terms strikingly similar to the earlier critique offered by Guillaume Budé : *Le Livre de l'Institution du Prince* (Paris: Jean Foucher, 1549).

[37] BNF, M Fr 15,494, final speech begins on f. 62.

for "your service, by true act of magnanimity of nobility," an interesting formulation that placed noble service in the realm of a freely given offer.[38]

Bauffremont turned next to what was arguably the most important topic for the nobility, particularly for men of his stature: *bienfaits*. Through his "natural instinct" the king "must make felt by the subjects his favors (*bienfaits*) and liberality." He needed to take care, however, to distribute these favors for due cause, avoiding doing so where there was more "ambition and presumption" than merit, "there being nothing in a republic or kingdom happier than when the *bienfaits* of a prince are never in vain, nor are they surpassed by the grandeur of services of his subjects." Speaker after speaker, especially the nobles, in the late sixteenth century would return to this theme of the need for balance between the services rendered by loyal *serviteurs* to their prince, and the *bienfaits* granted by that prince to deserving *serviteurs*.[39] For the nobility in particular, this attribute of monarchy – emphasized by Simon de Bucy in his 1356 memorandum against Robert le Coq – was surely the most important.

In his second, longer speech, Bauffremont showed the profound depth of his noble commonwealth ideology. Bauffremont was a **politician** – one of the three or four most important noble leaders in Burgundy – and he created the principles for his political action by melding Classical education and long-standing noble commonwealth ideology. Saint-Julien praised Nicolas' abundant knowledge and study and the long experience he had in affairs of State, which enabled him to form a theory [*théorique*] and an "art" of knowing how to love the *pays*.[40] As a result of his success on behalf of his *patrie* [Burgundy], "you have made it clear that the good of the King, cannot and must not be separated from the public utility." Saint-Julien here moved away from the more traditional "bien public," which he cited in other contexts, and to "public utility," a phrase increasingly cited both by elites and by the Crown.[41] Shifting to "public utility" moved the practical benefits of a given policy into the amoral

---

[38] Similar sentiments in the November 1560 *cahier* of the nobility of the bailiwick of Dijon. ADCO, B 3469.

[39] N. Le Roux, *La faveur du roi: mignons et courtisans au temps des derniers Valois (vers 1547 – vers 1589)* (Seyssel: Champ Vallon, 2000), demonstrates the catastrophic impact on relations with the Guise and other leading aristocrats of Henry III's distribution of *bienfaits* to his *mignons* and their clients in the 1580s.

[40] "la longue experience, que vous avez des affaires d'Estat, ont formé en vous une theorique, & art de sçavoir aimer le païs, pour luy profiter [. . .] vous avez fait paroistre que le bien du Roy, ne peut, ny ne doit estre separé de l'utilité publique : dont vostre patrie a receu tant de secours," Saint-Julien de Balleure, *De l'Origine des Bourgongnons*, dedication. Bauffremont and his circle dominated the Estates of Burgundy and reformed the Customs; from the mid-1550s to the late 1570s, he was the province's main emissary to the royal government.

[41] Saint-Julien, *De l'Origine*, 261, calls the bourgeois of Macon who had, in the past, so willingly served as *échevins*, "zelateurs du bien publicq." He contrasted that situation with

dimension we associate with reason of State, as it developed from Machiavelli to Richelieu. Saint-Julien regularly referred [writing in 1581] to "the State," a term that virtually unknown at the time of Bauffremont's 1561 speech. This new combination – public utility and the bien de l'État – completely elided the moral and ethical dimensions deeply embedded in the term *bien public*.

Saint-Julien explicitly connected Bauffremont to Geoffroi de Charny, who died at Poitiers bearing the Oriflamme, to Geoffroi's father, Jean, one of the leaders of the Burgundian noble league of 1314, and to Geoffroi's grandfather, Jean de Joinville. Geoffroi wrote a *Livre de chevalrie*, in which he laid down principles both for knights and for princes. In his work, Geoffroi continuously repeated a simple dictum: "Qui plus fait, mie[u]x vault" [who does more, is worth more]. Just like Nicolas in 1561, Geoffroi in the 1350s emphasized that great lords who reward their best men will be well served, because others will see that merit is rewarded, and seek out their service.

As for the prince, was he chosen so that he could "enjoy delicacies" and put on airs, or do damage to the common people for his own profit? "Certes nennil" [Indeed not!] Geoffroi's prince acted bravely and honestly, served his people, and kept his word. Joinville, in his long list of Saint Louis' estimable qualities, brought up the king's deathbed instruction to his son Philip: to love God, to maintain "the good customs of your kingdom, and tear down the bad ones." Philip should not covet the goods of his people and should levy *tailles* on them only for "great necessity."[42]

What register did Nicolas' grandson, Henri, use in 1615?[43] We hear continuities going back to Joinville or Geoffroi de Charny: "our kings were not among those princes ... who prefer flattery to the truth, or who rarely shared their counsels as little as their authority with their subjects." He cited the difference between "princes who reign too imperiously, and those who moderate their power by reason." We hear new words, too, in his comparison of "violent sovereignties" to raging torrents, which ravaged instead of watering plants. Obedience forced upon subjects did not last: on the first occasion of discontent, "courage is intimidated, wills are altered." Just as the term "sovereignty" was new, in comparison to 1561, so, too, Henri spoke of how the nobility had always helped kings affirm and expand "the empire of the French." Henri here used a word similarly slipped into keeper of the seals François II de Montholon's 1588 speech for Henry III: empire.[44] Francis I and Henry II had adopted an imperial (closed) crown, but the verbal emphasis on their "empire,"

---

the current (1581) one, in which the constant royal demands for money meant no one wanted to serve.

[42] Joinville, *Histoire de Saint Louis* (Paris, 1874), 378–379.

[43] Lalourcé and Duval, *Recueil de pièces originales*, VIII, 240–249.

[44] Montholon's cousin, Philippe, chief judge at Chalon, witnessed the marriage of N. de Bauffremont's daughter.

as opposed simply to their kingdom, took root only in the period in which the State achieved rhetorical preeminence.[45]

Henri de Bauffremont suddenly shifted gears, launching a virulent attack on venality of office – the true plague of the State – in terms much harsher than any noble had used in 1560–1561 or 1576. Venality had spread "by a pernicious contagion," to positions in the king's household and the military.

> Stifle, Sire, like a Gallic Hercules, this monster that ravages your kingdom, and swallows your authority, stripping it of the distribution of honors, the sole prize of virtue; it would mean recovering the most beautiful fleuron of your crown, and replacing your full scepter in your hands and reestablishing the dignity of your empire

Where once the "fleurons" in the Crown were peerage fiefs like Burgundy and Flanders, now the "distribution of honors" had reached that rarified status.

Bauffremont quickly expressed the nobility's approval of the Spanish marriages, because the "happiness of the kingdom consists in the life of the prince, and the surety of the State in posterity."[46] He ended with a request to restore the splendor of the nobility, which would make them worthy [digne] of the most eminent positions in the kingdom. The nobility was the force of royalty, "represented by the scepter monarchs carry, solid foundation on which is built this admirable edifice of your State."

"Empire," "State," "sovereignty" – this was the vocabulary of an entirely new political discourse that had to incorporate some elements of the old commonwealth vocabulary. The sly shift from "bien public" to "bien du public," the revival of the "public utility," the complete shift over to "the State" as the term of choice for the political body of the kingdom – all these elements built upon the gradual transition evident in the first half of the sixteenth century and brought into the open by the crises of 1559–1561, radically compounded by the civil wars. These fundamental philosophical shifts, however, must be contextualized first in the practical political changes that made the older vocabulary anachronistic, indeed obsolete. The French commonwealth tradition died not simply on the pens of political philosophers, or at the failed Estates Generals, but in the assembly rooms of town councils and bailiwick estates.

---

[45] The global dimension of "empire" took on progressively greater importance, especially in the seventeenth century.

[46] Louis XIII married Philip III's daughter, Anne, while Louis' sister, Elisabeth, married the future Philip IV.

BIBLIOGRAPHY

Abbreviations used in the notes

AD:	Archives départementales
AM:	Archives municipales
Beaumanoir, *Coutumes*:	P. de Beaumanoir, *Coutumes de Beauvaisis*, ed. A. Salmon. Paris, 1899. 2 vols.
BEC:	Bibliothèque de l'École des Chartes
	Bernier, A. ed., *Journal des États Généraux tenus à Tours en 1484 sous le règne de Charles VIII par Jehan Masselin* (Paris, 1835).
BNF:	Bibliothèque Nationale de France
M Fr:	Manuscrits Français
CAF:	*Catalogue des Actes de François Ier* (Paris, 1887–1908), 10 vols. cour-de-france.fr has links to all ten volumes.
Cosneau, *Grandes Traités*:	E. Cosneau, *Les Grandes Traités de la Guerre de Cent Ans*. Paris, 1889.
J. Froissart, *Chroniques*:	J. Kervyn de Lettenhove, *Œuvres de Froissart*. Brussels, 1867–1877; reiussue, Osnabruck, 1967, available online; using this edition of *Froissart's Chronicles*, citing by chapter number.
	Histoire de France, Paul-François Velly, Claude Villaret, and J.-J. Garnier. Paris, 1753–1776. By last name and volume number
HGL:	C. Devic, J. Vaissette, et al.,*Histoire Générale de Languedoc*. Toulouse: Privat, 1872–1904. 16 vols. Gallica has an earlier, inferior edition.
Isambert, *Recueil*:	F.-A. Isambert et al., *Recueil général des anciennes lois françaises*. Paris, 1821–1833. 29 vols., links available on cour-de-france.fr
Le Jouvencel:	Bueil, Jean de. *Le Jouvencel de Jean de Bueill*, ed. C. Favre and L. Lecestre. Paris, 1887–1889, 2 vols.

LTC: *Layettes du Trésor des Chartes*, ed. A. Teulat. Paris, 1863–1866, vols. I-II of nine.

Monstrelet: *Chroniques d'Enguerrand de Monstrelet*, ed. L. Douëe-d'Arcq Paris, 1857–1862. 6 vols.

Ordonnances: *Ordonnances des rois de France de la troisième race* (Paris, 1723–1849), 21 vols. Cour-de-france.fr has links.

PU: Presses universitaires

PUR: Presses universitaires de Rennes

Thierry, *Recueil*: A. Thierry, *Recueil des monuments inédites des l'histoire du Tiers État* (Paris, 1850–1870), 4 vols.; vols. 1–3, Amiens and its region; v. 4, Abbeville and other towns.

UP: University Press – CUP (Cambridge); OUP (Oxford)

Varin, *Archives administratives/legislatives: Archives administratives de la ville de Reims*, 9 vols. (Paris, 1839–1853). And *Archives legislatives de la ville de Reims*, 2 vols. (Paris, 1839, 1844). Volumes 3 and 4 deal with a later period.

Christine de Pizan

Remarkably, Christine de Pizan does not yet have a Pléiade edition of her works, so her writings appear in scattered editions and manuscripts best presented separately.

Le livre de la paix of Christine de Pizan. ed. C. Cannon Willard. S'Gravenhage: Mouton, 1958. A seventeenth-century manuscript copy is available on Gallica: BNF, M Fr 1182, which also contains a copy of *La Cité des Dames*. The compiler, in Latin, calls her "Puella doctissima," but in French just refers to her as the daughter of a royal councilor. K. Green, C. Mews, and J. Pinder have translated the text, *The Book of Peace*. University Park, PA: Penn State UP, 2008.

Le livre des fais d'armes et de chevalerie: BNF, M Fr 23997 [Gallica]

Livre des fais et bonnes meurs du saige roy Charles V (1404), ed. S. Solente. Paris, 1936–1940. 2 vols. [Gallica has multiple manuscript versions.]

Le tresor de la cité des dames: www.gutenberg.org/files/26608/26608-h/26608-h.htm

Le livre du corps de policie, ed. A. Kennedy. Paris: Champion, 1998. Modern critical edition, with a glossary, based on a manuscript held at Chantilly (Musée Condé 294).

Le livre du corps de policie, ed. R Lucas. Geneva and Paris: Droz, Minard, 1967. Based on BNF, M Fr 12439 [original available on gallica]. Gallica also has

several other manuscripts, including one the catalog identifies as in the hand of one of Christine's known scribes: BNF, Arsenal, Manuscrit 2681.
Selected Writings of Christine de Pizan, ed. R. Blumenfeld-Koskinki. NY: Norton, 1997.

Online resources:

Online sites for many of the older books are: archive.org; cour-de-france; Gallica [BNF]; Hathi Trust; and Google Books. The BNF has also put online many manuscripts, including the magnificent *Grandes Chroniques de France* of Charles V (Manuscrit Français 2813).

Many archives in France have digitalized records; in addition to the municipal archives cited below, some departmental archives, such as those of the Côte d'Or, have put online some exceptionally rich sources, going far beyond the baptism-marriage-burial records now commonly available for many departments. As with respect to the towns, I have read many other financial records from this period for my earlier publications; I do not include them here.

Archival Sources

Municipal Deliberations and Town Archives

I consulted municipal deliberations and other town records in many cities: some on site; some in digital form; some in printed versions, often published in the nineteenth century and now available online. Deliberations are found in series BB in all cases, except Rouen. They are always arranged chronologically. Rouen has its own idiosyncratic system created in the early nineteenth century. Series AA has municipal correspondence and documents emanating from the royal government including, in some cases, those related to meetings of the Estates General. Series CC has the financial information, which I have consulted for many of these towns – and about twenty others – during previous projects.

On site: Chalon-sur-Saône, Dijon, Macon, Nantes, Rennes, Rouen, St-Malo, Troyes

Online (digitalized deliberations): Arles, Blois, Lyon, Rennes, Toulouse

Published form: Poitiers, complete, print only: René Favreau, ed., starting from 1412, in three volumes: tome I: *Poitiers, de Jean de Berry à Charles VII. Registres des délibérations du corps de ville* (n. 1–3); tome II: *Poitiers, de Charles VII à Louis XI, registres des délibérations du corps de ville* (n. 4–5); tome III: *Poitiers sous le règne de Louis XI de 1466 à 1471. Registre des délibérations du corps de ville* (n. 5–6). Poitiers: Société des Antiquitaires de l'Ouest, 2014–2015.

Published and now online (often partial): Abbeville, Amiens, Arles, Autun, Bergerac, Bordeaux, Chalon-sur-Saône, Dijon, Ghent, Limoges, Lyon, Paris, Poitiers, Reims, Rouen, Saint-Flour, Saint-Jean-d'Angély, Toulouse, Troyes, Ypres.

Abbeville: Thierry, A., ed. *Recueil de monuments inédits de l'histoire du Tiers Etat, région du Nord*, t. IV. Paris, 1870.

Amiens: Thierry, A., ed. *Recueil de monuments inédits de l'histoire du Tiers Etat, région du Nord*, t. I-II. Paris, 1850, 1853.

Arles: Anibert, N. *Mémoires historiques et critiques, sur l'ancienne république d'Arles*, 3 vols. Avignon, 1779–1781.

Autun: Abord, H. *Histoire de la Réforme et de la Ligue dans la ville d'Autun: précédée d'une introduction et suivie de pièces justificatives* (Paris, 1855), 3 vols.

Bergerac: Charrier, G. *Les Jurades de la ville de Bergerac*. Bergerac, 1892.

Bordeaux: Registres de la Jurade , *Délibérations de 1414 à 1416 et de 1420 à 1422* (Bordeaux: G. Gounouilhou, 1883.

Dast Le Vacher de Boisville, J. N. et al. *Inventaire Sommaire des Registres de la Jurade, 1520 à 1783*. Bordeaux, 1896–1947. 8 vols. V. 1–6 online. Alphabetical presentation by subject, such as "grains," but which cuts off about halfway through the alphabet. A group of local officials drew up this inventory, at royal command, starting in 1751. A fire destroyed most of Bordeaux's archives in 1862, so this summary is our main source about deliberations.

Lurbe, Gabriel de. *Chronique Bourdeloise*. Bordeaux, 1619–1620.

Chalon-sur-Saône: Perry, C. *Histoire civile et ecclesiastique, ancienne et moderne de la ville et cité de Chalon*. Chalon, 1659. Perry cites extensively from the municipal deliberations.

Dijon: Garnier, J., ed. *Correspondance de la mairie de Dijon* (Dijon, 1868–1870), 3 vols.

Ghent: Diericx, C. I. *Mémoires sur Les Lois, les Coutumes et les Privilèges des Gantois* (Ghent, 1818), 2 vols.

Limoges: Ruben, E. and L. Guibert, eds. *Registres consulaires de la ville de Limoges*, t. I, 1504–1552. II, 1552–1581. Limoges, 1867, 1869.

Lyon: Guigue, G. *Registres consulaires de la Ville de Lyon. I: 1416–1423; II: 1422–1450*. 2 vols. Lyon, 1882, 1926. [These registers are now online.]

Paris: *Registres des délibérations du bureau de la ville de Paris*. Paris, 1883–1894, vols. 1–8.

[abbreviated in notes as RDBVP]

Viard, J. *Documents parisiens du règne de Philippe de Valois*, 2 vols. Paris, 1899, 1902.

Poitiers: Audoin, E., ed. *Recueil de documents concernant la commune et la ville de Poitiers. Archives Historiques du Poitou* XLIV, XLVI. Poitiers, 1923, 1928.

Reims: Guibert, S., ed. *Registre de deliberations du conseil de ville de Reims (1422–1436)*. Académie nationale de Reims, 1993.

Varin, P. *Archives administratives de la ville de Reims*. Paris, 1839–1848, 5 vols.
Archives legislatives de la ville de Reims. Paris, 1840–1852, 4 vols.

Rouen: Giry, A., ed. *Les établissements de Rouen*. Paris: BEC, 1883–1885.

Saint-Flour: Boudet, M., ed. *Registres consulaires de Saint-Flour (1376–1405)*. Paris and Riom: Champion; Jouvet, 1900.

Saint-Jean d'Angély: d'Aussy, D. and L.-C. Saudau., "Registres de l'echevinage de Saint-Jean-d'Angély, 1332–1496" *Archives historiques de la Saintonge et l'Aunis*, XXIV, XXVI, and XXXII. Paris and Saint-Jean d'Angély, 1895, 1897, 1904: online at Gallica under "Registres de l'échevinage" and not through *Archives historiques de la Saintonge*.

Toulouse: La Faille, G. de. *Annales de la ville de Toulouse*. Paris, 1701.

Durosoy, B. *Annales de la ville de Toulouse*. Paris, 1772. T. II: *Divers titres et actes, pour servir de preuves*. [The original manuscript is now online.]

Troyes: Roserot, A. *Le plus ancien registre des délibérations du conseil de la Ville de Troyes (1429–1433)*. Troyes, 1886.

Ypres: Diegerick, I. *Inventaire analytique et chronologique des chartes et documents appartenant aux archives de la ville d'Ypres*. 7 vols. Bruges, 1853–1868.

Neil Murphy, *Ceremonial Entries, Municipal Liberties and the Negotiation of Power in Valois France, 1328–1589*. Leiden: Brill, 2016, has an extensive list of other available sources.

Municipal Archives [aside from deliberations]

Blois

BB 5 cahier and documents (in the deliberations), Estates General of 1576

Bourges

AA 13 Royal letters to the town government

Dijon

AA 6, royal letters to town government
AA 12, royal letters to town government
AA 20 letters of Jean II ordering city of Dijon to turn over city to *bailli* of Macon, 1361 [Jean inheriting from duke Philippe le Rouvre]
BB 450, letters of Charles IX, April 1561, about holding new local estates
BB 452, letters of Francis I, 1523, about Charles de Bourbon, violating his "foy et serement fais a nous et a la chose publique de nostre royaulme"; about "ennemys de la chose publicque [de nostre royaulme], 1524; letter from Louise of Savoy about capture of Francis I, March 3, 1525
GG 1–3, guild statutes, fourteenth to eighteenth centuries

Macon

AA 10 Signed cahier of the Third Estate, Estates at Pontoise, August 1561

Troyes

BB 15 Cahiers of guilds, groups, and nearby castellanies, Estates General of 1576

Bibliothèque Nationale de France (BNF)

The following two documents, not in the BNF, were consulted through its digital collection, Gallica:

Bibliothèque Sainte-Geneviève

OEXV 558 Documents on Estates General of 1484 [also uploaded onto archive .org]

Municipal Library of Besançon

434 Fourteenth-century French translation of Giles of Rome, *De regimine*, and other works

Arsenal (BNF)

744 Giles of Rome, *De regimine* [fourteenth-century manuscript]
2189 Procès-verbal of clergy, Estates General of 1560
2190 Procès-verbal of clergy, Estates General of 1576
2648 documents of famous trials, starting with Jeanne d'Arc [seventeenth-century copies]
2655 trial of chancellor Poyet [seventeenth-century copies]
2681 *Le livre du corps de policie* of Christine de Pizan, in the hand of one of her known secretaries
2831 Eighteenth-century collection of documents about trials for lèse-majesté
3970 Cahier of the nobility, Estates at Pontoise, 1561
4058 Achilles de Harlay, speech on royal scepter, coronation of Louis XIII, 1613
4084 Letters making Louise regent during Francis I's absence; 1523; speech of de Selve on deliverance of Francis I; speech of Francis I at hotel de Bourbon, 28-IX -1529; letters to *bailli* of St-Pierre les Moutiers to call local estates, X-1529, to ratify Treaty of Cambrai, with text of the oath the citizens had to take
5199 Jean Golein, French rendering of *De l'informacione principum*, 1379

Richelieu (BNF)

Manuscrits Dupuy

539 Documents on War of Public Good, seventeenth-century compilation
646 Documents on the 1350s, seventeenth-century compilation
3888 Achilles de Harlay, speech to Henry IV, 1594, on the king surviving Jean Chastel's attempted regicide

Manuscrits Français

203 Parlementaire treatise on Pragmatic Sanction, c. 1500

1182 Christine de Pizan, *Livre de la Paix*, fifteenth-century manuscript

2608 *Grandes Chroniques de France*, c. 1390s (copy of Wenceslaus IV of Bohemia)

2813 *Grandes Chroniques de France*, c. 1380 (copy of Charles V)

4875 Remonstrance on disorders in justice, not dated [probably early 1572]. Internal evidence suggests the author might have been Pomponne de Bellièvre.

5079 Documents of lawsuit of Louise of Savoy about the Auvergne, 1520s

12439 *Le livre du corps de policie*, Christine de Pizan (fifteenth-century)

15494 Jacques Montaigne, *Histoire de France*, c. 1570

16250 Journal of Pierre de Blanchefort, noble deputy of St-Pierre-le-Moutier, Estates General of 1576, seventeenth-century copy [original in municipal library of Blois]

16624 Election to Estates General of 1588, provosty of Paris

23926 Nicole Oresme, *Petite traicté de la premiere invention des monnoies* [sixteenth-century copy]

23927 Oresme, *Petite traicté de la premiere invention des monnoies* [fifteenth-century copy]

24287 Denis Foulechat, French translation of John of Salisbury *Policraticus*, 1372

Departmental Archives (AD)

At the AD of Ille-et-Vilaine, I have extensively researched the papers of the Estates of Brittany for my earlier publications. See the bibliography in *Classes, Estates and Order in Early Modern Brittany*. Cambridge: CUP, 1994. For ongoing projects, I have also extensively researched the papers of the Estates of Burgundy, series B of the AD Côte d'Or. Many of these documents are now online at: https://archives.cotedor.fr/v2/site/AD21/Rechercher/Archives_en_ligne

My earlier work on the French state has involved research in the departmental archives at Amiens, Angers, Bordeaux, Bourges, Caen, Châlons-en-Champagne, Evreux, Limoges, Lyon, Nantes, Niort, Quimper, Rennes, Rouen, Saint-Brieuc, Troyes, and Vannes: I draw my knowledge of issues like local administrative practice and taxation from that research.

Côte d'Or

B 3062 Papers of the Estates of Burgundy, 1550s

B 3063 Papers of the Estates of Burgundy, 1560–1565

B 3469 Cahier of the nobility of the bailiwick of Dijon, November 1560

Eure-et-Loir

E 3000 Châteaudun, 1555, deliberation on tailles, complaint that only 27 of the 1200 heads of households attended

E 3040 Châteaudun, October 1560, complaint of local *élus* that an assembly (called for the coming Estates General) had vilified them in its *cahier*

Printed primary sources

General

Two vast nineteenth-century projects are now available online:

Documents inédits sur l'histoire de France:

https://gallica.bnf.fr/html/und/livres/documents-inedits-sur-lhistoire-de-france?mode=desktop

Choix de chroniques et mémoires sur l'histoire de France.

Avis au roy (c. 1347–1350): Morgan Library, Ms 456

Bardonnet, A., ed. *Procès-verbal de déliverance à Jean Chandos*. Niort, n.d.

Bernier, A. ed., *Journal des Etats Généraux tenus à Tours en 1484 sous le règne de Charles VIII par Jehan Masselin* (Paris, 1835).

With this text, see also: *États de Tours*, Bibliothèque Sainte-Geneviève, OEXV 558, image 68 of 132 (unpaginated). Online: https://archive.org/stream/OEXV558_P3#page/n0/mode/2up

Besse, G. *Recueil de diverses pieces servant à l'histoire du roy Charles VI*. Paris, 1660.

Blanchard, R. *Lettres et mandements de Jean V, duc de Bretagne*. 5 vols (Nantes, 1889–1895).

Bourdot de Richebourg, C. *Nouveau coutumier général ou corps des coutume générales et particulières de France et de ses provinces*. Paris, 1724. 8 vols.

Boutiot and Babeau, eds. *Documents inédits tirés des archives de Troyes et relatifs aux États-Généraux*. Troyes, 1878.

Bouviers des Noes,F. *Procédures politiques du règne de Louis XI*: Le procès de René d'Alençon, comte de Perche, 1481–1483. Lille, 2004. 2 vols.

Budé, G. *Le Livre de l'Institution du Prince*. Paris: Jean Foucher, 1549.

De Asse et partibus euis. Paris, 1514.

Summaire ou Epitome du livre de Asse fait par commandme[n]t du Roy, par maistre Guillaume Bude. Paris, 1522. Both versions on Gallica.

Buridan, J. *Quætiones super octo libros politicorum Aristotelis*. Paris: Jean Petit, 1524.

Cauchies, J.-M. *Ordonnances de Jean sans Peur 1405–1419. Recueil des ordonnances des Pays-Bas, 1ᵉ section, T. 3*. Brussels: Ministère de Justice, 2001.

Chabert, F.-M., ed. *Journal du siège de Metz en 1552: documents relatifs à l'organisation de l'armée de l'empereur Charles-Quint et à ses travaux devant cette place, et description des médailles frappées à l'occasion de la levée du siège.* Metz, 1856.

Chapuis, G. trans., *Le parfait Courtisan du comte Baltasar Castillonois.* Lyon, 1585. http://gallica.bnf.fr/ark:/12148/bpt6k754790/f6.image.r=Courtisan%20casti glione.langFR

Chevalier, C.-U. *Ordonnances des rois de France et autres princes souverains relatives au Dauphiné: précédées d'un Catalogue des registres de l'ancienne Chambre des comptes de cette province.* Colmar, 1871.

Delisle, L., ed. *Mandements et actes divers de Charles V.* Paris, 1874.

Dewick, E. S. *The Coronation Book of Charles V of France.* London: Henry Bradshaw Society, 1899.

Douët d'Arcq,L. ed., *Choix des pièces inédites relatives au règne de Charles VI.* Paris, 1864.

Du Chesne, F. *Histoire des chancelliers de France et des gardes des sçeaux de France.* Paris, 1686.

Dupuy, P. *Traité de la majorité de nos rois.* Paris, 1655.

Foulechat, D. *Le Policratique de Jean de Salisbury (1372), livres I–III,* ed. C. Brucker. Geneva: Droz, 1994.

Gerson, J. *Vivat Rex.* Paris, 1561.

Godefroy, T. and D. *Le ceremonial François,* 2 vols. Paris: Sebastien Cramoisy, 1649.

Grandmaison, C., ed. *Plaintes et doléances de la province de Touraine aux États généraux du royaume.* Tours, 1890.

Grassaille, C. *Regalium Franciæ libri duo, iura monia & dignitates Christianiss. Galliæ Regum, continents.* Lyon 1545.

Jackson, R., ed. *Ordines Coronationis Franciae,* 2 vols. Philadelphia: University of Pennsylvania Press, 1995, 2000.

Jones, M. *Recueil des actes de Jean IV, duc de Bretagne.* 2 vols. Paris: Klincksieck, 1980, 1983.

Recueil des actes de Charles de Blois et de Jeanne de Penthièvre. Rennes: PUR, 1996, available on open edition.

Juvénal des Ursins, J. *Écrits Politiques de Jean Juvénal des Ursins,* ed. P. S. Lewis. 3 vols. Paris: Klincksieck, 1978–1992.

"Juvénal des Ursins, J." *Histoire de Charles VI, roi de France.* Paris, 1841. Peter Lewis has raised fundamental doubts about whether Juvénal des Ursins wrote this text: "L'Histoire de Charles VI attribué à Jean Juvénal des Ursins: pour une édition nouvelle," *Comptes-rendus de l'Académie des Inscriptions et des Belles-Lettres* 140, n. 2 (1996): 565–569.

Longnon, A. *Documents relatifs au comté de Champagne et de Brie, 1172–1361.* Paris: Imprimerie Nationale, 1901–14. 3 vols.

Mézières, P. de. *Le Songe du Vieil Pelerin,* ed. G. W. Coopland. Cambridge: CUP, 1969. 2 vols.

Oresme, N. *De Moneta of Nicholas Oresme*, trans C. Johnson. London, 1956; Auburn, AL, 2009.

L. Wolowski published an edition of the French translation: *Traictie des la première invention des monnoies de Nicole Oresme.* Paris, 1864. The original is available on gallica.

Ordonnances des rois de France: règne de François Ier. 9 vols. [some with multiple parts] Paris: Imprimerie nationale, 1902–1989. Through December 1539.

Les ordonnances Royaulx nouvellement publiées à Paris de par le Roy Loys douziesme de ce nom le 13 juin 1499.

Pélicier, P. ed., *Lettres de Charles VIII, roi de France.* 5 vols. Paris: Renouard, 1898–1905.

Pithou, P. and P. Dupuy, ed., *Traitez des droits et libertez de l'Eglise gallicane.* Paris, 1731; original edition 1594.

Recueil des édits, déclarations, lettres-patentes [. . .] concernant l'Administration des Etats de Bourgogne. Dijon, 1784.

Rymer, T. *Fœdera.* London, 1739–1745. 12 vols. Online at British History Online, www.british-history.ac.uk/rymer-foedera

Secousse, D.-F. *Recueil des pièces servant de preuves aux mémoires sur les Troubles excités en France par Charles de Navarre dit le Mauvais.* Paris, 1755.

Seyssel, C. de. *Les louenges du roy Louis XII*, ed. P. Eichel-Loikine and L. Vissière. Geneva: Droz, 2009.

Seyssel, C. *La monarchie de France*, ed. J. Poujol. Paris: Librairie d'Argences, 1961. Poujol went back to the manuscripts to check against the corrupted early editions. Gallica has the 1519 edition, *La grant monarchie de France*, and the 1557 edition, published by Galliot du Pré

Trémaugon, E. de, *Le Songe du Vergier*, ed. M. Schnerb-Lièvre, 2 vols. Paris: CNRS, 1982.

Somnium viridarii, ed. M. Schnerb-Lièvre Paris: CNRS, 1996.

Trésor des Chartes JJ 54, online at: www.culture.gouv.fr/Wave/image/archim/JJ/PG/frchanjj_jj054a_0003r.htm

Vaesen, J. and E. Charavay, *Lettres de Louis XI*, 11 vols. Paris: Renouard 1883–1909.

"Voyage de Nicolas de Bosc," in Voyage *littéraire de deux religieux bénédictins de la Congrégation de Saint-Maur*, ed. E. Martène and U. Durand. Paris, 1724.

Early Modern Historians

Basin, T. *Histoire de Louis XI.* Ed. and trans. C. Samaran. Paris: Société d'édition "Les Belles Lettres," 1963–1972, 3 vols.: vols. 2–3 co-edited by M.-C. Garand.

Advis de Monseigneur de Lysieux au roi. Epistola . . .. Domini Lexoviensis ad Ludovicum regem francorum [509–521). In Theodore of Canterbury, *Theodori sanctissimi ac doctissimi archiepiscopi Cantuariensis Poenitentiale.* Paris 1677. Basin's text written in 1464 against *graces expéditives*, and to restore the Pragmatic Sanction of 1438.

Champier, S. *Les gestes ensemble la vie du preulx chevalier Bayard*, ed. D. Crouzet. Paris: Imprimerie Nationale, 1992.

L'antiquité de la ville de Lyon, ensemble la rebeine ou rebellion du populaire contre les conseillers de la cité en 1529. Ed. M.-C. Guigue. Lyon, 1884.

*Ung petit traicté de la noblesse et ancien[n]été de la ville de lyo[n].*Paris, 1529.

Chartier, Jean. *Histoire de Charles VII.* Ed. D. Godefroy. Paris, 1661.

Chorier, N. *Histoire Générale de Dauphiné.* Lyon: J. Thioly, 1672.

D'Argentré, B. *Histoire de Bretaigne* (1583). The royal government forced d'Argentré to modify this text and re-issue it several years later. In the seventeenth century, multiple printings took place, supposedly of "new" editions but in fact restoring the 1583 original. Gallica has several of them online.

Dumont, J. *Corps universel diplomatique du droit des gens contenant un recueil des traitez d'alliance, de paix, de treve* . . . . Amsterdam, The Hague:Brunel et al., Husson and Levier, 1726.

Hotman, F. *La Gaule françoise.* Cologne, 1574.

Mézeray, F. de. *Histoire de France depuis Faramond jusqu'au règne de Louis le juste: enrichie de plusieurs belles & rares antiquitez & de la vie des reynes.* Paris, 1685.

Abrégé chronologique de l'Histoire de France. Amsterdam, 1755. 4 vols.

Morice, P.-H. *Histoire Ecclesiastique et Civile de Bretagne.* Paris, 1750, 1756. 2 vols.

Mémoires pour servir de Preuves de l'Histoire Ecclesiastique et Civile de Bretagne. Paris, 1742–1746. 3 vols. These volumes reproduce the original documents.

Pasquier, E. *Recherches de la France.* Paris, 1622. 3 Vols.

Recherches de la France. Livre Premier. Paris: Vincent Sertanas, 1560. Both editions on Gallica.

Ribier, G. *Lettres et Mémoires d'Estat.* Paris, 1666. 2 vols.

Rubys, C. de. *Histoire véritable de la ville de Lyon.* Lyon, 1604

Saint-Julien de Balleure, P. *De l'Origine des Bourgongnons et antiquité des estats de Bourgogne.* Paris: N. Chesneau, 1581.

Meslanges Historiques. Lyon, 1588.

Thou, J. de. *Histoire universelle.* "London" [Paris], 1734. 16 vols.

Valbonnais, J.-P. *Mémoires pour servir à l'histoire de Dauphiné.* Grenoble, 1711.

Chronicles, Memoirs, and Journals

Grandes Chroniques de France

Three manuscripts on Gallica –

BNF, M Fr 2813 [copy made for Charles V, c. 1380]

BNF, M Fr 2608 [late fourteenth-century copy, probably made for Wenceslas of Bohemia]

BNF, M Fr 6465 [mid-fifteenth-century copy, with illustrations by Jean Fouquet, text often badly damaged]

Delachenal, R. *Chronique des règnes de Jean II et de Charles V*. Paris, 1910, 1916.
    V. I: 1350–1364; V. II: 1364–1380.

Viard, J. ed., *Les grandes chroniques de France*. Paris, 1920. 5 vols

Guénée, B. "Les Grandes Chroniques de France," in *Les lieux de mémoire*, under
    the direction of P. Nora. Paris: Gallimard, 1984–1986, 3 vols, v. I, part 2,
    189–214, for an introduction to the history of the more than 100 surviving
    manuscript versions from before 1500.

I have largely omitted the dozens of journals and memoirs available for the
sixteenth century. The Petitot editions, *Collection complète des mémoires relatifs à
l'histoire de France*, which contains fifty-two volumes in its first series – most of
them about the sixteenth century – is available online through multiple sites. If
modern critical editions of these texts exist, I have consulted them.

Chartier, Jean. *Chronique de Charles VII*, ed. Vallet de Viriville. Paris, 1858, 3 vols.
    (fifteenth-century manuscript online at gallica: BNF, M Fr 5051).

Chronique de Jean le Bel, ed. J. Viard and E. Déprez. Paris, 1905.

Chronique de Jean le Fèvre, seigneur de Saint-Rémy, ed. F. Morand. Paris:
    Renouard, 1876.

Chroniques d'Enguerrand de Monstrelet, ed. L. Douët-D'Arcq. Paris, 1857–1862. 6
    vols

Chronique des abbés de Saint-Ouen de Rouen, ed. F. Michel. Rouen, 1840.

Chronique des quatre premiers Valois (1327–1393), ed. S. Luce. Paris, 1862.

Chronique du Religieux de Saint-Denys, le règne de Charles VI, de 1380 à 1422. Ed.
    and trans. L. Bellaguet. Paris, 1839–1852. 6 vols. Bilingual edition.

Useful introductory material about the overall Chronicle of Saint-Denis in the
    "Introduction" to the earliest segments of the Chronicle, *Chroniques latines
    de Saint-Denis:* http://elec.enc.sorbonne.fr/chroniqueslatines/intro

Chronique normande du XIVᵉ Siècle. Ed. A. and E. Molinier. Paris, 1882.

Commynes, P. de. *Mémoires de Philippe de Commynes*, ed. É. Dupont. Paris, 1840–
    1847. 3 vols.

    Mémoires. Ed. J. Calmette and G. Durville. Paris, 1924–1925. 3 vols.

    Mémoires. Ed. J. Blanchard. Paris: Droz, 2007. 2 vols.

The manuscript copy owned by Henry III is on Gallica: M Français 10156. A note
    at the beginning says it belonged to Mgr. Sourdis, grand master of the garde-
    robe of Francis I.

Coulon, A. "Fragment d'un chronique du règne de Louis XI," *Mélanges d'histoire et
    d'archéologie* (1895): 103–140.

Deux chroniques de Rouen. Ed. A. Héron. Rouen: Lestringant; Paris: Picard, 1900.

Haton, C. *Mémoires de Claude Haton*. Dir. L. Bourquin. 4 vols. Paris: Collection
    des documents inédits sur l'histoire de la France, 2001–2007.

    Mémoires de Claude Haton. Ed. F. Bourquelot. Paris: Comité des Travaux
    Historiques et Scientifiques, 1857.

Journal de Jean Barrillon, secrétaire du chancelier Duprat, 1515–1521. Ed. P. de
    Vaissière. Paris. 1897–1899. 2 vols.

Journal de Jean de Roye connu sous le nom de Chronique Scandaleuse 1460-1483. Ed. B. de Mandrot. Paris, 1894–1896.

Journal de Jean Le Fèvre, évêque de Chartres. Ed. H. Moranville. Paris, 1887.

Journal de Jean Maupoint, prieur de Sainte-Catherine-de-la-Couture. Ed. G. Fagniez Paris, 1878.

Journal d'un bourgeois de Paris sous le règne de François Ier (1515–1536). Ed. V.-L. Bourrilly. Paris, 1910.

La Marche, Olivier de. *Mémoires d'Olivier de la Marche.* Ed. H. Beaune and J. d'Arbaumont. Paris, 1883–1888. 4 vols.

Le Bouvier, Gilles (Le Hérault Berry), *Les Chroniques du roi Charles VII.* Ed. L. Celier and H. Courteault. Paris: Klincksieck, 1979.

Œuvres de Georges Chastellain: Chronique. Ed. J. Kervyn de Lettenhove. Brussels, 1863–1865. 7 vols,

Ordonnance faict par messire Pierre d'Urfé pour l'enterrement du roi Charles VIII. Paris, 1498. http://cartelfr.louvre.fr/cartelfr/visite?srv=car_not_frame&idNotice=4850

Pichon, J. ed. *Partie inédite des chroniques Saint-Denis.* Paris, 1864.

Tuetey, A. *Journal d'un bourgeois de Paris, 1405–1449.* Paris, 1881.

Villani, M. *Cronica di Matteo Villani.* Ed. F. Dragomanni. 2 vols. Florence, 1846.

Selected Secondary Works

Abord, H. *Histoire de la Réforme et de la Ligue dans la ville d'Autun: précédée d'une introduction et suivie de pièces justificatives.* Paris, 1855. 3 vols.

Adams, T. *Christine de Pizan and the Fight for France.* University Park, PA: Pennsylvania State UP, 2014.

The Life and Afterlife of Isabeau of Bavaria. Baltimore, MD: Johns Hopkins UP, 2010.

"The political significance of Christine de Pizan's third estate in the *Livre du corps de policie,*" *J. of Medieval History* 35, n. 4 (2009): 385–398

Autrand, F. *Charles V.* Paris: Fayard, 1994.

Christine de Pizan. Une femme en politique. Paris: Fayard, 2009.

Naissance d'un grand corps de l'État, les gens du Parlement, 1346-1454. Paris, 1981.

"Noblesse ancienne et nouvelle noblesse dans le service de l'Etat en France: les tensions du début du XVe siècle," in *Gererchie economiche e gerarchie sociali secoli XII–XVIII.* Florence, 1990.

Bakos, A. *Images of Kingship in Early Modern France: Louis XI in Political Thought 1560–1789.* London: Routledge, 1997.

Barbey, J. *Être roi. Le roi et son gouvernement en France de Clovis à Louis XVI.* Paris: Fayard, 1992.

La fonction royale. Essence et légitimité d'après les Tractatus de Jean de Terrevermeille. Paris: Nouvelles éditions latines, 1983.

Bart, J. *Histoire du droit privé de la chute de l'Empire romain au XIXe siècle*. Paris: Montchrestien, 2009, 2nd edition.

Bercé, Y.-M. ed., *Les procès politiques*. Rome: École Française de Rome, 2007.

Bourdieu, P. "La production et la reproduction de la langue légitime," in *Langage et Pouvoir symbolique* (Paris: Seuil, 2001). English translation by G. Raymond, *Language and Symbolic Power*. Cambridge, MA: Harvard UP, 1993.

  Sur l'État. Cours au Collège de France, 1989–1992. Paris: Seuil, 2012.

Bove, B. *Dominer la ville. Prévôts des marchands et échevins parisiens de 1260 à 1350*. Paris, 2004.

Bridrey, E. *La théorie de la monnaie au XIVe siècle. Nicole Oresme*. Paris, 1906.

Briggs, C. *Giles of Rome's De Regimine Principum. Reading and writing Politics at Court and University, ca. 1275–ca. 1525*. Cambridge: CUP, 1999.

Brown, C. ed., *The Cultural and Political Legacy of Anne de Bretagne. Negotiating Convention in Books and Documents*. Cambridge: D.S. Brewer, 2010.

Brown, E. A. R. "The Ceremonial of Royal Succession in Capetian France: The Double Funeral of Louis X," *Traditio* 34 (1978): 227–271.

  "Subsidy and Reform in 1321: The Accounts of Najac and the Politics of Philip V," *Traditio* 27 (1971): 399–431.

  "The Tyranny of a Construct: Feudalism and Historians of Medieval Europe," *American Historical Review* (1974), now available online: http://isites .harvard.edu/fs/docs/icb.topic1350026.files/Brown-Tyranny-of -a-Construct.pdf

  and R. Famiglietti. *The Lit de Justice: Semantics, Ceremonial, and the Parlement of Paris 1300–1600*. Sigmaringen: Jan Thorbecke Verlag, 1994.

Bulst, N. *Die französischen Generalstände von 1468 under 1484. Prosopographische Untersuchungen zu den Delegierten*. Sigmaringen, 1992.

Canning, J. *Ideas of Power in the Late Middle Ages, 1296–1417*. Cambridge: Cambridge UP, 2011.

Cazelles, R. "Étienne Marcel au sein de la haute bourgeoisie d'affaires," *Journal des Savants* 1, n. 1 (1963): 413–427.

  "La Jacquerie fut-elle un mouvement paysan?" *Comptes rendus des séances de l'Académie des Inscriptions et Belles-Lettres*, 122, n. 3 (1978): 654–666.

  "Mouvements révolutionaires au milieu du XIV siècle," *Revue Historique*, 229 (1962): 279–312.

  "Quelques réflexions à propos des mutations de la monnaie royale française (1295–1360)," *Le Moyen Âge* (1966): 83–105; 251–278.

  Société politique, noblesse et royauté sous Jean II et Charles V. Geneva: Droz, 1982.

P. Chaplais, "Some Documents Regarding Fulfilment and interpretation of the Treaty of Brétigny, 1361–1369," *Camden Miscellany*, vol. XIX (Third Series, v. LXX). London: Royal Historical Society, 1952.

Charbonnel, N. "Corps Politique, Corps Mystique." www.editions-areopage.com /html/chronologie.pdf

Chauou, A. *L'idéologie plantagenêt. Royauté arthurienne et monarchie politique dans l'espace Plantagenêt (XIIe-XIIIe siècles).* Rennes: PUR, 2001.

Chevalier, B. *Les bonnes villes de France du XIVe au XVIe siècle.* Paris: Aubier, 1982.

Coleman, J. "El concepto de república. Continuidad mítica y continuidad real," *Res Publica* 15 (1) (2005), for a nice presentation of the problems with respect to the term "*res publica.*"

"The Practical Uses of Begriffsgeschichte," 30. www.jyu.fi/yhtfil/redescriptions/ Yearbook%201999/Coleman%20J%201999.pdf

Collins, J. *From Monarchical Commonwealth to Royal State, 1561–1651.* Cambridge: CUP, forthcoming.

Combet, J. *Louis XI et le Saint-Siège.* Paris: Hachette, 1903.

Contamine, P. *Des Pouvoirs en France, 1300–1500.* Paris: P. de l'École Normale Supérieur, 1992.

Cosandey, F. *La Reine de France, Symbole et pouvoir, XVe-XVIIIe siècle.* Paris: Gallimard, 2000.

Coville, A. *Les cabochiens et l'ordonnance de 1413.* Paris: Hachette, 1888.

Les États de Normandie: leurs origines et leur développement au XIVe siècle. Paris, 1894.

Jean Petit. Paris, 1935.

Crest, A. du. *Modèle familial et pouvoir monarchique (XVIe - XVIIIe siècles).* Aix: PU d'Aix-Marseille, 2002.

Croix, A. *L'âge d'or de la Bretagne.* Rennes: Éditions Ouest-France, 1993.

Daubresse, S. *Le Parlement de Paris ou la Voix de la Raison (1559–1589).* Geneva: Droz, 2005.

"Christophe de Thou et Charles IX: recherches sur les rapports entre le parlement et le prince (1560–1574), *Histoire, économie et société* 17, n. 3 (1997): 389–422.

Daussy, H. *Le parti Huguenot.* Geneva: Droz, 2014

Delachenal, R. *Histoire de Charles V.* 5 vols. Paris: A. Picard, 1909–1931.

"La bibliothèque d'un avocat au XIVe siècle," *Nouvelle revue historique de droit français et étranger* (1887): 524–537.

Deslisle, L. *Testament de Blanche de Navarre, reine de France.* Paris, 1885.

Descimon, R. "Declareuil (1913) contre Hauser (1912). Les rendez-vous manqués de l'histoire et de l'histoire du droit," *Annales. Histoire. Sciences Sociales* 57, n. 6 (2002): 1615–1636.

"Les fonctions de la métaphore du mariage politique du roi et de la république. France, XVe-XVIIIe siècles," *Annales. Histoire, Sciences Sociales,* 47, n.6 (1992): 1127–1147, 1129.

"La vénalité des offices comme dette publique sous l'ancien régime français. Le bien commun au pays des intérêts privés," in *La dette publique dans l'histoire,* ed. J.-Y. Grenier Paris: CHEFF, 2006: 177–242.

and F. Cosandey. *L'absolutisme en France.* Paris: Seuil, 2002.

and Demonet, M. "L'exercice politique de la bourgeoisie: les assemblées de Ville de Paris de 1528 à 1679," in C. Dolan, ed., *Les pratiques politiques dans les villes françaises d'Ancien Régime* Rennes: PUR, 2018, 113–163.

Doucet, R. "Le Grand Parti de Lyon au 16ème siècle," *Revue Historique* 171 (1933): 473–513 and 172 (1933): 1–41.

Douët-d'Arcq, L. "Acte d'accusation contre Robert le Coq, évêque de Laon," *BEC*, v. 2 (1841): 350–388.

Dupont-Ferrier, G. *Les officiers royaux des bailliages et sénéchaussées.* Paris: Émile Bouillon, 1902.

Édouard, S. *Les Devoirs du prince. L'éducation princière à la Renaissance.* Paris: Classics Garnier, 2014.

Eichel-Lojkine, P. ed., *Claude de Seyssel. Écrire l'histoire, penser le politique en France, à l'aube des temps modernes.* Rennes: PUR, 2010.

Ellenius, A. ed., *Iconography, Propaganda, and Legitimation.* Oxford and NY: OUP, 1999.

Équipe Golein, "Remarques sur la traduction de Jean Golein du '*De Informacione principum,*" *Neuphilologische Mitteilungen* 95, n. 1 (1994): 19–30,

Fargeix, C. *Les élites lyonnaises du XVe siècle au miroir de leur langage. Pratiques et représentations culturelles des conseillers de Lyon, d'après les registres de délibérations consulaires.* Paris: De Boccard, 2007.

Fasolt, C. *Council and Hierarchy: The Political Thought of William Durant the Younger.* Cambridge; New York: CUP, 1991.

   Past Sense – Studies in Medieval and Early Modern European History. Leiden: Brill, 2014.

Favier, J. *Louis XI.* Paris: Fayard, 2001.

Favreau, R. *La ville de Poitiers à la fin du Moyen Âge. Un capital regional.* Poitiers: MSA Ouest, 1977–1978. 2 vols.

Forhan, K. Langdon. *The Political Theory of Christine de Pizan.* Burlington, VT: Ashgate, 2002.

Fumaroli, M. *L'âge de l'éloquence.* Paris and Geneva: Droz, 1980.

Funk, A. "Robert Le Coq and Etienne Marcel," *Speculum,* vol. 19, No. 4 (Oct., 1944): 470–487.

Gaude-Ferragu, M. *La Reine au Moyen Âge. Le pouvoir au féminin, XIVe – XVe siècle.* Paris: Taillandier, 2014.

Gaussin, P.-R. *Louis XI, un roi entre deux mondes.* Paris, 1976.

   "Les conseillers de Louis XI," in *La France de la fin du XVe siècle. Renouveau et apogée,* ed. B. Chevalier and P. Contamine. Paris: CNRS, 1985.

   "Les conseillers de Charles VII," *Francia* (1983): 67–127.

Gauvard, C. *"De grace especial" Crime, état et société en France à la fin du Moyen Âge.* Paris: Publications de la Sorbonne, 1991, 2010.

Giesey, R. "When and Why Hotman wrote the *Francogallia,*" *Bibliothèque d'Humanisme et Renaissance,* 29, n. 3 (1967): 581–611.

   The Juristic Basis of Dynastic Right to the French Throne. Transactions of the American Philosophical Society, new series, v. 51, n. 9. Philadelphia, 1961.

The Royal Funeral Ceremony in Renaissance France. Geneva: Droz, 1960.

Gorochov, N. *Le Collège de Navarre, de sa fondation (1305) au début du XVe siècle (1418). Histoire de l'institution, de sa vie intellectuelle et de son recrutement.* Paris: Honoré Champion, 1997.

Graham-Goering, E. Maëlan. "Negotiating princely power in late medieval France: Jeanne de Penthièvre, duchess of Brittany (c. 1325–1384)," Ph.D. thesis, University of York, 2014.

Princely Power in Late Medieval France: Jeanne de Penthièvre and the War for Brittany. Cambridge: CUP, 2020.

Grant, E. *God & Reason in the Middle Ages.* Cambridge: CUP, 2001.

Greengrass, M. *Governing Passions. Peace and Reform in the French Kingdom.* Oxford: OUP, 2007.

Grévy-Pons, N. *L'Honneur de la Couronne de France: Quatre libelles contre les Anglais (vers 1419 – vers 1429).* Paris: Société de l'Histoire de France, 1990.

"Propagande et sentiment national pendant le règne de Charles VI: L'exemple de Jean de Montreuil," *Francia – Forschungen zur westeuropäischen Geschichte,* vol. 8 (1980): 127–146.

Guenée, B. *Between Church and State: The Lives of Four French Bishops in Late Middle Ages,* trans. A. Goldhammer. Chicago: UCP, 1991.

L'opinion publique à la fin du Moyen Âge d'après la chronique du religieux de Saint-Denis. Paris: Perrin, 2002.

"Y a-t-il un État aux XIVe et XVe siècles?" *Annales E.S.C.* (1971).

Guillot, O., A. Rigaudière, and Y. Sassier, *Pouvoirs et institutions dans la France médiévale. T. 2. Des temps féodaux aux temps de l'État.* Paris: Armand Colin, 1994, 1999.

Haemers, J. *For the Common Good: State Power and Urban Revolts in the Reign of Mary of Burgundy, 1477–1482.* Turnhout: Brepols, 2009.

Hamon, P. *L'argent du roi.* Paris: CHEFF, 1994.

Messieurs des finances. Paris: CHEFF, 1999.

Les Renaissances 1453–1559. Paris: Éditions Belin, 2009.

Hanley, S. *The Lit de Justice of the Kings of France. Constitutional Ideology in Legend, Ritual, and Discourse.* Princeton, NJ: Princeton UP, 1983; re-issue 2014.

Hauser, H. "Le Traité de Madrid et la cession de la Bourgogne à Charles-Quint. Étude sur le sentiment national bourguignon en 1525–1526," *Revue Bourguignonne* t. XXII (1912).

Hayden, J. M. and M. Greenshields. *Six Hundred Years of Reform: French Bishops and the French Church, 1190–1789.* Montreal: McGill-Queen's UP, 2005.

Henneman, J. B. *Royal Taxation in Fourteen-Century France: The Captivity and Ransom of John II, 1356–1370.* Philadelphia: Transactions of the American Philosophical Society, 1976

Royal Taxation in Fourteenth-Century France: The Development of War Financing, 1322–1356. Princeton, NJ: Princeton UP, 1971.

Hébert, M. *Parlementer. Assemblées représentatives et échange politique en Europe occidentale à la fin du Moyen Âge.* Paris: De Boccard, 2014.

Hochner, N. *Louis XII. Les dérèglements de l'image royal (1498–1515).* Seyssel: Champ Vallon, 2006.

Holt, M. "Attitudes of the French Nobility at the Estates-General of 1576," *The Sixteenth Century Journal*, vol. 18, No. 4 (Winter, 1987): 489–504.

The Politics of Wine in Early Modern France. Cambridge: CUP, 2018.

Hollenbach, D. *The Common Good and Christian Ethics.* Cambridge: CUP, 2002.

Houllemare, M. *Politiques de la parole. Le parlement de Paris au XVIᵉ siècle.* Geneva: Droz, 2011.

"L'imaginaire politique du Parlement de Paris sous Henri II, Sénat de la capitale," in *Cités Humanistes, Cités Politiques (1400–1600).* Ed. E. Crouzet-Pavan, D. Crouzet, P. Desan Paris: PU Sorbonne, 2014.

Janvier, A. *Livre d'or de la municipalité amiénoise.* Amiens, 1892.

Jordan W. C., The French Monarchy and the Jews. Philadelphia: University of Pennsylvania Press, 1989.

Jackson, R. *Vive le Roi! A History of the French Coronation from Charles V to Charles X.* Chapel Hill: University of North Carolina Press, 1984.

Jouanna, A. *Le devoir de révolte.* Paris: Fayard, 1989.

Le pouvoir absolu. Paris: Gallimard, 2013.

Le prince absolu: apogée et déclin de l'imaginaire monarchique. Paris: Gallimard, 2014.

Julerot, V. *"y a ung grant desordre; élections épiscopales et schismes diocésains en France sous Charles VIII".* Paris: PU Sorbonne, 2006.

Kaye, J. *Economy and Nature in the Fourteenth Century: Money, Market Exchange, and the Emergence of Scientific Thought.* Cambridge: CUP, 1998.

Keane, M. *Material Culture and Queenship in Fourteenth-Century France: The Testament of Blanche of Navarre.* Leiden: Brill, 2016.

Kekewich, M. *The Good King: René of Anjou and Fifteenth Century Europe.* Houndsmill: Palgrave, 2008.

Kelley, D. *The Beginning of Ideology.* Cambridge: CUP, 1981.

Kempshall, M. S. *The Common Good in Late Medieval Political Thought.* Oxford: Clarendon Press, 1999.

Kerhervé, J. "Écriture et récriture de l'histoire dans *l'Histoire de Bretaigne* de Bertrand d'Argentré. L'exemple du Livre XII," in N.-Y. Tonnerre, ed., *Chroniqueurs et historiens de la Bretagne* Rennes: PUR, 2001, 77–109.

Keys, M. *Aquinas, Aristotle and the Promise of the Common Good.* Cambridge: CUP, 2006.

Knecht, R. J. *Francis I.* Cambridge: CUP, 1982.

"Francis I and the 'Lit de Justice': A Legend Defended," *French History* 7, n. 1 (1993): 53–83.

Koselleck, R. *Futures Past: On the Semantics of Historical Time.* Trans. K. Tribe. Cambridge, MA: MIT Press, 1985.

Krynen, J. *L'empire du roi: Idées et croyances politiques en France XIIIᵉ-XVᵉ siècle.* Paris: Gallimard, 1993.

Idéal du prince et pouvoir royal en France à la fin du Moyen Âge (1380-1440): étude de la littérature politique du temps. Paris: A. and J. Picard, 1981.

L'idéologie de la magistrature ancienne. Paris: Gallimard, 2009.

"Les légistes 'idiots politiques'. Sur l'hostilité des théologiens à l'égard des juristes, en France, au temps de Charles V," in *Théologie et droit dans la science politique de L'État moderne.* Rome: Mélanges de l'École Française de Rome, 1991. 171–198.

"Rex Christianissimus: A Medieval Theme at the Roots of French Absolutism," *History and Anthropology* 4, 1 (1989): 79–96.

Labande-Mailfert, Y. *Charles VIII.* Paris: Fayard, 1986.

Lange, T. *The First French Reformation. Church Reform and the Origins of the Old Regime.* NY and Cambridge: CUP, 2014.

Leguay, J.-P. *Vivre dans les villes bretonnes au Moyen Âge.* Rennes: PUR, 2009.

and H. Martin, *Fastes et malheurs de la Bretagne ducale.* Rennes: Éditions Ouest-France, 1997.

Lehugeur, P. *Histoire de Philippe le Long.* Paris, 1897, 2 vols.

Le Page, D. and Loiseau, J. *Pouvoir royal et institutions dans la France moderne.* Paris: Armand Colin, 2019.

Le Roux, N. *La faveur du roi: mignons et courtisans au temps des derniers Valois (vers 1547 – vers 1589).* Seyssel: Champ Vallon, 2000.

Le Roy Ladurie, E. *L'état royal, 1460–1610.* Paris: Hachette, 1987.

Lethenet, B. "'Comment l'on doit se gouverner': La ville, la guerre et le pouvoir. Macon (vers 1380 – vers 1422)," Ph.D. thesis, Université de Strasbourg, 2012.

Lewis, P. S. *Essays in Later Medieval French History.* London, 1985.

Later Mediaeval France: The Polity. London: Macmillan, 1968.

Leyte, G. *Domaine et domanialité publique dans la France medieval (XIIe – XVe siècles).* Strasbourg: PU Strasbourg, 1996.

Lurie, G. "Citizenship in late medieval Champagne: the towns of Châlons, Reims, and Troyes, 1417 – c. 1435," *French Historical Studies* 38, n. 3 (2015): 365–390.

"French Citizenship and the Uprisings of 1380–1383," *The Medieval Chronicle* X (2015): 119–140.

Lusignan, S. *La langue des rois au Moyen Âge. Le français en France et en Angleterre.* Paris: PUF, 2004.

Maiolo, F. *Medieval Sovereignty. Marsilius of Padua and Bartolus of Saxoferrato.* Delft: Eburon, 2007.

Major, J. R. *The Deputies to the Estates General in Renaissance France* (Madison: University of Wisconsin Press, 1960.

Representatives Government in Early Modern France. New Haven and London: Yale UP, 1980.

McGuire, B. *Jean Gerson and the Last Medieval Reformation* University Park: Pennsylvania State University Press, 2005.

Michon, C. ed. *Les Conseillers de François Ier*. Rennes: PUR 2011.

Mirot, L. *Les insurrections urbaines au début du règne de Charles VI*. Paris, 1907.

Miskimin, H. *Money and Power in 15th-century France*. New Haven and London: Yale UP, 1984.

Murphy, N. *Ceremonial Entries, Municipal Liberties and the Negotiation of Power in Valois France, 1328–1589*. Leiden: Brill, 2016.

Nederman, C. "Christine de Pizan and Jean Gerson on the Body Politic: Inclusion, Hierarchy, and the Limits of Intellectual Influence," *Del Storia Pensaro Politico* (2013): 465–480.

   Community and Consent: The Secular Political Theory of Marsiglio of Padua's Defensor Pacis. London: Rowman and Littlefield, 1995.

   and G. Moreno-Riaño, eds. *A Companion to Marsilius of Padua*. Leiden: Brill, 2012.

Oakley, F. *The Political Thought of Pierre d'Ailly*. New Haven and London: Yale UP, 1964.

Olivier-Martin, F. *Histoire du droit français des origines à la Révolution*. Paris: Domat Monchrétien, 1948.

Oudart, H., J.-M. Picard, and J. Quaghebeur, eds. *Le Prince, son peuple et le bien commun. De l'Antiquité tardive à la fin du Moyen Âge*. Rennes: PUR, 2013.

Pagden, A. ed., *The Languages of Political Discourse in Early-Modern Europe*. Cambridge: CUP, 1987.

Parsons, J. *The Church in the Republic: Gallicanism and Political Ideology in Renaissance France*. Washington: Catholic University of America Press, 2005.

Pennington, K. *Popes and Bishops. The Papal Monarchy in the Twelfth and Thirteenth Centuries*. Philadelphia: University of Pennsylvania Press, 1984.

   The Prince and the Law, 1200–1600: Sovereignty and Rights in the Western Legal Tradition. Berkeley: University of California Press, 1993.

Perret, N.-L. *Les traductions françaises du De regimine principum de Gilles de Rome: Parcours matériel, culturel et intellectuel d'un discours sur l'éducation*. Leiden: Brill, 2011.

Perroy, E. "The Anglo-French Negotiations at Bruges, 1374–1377," in *Camden Miscellany*, v. XIX (1952).

Petit, E. *Histoire des ducs de Bourgogne de la race capétienne*, 9 vols. Paris, 1885–1905.

Petit-Renaud, S. "Le roi, les légistes et le parlement de Paris aux XIVe et XVe siècles: contradictions dans la perception du pouvoir de 'faire loy'?," *Cahiers de recherches médiévales et humanistes*, 7 (2000).

Pocock, J. *The Machiavellian Moment*. Princeton, NJ: Princeton UP, 1975.

Potter, D. *A History of France, 1460–1560: The Emergence of a Nation State*. London: Macmillan, 1995.

War and Government in the French Provinces. *Picardy, 1470–1560.* Cambridge: CUP, 1993.

Randall, M. *The Gargantuan Polity: On the Individual and the Community in the French Renaissance.* Toronto: UT Press, 2008.

Ribémont, B. "Jean Corbechon, un traducteur encyclopédiste au XIVe siècle," *Cahiers de recherches médiévales* [Online], 6 | 1999. URL: http://crm.revues.org/932.

Rigaudière, A. *Penser et construire l'État au Moyen Âge.* Paris: CHEFF, 2003.

"Un grand moment pour l'histoire du droit constitutionnel français: 1374–1409," *Journal des Savants* (2012): 281–370.

Rigby, S. "The Body Politic in the Social and Political Thought of Christine de Pizan: Reciprocity, Hierarchy and Political Authority," *Cahiers de recherches médiévales et humanists* [On line], *Études christiniennes,* URL: http://crm.revues.org/12965

Rivaud, D. *Les villes et le roi. Les municipalités de Bourges, Poitiers et Tours et l'émergence de l'État moderne (v. 1440 – v. 1560).* Rennes: PUR, 2007.

Robertson, A. W. *Guillaume de Machaut and Reims. Context and Meaning in his Musical Works.* Cambridge: CUP, 2002.

Rohr, Z. *Yolande of Aragon (1381–1442). Family and Power.* Houndmills: Palgrave, 2016.

Ryan, J. *The Apostolic Conciliarism of Jean Gerson.* Oxford and NY: OUP, 2012.

Sabatier, G. *Le Prince et les Arts. Stratégies figuratives et monarchie française de la Renaissance aux Lumières.* Seyssel: Champ Vallon, 2010.

Sassier, Y. *Structures du pouvoir, royauté et res publica; France, IX–XII siècle.* Rouen: PU de Rouen, 2004.

Scordia, L. "Le bien commun, argument "pro et contra" de la fiscalité royale, dans la France de la fin du Moyen Âge," *Revue Française d'Histoire des Idées Politiques,* 32 (2010): 293–309. Special issue devoted to "Pouvoir d'un seul et bien commun (VIIe–XVIe siècles).

"*Le roi doit vivre du sien": La théorie de l'impôt en France (XIIIe–XVe siècle).* Paris: Institut d'Études Augustiniennes, 2005.

Schnerb, B. *L'état bourguignon.* Paris: Perrin, 2005.

Sherman, C. *Imaging Aristotle: Verbal and Visual Representation in Fourteenth-century France.* Berkeley: University of California Press, 1995.

Skinner, Q. *Foundations of Modern Political Thought.* Cambridge: CUP, 1978, 2 vols.

and R. Van Gelderen, eds., *Republicanism: A Shared European Heritage.* Cambridge: CUP, 2002, 2 vols.

Strayer, J. *The Reign of Philip the Fair.* Princeton, NJ: Princeton UP, 1980.

Taylor, C. "The Salic Law and the Valois Succession to the French Crown,"*French History* 15, n. 4 (2001): 358–377, which contains an extensive bibliography on Salic Law.

Taylor, C. H., "Assemblies of French Towns in 1316," *Speculum* XIV, n. 3 (1939): 275–299.

"French Assemblies and Subsidy in 1321," *Speculum* 43 (1968): 217–244.

Thomas, A. *Jean Gerson et l'éducation des dauphins de France*. Paris, 1930.

Valois, N. de. "Les états de Pontoise (1561)" *Revue de l'histoire de l'Église de France* 29 (1943): 257–276.

"Notes sur la révolution parisienne de 1356–1358: la revanche des frères Braque," *Bulletin de la société historiques de Paris et d'Ile-de-France* X (1883): 100–126.

Histoire de la Pragmatique sanction de Bourges sous Charles VII. Paris, 1906.

Verdon, J. *L'information et désinformation au Moyen Âge*. Paris: Perrin, 2014.

Viennot, E. *La France, les femmes et le pouvoir, Volume 1, L'invention de la loi salique (V^e–XVIe siècle)*. Paris: Perrin, 2006.

Watts, J. *The Making of Polities: Europe, 1300–1500*. Cambridge: CUP, 2009.

Georgetown University Ph.D. Dissertations

Kern, D. "The Political Kingdom: Parliamentary Institutions and Languages of Political Legitimacy in England and Castile, 1450–1520," 2012.

Lurie, G. "Citizenship in Later Medieval France, c. 1370 – c. 1480," 2012.

INDEX

Milton Keynes UK
Ingram Content Group UK Ltd.
UKHW021209030624
443304UK00020B/131

9 781108 461283